DATE			

THEORY OF PERSONALITY AND INDIVIDUAL DIFFERENCES

Factors, Systems, and Processes

JOSEPH R. ROYCE

Center for Advanced Study in Theoretical Psychology
University of Alberta

ARNOLD POWELL

Columbus College
and
Center for Advanced Study in Theoretical Psychology
University of Alberta

PRENTICE-HALL, INC., *Englewood Cliffs, New Jersey 07632*

Library of Congress Cataloging in Publication Data

ROYCE, JOSEPH R.
   Theory of personality and individual differences.

   (The Century psychology series)
   Bibliography: p.
   Includes indexes.
   1. Personality. 2. Individuality. I. Powell,
Arnold. II. Title. III. Series.
BF698.R8873 1983   155.2   82–21475
ISBN 0-13-914473-0

THE CENTURY PSYCHOLOGY SERIES

James J. Jenkins
Walter Mischel
Willard W. Hartup

Editors

© 1983 by PRENTICE-HALL, INC. *Englewood Cliffs, N.J. 07632*

Printed in the United States of America

10 9 8 7 6 5 4 3 2 1

ISBN 0-13-914473-0

PRENTICE-HALL INTERNATIONAL, INC., *London*
PRENTICE-HALL OF AUSTRALIA PTY. LIMITED, *Sydney*
EDITORA PRENTICE-HALL DO BRASIL LTDA., *Rio de Janeiro*
PRENTICE-HALL CANADA, INC., *Toronto*
PRENTICE-HALL OF INDIA PRIVATE LIMITED, *New Delhi*
PRENTICE-HALL OF JAPAN, INC., *Tokyo*
PRENTICE-HALL OF SOUTHEAST ASIA PTE. LTD., *Singapore*
WHITEHALL BOOKS LIMITED, *Wellington, New Zealand*

Acknowledgments

We wish to thank the following publishers and individuals for permission to reproduce
materials as indicated: Duke University Press, Fig. 1, p. 482; Fig. 2, p. 485; Fig. 3, p. 487;
and paraphrasing of pp. 478–488; reprinted from D. Wardell and J. R. Royce, Toward a
multifactor theory of styles and their relationships to cognition and affect, *Journal of Personality,* 1978, *46,* 474–505. The Society of Multivariate Experimental Psychology, Fig. 1, p. 37,
and paraphrasing of pp. 36–41, reprinted from S. R. Diamond and J. R. Royce, Cognitive
abilities as expressions of three "ways of knowing," *Multivariate Behavioral Research,* 1980,

and Noordhoff International Publishers have recently been taken over by Martinus Nijhoff Publishers; all future titles in the NATO ASI Series on Behavioral and Social Sciences will appear under the Martinus Nijhoff imprint), Fig. 14, p. 606; pages 603, 605, 607-8, 614, 619, 627-28, 630-32, and paraphrasing of pp. 632-35; reprinted from J. R. Royce, The factor gene basis of individuality, in J. R. Royce and L. P. Mos (Eds.), *Theoretical advances in behavior genetics* (Alphen aan den Rijn, The Netherlands, Sijthoff & Noordhoff, 1979); paraphrasing of pages 415-18; reprinted from J. R. Royce, G. P. Kearsley, and W. Klare, The relationship between factors and psychological processes, in J. M. Scandura and C. J. Brainerd (Eds.), *Structural/Process Models of Complex Human Behavior* (Alphen aan den Rijn, The Netherlands: Sijthoff & Noordhoff, 1978). International Cultural Foundation Press, Fig. 1, p. 1126; Fig. 8, p. 1139; pp. 1125-28, reprinted from J. R. Royce and A. Powell, Toward a theory of man: A multi-disciplinary, multi-systems multi-dimensional approach, in *The Search for Absolute Values in a Changing World* (New York: International Cultural Foundation Press, 1978); Fig. 2, p. 449, paraphrasing of pages 448, 450, reprinted from J. R. Royce and A. Powell, Human nature, metaphoric invariance, and the search for self-knowledge, in *The Re-Evaluation of Existing Values and the Search for Absolute Values* (New York: International Cultural Foundation Press, 1979). Pantheon Books, Inc., quote from S. Terkel, *Working,* p. 10 (New York: Pantheon Books, Inc., 1976). Random House, quote from J. A. Michener and A. G. Day, *Rascals in Paradise,* pp. 358-59 (New York: Random House/Martin Secker & Warburg, Limited, 1957). Black Publishers, Limited (originally published by Harper & Row Publishers), quote from G. Seaver, *Albert Schweitzer: The Man and His Mind,* p. 334 (London: Black Publishers, Limited, 1947). Academic Psychology Bulletin, Figure 3, p. 265; Figure 4, p. 267; reprinted from A. Powell and J. R. Royce, Cognitive information processing: The role of individual differences in the search for invariants, *Academic Psychology Bulletin,* 1982, *4,* 255-89.

Contents

11

12

13

We dedicate this book to the memory of

L. L. Thurstone

and to

William J. Arnold

Preface

This book constitutes the culmination of a long-term project on the nature of individuality. Our concern in this book is to provide a scientific account of the full range of individual differences and, at the same time, to explain the uniqueness of personality. The individuality project is massive in scope and intent—it reaches for no less than a general theory of individual differences. It reaches toward this goal via three major syntheses:

1. *methodological*—the relevant findings from psychology's two sciences (i.e., experimental and correlational psychology)
2. *conceptual*—the integration of concepts from factor theory, systems theory, and information-processing theory
3. *empirical*—the relevant empirical findings from all sources

However, it was clear to us from the start that there was little point to putting forward the general theory until we could articulate several critical minitheories (e.g., a development model and a model for each of the six systems). We therefore adopted the strategy of breaking down the total effort into 16 smaller projects before taking on the overall synthesis. This prebook effort required some 15 years to complete and resulted in some three dozen publications (they are included in the References) that provided a solid basis for the various parts of the book.

Although this book focuses on substantive theory, it is always done in the context of the relevant empirical findings. Thus, while substantive theory is primary, we also consider relevant empirical, methodological, and metatheoretic issues. However, because of space limitations we have not presented the empirical evidence in detail. This included the deletion of references in addition to text, figures, and tables that had previously been published as part of the overall project. Instead, we adopted the general policy of summarizing those aspects of the empirical evidence that are most germane to the theoretical point at issue and referring the reader who wants more detail to the appropriate paper.

Although the individuality project represents the major lifetime commitment of the senior author, it did not become a formal, grant-supported project until 1965. Since that date it has been supported by grants to J. R. Royce from the National Research Council, the Alberta Human Resources Research Council, and the University of Alberta. However, the major financial support was provided by the Canada Council, including Sabbatical Leave Grants in 1965–1966, 1972–1973, and 1981–1982.

Thus, the project has been a group effort involving some 20 theoretical researchers over the years. However, Arnold Powell, the coauthor of this book, has been the principal collaborator on the project. Other major contributors include research associates Stephen Diamond, Allan Buss, and Burt Voorhees, and graduate research assistants Gregory Kearsley, Donald Schopflocher, Michael Katzko, and Douglas Wardell. Less extensive contributions were made by research associates George Kawash and Warren Klare, and graduate research assistants Frederick Bell, Paul Enabnit, Peter Holt, John McDermott, Kenneth Meehan, Steve Nicely, and John Wozny. The project has also profited by continual critical feedback from the following Center staff: Richard Jung, W. W. Rozeboom, Herman Tennessen, Thaddeus Weckowicz, and Kellogg Wilson. We owe a special indebtedness to Leendert Mos, Center Professional Officer, who, with Chris Chambers, prepared both the author and subject indexes, and also contributed directly to empirical aspects of the project and indirectly as a friendly and constructive critic during our weekly individuality seminars. The specific contributions made by each participant are indicated via authorship in the References. Although we have drawn on most of the papers that have been produced by the 20 contributors to the individuality project, we have not reproduced or summarized large segments of previously published material unless one or both of us was an author. We have indicated authorship in all cases, and we hereby express our deep appreciation of each of the contributors to the project. The job could not have been completed without their help. Nor could the task of preparing finished copy of the book have been possible without the help of our two Center secretaries, Evelyn Murison and Frances Rowe, who have been typing individuality papers and book chapters since 1974. Their contribution includes the preparation of tables and figures, manuscript duplication, and general assistance, in addition to typing the book manuscript. We are grateful to Evelyn and Frances for their loyal, proficient, and cheerful assistance on the production aspect of the book.

In effect, the research of the past 15 years has provided us with the parts of the theory, and the book constitutes the whole. We have found this overall synthesizing task to be difficult but rewarding. The major difficulty was the sheer complexity of the task. We were able to overcome some of this complexity by our early commitment to factor analysis as the basis for identifying personality dimensions. And factor analysis was also helpful in resolving the problem of how these basic dimensions of personality are organized. However, we had to look elsewhere for answers concerning the more molar aspects of behavior. Although we were aware of the possible relevance of systems theory because of the influence of von Bertalanffy when he was on staff at the Center in the 1960s, there was no precedent available to guide us in applying systems theory to psychology. However, as we delved further into systems theory, it became increasingly clear that it was the best conceptual framework available for our problem. For example, prior to our decision to cast our substantive findings into the framework of systems theory, we merely had an inventory of invariant factors, but we were not clear as to how to organize them. Once we began to think in terms of systems, however, we were able to make our first important step in the direction of evolving a viable theoretical structure—that is, to allocate factors to different systems on the basis of functional role. Fortunately, previous work Royce had been conducting in an entirely different vein now became relevant to the individuality project—namely, the work on psychological epistemology. The major conclusion from this line of investigation was that there are three ways of knowing—rationalism, empiricism, and metaphorism. However, we did not know how to account for these variations except to indicate that it was a matter of psychological processing. But the individuality project had moved us into the style domain, and Royce slowly came to the realization that a way of knowing can best be conceptualized as an epistemic style.

The subsequent elaboration of the cooperative functioning of the style and cognitive systems constituted our first analysis of how systems interact to account for complex psychological phenomena. This led us to look explicitly at the more general issue of system interactions and integrations. At this juncture we were engaged in systems thinking in a very serious way. By this time we were also nearing the completion of the structural aspects of our analysis—namely, filling in the hierarchies of each of the six systems. But, as with other factor approaches, we had not made much headway with the process aspects of the theory, and we subsequently decided that information processing was the best way to accomplish this task. All of this meant that we would get at dynamics via an appropriate synthesis of factor analysis, systems theory, and information-processing theory. Providing this synthesis has proved to be the most difficult aspect of the project. We will cite two examples—the analyses of emotion in Chapter 8 and personality integration over the life span in Chapter 12. Royce had initiated experimental research in the emotionality domain in the form of a doctoral dissertation in 1948 and had wanted to propose a theory of emotion ever since. However, he was never able to determine how to attack the problem until we evolved individuality theory. And, at that juncture the appropriate approach became obvious—emotion involves the cooperative functioning of the cognitive and affective systems. The second example, personality integration over the life span, constitutes an excellent example of the power and relevance of systems theory for understanding organized complexity. Its richness lies in the fact that it leads to plausible and testable insights about questions that have not been convincingly attacked heretofore.

Systems thinking grew out of Bertalanffy's early theoretical work in embryonic biology and, in retrospect, it seems appropriate that our developmental model should draw so heavily on systems theory. The real breakthrough in our thinking came when we recognized that development could be conceived as a complex of interrelated transformations that are all related to the increasing systematic organization of personality. When this was combined with our ideas about the importance of uncertainty and risk management, we were then able to gain some real insight into the ebb and flow of life-span development. The basic problem with development and the complex transformations that individuals undergo is that the theoretical model has to "come alive" in a sense in order to model personality adequately. Clear recognition of this problem proved to be of tremendous importance in the evolution of our thinking.

In writing the book we have tried always to keep the reader in mind. We have done our best to communicate without sacrificing content. But we have worked for so long with the concepts and complexities of this project that our ideas now seem obvious and straightforward to us. Therefore, communication is apt to be difficult at times, particularly when dealing with something as complex as personality. Furthermore, the complexity of individuality theory increases as the book develops. Because of this complexity, it is difficult to keep everything in mind. We have, therefore, presented figures and tables throughout the text as aids to understanding what we have to say. We recommend, therefore, that the reader refer to figures and tables in the earlier chapters that are relevant to later chapters. For example, in Part III we discuss interactions between the six systems described in Part II. The complexities of Part III will be easier to grasp if the reader will review the relevant material from Part II. Usually it will not be necessary to review the text; a quick review of the relevant figures and tables should suffice. In fact, we urge that the reader do this kind of cross-referencing by looking ahead as well as looking back. All the parts of the theory are so interrelated that it will be easier to see the functional role of a given part if one knows the total context in which it is embedded.

While you will find that a given table or figure is a visual aid for understanding the text, you will also find that it is frequently more than that because we have found that the pictorial mode of presentation is the only way to understand and communicate many complex interrelationships. Some of the tables and figures provide models and explanations of a segment of the total theory. Some examples are the hierarchical structure of each of the six systems and of the suprasystem, life-span shifts in personality organization, and the relationships between factors and genes.

Despite our familiarity with the concepts and complexities of individuality theory, we have found that we have a better understanding of basic relationships and subtleties if we know the functional role of a given segment of the theory in the context of the total theory. This means that a second reading is desirable. One way to handle this problem is to make a relatively rapid first reading with the intent of identifying the total scope of the theory. A second reading then will allow you to fill in the details of the several subterrains. It is much easier to fill in such terrain details given an understanding of the total theoretical structure. This kind of close reading will also reveal the cracks in the edifice we have constructed.

Because of the strategies we have followed in this project we believe we have at least confronted the full complexity of the subject matter. We are also of the opinion that the theory constitutes a valuable synthesis concerning the nature of personality. Exactly how viable a synthesis it is will be determined by its further development. It is our hope that it will eventually evolve into an explanatory theory, and it is our belief that it has a sufficiently solid basis for at least initiating such a quest.

I

THE CONCEPTUAL
FRAMEWORK
OF THE THEORY

The three chapters in Part I of the book provide an overview of our theory of personality and individual differences. We also discuss some of the meta-theoretical issues that must be confronted by such a theory. Our basic concern is with constructing a general theory of how individuals differ from each other psychologically. The approach we have taken in reaching this goal involves a combination of factor analysis and systems and information-processing theory. Factor analysis provides the empirical basis for our effort inasmuch as it aids in identifying important personality traits. Systems and information-processing theory provide a conceptual model for dealing with the organized complexities of personality. Other elements of our theory include a model of life-span developmental change and models of the hereditary and environmental sources for such change.

1

Introduction and Overview

Personal meaning refers to the significance that each person attaches to life. While the search for personal meaning may not always be verbalized, it permeates people's thoughts and lurks in the background of most of their behaviors. The search for personal meaning leads some individuals to celebrate life; the failure to find it leads others to withdraw from living. Frustrated in the attempt to create meaning, some individuals create corners merely to exist in, or they encapsulate themselves in narrow but seemingly comfortable views of themselves and the world around them. Sometimes the search for significance in life leads individuals to produce great works of art or to make new discoveries in the worlds of science or business, and for some individuals the search leads to the betterment of the human condition. In nearly everything people do, there is always the question in the background as to whether their activities and their lives are "meaningful."

In the search for personal meaning all individuals must wrestle with three important questions: (1) What kind of world is this I live in? (2) How can I best live my life so that my needs and values can be satisfied? and (3) Who am I? In attempting to find acceptable answers to the first of these three questions, individuals develop *world views,* or general images of what the world is like. In trying to answer the second question, they develop individual *life styles,* or value-engaging patterns in living. And in answering the third question, they gain self-knowledge, which results in individual *images of their selves* in relation to the world and life.

The search to find answers to these three questions is just that—a *search*. Although the meaning each individual seeks to find in or create out of life hinges on answers to them, each one's answers are always tentative. One can never know what new event will take place in the next moment or how some new reaction may change one's self-image. To paraphrase Carl Rogers, we might say that the quest for personal meaning in life is a "journey, not a destination."

Although each individual must struggle or wrestle with the same three questions, the answers that each arrives at are unique. Uniqueness in world views, life styles, and self-images is pervasive because the way in which individuals differ from each other psychologically are so pervasive. We differ, for example, in the acuity of the senses we possess and through which we pick up information from the environment. We differ in the cognitive abilities that enable us to interpret, analyze, and elaborate on the information that the senses take in. The differences extend to all important psychological domains—styles, values, affect, and motor skills.

In the lives of three very different individuals we can find prototypic examples of different approaches to the search for personal meaning.

Albert Einstein   The life and work of Albert Einstein illustrates better than that of any other individual the commitment to a *rational* view of the world and to a life style based on the need for *mastery* and achievement. The image of reality that Einstein developed and impressed on the rest of the world was based on rational considerations; his approach to living was one of respect for the nature of things around him and his own value for mastering the mysteries of the universe. Although in his later years Einstein developed a deep interest in the social conditions that surrounded him, his primary commitment was to a rational understanding of the universe.

Mahatma Gandhi   The life and death (at the hands of an assassin) of Mahatma Gandhi exemplifies the commitment to a more *empirical* observation of the conditions that surround humankind and the need to give of oneself *altruistically*. Gandhi was pushed toward his more altruistic approach to life by his perceptual sensitivity to the social injustices that surrounded him—for example, in South Africa during his early career as a lawyer. Although rational and metaphoric understandings of the universe were at his disposal, his primary way of relating to the world was through this perceptual sensitivity, and his principal way of creating meaning out of life was through an altruistic commitment to humankind.

Henry David Thoreau   Thoreau, who is probably more celebrated in the present century than he was during his own (nineteenth) century, exemplifies a more *symbolic,* or metaphoric, way of understanding the world and a commitment to the life of the *individualist.* Thoreau most wanted to be able to realize his own individual potentials and to express them in his own way. His interest in the art of living was expressed most effectively in his metaphors about life and how individuals should choose to live it.

This book represents our attempt to present a comprehensive theory about how individuals differ from each other psychologically and how such differences give rise to differences in integrative personality, including world view, life style, and self-image. In the remainder of this first chapter we present a highly condensed overview of the theory. We begin with some orienting attitudes that have guided our efforts throughout.

ORIENTING ATTITUDES TOWARD PERSONALITY AND INDIVIDUAL DIFFERENCES

The orienting attitudes that have guided this project over the years can be stated in the form of a few simple maxims.

Maxim I.
Individual differences pervade all areas of psychological functioning.

This first maxim would seem to need little justification or elaboration to those, like ourselves, who have worked in the area of differential psychology or to anyone who observes other individuals on a daily basis. On the other hand, to anyone approaching such a statement from the standpoint of mainstream experimental or theoretical psychology, our dogmatic statement would seem to require a great deal of justification. That is, mainstream experimental psychology deals very little with individual differences, focusing instead on differences among treatment groups in various experimental arrangements. Most often in such experimental arrangements the differences among subjects are ignored and allowed to contribute variation to various "error terms" in statistical analyses. For differential psychologists, however, individual differences are the heart of the matter—they are the starting point for understanding psychological processes. The goal of the experimental psychologist and the differential psychologist is usually the same: namely, to discover general laws that apply to psychological processes. Even so, a differential psychologist is more apt to start by examining the many ways in which individuals may differ with respect to some task or process in order to discover the generalities.

Whenever one searches for them, it is possible to find important differences among individuals in *any* psychological process one cares to examine. Why, then, do experimental (bivariate) psychology and differential (multivariate) psychology continue to develop in relative isolation from each other? First, the technical demands for working in either bivariate or multivariate psychology still serve as deterrents to building bridges between the two approaches. That is, the demands in either one of these two traditions are so great that it is difficult for a single researcher to combine the necessary skills and know-how of both approaches. Second, psychology is still immature theoretically. That is, the zeitgeist has been so heavily focused on data that theory has been neglected. This means that the general level of sophistication in theory construction has not kept pace with competence in experimentation and statistical-methodological analysis. Several factors suggest that further scientific progress in psychology is crucially dependent on advances in the construction of *viable* theory (Royce, 1970a, 1976, 1977a, 1978a). These include the current overload of uninterpreted data, psychology's conceptual pluralism, the increasing acceptance of the theory-laden view of science, and psychology's current stage in its historical development. We present a general perspective on the nature of theory and metatheory in psychology in Chapter 2.

Despite these obstructions to a unification of psychology's two sciences, a number of seminal efforts have been made to close the gap between traditional experimental psychology and the study of individual differences. Multivariate researchers (e.g., Glaser, 1972; Messick, 1973) have pointed out the need to study the *dynamics* of individual differences rather than remain content with a static trait-theory approach, which has been prominent in differential psychology. On the other hand, experimental psychologists (e.g., Melton, 1967; Underwood, 1975) have acknowledged that theories of behavior that fail to account for individual differences are inadequate. And a few investigators, such as H. J. Eysenck (e.g., 1967, 1970, 1973) and Royce (e.g., 1977a,b,c, 1978b), have devoted much of their professional careers to research programs that combine both approaches.

Systems and information processing approaches have provided a much needed conceptual framework for bringing the two psychological sciences together, although they have led to concentration of research in the cognitive domain (e.g., Carroll, 1976; Gagné, 1967; Glaser, 1972; Hunt, 1974; Hunt, Frost, & Lunneborg, 1973; Snow, 1976a, b; Sternberg, 1977; Underwood, 1975). Even so, attempts to provide theoretical linkages between the two approaches are limited in scope and are still rare. Studies concentrating on the multivariate approach (e.g., Guilford, 1959) tend to obscure process, and contributions from the experimental tradition (e.g., Sternberg, 1977) tend to deny the multidimensionality of the problem. And, although we get both structure and dynamics from Eysenck's work (e.g., H. J. Eysenck, 1970), his analyses are limited to the affective domain and to three theoretical constructs. Although the theory we present in this book also falls short of the ultimate goal, we see it as a significant step in the direction of unification.

Maxim II.
Personality and its component processes
are extremely complex
from a theoretical-scientific perspective.

It is important to remember that there are no simplistic solutions to the problem we have undertaken. Our claim is that the individual human organism is the most complex problem area ever subjected to scientific observation and analysis. Consider, for example, that some 10 billion individual nerve cells, each highly sensitive to events around it and each having as many as 2,000 to 4,000 connections to other individual nerve cells, are packed into the human head—a space considerably smaller than a basketball! Consider further that this complex mass of interacting cells is influenced by heredity, nutrition, the individual's psychological makeup, the surrounding culture, information about events that have taken place in remote times, dreams about the future, and so forth. The permutations and combinations of events that might be critical in understanding even the simplest of processes are truly staggering. Therefore, we feel no need to apologize for having introduced a somewhat complex theory of personality and individual differences and for saying, in the same breath, that this complex theory has only begun to scratch the surface of the problem.

We have evolved several strategies for dealing with the problem of complexity. First, we relied on the results of factor-analytic investigations to provide an empirical guide to the *structure* of individual differences (Chapter 3 outlines the factor-analytic model). Like any empirical results, factor-analytic findings suggest ways of thinking about the problems at hand. Since no empirical procedure or result is beyond reproach, any theorist should be prepared to follow whatever lead is made available, whether the lead comes from the bivariate, experimental laboratory or the multivariate, differential psychology approach. Therefore, our second major strategy has involved combing the experimental literature in the domains of concern for additional leads as to how individual difference variables might be construed to influence integrative personality. This strategy was particularly important in those domains where individual difference studies were meager or inadequate in other ways. For example, as will be discussed in subsequent chapters, differential psychologists have concentrated their efforts on such domains as cognition and affect; they have undertaken relatively few investigations in other areas. In such cases, the experimental literature has provided an important source of information about how individual differences might be structured and how they might influence information processing.

Our third strategy has used constructs from general systems theory—an approach originally developed as a conceptual framework for dealing with "organized complexities," regardless of subject matter. For example, a very important simplifying strategy involved the conceptualization of the various domains of personality and individual differences (e.g., cognition, affect) as separate (but complexly interactive) systems making up the total psychological suprasystem. This was initially helpful because the overall domain of personality was thus divided into more manageable units. As the theory developed we began to ask more interesting questions about the outcomes of various interactions among these smaller units. The systems approach was also of great value in answering questions about characteristics of the various domains of individuality.

Our final major strategy involved an attempt to wed modern information-processing concepts with factor theory. Chapter 3 includes a summary of important concepts from systems and information-processing theory.

An additional idea related to our view that personality is extremely complex is that human behavior (and the internal events that can only be inferred) is *multiply determined*. We think personality is more appropriately construed as a complex network of causal influences rather than as simple chains of causal events. With such a perspective personality will always be unpredictable and the effect of external influences highly uncertain. Not even a rigidly totalitarian or a Utopian society (such as might exist in the mind of a Skinnerian) can rid us completely of such uncertainties concerning the behaviors, thoughts, and feelings of the individual human organism.

Maxim III.
Personality and its component systems
are goal directed.

As Henry Murray (1938) and many others after him were fond of pointing out, the human individual is not merely *reactive,* but *proactive*. Individuals are not merely "pushed around" by various environmental forces (stimuli) but more often are pulled, encouraged, driven, cajoled, or otherwise led to pursue goals that may be nonexistent or that frequently require a concerted, concentrated, and even creative effort for their attainment. A fairly simple drive-reduction model of motivated behavior may well apply to imprisoned animals in restricted experimental environments, and principles of operant or respondent conditioning may significantly contribute to our understanding of complex behavior in various laboratory situations, but a better understanding of complex human behavior requires a search that goes deeper below the surface. For example, as we indicated at the beginning of this chapter, humans are directed to find or create personal meaning in their lives—a notion that goes far beyond the confines of restricted laboratory environments. Personal meaning is not something that exists in the external world or confronts individuals from outside their skin and dictates the next step to take. It is a vision that each of us must create anew for ourselves. Moreover, this vision might underlie even the most mundane of behavioral acts.

A *teleogenic* system is goal-directed; a *teleogenetic* system can generate its own goals (Coulter, 1968). We see human personality and its component systems as teleogenetic systems, inasmuch as individuals can and do generate for themselves life-long goals that guide and direct their thoughts and actions for many decades. They choose mates and careers, for example, that structure their lives for many years.

The major implication is that, in order to understand personality or its component systems, we have had to inquire into the particular goals that occupy these systems.

It is important to emphasize that our model of individuals as goal-directed does not mean that the organism always acts to reduce tension. To the contrary, human goals more frequently require the creation of tension. Whether the task involves pursuing a graduate degree, trying to understand human individuality, exploring the North Pole, enjoying rides at a fair, or organizing a hunt in a hunting-gathering society, the undertakings of most individuals lead to increases in the overall tension level, at least initially. As we shall discuss in a number of places throughout the book, it is more appropriate to describe individuals as *manipulating* tension rather than merely reducing it.

Maxim IV.
Each person is in some ways
the same individual throughout the life span,
and in other ways very different individuals
throughout the life span.

One of the most obvious characteristics of the behavior of any individual is that it changes in many important respects over the life span and yet remains the same in many other respects. The stability of some personality characteristics presents no real problem to theorizing about personality, but radical changes present a major challenge to theoretical attempts to describe and explain complex human behavior. The challenge stems from the fact that most information-processing (and other) models of behavior are *synchronic* as opposed to *diachronic*. Synchronic changes are cross-sectional changes within a system at any given moment, whereas diachronic changes are the longitudinal changes of a system over extended periods of time. This distinction is important because, in part, any *change in structure* requires a change in the model used to represent that structure. As outlined in Chapter 3, we think the various systems of personality undergo both synchronic and diachronic changes from birth to death. The synchronic are relatively easy to deal with conceptually; the diachronic are more problematic.

A critical aspect of the challenge presented by developmental change concerns problems of how to describe the overall organization of personality and individual differences. Our approach has been to focus on the middle period of life (from early to late adulthood) because personality and its various components are most stable during this period. At the same time we have tried to keep in mind that the descriptions we develop in this manner apply to only a portion of the total life span. The other point to consider in this context is that most of the empirical research in individual differences, as in other areas of psychology, is based on samples from adult populations. In any case, Chapter 7 summarizes the available research on life span changes in individual difference variables relevant to our theory. We further propose a model of changes in the structural organization of personality that occur from birth to death (Chapter 12).

Personality changes are propelled by a variety of forces. Some are genetic, others reside in the environment, and still others result as a complex interaction among genetic and environmental forces. In Chapter 3 we describe a factor-gene model that makes it possible to analyze the extent of hereditary contribution to any particular individual difference. We also present a factor-learning model wherein a variety of learning processes related to individual differences are discussed, and in Chapter 7 we summarize the empirical evidence regarding the hereditary and environmental contributions to personality and individual differences.

BRIEF OVERVIEW
OF MULTIFACTOR-SYSTEMS
THEORY OF INDIVIDUALITY

Our theory of individuality and personality is referred to as multifactor-systems theory since the dimensions of individual differences in each of six personality systems are identified through the method and theory of factor analysis. Personality is hypothesized to be composed of six interacting systems: *sensory, motor, cognition, affect, style,* and *value.* Definitions of each are provided in Table 1-1, where, for example, the total psychological system is defined as ''a hierarchical organization of systems, subsystems, and traits that transduce, transform, and integrate psychological information.'' Within this scheme, the sensory (Kearsley & Royce, 1977) and motor (Powell, Katzko, & Royce, 1978) systems are at the periphery of personality, but they nevertheless filter and transduce energy into information and vice versa. As will be discussed in Chapter 4, the sensory and motor components can be thought of as input-output components. The cognitive (Diamond & Royce, 1980; Powell & Royce, 1982) and affective (Royce & McDermott, 1977) systems are more central aspects of integrative personality that engage in the active transformation of information. As will be discussed in Chapter 5, the primary function of the cognitive system is to identify ecological invariants by transforming information in various ways, and the affective system transforms information in order to establish optimal levels of internal arousal. The style (Wardell & Royce, 1978) and value systems are also central processing components of personality, but they are postulated to have more of an integrative or self-organizing role in overall functioning. As will be discussed in Chapter 6, styles exercise a coordinating influence over various *modes* of information process-

TABLE 1-1 Definitions of the Basic Systems Postulated to be the Components of Integrative Personality

SYSTEM LEVELS	DEFINITIONS	
Suprasystem	Integrative personality (the total psychological system) is a hierarchical organization of systems, subsystems, and traits that transduce, transform, and integrate information.	
Self-organizing or integrative	STYLE A multidimensional, hierarchical system that integrates and modulates information by coordinating cognition and affect, and by selecting particular modes of processing	VALUE A multidimensional, hierarchical system that integrates and modulates information by coordinating cognition and affect to achieve specifiable goals, by satisfying specified needs, or by selecting specifiable information content
Learning-adaptive or transformational	COGNITION A multidimensional, hierarchical system that transforms psychological information in order to identify environmental invariants.	AFFECT A multidimensional, hierarchical system that transforms psychological information in order to attain optimal arousal states
Controlled-process, or transductional (Encoding and decoding)	SENSORY A multidimensional, hierarchical system that transduces physical energy into psychological information	MOTOR A multidimensional, hierarchical system that transduces psychological information into physical energy.

ing; values are more concerned with the *content* of information processing activities and with long-range goals.

Each of the six basic systems of individuality are described in terms of dimensions of individual differences that have been reliably identified in factor-analytic investigations. However, as indicated earlier, the research literature has been found to be lacking in several areas, and it was necessary to use leads from non-factor-analytic research in constructing hypotheses about the structure of individual differences in some of these areas. To date in our research on the structure, dynamics, and development of the six systems, 153 factors have been identified as reliable dimensions of individual differences, and an additional 32 have been postulated on the basis of non-factor-analytic research.

The six major systems hypothesized to make up personality are diagramed in relationship to each other in Figure 1-1, and the major subsystems within each are also shown. Thus, for example, cognition is hypothesized to be composed of *perceiving, conceptualizing,* and *symbolizing.* Similarly, the motor system is composed of the *spatiality* and *temporality* subsystems. These various subsystems can also be characterized as higher-order factors or source traits of individual differences. More specifically, the various subsystems depicted in Figure 1-1 are identified via third-order factors that subsume a variety of second- and first-order (or primary) factors.

Overall, personality has been conceptualized as *hierarchically* organized since there are events that intervene in the functioning or control of other events. For example, an individual's cognitive styles have a coordinating influence on how information is processed by the cognitive system, and an individual's values have a coordinating influence on what is felt in various situations—that is, on affective arousal for given inputs and processed information. Such inputs are depicted in Figure 1-1 as arrows pointing from higher-level systems to lower-level systems; feedback is represented by arrows pointing in the opposite direction.

The higher-level systems of integrative personality depicted in Figure 1-1, in comparison with lower-level systems, (1) are more important with respect to the processes involved in personality integration; (2) can input coordinating information; (3) are concerned with longer units of time; (4) have a higher priority of action; and (5) are more closely related to the deeper (in the sense of significant) levels or aspects of personality.

Personality and its component systems are considered to be goal-seeking systems (Bertalanffy, 1955; Mesarovic, Macko, & Takahara, 1970; Sommerhof, 1969) with internal norms for evaluating whether actions are "successful." Furthermore, the goals of these systems are decomposable, as when plans are decomposed into strategies, strategies into tactics, and so on (Miller, Galanter, & Pribram, 1960; Singer, 1975). For example, at the highest level of personality, the goal is to optimize personal meaning (see Figure 1-1), which involves such subgoals as establishing a satisfactory life style, evolving an adequate world view, and maintaining acceptable self-images.

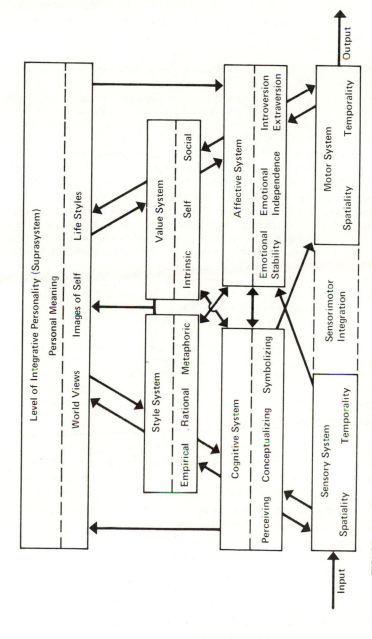

FIGURE 1-1 The basic systems and interactive relationships of integrative personality. (From Powell & Royce, 1978)

13

Developmental Change

According to our metamorphogenetic model presented in Chapter 3, these structures of personality undergo a variety of transformations that can be summarized in the following ways:

1. *Quantitative change.* There are measurable increases and decreases in individual differences over the life span; such changes are typically described as *growth* and *aging.*

2. *Differentiation and consolidation.* During early development there is increasing differentiation among the various components of personality. In other words, the more mature individual is expected to be more psychologically differentiated and articulated than the child (e.g., Witkin, 1974).

3. *Increasing integration and hierarchical organization.* Accompanying the above changes in personality over the life span, one might expect to find increasing hierarchical organization both within and between the various subsystems and components.

4. *Self-organization.* Another important characteristic of development relates to progressive changes in the overall *goals* of personality. With increasing differentiation and hierarchicalization, the critical decisions that an individual must face also change. For example, one would not expect a child to maintain the same general goals as an adult unless the adult is retarded in development or the child is very advanced.

5. *Increasing capacity for the self-generation of goals and norms.* For example, individuals plan life styles and careers that extend over the entire life span and can plan for the kind of persons they will become in the future. The choices a person makes throughout life determine the course of individual development, in some cases including the roles that environment and genes may play in the process. Many individuals make career choices early in adolescence, or even childhood, that influence the rest of their lives, including how their inherited abilities are developed, how their abilities interact with the environment, and the range of choices they will be able to make later in life.

Levels of Analysis
and System Interactions

One of the most central aspects of our theoretical analysis of overall personality that serves to integrate factor and systems constructs is our conception of personality as being organized at various levels of functioning. As outlined in Table 1–2, we require five levels of abstraction from the perspectives of both factor theory and systems analysis. Thus, at the apex we have the total psychological system, or personality, as the functioning unit. Level IV refers to each of the six systems that compose the total system. These are relatively autonomous functional units that subsume the factor-identified, interactive components of an entire domain (such as cognition or affect), and that represent the basic units of integrative personality. From the standpoint of factor theory, the important construct at this level is that of personality type, which refers to the overall dimensional characteristics of an entire domain of functioning (e.g., cognitive type or affective type). The functional significance of each of the levels of personality are identified in the right-hand column. For example, the integrative suprasystem of personality is primarily concerned with the maintenance of personal meaning,

TABLE 1–2   Overall Comparison Among the Integrative Units of Personality

LEVEL OF ANALYSIS	SYSTEMS THEORY CONSTRUCTS	PSYCHOLOGICAL (AND FACTOR) EQUIVALENTS	FUNCTIONAL SIGNIFICANCE
V	Suprasystem	Personality (Psychological Integration)	Maintenance of personal meaning
IV	Systems	Psychological type (profile)	Adaptation under varying conditions
III	Subsystems	Tertiary traits (Third-order factors)	Integrative goal attainment
II	Subsystem components	Secondary traits (Second-order factors)	Specific goal achievement
I	Subsystem elements	Primary traits (First-order factors)	Specific operations

while the significance of a system (and type, as reflected in the dimensional characteristics) lies in its adaptive role to changing environmental conditions. At issue here is the transduction, transformation, and integration of psychological information, given particular environmental inputs and a particular personality type.

There are a variety of subtotal integrations that are a consequence of interactions among two or more of the six systems. Among the 15 possible paired combinations of the six systems we have identified several of these subtotal integrations that involve various combinations of style, value, cognition, and affect (see Figure 1–2). For example, we think world view is generated primarily as an outcome of the interaction of cognition and style. Similarly, variations in life style are the result of affective-value interaction, emotion a consequence of cognitive-affective interaction, and self-image an outcome of style and value interaction. For the sake of completeness we have also shown sensory-motor integration in Figure 1–2.

The subsystems, indicated at level III of Table 1–2, are the major subclasses of each of the major systems. For example, the three subcategories of the cognitive system have been identified as perceiving, conceptualizing, and symbolizing. Psychologically, they are integrative components of personality, in systems terminology they are subsystems, and from the standpoint of factor analysis they are third-order factors. These tertiary traits emerge out of the second-order factors of level II, which, in turn, emerge out of the primary traits of level I. From the systems perspective, second-order factors refer to the processing dimensions of subsystem components, whereas first-order factors reflect the processing dimensions of subsystem elements.

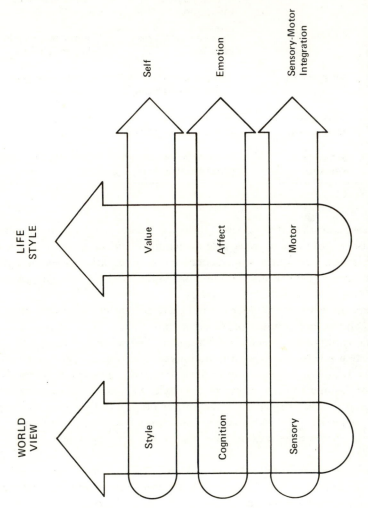

FIGURE 1-2 The major constructions resulting from various combinations of system interactions.

16

The whole problem of system interactions and integrations is addressed in Part 3 of the book. Chapter 8 considers all the possible interactive combinations, the general problem of interactions, belief systems as an outcome of value and cognition, and emotion as an outcome of affect and cognition. Chapters 9 and 10 are directed more specifically at the system interactions we consider to be most important in integrative personality. In Chapter 9 the combination of cognition and style is shown to yield world views, and life styles are shown to emerge out of the value-affect interaction. How style and value give rise to self-images is discussed in Chapter 10. Finally, the concept of personality type, the general problem of personality integration, and the concept of personal meaning are discussed in Chapter 11, and Chapter 12 presents the life-span development of integrative personality.

2

On Theory and Metatheory
and Their Relevance
to Individuality Theory

Since our efforts are primarily theoretical, it seems important to make some introductory remarks concerning the role of theory in psychology and science in general, as well as some of the metatheoretical (i.e., theory of theory) aspects of individuality theory. In this chapter we address several important metatheoretical issues. The first, dealing with the role of theory in psychology, is the most general one and is the concern of the major portion of this chapter. The remaining issues are more directly relevant to our specific theory and concern some metatheoretical aspects of factor analysis, the general context of individuality theory, humanism versus mechanism, the problem of determinism, the part–whole problem, and the question of mind versus body. Our concern in this chapter is to discuss briefly the major background issues rather than present an exhaustive metatheoretic analysis.

THE ROLE OF THEORY
IN SCIENTIFIC PSYCHOLOGY

Albert Einstein summed up our position with respect to the role of theory in scientific undertakings in a succinct and very elegant statement: ''Science is the attempt to make the chaotic diversity of our own sense experience correspond to a logically uniform system of thought'' (Einstein, 1940, p. 487). This statement implies that the ultimate goal of science is theory (''a logically uniform system of thought'') that makes logical sense of empirical observation (''our sense impressions''). Science is not just endlessly collecting empirical data; it is an explicit attempt to understand and explain what it is that empirical observations yield. This point was made in several earlier publications by Royce (e.g., 1976, 1978): '' . . .*the ultimate goal of science is to develop powerful theory.*'' The key terms in this statement are *powerful* and *ultimate.* The term *ultimate* has to do with what science is trying to accomplish. The view here espoused is that science is reaching for those theoretical generalizations that ''explain'' observables as ''for instances.'' But theory will not be adequate to the task unless it takes on conceptual ''power,'' where *power* refers to the more advanced or perfected forms of theory.

Although no scientific discipline has achieved complete theoretical unification, this is the ideal toward which science strives. Nevertheless, the natural sciences have generated highly advanced theories such as Newtonian or Einsteinian theory in physics and genetic-evolutionary theory in biology. When the final chapter is written, psychology may have to settle for theory of relatively limited scope, although psychology's immediate problem is to get beyond its first chapter as a theoretical science.

In their historical development sciences go through several stages during which there is differential development of the empirical and theoretical aspects. When traced back to its earliest origins, each science has evolved out of a philosophic context. But between philosophic origins and the final stage of theoretical explanation, scientific methods of observation and measurement are developed. Although a given science may go through more or fewer stages in its development, and although the sequentiality of stages may vary (i.e., there is no fixed sequence), it is our view that the total spectrum of scientific development can be spanned in terms of the following four stages: (a) prescientific philosophic speculation, (b) empirical exploration, (c) sophistication of methods of controlled observation and quantification, and (d) theoretical formalization and unification.[1]

This leads to the conclusion that

> *contemporary psychology can be described as being in an empirical-experimental stage.* In terms of the four stages indicated, psychology is somewhere between stages (b) and (c), empirical exploration and the development of better methods of observation and quantification. For a more complete elaboration of this conclusion the reader is referred to

[1]The concept of stage is not meant to convey a sequence of clearly definable points that must occur in the development of all sciences. Rather, it is being used in the sense of identifiable phases or periods that typically fall in the specified sequence (but do not have to). For example, it is possible for a theory (stage d) to be formulated prior to the gathering of data (stages b and c). However, such empirically empty formulations are usually regarded as philosophical speculation (stage a). The important point is that powerful theory is the ultimate goal, whatever the variations in prior developmental sequence. The suggested sequence of phases or stages is put forth in the context of historical evidence; it is not put forth as an analogue of embryological development.

previous analyses (Royce, 1957c, 1970a, 1976). A major point of these earlier analyses is that the various areas of psychology are in different stages of development. For example, areas such as sensation, perception, learning, and biopsychology can be characterized as experimental and semi-explanatory, whereas areas such as personality and social are characterized as correlational-descriptive. Thus, while subdomains range over all four stages, the central tendency of the entire field is assessed to be between stages (b) and (c). The most obvious manifestations of this claim are the tons of data which psychologists have amassed during the 20th century. (Royce, 1978a, p. 260)

From the above points, it follows that *psychology at present is a theoretically immature science*. If the ultimate goal of science is to evolve advanced forms of theory (e.g., explanatory theory), and if psychology is still focused on the problems of gathering and quantifying data, then it is clear that psychology has devoted a relatively small proportion of its total effort to the development of theory. If we assume there is validity to this line of reasoning, then it also follows that *at this stage of its development further scientific progress in psychology is crucially dependent on advances in the construction of theory.*

There are other reasons for believing that further progress is dependent on theoretical work. For example, the vacuum left by the demise of logical positivism is being filled by *theory-laden constructivism* (Royce, 1976). [2] This view emerges out of the writings of such philosophers of science as Polanyi (1958), Feyerabend (1965, 1970), Habermas (1971), and Radnitzky (1970), and such historians of science as Hanson (1961) and Kuhn (1970). The major claims of this new philosophy are:

1. All observations are theory-laden; that is, an observation is made within an overall conceptual framework. Thus, the same observation might have different meanings if embedded in different theoretical contexts.
2. Furthermore, the basic concepts of a theory are *constructed* by the investigator.
3. Thus, scientific findings are, in some sense, human inventions or constructions.
4. We choose between competing theories primarily on theoretical grounds, only secondarily on empirical grounds, via such criteria as exhaustiveness, reliability, fruitfulness, and interpretability (hermeneutics).
5. The role of observation is not that of arbiter between competing theories, as was claimed by the logical positivists and others. In fact, historical analysis shows that no theory has ever been dropped because of a so-called crucial experiment or because of inadequate or insufficient data (Frank, 1964).
6. The primary role of empirical observation is to provide the empirical correlates of one or another theory-laden construct; that is, observation provides the substantive content of the conceptual abstractions of the theoretician (Royce, 1976, p. 5).

[2] Realism is another postpositivistic metatheoretic approach that has contemporary relevance (e.g., see Harré, 1976). Although it takes a variety of forms, such as naive realism and critical, or Popperian, realism, a major tenet of this view is that theoretical terms are not reducible to observation terms (as claimed by the logical positivists), and further, that they refer to external reality with as much force as observation terms. Thus, critical realism is in agreement with constructivism regarding the importance of theoretical concepts. However, further analysis is bound to lead to several disagreements. For example, theory-laden constructivism appears to be open on the issue of the ontological status of theoretical terms—that is, construing theoretical terms as either useful conventions (instrumentalism) or as "real"—whereas realism clearly must adopt the latter stance.

The argument is that theory-laden constructivism is the most adequate metatheory available for science, and that this state of affairs has implications for psychology, the most obvious one being *"that scientific advancement is more dependent upon theory construction per se than was heretofore realized"* (Royce, 1976, p. 6).

> More specifically, the argument is that, since understanding of psychological phenomena is crucially dependent upon adequacy of conceptualization, continuation of psychology's present overcommitment to empiricism would be a blatant error! Furthermore, if we combine this metatheoretic point with the fact that psychology is in a pre-theoretical (or, at least, theoretically muddled) phase of its historical development, then it follows that scientific advancement in psychology is being severely retarded because of theoretical inadequacies. (Royce, 1978a, p. 261)

Koch (1976, pp. 6–7 and 1976, pp. 480–495) reviews psychology's hundred-year history and regards it as an enterprise that

1. is not, and cannot (in principle) be coherent
2. is a victim of scientism
3. has either given us pseudo or negative knowledge.[3]

In short, Koch concludes that scientific psychology has failed. He argues that, since what psychology has to offer are various images of humankind instead of explanatory theory, the scientific charade should be dropped and psychology reconceived as "psychological studies." We agree with most of Koch's critique concerning psychology's inadequacies, including his claim that the field is too conceptually diverse to yield to complete unification, and Royce has offered similar prescriptions concerning the redefinition of psychology (Royce, 1960, 1976). However, we disagree with Koch's readiness to concede defeat at this juncture. Our major argument against Koch's position is that his conclusion is premature because psychology as theoretical science has not been put to the test of theoretical adequacy for the simple reason that its practitioners have been focusing their attention on gathering data at the expense of pursuing theory.[4] That is, the psychology zeitgeist has been so focused on data that theory has been neglected. As a result the general level of sophistication in theory construction simply has not

---

[3]Negative knowledge demonstrates what is not the case, in contrast to positive knowledge, which demonstrates what is the case. It can, of course, be argued that demonstrations of what is not the case help advance knowledge. In fact, this is Popper's (1963) position in his "conjectures and refutations" view of how science progresses. He argues that it is not possible to inductively confirm a theory—rather, one determines its degree of corroborability, where corroborability depends on the severity of the empirical tests to which a theory has been subjected. In short, negative knowledge is useful in refuting weak theory, but strong theory requires positive knowledge. Thus, the force of Koch's position remains—a science cannot move toward theoretical maturity solely on the basis of negative knowledge.

[4]This statement should not be construed as antiempirical. Solid data is crucial to the scientific enterprise. The mere gathering of data, while necessary, is not sufficient. That is, empiricism for the sake of empiricism cannot resolve the conceptual issues of science. In short, sophistication in both the rational aspects of theory construction and the empirical aspects of data gathering are crucial to the advancement of science.

kept pace with the technical advances in experimentation and statistical-methodological analysis. To put it conversely, advancements in experimentation and statistical-methodological analysis have resulted in a sophisticated research technology, but comparable advancements in theory construction are necessary to move psychology in the direction of explanatory science (Royce, 1976).[5]

Differential Strategies of Theory Construction

The most important point to be made in this section is

> that the construction of psychological theory will require a variety of strategies, and further, that the optimal strategy for developing a theory of any phenomenon is dependent upon the degree of maturity of the domain in question. Figure 2-1 indicates that theoretic maturity or power can be regarded as a continuum, and that it has a wide range. However, it also indicates that we can identify three points on this continuum which have been referred to as programmatic, descriptive, and explanatory. What theory construction strategy is indicated for each of these three metatheoretic categories?
>
> We begin with the explanatory category, which is the most difficult to achieve but the easiest to discuss. One reason it is relatively easy to discuss is because it is unlikely that psychology is ready for this kind of theory. In any event, no such psychological theory is available. Theory of this degree of power involves the mutual meshing of rigorous formalism (usually some form of mathematics), a highly replicable empiricism, and a relatively broad scope. Furthermore, such theory, which can be characterized as having achieved considerable "thinghood," has the potential for continued broadening of its scope. Therefore, the relevant strategy for explanatory theory is to press for the limits of its applicability. However, the issue of theoretical scope also raises the question of parsimony—that is, stating the theory via the smallest possible set of constructs, principles, and axioms. Hence, optimality of strategy for explanatory theory will occur at that juncture where scope is maximized and the number of required theoretical principles is minimized. (Royce, 1978a, pp. 271-72)

[5]In fact, a case could be made for the claim that psychology's greatest contribution to date lies in the realm of methodology—both statistical and observational. Perhaps the most obvious statistical example is analysis of variance. Although this procedure for data analysis originated in agriculture, it has received an impressive elaboration by psychologists. Observational examples range all the way from the development of the standardized test to monitoring dreams via rapid eye movements. The point here is that psychologists have shown tremendous ingenuity in devising methodology that allows them to observe the previously unobservable. Finally, factor analysis is an example of methodological innovation that combined both statistical and observational ingenuity. Furthermore, it constitutes one of the few examples of the exportation of psychological expertise—i.e., although it originated in psychology, it has been applied to all the sciences, including physics, biology, and the social sciences (Royce, 1958; Harman, 1976).

The major point is that, despite its methodological sophistication, psychology has been held back primarily because of its lack of sophistication in theory construction. The point is made doubly important in the context of a theory-laden view of science. This view says that, since observations are dependent on the theoretical constructs we use, empirical adequacy is a direct consequence of the scientist's conceptual framework. Thus, the appropriate conclusion is that observations of psychological phenomena are directly dependent on the adequacy of the psychologist's theories.

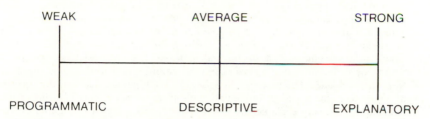

THEORETICAL POWER

WEAK   AVERAGE   STRONG

PROGRAMMATIC   DESCRIPTIVE   EXPLANATORY

FIGURE 2-1   A continuum of theoretical power showing the relationships among programmatic, descriptive, and explanatory theory. (From Royce, 1978a)

The next category to be analyzed, labeled *descriptive,*

> should be thought of as being at an average level of theoretical power. Such theory has a relatively solid empirical base, but the rational structure is relatively underdeveloped. Exemplars of such theory in psychology can be found most readily in the areas of sensory processes, perception, learning, and biopsychology. (Royce 1970a, pp. 20–22).

The crucial task of descriptive theory is to develop a nomological network that can accommodate a relatively limited domain. Although a rigorous formalism is desirable, it is not crucial. What is crucial is to establish a network of relationships (i.e., lawful relationships among theoretical constructs) and a body of generalizations and principles. This means that descriptive theory must become more abstract. It must run the risk of conceptualizing at increasing distances from the data but without losing sufficient contact with the data. Thus, optimality of strategy in this case involves developing a tight nomological network while minimizing relatively weak connections.

The weakest category of theory is designated as programmatic. It characterizes most of the theory in psychology, particularly in highly complex areas such as motivation, emotion, psychopathology, and social behavior (Royce, 1970a).

> The most obvious problem for these areas of investigation is the quality of the data base. Without a solid empirical foundation theory reduces to empty speculation. And, while we do not deny the value of speculation (e.g., see Bakan, 1975), the history of pre-scientific psychology constitutes a clear demonstration of the dangers of empirically empty theorizing. The greatest risk of unbridled speculation is the attempt to evolve explanatory theory prematurely. Thus, while it might be reasonable to demand stronger formalisms and greater explicitness of constructs and relationships in the case of the more mature theories (i.e., in the areas of sensation, perception, learning, and biopsychology), the history of science shows that it is rare, if not impossible, for a science to leapfrog into theoretical maturity. On the contrary, the history of science suggests that progress, although cumulative within a given conceptual framework, is usually painful and slow. Thus, weak, programmatic theory may

eventually evolve into more explicit and adequate theory, but such an evolution means that certain requirements will have been met. It means, for example, the identification of empirically based theoretical constructs, the generation of many, highly reliable, empirical laws, the development of a viable taxonomy, and an inventory of generalizations. In short, the simpler forms of theory construction are called for when developing primitive theory. However, the long-range implications of such relatively simple achievements should not be underestimated, for the establishment of any degree of order amidst the chaos of raw empiricism constitutes a significant theoretical advance. Furthermore, as Eysenck (1960) has pointed out, the successes of weak theory have a larger immediate pay-off (in terms of "bits" of information) than the successes of explanatory theory. More specifically, the potential of weak theory is that it can provide a direction which was not previously available. This means that theory construction strategy in the case of weak theory is primarily a matter of heuristics. But the typical situation, especially in the case of programmatic theory, is that many alternative theories are available. Good heuristics in this context includes the critical analysis of alternatives, with the implication that most programmatic theories will be discarded. This point highlights one of the most devastating manifestations of the immaturity of contemporary psychology as theoretical science—namely, its failure to reject and retain selectively. The weakness of programmatic psychological theory does *not* lie in the fact that many alternatives have been produced. Rather, it lies in the fact that so few of the alternatives have been weeded out (e.g., over 20 theories of motivation [Madsen, 1974], and a similarly large number of mental illness models [Weckowicz, 1982], and with little basis available for deciding which ones should be rejected or retained).

Although programmatic theory includes elements of empiricism and rationalism, it is typically dominated by analogical metatheory. And, since the point of focus is heuristic rather than explanatory, there is insufficient epistemological basis for regarding such theory as "true." The more justifiable concern is whether it carries sufficient weight to warrant further research. Thus, the major thrust of weak theory is to move beyond pure metaphor or analogy to increasing degrees of empirical and rational potency in the hope that the theory will become more explanatory.[6] This means that programmatic theory construction strategy should be focused on how to initiate an attack on the domain in question. Thus, the optimal strategy in this case involves trying to get a nomological network started; that is, identifying some of the relevant theoretical constructs and ascertaining their theoretical relationships. (Royce, 1978a, pp. 272–73)

Our multifactor-systems theory has elements of all three categories of theory we have been describing. For example, the empirical basis in factor analysis gives it *descriptive* status; the factor-gene and factor-learning models and our models of development, cognition, affect, emotion, world view, life style, and personal meaning provide it with explanatory status. However, the many attempts at integrating concepts from a variety of different research traditions suggest that much of our theoretical effort is still in the realm of programmatic theory. Overall, we assess our theory as descriptive, with some explanatory characteristics. This means that the theory has a relatively solid empirical basis but that it carries only average theoretical power. Perhaps our major theoretical accomplishment has

---

[6]For an elaboration of the role of the metaphor in science see Oppenheimer (1956). For a similar analysis that is focused on psychology, see Nash (1963).

been to put forward a viable nomological network that covers the full range of individual differences. We also provide the beginnings of a more powerful theory by virtue of a few unifying constructs. For example, third-order factor constructs, system properties and principles, and the concept of personality type are all constructs with considerable potential. A full elaboration of these unifying constructs could well evolve into a more parsimonious theory with greater explanatory power.

Conceptual Pluralism

Conceptual pluralism refers to the claim that psychology is "multi" (see Royce, 1976)—in particular, that it is multitheoretic.

> The traditional stance has been to view pluralism as a sign of theoretic weakness, and to view it with alarm (e.g., Koch, 1974). However, contemporary counter-thought regarding such matters suggests that the prolific spinning of conceptual alternatives is a more accurate reflection of the realities of doing science (Naess, 1972). Furthermore, theoretical pluralism is consistent with the logical argument that different theoretical structures can accommodate the same set of data. And theoretical pluralism is consistent with the view that *no theory can be verified.* On the other hand, Popper (1959) argues that theories can be refuted. Furthermore, he argues that theories which are, in principle, not refutable (e.g., psychoanalysis) are irrelevant to science. However, attempts to refute viable alternatives constitute a major concern of the scientist. Such refutations of theoretical conjectures (Popper, 1963) establish the boundary conditions of a given theory. For example, if a theory were to survive all possible refutations (past, present, and future), it would be reasonable to conclude that the theory has been confirmed. However, Popper argues that, since there are always potential refutations via observations not yet made (i.e., in the future), we can never know whether a given theory will survive them. Thus, we are left with degrees of corroboration via the principle of falsifiability rather than total verifiability as the epistemic basis for the validity of a theory. And this also means we must grapple with theoretical pluralism as a scientific reality, particularly in highly complex fields (such as psychology) where the scope of a particular theory is likely to be relatively limited. (Royce, 1978a, p. 273)

In Royce's Nebraska Symposium paper (1976) and elsewhere (Royce, 1977c), the stance is taken that psychology must develop a philosophy that takes conceptual pluralism into account, and that such a philosophy will take some form of *constructive dialectic.* In this view the term *dialectic* refers to maintaining the tension between viable alternatives, and the term *constructive* refers to "invented" or "created" (i.e., not "discovered") theories. In short, such a philosophy regards the creative production of theoretical alternatives as normal science. However, normal science also involves the development of pragmatic strategies for the selective rejection and retention of proliferated theory (Royce, 1978a, p. 273).

Our general hope for individuality theory is that it will be a part of some "constructive dialectic" analysis. We recognize that no theory in contemporary psychology that attempts to look at so much of the terrain as ours does can survive in total. But we do think that some of the insights presented here will be selectively retained as part of the small number of viable alternatives.

Two Major Obstacles to Developing a Viable Theory of Individual Differences

Although it has long been recognized that differential psychology might provide important insights to understanding personality, the Achilles' heel of this approach has been the problem of identifying the fundamental dimensions that account for observed differences. Although factor analysis is the best available scientific method for identifying the dimensions of organized complexity, and although it has reduced the number of required personality constructs from thousands to hundreds, the current state of the art is such that there is no mechanical algorithm available for deciding which dimensions are invariant. This means it is necessary to make qualitative judgements concerning this issue. It is our view that *the problem of factor invariance (i.e., factors that are repeatable despite variations in investigators, subjects, and measurements) underlies the substantive conflicts and confusions concerning factors and their organization* (Royce, 1979b).

The mere inventorying of invariant factors, although an important and necessary step, cannot generate advanced forms of science because explanatory theory requires viable conceptual frameworks as a basis for interpreting empirical observables (Royce, 1976, 1978a). The point is that factor analysis per se is incapable of providing the prerequisite conceptual framework for its substantive findings. It can identify potentially unifying components of such a framework (Royce, 1963), but the subsuming model (of which factors are critical parts) must come from elsewhere. This point has not been adequately perceived by either the factor analysts or their critics. The major shortcoming of the factor-analytic proponents is their belief that a theoretical structure could somehow be automatically generated as a natural consequence of inventorying invariant factors. A major consequence of this conceptual commitment is that personality theory too heavily based on factor analysis has not been able to go beyond structure to dynamics (Royce, 1979b).

Although occasional voices from within the factor subcommunity have mentioned the need to deal with process (e.g., see Messick, 1973), it is the current interaction between multivariate and experimental psychology that is forcing the issue of conceptual framework into such sharp focus. That is, the experimental tradition has kept its eye on process. But the importation of a new ingredient, the information-processing and systems paradigm, is of particular importance in this context. For this new paradigm is the conceptual framework that is bringing multivariate and experimental psychology together in an effort to understand complex psychological phenomena.

Multifactor-systems theory represents an attempt to embed factors as source traits of individual differences within the context of complex information processing systems. In short, we are attempting to deal with both the structural and the processing dynamics of personality.

THE GENERAL CONTEXT
OF INDIVIDUALITY THEORY

We view individuality theory as being part of the total effort to gain theoretical insight into the nature of humankind and the human condition. We think that most attempts to gain such insights have ended far short of their goals because they fail to consider humankind from sufficiently rich and varied perspectives. Although some disciplines are more central than others, all of the humanities and the social and natural sciences shed light on what it means to be human, and attempts to understand the human condition will continue to be frustrated if the insights each speciality has to offer are not taken into account. However, there are many hurdles to overcome in attempting a synthesis of such insights. For example, one individual cannot expect to master the language, knowledge, and perceptual sensitivities of more than a few specialized disciplines. Indeed, in today's specialized world it is a major feat to master a single *sub*discipline of knowledge (Royce, 1970b).

In Figure 2-2 we present an overall view of a sampling of knowledge specialties which have something insightful to say about the nature of the human condition. The various disciplines have been placed along a continuum which orders them in terms of the relative importance of cultural or physical constraints considered to be important in the focus of their investigations. We have attempted to identify a major controversy within each of these disciplines which expresses an issue of central importance regarding the nature of the human condition.[7] In psychology, for example, a host of issues are entailed by the controversy surrounding the question as to whether humans should be conceptualized in mechanistic or humanistic terms. Similarly, in many other disciplines which have something meaningful to say about humankind there are controversies concerning the nature of humankind which are deeply rooted in historical traditions of scholarship. In art and literature, for example, the continuum we have identified is labeled universal-idiosyncratic. The key to this conceptualization is that universality (like the Platonic idea) is embodied in the single, concrete case. The works of such fine artists as Dianne Arbus (1972) exemplify this paradox—in her photographic work she focuses penetratingly upon individuals and, in the process, we find ourselves examining the universal qualities of [humankind].

Although the disciplines indicated in the upper half of Figure 2-2 deal directly with humankind, it should be noted that the physical sciences (shown in the lower half) are not irrelevant. The issues indicated for physics and chemistry, for example, have a direct bearing on the human condition. Let us take the predictability-uncertainty continuum shown for physics as an example. This issue has a direct bearing on the free will-determinism problem. That is, that there is at least as much indeterminacy

[7]A preliminary version of Figure 2-2 was worked out during an involved discussion with Leendert Mos. We appreciate his suggestions and insights.

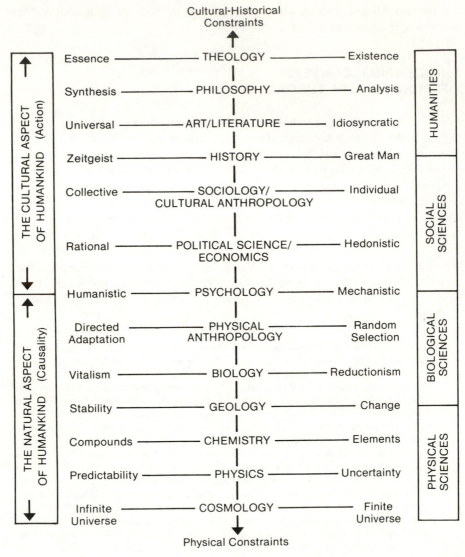

FIGURE 2-2 A sampling of knowledge disciplines and the major controversies from these disciplines regarding the human condition. (From Royce & Powell, 1978)

at the supra-physical level of investigation as there is at the relatively micro level of physics. Furthermore, aligning this continuum with the essence–existence contrast of theology, it can be seen that the uncertainty principle from physics has to do with existence (in contrast to the predictability–essence alignment at the opposite ends of the two continua). The point is that all forms of existence, whether they are at the relatively micro levels of the physical sciences or the molar levels of the social sciences and the humanities, are characterized by varying degrees of indeterminacy. For example, as one moves to the more abstract worlds of reason and essence, epitomized by mathematics, one also moves toward greater precision of prediction. The suggestion is that "essential man" is relatively determined whereas "existential man" is not. The analysis of how genes determine human mental and physical characteristics is an example of man as essence. But the history of [humankind's] metaphysical demands for meaning in the universe, while partially analyzable in terms of . . . "essential" characteristics, is primarily a manifestation of [our] existential nature.

There are additional points to be made regarding the various perspectives represented in Figure 2–2. [For example,]as noted on the left hand side of the figure, there is a global distinction to be made between those disciplines in the upper half of the figure and those in the lower half. One way of characterizing this global distinction is in terms of causality and action. That is, in the progression from the bottom to the top of the figure one is forced to construct explanations more in terms of teleological *action* or intentionality (i.e., goal-seeking) and less in terms of traditional causal explanations. Another distinction that applies generally in proceeding from the bottom to the top is the molarity of focus. That is, disciplines toward the bottom (excepting Cosmology) are focused on more molecular problems of the human condition, and as one proceeds upward, the concern is with increasingly molar problems.

There are also distinctions to be made with respect to temporal considerations entailed in Figure 2–2. Regarding the most global distinction, namely change, principles of cultural evolution would be invoked in the case of the cultural aspect of [humankind], while principles of physical evolution would be invoked in the case of the natural aspect of [humankind]. Furthermore, the temporal focus changes as one moves from the center of the figure (psychology) to the extremes (cosmology and theology). [With a shift] in focus from disciplines nearer the center to those toward the extremes, the time focus increases. Thus, for example, the temporal focus of both theology and cosmology is greater than for sociology and geology, respectively. And while physics is concerned with the laws of the physical universe, cosmology may even be interested in the existence of other universes. This contrast in time frames is also reflected in the fast reactions of atomic and chemical phenomena, and the rise and fall of cultures and civilizations which require centuries and millennia at the level of social, economic, and political systems, and the eons of time which are characteristic of the cultural evolution of history and the physical evolution of life and the cosmos. (Royce & Powell, 1978, pp. 1125–28)

To summarize, we see individuality theory as one part of a total effort to develop viable theories of the nature of humankind. As a psychological theory, it is part of the bridge that joins the physical and biological sciences with the social sciences and the humanities. Also, as a psychological theory, it must touch on the issue of mechanism versus humanism and other such issues, which we consider in the following subsections. We offer no new solutions to these issues, but they are related to many of the specific concepts and models presented throughout the remainder of the book. Therefore, out of respect for these perennial philosophical problems, it is important that we at least articulate their relationships to individuality theory.

Humanism Versus Mechanism

As noted in the preceding section, one of the major issues in contemporary psychology, as we view it, concerns the mechanistic versus humanistic conceptions of individual personality and behavior. For example, at one extreme are radical behaviorists who insist on conceiving humans as complex input-output devices who are "pushed around" by environmental forces. At the other extreme are third-force, humanistic psychologists who project an image of individuals as symbolizers who strive for fulfillment, are confronted by questions of meaning and morality, and who are quantum leaps beyond the rest of the animal world in their capacity to dream.

One fundamental difference between the mechanistic and the humanistic models of individual personality concerns what is being processed (Coward & Royce, 1981). For example, mechanistic models deal with matter-energy processing, while humanistic models focus on value processing and meaning. If we add information processing to the matter-energy and meaning categories, we have a three-class taxonomy for describing process (see Miller, 1978). If we also introduce different levels of investigation, such as the inorganic, the behavioral, and the cultural, we can elaborate further on what is being processed. All this is summarized in Table 2-1.

According to this table (see the center) psychology is, in principle, primarily concerned with information processing. While there is increasing awareness that it is information which is crucial at the behavioral level, psychology has tended to follow the inorganic-organismic, matter-energy paradigm of traditional science. Although scientific psychology has been aware of how important it is to process meaning, it has found this problem to be essentially intractable. Humanistic psychology is focused on meaning, regardless of its intractability; [but] most psychologists, including the humanists, have uncritically accepted epistemic attitudes which were originally developed for dealing with matter-energy processing. Unfortunately, humanistic psychologists have not been any more successful in dealing with the problem of meaning than their predecessors. According to Table 2-1 information processing constitutes a bridge between the processing of matter-energy and meaning, and psychology constitutes a bridge between the organismic and cultural levels of analysis. It is conceivable that investigations which involve an appropriate adaptation of information concepts could move toward the processing of meaning. [The

TABLE 2-1   The Relationship between Level of Investigation and What Is Being Processed

LEVEL OF INVESTIGATION	PROCESSING CATEGORIES		
	MATTER-ENERGY	INFORMATION	MEANING
Inorganic	+ +		
Organismic	+ +	+	
Behavioral-mental		+ +	+
Behavioral-social		+ +	+ +
Social-cultural		+	+ +

point we alluded to in Chapter 1] is that the psychology *Zeitgeist* is currently undergoing a paradigm shift away from behavioral, matter-energy processing toward information-meaning processing (e.g., the emergence of cognitive psychology), [it can be anticipated, therefore,] that this issue will at least receive more attention. However, the concern for meaning continues to be 'the' problem, whether psychologists call themselves scientific or humanistic (e.g., see Koch, 1976). (Coward & Royce, 1981, pp. 118–19)

As described in Chapter 1, individuality theory confronts both ends of the continuum we have been discussing. For example, at the lowest level of integrative personality, we are concerned with those characteristics of the individual related to the transduction of matter-energy into information. At the other extreme, when concerned with the integrative, or self-organizing, aspects of personality, we are clearly focused on the problem of meaning and how individuals proceed to create it in their lives.

Determinism Versus Free Will

Another interrelated issue is the role of causality or determinism in complex human behavior. Causality and determinism lie at the conceptual foundations of scientific explanation. The fact that the traditional deterministic principle has had to give way to probabilism does not diminish the underlying commitment to causality. However, there have been challenges to the "billiard ball" conception of causality, a conception that calls for an invariant sequence of univariate causes and effects. The challenges from individuality theory come from both factor theory and systems-information theory. The challenge to univariate determination is particularly potent from factor theory, which is based on the assumption of multivariate determination. But a further challenge to a simplistic conception of causality also arises from the teleological purposivism of cybernetic-feedback-information theory.

The major difference between mechanistic, or billiard ball, causality and telenomic causality is that the latter is focused on a "pull from in front" whereas the former is focused on a "push from behind." The telenomic version of causality is accommodated via the concept of feedback, wherein a system can achieve any steady state within its range of capability via a continuous interplay between positive and negative feedback. Such achievements are called purposes and goals, where these purposes and goals are achieved by the matching of a *comparison norm* (i.e., a preferred steady state) to information received by negative feedback.

What can be said about causality in this context? As we see it, causality remains important, but it is not the simple, traditional, one-way, mechanistic determinism. Feedback loops allow for an enormous variety of connections among parts, and the fact that information rather than energy is being processed, introduces additional complications. This point has to do with whether transformations of information are causally connected in a manner comparable to energy transformations, as was alluded to in our preceding discussion of humanism versus mechanism, and as we will discuss further in the context of the mind-body issue (to follow).

Our view is that some form of causality and determinism is at work in complex systems but that its exact nature is complicated. These complications can be illustrated by way of the following properties of complex, open systems that we consider relevant to a better understanding of causality in complex systems.

1. *Causality can be nonmechanistic.* Causality need not follow the linear cause–effect sequence of billiard balls, since cause–effect sequences can allow for feedback loops and comparison norms that accommodate goals and purposes in addition to linear, mechanical, causal sequences.

2. *Causality can be multiply determined.* There can be many causes of a single effect, many effects from a single cause, and many effects from many causes. In general, we expect such one-many, many-one, and many-many causal relationships in complex systems.

3. *Complex systems are interdeterministic.* This principle says that information flow outputs are a consequence of the interaction between a given input and the multiple interactions of the functional units of interacting systems.

4. *Functional relationships are a crucial property of complex systems.* This principle is focused on identifying invariants among the parts of the total system. The point is that invariance is indicative of lawfulness and replicable regularity and, thus, the concern is with underlying patterns in the transmission of information rather than causality per se.

The Part–Whole Problem

The problem at issue concerns the relationships between the parts and wholes of complex phenomena. The key question is the extent to which a whole can be accounted for by its parts. If a whole can be completely accounted for by its parts, then it is simply a conglomerate, which is reducible to the parts. Examples of conglomerate wholes are a pile of bricks or a pocketful of coins. If a whole is not reducible to additive parts, it is said to have emergent properties—that is, properties that cannot be accounted for by the properties of the parts. Elementism claims that a whole is nothing but the sum of the parts, whereas holism claims that a whole is more than the sum of the parts.

Perhaps the key to the eventual resolution of this problem lies in our understanding of the relationships among the parts. Elementism posits no special relatedness among the parts, which are viewed as replaceable and additive—that is, any part can be replaced without effect on the whole. Holism, on the other hand, posits a high degree of interdependence among the parts, such that the removal of any part will radically affect the whole—for example, removal of any part of a soap bubble will destroy the bubble (Wertheimer, 1972, p. 69).

As we see it, every personality theory is entangled in the part–whole problem, and, in fact, this issue constitutes the most difficult metatheoretic issue for any such theory. The reason is that, no matter what the conceptual framework, all theories of personality face the same problem—namely, to account for the organized complexity called personality. This means such theories must eventually specify the parts and how they are put together. In the case of individuality theory, personality is regarded as a hierarchical composite of systems, subsystems, and factors. And we simply do not know the extent to which such systemic and factor parts can account for the suprasystem composite. However, our guess is that the relationships among the parts do not constitute a simple, additive conglomerate, like a heap of coins. Rather, we suspect that there are many multiplicative and other complex interactions among the parts, and that a thorough understanding of the nature of these complex relationships is the key to evolving a more explanatory theory of personality and individual differences. Cases in point are the inverted-U relationship between arousal and performance (see Chapter 5) and the integrative role of the style and value systems (see Chapter 6). In our opinion the eventual answer to such complexities will be implemented by a better understanding of hierarchy theory (Whyte, Wilson, & Wilson, 1969; Mesarovic, Macko, & Takahara, 1970; and Weiss, 1971), a recent interdisciplinary development that indicates that the problems of hierarchical organization are common to the complex phenomena of all the sciences, including the biological and physical sciences.

We have made a beginning at bringing hierarchy theory to bear on the part–whole problem by regarding the Janus-faced units summarized in Table 1–2 (Chapter 1) as holons. Holons constitute the basic units of individuality theory, regardless of level, and they are defined as functional units that are simultaneously a part and a whole (Koestler, 1969; Laszlo, 1972a). They are parts when they are functionally subsumed by a larger functional unit, and they are wholes when they do the subsuming. For example, the cognitive functional unit is part of the total psychological system (i.e., it is a subsystem of personality), and it is simultaneously the system that subsumes all cognitive subunits (i.e., all cognitive traits are subunits of the cognitive system).

Holons are distributed at the five levels discussed in Table 1–2 (see column 2). Proceeding from the smallest to the largest units, holons range from its most elemental units, first-order factors, through the second- and third-order factors, or subsystems, to systems at the fourth level (e.g., cognition, affect), and the most molar holon at the apex, the suprasystem or personality. These are increasingly molar units. But they are all interpreted as functional unities, meaning that the holon is always a functioning entity—whether it be a relatively molecular entity, such as a first-order factor, or the total personality. The relevant point we make in Chapter 3 is that factor analysis is not capable of generating a viable theoretical structure all by itself. Thus, the factor model is limited to generating an inventory of potentially useful theoretical constructs, which can then be used in an appropriate conceptual framework. We are taking systems and information theory as our general paradigm for encompassing the constructs produced by the factor model, which means, for example, that when the factor analysts identify an invariant higher-order factor they may be identifying a subsystem. Introversion–extraversion and emotional stability are cases in point. They are regarded as two of the three subsystems of the affective system (see Chapter 5), but they were also empirically identified as third-order factors.

Proceeding upward in Table 1–2, it can be seen that the more encompassing the holon, the more it functions holistically. Thus, in moving from the first-order and second-order factors to third-order factors, or subsystems, to systems and the total system, one moves from factor-identified dimensions to the six systems and their interactions and integrations.

We regard adopting the concept of holon as the basic functional unit of individuality as a small but appropriate first step toward an eventual resolution of the part–whole problem. The point is that the problem of complex organization is simply too difficult to resolve, given the present state of the science. However, the issue must eventually be tackled if we are to evolve an explanatory theory of personality. Thus, although our attempts to date constitute a primitive beginning, factor-system theory is an approach that is at least capable of addressing the problem.

Mind Versus Body

The fact that we are focused at the *psychological* level of analysis (although the factor-gene and developmental models make contact with the biological realm) raises the question of the relation between "mind" and "body." We view both mind and body as valid and distinguishable realities. That is, we consider *mind* to refer to the nonphysical, intentional aspects of psychological structure and functioning. This includes all forms of sensory and cognitive functioning, plus all forms of wanting, wishing, feeling, and believing. Despite the difficulty of being clear about what should be meant by *mind,* there is massive evidence in the psychological literature providing details of the mental processing that occurs during cognizing, believing, and other mental events. Whatever the eventual nature of *mind,* we see the processing of energy and matter as the key to what is meant by *body* and the processing of information as the key to what is meant by *mind.*

To illustrate, consider the analogy of the computer. Following this analogy, the hardware is what we mean by *body* and the program is the equivalent of *mind.* Of course, a program is impossible without the computer hardware, and a mind is impossible without a brain. However, while the brain is necessary for a mind, it is clearly not sufficient. The different ways in which a computer can be programmed are comparable to the different ways that brains can be programmed. This is done via varying forms of acculturation, as in the case of different cultures in various parts of the world, and via a variety of subcultures within the same general culture.

Thus, we view brain or body as the biological substrate, or prerequisite, for mind. But, depending on what information is fed into given brains, as well as how it is organized within them, we get different "minds."

As we said, it is our view that mind and body constitute equally valid and distinguishable realities. Each carries causal weight within its own domain—that is, mental effects have mental causes, and physical effects have physical causes. But what about the possibility of mind–body interaction—the physical causing mental phenomena and the reverse? Although nobody has been able to offer an adequate statement of such mind–body interactions, it can no longer be doubted that such events do occur. The massive evidence from the neural and pharmacological sciences, for example, makes it clear that there are physical causes of mental states. The effects of brain stimulation and the effects of drugs on mood states are the most dramatic and convincing cases in point. And the effects of psychological stress and biofeedback on various organs of the body constitute striking evidence of psychological causes of physical effects. Biofeedback control over heart rate and other autonomic variables constitute the most convincing cases in point. Psychogenic ulcers and psychologically induced high blood pressure are also well-documented examples of psychological causation.

All of these findings point convincingly to a two-way interaction between mind and body. Yet, there is no adequate account of the nature of the interaction. Although we cannot offer an adequate statement, we can point to where we think the answer lies. We begin with the acceptance of both mental and physical causation. However, whereas physical causation is based on physical laws and the processing of energy, mental causation is based on psychological laws (mostly unknown) and the processing of information, as suggested in our earlier discussion. The interaction between the two is to be found in the (unexplored) relationships between energy and information.

Normality Versus Abnormality

Although we have not addressed the problem of "normality" versus "abnormality" in the development of individual theory, this issue confronts any personality theory, at least implicitly. From the standpoint of individuality theory we think this problem has two facets: (1) from the broadest perspective, it is a multidisciplinary problem; and (2) from the perspective of the individual, it involves existential questions.

As can be seen in Figure 2–2, many diverse disciplines of knowledge have something of importance to say about the nature of the human condition. Correspondingly, the issue of mental "health" versus mental "illness" must also be seen as a multifaceted problem. No one model, such as the medical or the behavioral model, of mental illness provides an adequate basis for understanding the complexities of "disturbed" behavior. Scheff (1966) suggested, for example, that social systems for amplifying deviance must also be considered relevant. "Mental illness," like other aspects of the human condition, is not a phenomenon that can be adequately dealt with from the perspective of a single model or a single discipline, such as psychology.

From the standpoint of the individual, existentialism has much to contribute to an understanding of the nature of mental health or mental illness. Mental illness, for example, can be viewed as individuals' attempts to make sense out of a meaningless universe. People cannot help but try to make sense out of the totality of things around them, but they find the futility of the twentieth century particularly devastating. The need for meaning, combined with the relativity of values, can lead to a state of existential ambiguity that, under particular conditions, overwhelms individuals. In short, we hypothesize that the search for meaning and values is at the center of the conceptual confusion regarding what is called mental illness.

3

The Basic Conceptual Models

Our general theory of personality and individual differences consists, in part, of five interrelated conceptual models that describe the structures, functions, and developmental changes of personality over the life-span: (1) *factor analysis*, (2) *systems and information processing*, (3) *development as metamorphogenesis*, (4) *factor-gene*, and (5) *factor-learning*. The first of these, the factor-analytic model, is employed in order to arrive at an empirical-theoretic description of the basic structures of personality. However, as discussed briefly in Chapter 2, models resulting from factor analysis tend to be static. Thus, we rely on a systems and information-processing approach in order to conceptualize the interactions and interrelations among the various structures of personality and in order to deal with the resulting "organized complexities." But even systems and information-processing models fall short when it comes to conceptualizing the complex changes that individuals undergo from birth to death. Such changes are approached from the perspective of a metamorphogenetic model of development, wherein personality is conceived as undergoing a variety of interrelated transformations. A broad understanding of these developmental changes requires an elaboration of the forces that propel such changes. Broadly conceived in terms of "heredity" and "environment," our conceptualization of the forces of developmental change consists of a factor-gene and a factor-learning model. Each of our five conceptual models is described, in turn, in each of the major sections of this chapter.

THE FACTOR-ANALYTIC MODEL

Factor analysis is a complex mathematical tool devised by psychologists to analyze the complexities of human behavioral and mental phenomena. Partly because of its inherent complexities, it has been misunderstood and misrepresented by its opponents and even by its proponents. The subtleties and technical issues involved in the methodology of factor analysis are covered in a variety of texts (e.g., Cattell, 1966a, 1978; Harman, 1976; Mulaik, 1972; and L. L. Thurstone, 1947) and are beyond the scope of the present book. However, it is critical to describe the applicability of the factor-analytic model to individuality theory. We do this in the present section.

The Basic Factor Model

As is well known, factor analysis operates on a matrix of intercorrelations such as might be generated in administering a large battery of psychometric tests to a group of subjects. The goal is to find a parsimonious model to account for the observed pattern of covariation in such a matrix. The existence of surface clusters indicates that there are common underlying sources of covariation. For example, it is possible to devise a variety of specific tasks that tap the span of immediate memory. Subjects can be required to perform a range of memory tasks, such as recalling a forward or backward string of digits presented only once auditorally, as is done in the administration of the Wechsler test of intelligence. Similarly, a string of verbal items could be presented visually with the same requirement that subjects recite them immediately after presentation, as is done in some information-processing experiments. Subjects who perform well on one of these tasks generally perform well on all similar tasks. Thus, the intercorrelations across subjects and tasks suggests that a general class of tasks such as this measures individuals' underlying capacities with respect to some factor such as "memory span." In other words, the common source of variation can be attributed to an underlying trait that distinguishes among individuals' performances in a variety of situations. In short, we consider factor analysis to be a mathematical technique for locating common sources of variation (identified as personality traits) that are considered to be structural components of individuality.

In mathematical form, factor analysis begins with the basic factor equation, which states that any behavior, indicated as a standard score Z_{ji} where

$$Z = \frac{Raw\ Score - Mean}{0}$$

is equal to the product of the loading (a_{jm}) of the measurement j on factor one, times the amount of this factor possessed by individual i (F_{1i}), plus the product involving the loading of the variable on factor two $(a_{j2}F_{2i})$, plus the product involving the loading of the variable on factor three, etc., until all the common factor variance is accounted for. In simplified mathematical terms (i.e., we have omitted all the correlational, specific factor, and error terms for purposes of exposition), this has been expressed as follows:[1]

$$Z_{ji} = a_{j1}F_{1i} + a_{j2}F_{2i} + a_{j3}F_{3i} + \ldots\ldots\ldots + a_{jm}F_{mi}. \tag{3.1}$$

If we now restate this in the more compact matrix (i.e., any rectangular arrangement of numbers) formalism, we get

$$Z = AF \tag{3.2}$$

where Z is a matrix of standardized test scores, A is a matrix of factor loadings, and F is a matrix of factor scores. However, since the focus of our attention is on the underlying factors rather than the original observations, we solve for F and get

$$F = A^{-1}Z. \tag{3.3}$$

However, since this involves an impractical form of F because there is no inverse for A, we turn to a variation of F (see Harman, 1976, p. 45), as follows:

$$F = A'R^{-1}Z \tag{3.4}$$

where A' refers to the transpose of the matrix of factor loadings, and R^{-1} is the inverse of the correlation matrix R.

A major aspect of individual difference theory (or individuality theory) involves an elaboration of hereditary and environmental sources of variation. Thus, we must find a way to link heredity and environment to factors. One approach is to decompose the A matrix (i.e., the factor loadings) into its hereditary, environmental, interaction, and correlated components, as follows:

$$A = H + E + I + C \tag{3.5}$$

Substituting in (3.4), we get

$$F = H'R^{-1}Z + E'R^{-1}Z + I'R^{-1}Z + C'R^{-1}Z. \tag{3.6}$$

---

[1]We have a problem of exposition at this juncture. The problem is that we require a little bit of matrix algebra in order to elaborate on the basics of the factor model. The dilemma is that our presentation is overly simplistic for those who are familiar with the model, but it may not be readable to those who are not familiar with matrix algebra. We have decided to meet this challenge via the compromise of explaining each step. We also recommend that the uninitiated but interested reader refer to an introductory text on factor analysis, such as Fruchter (1954) or Gorsuch (1974). After a relatively brief exposure to such a text, the reader will have no difficulty in following our presentation because we have confined ourselves to the elementary mathematical basis of the factor model.

Thus, the factor-gene model involves an elaboration of the first term,

$$F_H = H' R^{-1} Z. \tag{3.7}$$

The second term is the basis for the factor-learning model,

$$F_E = E' R^{-1} Z. \tag{3.8}$$

The third term deals with heredity-environment interaction effects,

$$F_I = I' R^{-1} Z, \tag{3.9}$$

and the fourth term deals with heredity-environment correlation effects

$$F_C = C' R^{-1} Z. \tag{3.10}$$

The factor-gene and factor-learning models discussed below will provide conceptual elaborations of equations (3.7) and (3.8) respectively.

Presentation of the factor model up to this point has been focused on structural aspects—factors as the components of behavioral complexes. The ultimate goal, however, involves going beyond structure to process or dynamics. The essence of process is change. Thus, there must also be a model of factor change. This can be indicated as:

$$F_\triangle = A_\triangle R_\triangle^{-1} Z_\triangle \tag{3.11}$$

(where $\triangle$ = change)

Factor change involves two general classes of phenomena, quantitative and qualitative. *Quantitative refers to change in the performance level of any one factor. Qualitative refers to change in the relationships (e.g., the correlations) between two or more factors.* Quantitative change is relatively easy to model both structurally and mathematically. Qualitative change, however, is a complex issue that has received relatively little attention (but see Royce, Kearsley, & Klare, 1978; and Buss & Royce, 1975). The analysis of change must also include how factor changes affect behavior. Thus, we need a change version of equation (3.2) such as:

$$Z_\triangle = A_\triangle F_\triangle. \tag{3.12}$$

The challenge here is to provide an understanding of temporality and factor change. This means that one must be able to specify the performance level of any factor of the n-dimensional system at any moment in time. It also requires an elaboration of factor interactions and integrations at any point in time.

Higher-order Factors

The complete factor model also includes the possibility of correlated factors. Thus, although the basic factor equation includes the correlated terms, they were purposely omitted in equation (3.1) for reasons of simplicity in the exploration of the factor model. It also should be pointed out that the details of organizational structure and dimensionality could differ from domain to domain. It could be, for example, that orthogonal (right angled, therefore uncorrelated) factors best describe an area such as sensory discrimination, whereas obliquity (correlated factors) may be required to account for the extensive correlations often reported among factors in the cognitive domain. Such structural details should be worked out along the way rather than imposed in an a priori manner. The advantage to such an approach is that it views the various factor solutions that have been put forward as special cases that apply to a particular subdomain of variables. This also means that a given hierarchy, strata, chain, simplex, or circumplex (Cattell, 1965) constitutes a subset of the more general lattice or reticular structure. The empirico-inductive strategy is, in fact, the basic strategy we followed in evolving our answer to the question of how factors are organized. What we found was that there were higher-order factors in five of the six domains under review. Because of the ubiquity of correlated primaries and, therefore, higher-order factors, we came to the conclusion that a hierarchical structure was required for each of the six systems. This means that we also postulated a hierarchical structure in the one domain where higher-order factors have not been reported—the motor domain. [2]

Thus, on both empirical and theoretical grounds we are now convinced that some form of hierarchical structure constitutes the best available hypothesis concerning the organization of factors. The theoretical justification is that the oblique factor solution is the most general solution of the various factor models. The oblique solution can accommodate the orthogonal solution, its only major competitor, as a special case. The empirical basis for favoring hierarchical structuring is that a viable theory must account for all the available evidence or, at least as much of it as possible, and this includes the fact that higher-order factors have been found repeatedly. Furthermore, some of the higher-order factors that have been found have received extensive experimental (non-factor-analytic) confirmation. Also, our general systems and information-processing model provides a theoretical expectation of hierarchical structure. In short, both the empirical and theoretical evidence is too compelling to ignore the demand for hierarchical structures. Of course, it is equally true that the details of these structures are not yet clear. There are, for example, such issues as the number of strata in a given domain and the number of factors at a given stratum. The major reason for these difficulties is the problem of factor invariance. Although we have attempted to in-

---

[2]The fact that no higher-order motor factors have been reported does not necessarily mean they will not be identified. It is most likely that they have not been reported because nobody has conducted a higher-order analysis in the motor domain. We anticipate that such factors will be identified if and when higher-order analyses are conducted in this domain.

clude only invariant factors in each of the six domains, there is no uniformity of factor invariance. For example, there are relatively few invariant factors identified for the sensory domain, but there is a relatively high degree of invariance in both the cognitive and affective domains.

Deciding on the number of factors for a given system or subsystem is an issue that may be intrinsically unresolvable. The difficulty is there is no way to know when one has exhaustively investigated a given domain. The only way we see for dealing with this kind of dilemma is an empirical as well as a theoretical answer, and it is similar to the dilemma that scientists face in any area of investigation. For example, the cutting edge of knowledge is such that no one ever knows whether a particular domain has been exhaustively investigated. The standard pragmatic guide, therefore, has been to continue investigation until no new information is discernible. What this means in the case of factor analysis is that one should continue the search for additional factors as long as such investigations continue to pay off in the form of identifying additional invariant factors.

The Generation of Theoretical Constructs

Our view that factor analysis is useful in generating structural models of personality implies that factor analysis can generate potentially useful theoretical constructs (Royce, 1963). We can best explicate what this means by assuming that science involves something like Cattell's inductive-deductive spiral (see Fig. 3–1). The lower segment of this model, the portion up to the term *hypothesis*, describes what we call the empirico-inductive–hypothesis-generating aspect of science, and the upper segment of the first loop of the spiral describes what has been generally referred to as the hypothetico-deductive aspect. The ascending spiral implies a never-ending process of empirico-inductive–hypothetico-deductive refinement.

A number of difficulties involved in generating theoretical constructs can be discussed in the context of this model of scientific investigation. For example, most empirical scientists concentrate their efforts toward the empirico-induction end of Cattell's spiral, exploring possibilities via varied laboratory and other observation techniques, but philosophers of science have spent more of their time analyzing the logical implications of hypothetico-deduction. The latter emphasis is concerned with the logic of justification, and the former relates to the logic of discovery. Unfortunately, too much has been written about *justification* and very little has been written about *discovery*.

Although the recent statements by a small number of historians of science such as Kuhn (1970) and Hanson (1961) are relevant, in general, they are not directly on target. Such statements are focused on what scientists do. However, more thought should be directed at what is logically possible, regardless of what scientists do in practice. In general, research on the logic of discovery seems to have been neglected by philosophers.

How does factor analysis fit into this picture? The most obvious point to be made is that the identification of factors is a problem in the logic of discovery. It is

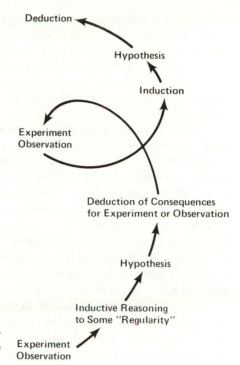

FIGURE 3-1   Cattell's inductive-hypothetico-
deductive spiral. (From Cattell, 1966, Fig. 1-1,
p. 16)

possible to employ factor analysis for confirming what is already known, or to
make deductions and perform experimental tests by using a specific criterion
variable (as in Eysenck's work with several variables). But a variety of other
deductive strategies are also available. On the other hand, by using large matrices
of empirical variables to cover a previously unexplored terrain (or a terrain where
the covariations are blurred), factor analysis provides a way for inductively
generating potentially useful theoretical constructs in complex domains where
observables are confusedly interrelated. This is particularly so if the analyses constitute an orderly and insightful progression of investigations that are attempting
to generate an explicit theoretical model.

From our experience in applications of the factor model, there seem to be
two phases of scientific inference in the typical exploratory factor investigation.
The first phase is focused on establishing that there are patterns in the observed
test data that can be replicated, and the second phase is concerned with the identification of *latent unknowns*.

Although the problem of construct identification is recognized as *the* problem in factor analysis, the fact that there are two general strategies for providing
plausible hypotheses does not seem to be common knowledge. One of these
strategies was developed from within the factor model, and the other evolved via
an alliance with traditional experimental psychology. The internal strategy involves *invariance analysis*. Cattell (1966a) and Royce (1973a,b) provide a broad

coverage of the theoretical and empirical aspects of this approach. Royce's contributions in this area are primarily in the comparative-physiological domain (Royce, 1966a), especially in the area of behavior genetics (Poley & Royce, 1973; Royce, Holmes, & Poley, 1975; Royce & Mos, 1980; Royce, Poley & Yeudall, 1973). These efforts have involved establishing whether or not investigators are talking about the same factor despite variations in investigators, test batteries, and subjects.

The external strategy involves *experimental manipulation of factors*—the effect of such variables as brain damage (Mos, Lukaweski, & Royce, 1977; Royce, Yeudall, & Bock, 1976), electric shock and drugs (Satinder, Royce, & Yeudall, 1970), maternal stimulation (Poley & Royce, 1970), early stress (Mos, Royce, & Poley, 1973), and the effect of light (Mos, Vriend, & Poley, 1974), and height (Royce & Poley, 1976) via the usual laboratory techniques. In both strategies the ultimate goal is to establish the boundary conditions or the range of effectiveness for each factorially identified unknown.

Although the *intent* of current efforts to find a mathematical solution to the invariance problem is to extend the *algorithmic* character of the factor model to a Phase II inference, current opinion among factor analysts is that a mathematical solution is not possible in principle, due to insufficiency of necessary information. For example, consider the difficulty of estimating factor invariance in the situation where two entirely different subsets of variables are involved. And the problem becomes even more horrendous if we introduce the complication of administering the test battery to two entirely different populations, and so forth. Thus, the factor approach will probably not be able to completely circumvent the subjective input of the investigator at the level of *factor identification*. Even so, it seems reasonable to conclude that as factor investigators increase their knowledge of the "boundary conditions" of factors these empirical constraints will increase the probability that the $n + 1^{th}$ interpretation of factor x is a more plausible hypothesis than the nth interpretation.

We can regard the two strategies just described as *empirical tenability;* that is, plausibility in terms of the weight of the empirical evidence. But there is another plausibility criterion available—namely, *theoretical tenability,* or the weight of the theoretical evidence. Examples of this from factor theory include the empirical search for missing entries in a taxonomic table, such as Guilford's (periodic-like) cubic table of cognitive elements (Guilford, 1967; Guilford & Hoepfner, 1971). Other examples include the usual deductions from a theoretical structure, such as Eysenck's (1967, 1970, 1973) many deductions involving the higher-order dimension of introversion–extraversion.[3]

---

[3]The theory-laden constructivist view (see Chapter 2) of the nature of science provides an insight at this juncture, namely, that no observation is devoid of an "interpretive context." In short, part of the subjective aspect of the factor-identification problem is the conceptual framework that the investigator brings to bear in making a Phase II inference. Thus, the same factor solution may elicit different conceptualizations for a given factor because of differences in world view, paradigm, and other cognitive commitments. This point is of particular importance in Phase II, for it is at this juncture that the factor analyst provides the "theoretical construction" as to the nature of a given factor.

Factors and Psychological Processes[4]

The core meaning of *process* as used in scientific explanation has to do with change. More precisely, process analysis is focused on what gives rise to change. This means specifying all the details of component interaction that intervene between successive system states. This requires the passage of time, although time per se is not part of the explanatory nexus of events. Rather, processes occur over specifiable time periods. When time intervals are of relatively short duration, the focus is on micro events (e.g., the perception of a color), and when the time intervals are of relatively long duration the focus is on more molar events (e.g., the life-span development of intelligence). In principle, "process" covers all time intervals. In the realm of psychological phenomena, process analysis is concerned with changes in stimulus (S), organism (O), and response (R). Thus, the basic process paradigm involves S inputs, O mediational processes, and R outputs.

The task that faces many psychologists of very different persuasions (psychology, personality, learning, etc.) is illustrated in Figure 3-2. In general,

---

Although this "inventive" interpretation is offered within the constraints of the pattern replicability provided by Phase I, thereby delimiting the number of "plausible hypotheses," the fact that Phase II involves cognitive constructions, and that more than one construction is feasible, suggests that it is not possible, in principle, to generate *the* hypothesis because a Phase II scientific inference actually involves generating a "construct"—a human invention. Although it is true that such plausible hypotheses are subsequently empirically tested via hypothetico-deductive procedures, and thereby receive further confirmation or disconfirmation, the constructivist or interpretive input remains.

Thus it would appear that "discovery," at least as it applies to the logic of factor analysis, involves interpretation or cognitive construction in addition to pattern replicability.

[4]The role of factors as psychological processes is discussed more thoroughly in Royce, Kearsley, and Klare (1978). We wish to acknowledge the important contributions of Greg Kearsley and Warren Klare to our understanding of this issue.

FIGURE 3-2 The expanded S-O-R model in which factors identify psychological or biological structures that intervene between changes in stimuli and changes in responses.

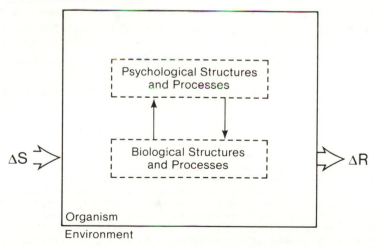

psychology is concerned with tracing out how the stimulus changes that result in changes in biological structure or processes affect psychological structures and processes, and how all this affects behavioral outputs. A specific example would be changes in emotionality factors due to limbic arousal effects that, in turn, are attributable to various stressors impinging on the organism.[5]

Factors are identified through the relationships existing in a correlation matrix. A derived factor dimension indicates that a subset of the initial variables are intercorrelated, and that it is possible to make the inference that this is due to some common underlying causal influence related to the internal processes of the organism. Furthermore, it is assumed that insofar as factor dimensions indicate differences among individuals on a set of variables, they must also reflect the common metric on which these differences can be scaled. Thus, factor dimensions reflect both differences and similarities. In short, a factor is a theoretical construct which may be viewed as:

> a variable, process, or determinant that accounts for covariation in a specified domain of observation. Within the standard paradigm of S-O-R, the conceptual focus of factor analysis is on the O variables. When the postfactorial focus is on the S-O relationships, factors can best be seen as dependent variables. When the postfactorial focus is on O-R relationships, factors can be best seen as predictors or independent variables. (Royce, 1963, p. 527)

A psychological factor dimension, then, can be thought of as a component of personality structure that can function in a nomological net as either *cause* or *effect*.

It is important to elaborate further on these two cases. First, consider the case where factors are independent variables, or the *causes* of some behavior. In this case detailed specification of how factorially identified components interact provides an explanation for the behavior. For example, if the task at hand involves a highly complex visual display such as might confront a pilot, the implication is that many of the perceptual dimensions will be processing simultaneously. On the other hand, the involvement of various conceptual and sensory-motor factors is dependent on the psychobiological idiosyncrasies of the pilot (i.e., his or her multidimensional profile on a variety of relevant factors) and when these mediational processors are needed as the pilot proceeds through take-off, ascent, level flight, descent, and landing.

The second case involves factors as dependent variables. In these instances the observed variation in factor scores is attributable to independent variables.

---

[5]It should be noted in passing that the concept of psychological structure is meant to apply to the individual. The fact that empirical factor analytic studies are based on populations is not relevant to the conceptual issues under discussion. However, there is no difficulty in any event, since individual profiles (which, of course, reflect the structure of factors for person *X*) can be obtained at a given point in time. Furthermore, the issue of intra-individual differences vs. inter-individual differences is also not inconsistent with the concept of psychological structure of factors. For example, *P* technique (factoring variables across occasions involving one individual) is available for the assessment of factor change in the single case (intra-individual differences), and, of course, *R* technique (factoring variables across individuals involving one occasion) is the standard procedure for assessing inter-individual differences.

Examples include factor performance level as a function of genotype (e.g., Royce, 1957a; Royce, Poley, & Yeudall, 1973), as a function of brain damage (e.g., Aftanas & Royce, 1969; Royce, Yeudall, & Bock, 1976), or as a function of environmental enrichment or deprivation (e.g., Mos, Royce, & Poley, 1973; Mos, Vriend, & Poley, 1974). Thus, factors as dependent variables do not provide a causal explanation, but rather, they reflect the effects of other process variables.

However, it is when factors as dependent variable and independent variable are combined that their importance as mediational processors can best be seen. Our attempt to develop a general theory of individual differences cannot succeed if it merely inventories all possible behavioral variations. The fact that behavioral variations also covary is the entry point for a more parsimonious description of observables. The important point is that a relatively small number of constructs can account for a very large number of observables. Also, the dependent and independent variable relationships of factors constitute extensions of the causal chain. For example, the chain of causal influences can be expanded to include hereditary, environmental, or even biological bases of the factors discovered in any domain.

Although most early contributors to the factor-analytic literature made the assumption that factors identify processors, there were relatively few attempts to follow-up on this idea. For example, L. L. Thurstone suggested:

> In the more fundamental factorial problem the object is to discover whether the variables can be made to exhibit some underlying order that *may throw light on the processes* that produce the individual differences shown in all the variables . . . . The derived variables [i.e., factors] are of scientific interest only insofar as *they represent processes or parameters* that involve the *fundamental concepts of the science involved*. (1947, p. 61)

There are at least two reasons why there has been little analysis of factors as processors: (1) the problem of factor interpretation, and (2) the relative lack of philosophic insight concerning the logic of discovery. Both of these problems have to do with the difficulty of *identifying unknowns* (see Royce, 1976, 1977a). In spite of the logical shortcomings, factor analysts have addressed the problem in terms of *factorial invariance*. And as we noted earlier, two classes of factor invariance have evolved—one from within factor analysis and the other through an alliance with experimental psychology.

SYSTEMS AND INFORMATION PROCESSING[6]

Although "general systems" and "information-processing" approaches are not incompatible, it should be noted that there are important differences, and these differences have consequences for the theoretical analysis of human personality.

---

[6]The relevant systems and information processing concepts are discussed more thoroughly in Royce and Buss (1976) and Powell, Royce, and Voorhees (in press).

Fundamentally, the differences stem from the fact that the "system" metaphor derives from the structural-functional orientation of organismic biology (e.g., Bertalanffy, 1967; Mesarovic, 1968; J. G. Miller, 1978) and other sciences (see also Nagel, 1961), while the "information-processing" metaphor stems from the functionalist orientation of behaviorism and neobehaviorism as well as the computing and information sciences. As a consequence of these divergent origins, architectural models of information-processing (e.g., Atkinson & Shiffrin, 1968; Blumenthal, 1977; Bower, 1975; Singer, 1975) are designed to explore relationships among system functions. Short-term memory, intermediate-term memory, buffers, consciousness (e.g., Hunt, 1971; Hunt & Lansman, 1975), and other architectural units reference system *functions* rather than psychological *structures*.

From a systems perspective, whether a system is thought to have, say, short-term memory, does not depend on the existence of a "short-term memory structure," but on the characteristic functions of the system. Thus, the systems perspective is concerned with structure as a basis for understanding function. Because the systems and information-processing approaches provide complementary frameworks, such complex mental functions as memory, learning, and perceiving are analyzed in terms of the system and subsystem architectural units.

There are several other reasons why we want to emphasize the value of systems theory. One reason is that the systems approach readily accommodates the findings of hierarchical factor analysis. Another reason is that hierarchical models seem to be applicable to most complex systems (Laszlo, 1974; Mesarovic, Macko, & Takahara, 1970; Mesarovic & Pestal, 1973; J. G. Miller, 1978; Pattee, 1973; Weiss, 1971; Whyte, Wilson, & Wilson, 1969). In addition, systems analysis makes possible a more comprehensive model of personality structures and functions.

Information Processing Significance
of Personality Systems

J. G. Miller's (1978) general systems theory is the most comprehensive and thorough in the literature related to systems and information processing. In his analysis of seven levels of systems, Miller has developed a schema for classifying the information-processing components of various systems. This is shown in the left column of Table 3–1. In the third column we provide brief descriptions of the structural and functional significance of these information-processing subsystems as they relate to an individual's brain. The second column describes the general function of the various components in terms of transduction, transformation, and integration. The fourth column provides brief examples of their psychological correlates from individuality theory. The entries in the third column of Table 3–1 show that sensory and motor functions are concentrated at the top and bottom. That is, the sensory and motor systems are transductional systems. Cognition, affect, style, and value, on the other hand, are concentrated more toward the center categories and thus deal with transformation and integration of information.

TABLE 3-1 The Psychological Correlates of Information-processing Subsystems (Modified from Royce & Buss, 1976)

INFORMATION PROCESSING SUBSYSTEM	GENERAL FUNCTION	MAJOR STRUCTURAL AND FUNCTIONAL SIGNIFICANCE	MAJOR PSYCHOLOGICAL CORRELATES
Input Transducer	Transduction	External sensory receptors; conversion of energy into neural events	Lower-order processes in the sensory system (e.g., visual hue, brightness)
Internal Transducer		Internal sensory receptors; conversion of internally generated sources of energy	Lower-order processes in the sensory system (e.g., kinesthetic sensitivity)
Channel and Net	Transformation	Peripheral and central neural networks for transmission of sensory information	Higher-order processes in the sensory system (e.g., visual, chemical, auditory)
Decoder		Primary sensory cortex, association areas of the cortex; translation into internal codes	Higher-order sensory processes (e.g., visual) and lower-order perceiving (e.g., spatial orientation)
Associator		Associative neural network; enduring associations among decoded items of information	Lower-order cognitive and affective processes (e.g., associative memory, memory for designs; conditionability)
Memory	Integration	Neurochemical systems of the brain for producing relatively permanent changes	Reconstructive cognitive memory processes (e.g., perceiving, conceptualizing)
Decider		Cortical, subcortical (e.g., limbic system), and peripheral neural centers; coordination and integration of information, and decision making	Higher-order cognitive abilities and affective traits (e.g., symbolizing, emotional stability); style and value systems
Encoder		Primary motor cortex and others such as the language cortex; translation of information into public code	Higher-order motor processes (e.g., motor speech and bodily orchestration)
Output Transducer	Transduction	Skeletal and muscular systems; information output to environment	Lower-order motor processes (e.g., motor discharge, reflexivity)

This summary comparison reveals several problems with applying Miller's analysis to psychological processes. First, while individual differences may be brought in, the schema does not explicitly make allowance for them. Second, and most important, the information processing subsystems identified by Miller seem to be more differentiated and more highly concentrated toward the periphery. That is, the more central components, such as the decider, are not sufficiently differentiated to allow us to distinguish among the central information-processing systems of personality. Even so, Table 3–1 serves to illustrate information-processing implications for the personality systems under consideration in this book.

The Characteristics of Complex Systems

Our systems and information-processing analysis of human personality focuses on the basic characteristics of what we have termed a "complex hierarchical information processing system" (CHIPS). A CHIPS is defined as follows:

A CHIPS is a nonrandom organization of subsystems and components among which:

1. *there is directive correlation with respect to the occurrence of certain end states and the initial states of the system and environment*;
2. *uncertainty and risk are regulated*;
3. *functioning is interdependent*;
4. *there is a multilevel, hierarchical structure*;
5. *there is increasing hierarchical organization over the life span of the system.*

Restriction 1 means that the system must be goal directed (see Sommerhof, 1969) in order to qualify as a CHIPS. The important point with regard to restriction 2 is that uncertainty and risk are regulated, *not simply reduced*. Restriction 3 merely specifies that units interact with each other. Restriction 4 implies that the system must be macrodeterministic—that there must be some subsystems that intervene in (or coordinate) the functioning of other subsystems or components. Taken together, restrictions 3 and 4 implicate internal feedback and feedforward processes in the functioning of a CHIPS. Lastly, restriction 5 means that the system undergoes development throughout its life span. This definition is sufficiently general to include all the complex, organismic, and social-psychological systems of concern to such general system theorists as Berrien (1968), Bertalanffy (1962), Laszlo (1972a, 1972b), and J. G. Miller (1978) but sufficiently restrictive to eliminate physicalistic and closed systems, as well as all but the most complex cybernetic devices (for example, extant cybernetic devices would most likely fail to meet restrictions 2 and 5).

The general systems literature has emphasized that complex, open systems can resolve decision problems in a variety of ways, a principle that accounts in part for their enormous adaptability. That is, according to the principle of equifinality, when the immediate goals cannot be readily attained according to one pathway of transformations, there are alternative paths available. One implication of this is that, unless two individual systems are *exact duplicates in every respect* (including past experience) and are exposed to exactly the same environmental demands, there will be identifiable differences manifested in processing activities. The surface manifestations of such differences in processing constitute the observables of differential psychology. Factor analysis comes in at this point because it is a tool for exploring the underlying sources of observable differences among individuals. In other words, factor analysis provides an important tool for identifying the processing components of complex systems.

Steady States and Goal Directedness

Both living and artificial cybernetic systems attract one's interest, in part, because they appear to engage in activities that can only be described as "goal seeking." And this aspect of the behaviors of all animals, as well as artificial intelligence, challenges the relevance of traditional mechanistic theories that have a long history in psychological theorizing (e.g., Day, 1976; Hull, 1931; T. Mischel, 1976). Such efforts to reduce goal seeking activities to simple mechanistic principles generally have resulted from a concern to avoid vitalistic or teleological concepts of causality. But, explanations of behavior that give emphasis to goal-directedness and goal seeking do not necessarily have to be *vitalistic* explanations (T. Mischel, 1976). Sommerhof (1969), for example, has shown how goal-directedness can be precisely defined in terms of a *directive correlation* with respect to the occurrence of certain end states (i.e., goals) and the initial states of the environment.

The dynamic balance that results from the many interacting variables and subsystems is called a steady state of a system (Brent, 1978c; Stagner, 1977). Steady-state mechanisms are operative at all levels, and, for each variable, component, or subsystem, there is a *range of stability*. *Strain* occurs when energy/information underload or overload results in the functioning of a variable, component, or subsystem that is beyond this range of stability. The reestablishment of equilibrium occurs through *adjustment processes,* which may involve the recruitment of other systems or subsystems (Royce & Buss, 1976; J. G. Miller, 1978). With sufficient stress, the entire system may be involved in coping, as in Selye's (1956) General Adaptation Syndrome (GAS) at the physiological level and the standard defense mechanisms at the psychological level.

A basic assumption in our general approach is that the personality suprasystem is in continual interaction with its environment; i.e., there are continuous inputs via the sensory system and continuous outputs via the motor system. In between are the transformational activities of cognition and affect and the integrative activities of styles and values. If we focus on any one of these systems, it is possible to describe the ongoing dynamics of information processing in terms of transitions among a set of discrete steady states. If the system is not operating in one of these steady states, it will alter its mode of processing until it is and then remain in that state until there is a sufficient change in its boundary conditions for another state to become more "attractive" (or until random fluctuations lead to a state transition).

Feedback processes   We have represented the functioning of a general open system in Figure 3–3. In this figure an information input (I) is processed by the sensory system(s) that flows into the control unit from the environment (E). N_2 refers to the systemic norm against which inputs must be compared, and O refers to motor system outputs that feed back into the external environment, E. Using the thermostat analogy, N_2 is comparable to the thermostat setting and E refers to the environmental conditions. For example, if the thermostat is set at 70° F (N_2) and the room temperature (E) is 65°, then the heating unit will be activated via negative feedback until there is a *match* between the input and N_2 (i.e., an identity between the thermostat setting of 70° F and the room temperature).

Positive feedback is also demonstrated in Figure 3–3. In this case a change in N is required. Thus, N_1, via positive feedback (i.e., increases in the deviating direction), constitutes a mismatch, or the need for a different norm. To follow through with the thermostat analogy, suppose that 65° F is selected. Thus, 65° F is the new norm (N_1) that, via negative feedback, results in a match, or reestablishment of a steady state.

This way of modeling feedback processes can be readily applied to individuality. Thus, in Figure 3–3 the psychological system (personality) is designated via the dotted-line rectangle, and the environment is indicated by E.

FIGURE 3-3   The basic system circuit, showing relationships between positive and negative feedback and assimilation and accommodation.

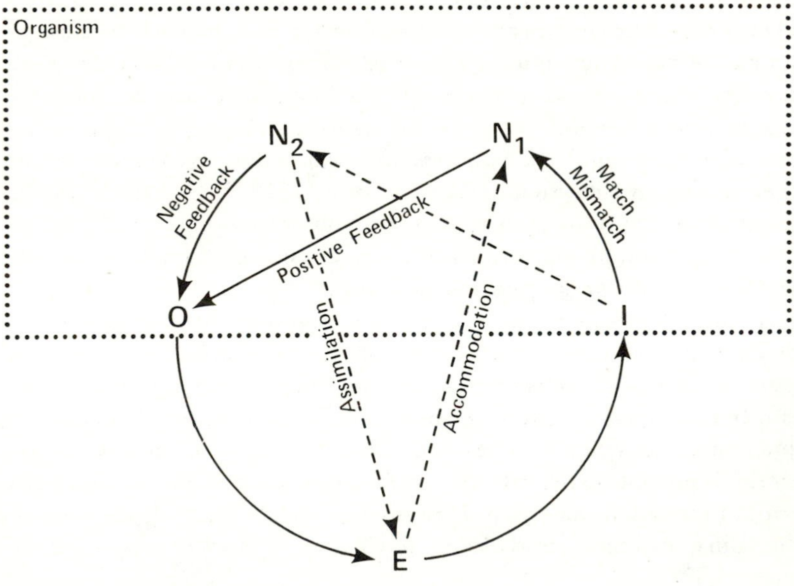

Inputs and outputs are handled via the sensory (I for input) and motor (O for output) systems respectively, and the remaining four systems are involved in "central processing." Psychologically, N may refer to either *external goals* or *internal purposes*, both of which provide direction for behavior. Figure 3–3 also incorporates the concepts of assimilation and accommodation. In the assimilation case (N_2) personality is in a steady state with the environment, and its norm (N_2) is "projected on to the environment." This means that new sensory inputs (I) are assimilated into the existing norm (N_2). In the accommodation case, a change in N is required in order to adapt to the environment. Thus, N_2 must be replaced by a different norm or internal need. By exploring various alternatives, a new norm, N_1, reestablishes the steady state. In this case the environment is "projected on to the norm." Such a norm shift reflects an accommodation to the environment. In brief, *assimilation involves adaptation by extension of the extant system state and accommodation involves adaptation by modification of the extant system state.*

Equifinality   The principle of equifinality (Bertalanffy, 1962) refers to the ability to achieve the same norm (i.e., goal or purpose) via a variety of routes. Behavioral equifinality refers to a wide range of outputs accomplishing the same goal—e.g., Lashley's (1941) rats were able to roll through a maze when the neural pathways to their limbs were severed. Internal processing equifinality refers to different subsets of components achieving the same information output. For example, if cognitive functioning is required, individuality theory indicates it can occur via three different subsystems—conceptualizing, perceiving, and symbolizing. A wide range of part–whole problems provide examples of the concept of part substitutability, including compensatory functioning (e.g., a one-armed baseball player; no loss of psychological functioning due to brain damage), vicarious functioning (e.g., planning before acting), and speed–accuracy trade-offs in skilled motor performance (e.g., Powell, Katzko, & Royce, 1978).

Information Processing and the Regulation of Uncertainty and Risk in a CHIPS

Information science is a new interdiscipline with all the trappings of a science, such as professional societies, annual meetings, conferences, and publications, but there is little unanimity regarding how the term *information* should be used. For example, although there is general acceptance of information as negative entropy or negative uncertainty (e.g., Garner, 1962), there is little insight available concerning the conceptual implications of that definition.

Regardless of future directions of information theory in the psychological sciences, it is important to recognize that individuals do not simply *reduce* uncertainty and risk to some minimum. Rather, they *regulate, control,* or *manage* uncertainty, as R. Jung (1965) outlined in his analysis of epistemic and telic systems. We regard the unqualified drive-reduction view as inadequate, for it is abundantly clear that humans search out stimulation and new information and engage in a wide variety of activities that temporarily increase the probability of risk or uncertainty. Scientific research provides an excellent example—scientists must expose themselves to uncertainty in their search for greater knowledge. Similarly, many scientists expose themselves to risks—both physical and mental—in that same quest for understanding.[7]

In general terms we view the information-processing activities of personality as involving the transformation of inputs into system states, where a *transformation is any change in physical, relational, or contextual characteristics of information*. It seems necessary for cognition to transform things in order to detect ecological invariants, and for affect to transform events in order to generate internal arousal states. But such transformations also expose an individual to uncertainty and risk (i.e., to changes with outcomes and risks that are potentially uncertain). If transforming information did not expose individuals to potential uncertainty or risk, such actions would hardly be "informative" or "arousing" in any meaningful sense, because the desired information would already be known. In short, the *search for invariants and optimal arousal, and the regulation of uncertainty and risk* are different sides of the same coin.

Interdependency within a CHIPS[8]

Interdependency refers to the combined functioning of two or more units (i.e., subsystems or other components) that compose the total system and implies that one part does not typically function independently of the other parts.

Since the total system provides an environment for its units, there must be continuous interaction among the various parts. Furthermore, in our description of goal-directedness, goals were described as involving the maintenance or achievement of steady states with respect to the dynamical laws governing energy and information flow. In the analysis of any particular system with respect to the interdependency of the subsystems, the important points are to identify the structure and function of each part, to describe the nature of the energy/information exchanges, to show how such exchanges alter the functioning of the subparts, and to determine overall system states produced by the cooperative interactions of the subsystems. In Part III of the book we present a detailed analysis of system interactions in the context of personality and individual differences (see especially Chapter 8).

Macrodeterminism and the Role of Decision-Control in a CHIPS

Models of interacting parts and multilevel, hierarchical organization raise the question of overall coordination and control of information flow. The standard answer to this problem has involved the postulation of an "executive" or

---

[7] It should be clear from our original definition of a CHIPS (above) that regulation of uncertainty and risk is a property of the total psychological system, not just cognition and affect, as most of our examples might imply.

[8] We wish to acknowledge the contribuiton of Burt Voorhees to our understanding of this issue.

"decider" unit (e.g., J. G. Miller, 1978; Mesarovic, Macko, & Takahara, 1970), that functionally coordinates the activity of the other parts of the system (see also Table 3–1). But extant information processing models have not been clear about the nature of such a decider unit.[9] Is it to be construed, for example, as a single unit, analogous to the chief executive of a large business corporation? In the following we provide a possible answer in terms of function rather than structure. By this we mean that control is viewed as distributed throughout the psychological system rather than concentrated in a single locus. For example, we have postulated four central processing units, two of which are construed as personality integrators (style and value). And coordination is based on a variety of mechanisms and principles—such as feedback, feedforward, equifinality, and stability, and within-system and between-system hierarchical organization.

Feedforward processes   In goal-seeking activities the central nervous system operates on the basis of preprogramming, or what Pribram (1971) has described as the feedforward mechanism or bias. According to this principle, response outcomes of a series of movements can be computed beforehand—before those outcomes become evident. Such preprogramming entails a rough specification of the various operations to be performed in a complex sequence. With a schematic specification, the fine grain of the actual sequence can then be monitored and controlled by positive and negative feedback mechanisms. Psychologists studying motor skills have become increasingly aware of the fact that feedforward mechanisms are as important in the control of skilled sequences as are feedback mechanisms (Powell, Katzko, & Royce, 1978; R. A. Schmidt, 1975; Stelmach, 1976). Feedforward processes also are involved in perceptual set and may account for some of the interactions between styles and cognitions.

Hierarchies and hierarchical templates   Hierarchy theory (e.g., see Pattee, 1973; Weiss, 1971; Whyte, Wilson, & Wilson, 1969) provides a powerful conceptual model for dealing with organized complexity. The most direct implication of hierarchy theory for individuality theory is captured in the following two principles (modified from Royce & Buss, 1976):

1. *The Within-System Hierarchical Principle*: In general, the closer a higher-order component is to the apex of a within-system hierarchy, the greater its potential influence on the processing activities of that hierarchy, and the greater its role as a system integrator.
2. *The Between-System Hierarchical Principle*: In general, the closer a higher-level system is to the apex of a hierarchy of systems, the greater its role as a personality integrator.

The major implication of these two principles is that higher-level system components provide some form of control over lower-level components, while still

---

[9]See, for example, Atkinson and Shiffrin (1968). A major consequence of this ambiguity is that decision making is accomplished by a little man in the head—a homunculus. In fact, philosophers have long held the view that this problem leads to an infinite regress and lies at the core of the decision-making process.

allowing for relative independence at each level. Furthermore, hierarchical structure implies the decomposition of goals, as when the suprasystem goals are decomposed into system goals, or *strategies*. There is also the further decomposition of goals into subsystem goals, or *tactics*, and the operations of the subsystem factor components. [10]

DEVELOPMENT
AS METAMORPHOGENESIS

The human individual undergoes a psychological "morphogenesis" in the sense that important structural changes take place throughout the life span. But other changes occur in addition to such structural changes—such as when a child's wishful aspirations evolve into a specific life style that, in turn, serves as a guideline for further growth and development. Such changes in an individual's integrative goals are influenced by environmental interactions not connoted by the term *morphogenesis*. Furthermore, human life-span changes evolve rather than change abruptly in form from one stage to the next. [11] For these reasons we require the *meta* prefix to the term *morphogenesis* when referring to our developmental model. The model has two parts: the transformations of personality, and the forces that determine these transformations.

Metamorphogenesis

The first part of our developmental model merely describes the many changes that an individual undergoes from birth to death:

> *Throughout the lifespan personality and its component systems undergo transformations involving: (a) quantitative increases and decreases in processing dimensions; (b) increasing differentiation and emergence, followed by increasing consolidation; (c) increasing integration and hierarchical organization among differentiated structures; (d) systematic evolution of integrative goals; and (e) increasing capacity for self-direction.* (Powell, Royce, & Voorhees, in press)

---

[10]Within the context of factor analysis, hierarchies have been offered by several investigators, especially in the cognitive domain (e.g., Burt, 1949; Cattell, 1971; Horn, 1968; Royce, 1973a; Vernon, 1950). While the British factor analysts have evolved nonoverlapping, neatly subdivided hierarchical models, researchers in North America have tended to prefer overlapping models (i.e., a given lower-order factor may have links to more than one higher-order factor). This difference in hierarchical models is related to differences in factor extraction, where the British have preferred extracting orthogonal centroids one after the other without rotation. Those in North America have opted for oblique rotation to simple structure, thereby building their hierarchies from the bottom up rather than the other way around. The logic of the latter necessitates overlapping hierarchies and is to be preferred to the extent one accepts L. L. Thurstone's (1947) argument that rotating to oblique simple structure is a necessary prerequisite in the search for useful theoretical constructs.

[11]Butterflies are traditionally the most dramatic examples of metamorphosis, since the stage transitions are so radical. Although humans undergo a kind of psychological metamorphosis, the changes and transformations are spread out in time, and there do not appear to be dramatically different stages when one examines the fine grain of psychological development.

Each of these transformations of personality has been the focus of large segments of developmental research and theorizing. In the first transformation the concern is with simple growth and aging, as in the growth and decline of intellectual abilities, or the ontogeny of particular skills such as walking, grasping, visual acuity, and tonal discrimination. Increasing differentiation (b), on the other hand, relates to the increasing articulation of various psychological processes, as in the increasing distinction among various affective reactions, emotions, grammatical structures, and concepts (see, e.g., Witkin, Dyk, Faterson, Goodenough, & Karp, 1962). With the loss of psychological functioning that occurs with aging (e.g., decline in memory span, rapidly decreasing sensory and motor abilities), there is compensation in the form of consolidation among the remaining psychological functions. (It should be noted that there is also *between-*system divergence as well as within-system dimensional divergence.) Developmental differentiation and consolidation can be empirically observed in terms of factor divergence and convergence (Buss & Royce, 1975; Kearsley, Buss, & Royce, 1977). That is, divergence and convergence can be defined in terms of changing correlations between factors over time.

Transformations involving increasing integration (c), relate to the overall organization of the differentiated structures of personality. For example, as an individual's values become increasingly more articulated, they also become more hierarchically organized—for example, some values come to have priority over others, and the overall organization of personality is increasingly dominated by the integrative action of styles and values. [12]

The first three transformations (a–c) are the focus of the *orthogenetic* principle of development (Werner, 1948, 1957), but the last two extend beyond Werner's principle. The evolution of the integrative goals of personality has been the focus of Erikson's (1968) studies of the developmental crises that individuals face throughout their life span. And the Piagetian emphasis on changing levels of equilibration also emphasizes the importance of type d transformations. The important point is that the goals that organize an individual's actions, thoughts, and feelings evolve over the course of the life span. For example, while the attainment of organized percepts may be adequate for cognition in the young child, an older child or an adult may search for conceptions that meet the criterion of "formal adequacy." Similarly, emotional balance may provide a sufficient goal for integrative personality in the young adolescent and neurotic adults, but more mature individuals attempt to articulate personally satisfying world views, life styles, and self-images.

The fifth characteristic (e) that we postulate as a characteristic of life-span

---

[12]It is important to note that development can proceed "from the top down," such as when cognitive abilities develop out of more global, higher-order cognitive structures (Kearsley, Buss, & Royce, 1977; Buss & Royce, 1975). However, it may also proceed "from the bottom up," as in the emergence of styles and values out of cognition and affect. We wish to acknowledge the important contribution of Allan Buss and Greg Kearsley to our understanding of the life-span development of cognitive abilities.

development—increasing capacity for self-direction—has been the focus of research and theorizing within clinical, personality, and humanistic psychologies. What is typically missing from such accounts, however, are the other kinds of transformations identified in the *metamorphogenetic* principle. That is, increasing self-direction is not a transformation in personality that can be divorced from all the other transformations. Rather, it is an aspect of development that emerges out of the other interrelated changes (a–d) that occur throughout the life span. For example, the goals that motivate children (in contrast to mature adults) tend to be more diffuse and unarticulated. And when a child's goals are highly specific (e.g., he or she wants to become a cartoonist), they tend not to be integrated with other aspects of personality, such as cognitive abilities, affect, and styles. Such goals cannot, therefore, serve as a basis for the development of world views, life styles, or self-images that organize one's actions over long periods of time. The mature adult, to a greater extent than the child, can make decisions that influence further development in a highly articulated and integrated fashion. Additionally, the adult's decisions tend to be more consistent with the evolving goals of integrative personality (i.e., emotional balance, personal meaning, life style, self-image, etc.).

Representation of quantitative changes   The prototypic, quantitative, life-span developmental curve for factor growth is shown in Figure 3–4. The abscissa is chronological age and the ordinate is the scaled score on a given factor. There are three parameters of psychological interest: K_1, K_2, and K_3. On the age dimension, maturity (M), or maximum performance, is indicated by K_2, and the

FIGURE 3-4   The generalized life-span development curve. (From Royce, 1973)

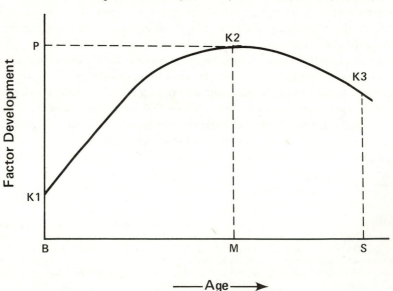

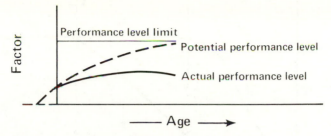

FIGURE 3-5 The relationship between performance level and performance limit. (From Royce, 1973)

onset of senescence (S), or performance level before death, is indicated by K_3. The
location of the y-intercept, K_1, indicates the extent of prenatal development, or
the degree to which the factor is present at birth (B).

The value of the parameter K_2 indicates the maximum factor performance
level (P), which occurs at maturity (M). If a factor does not reach optimal development in the life span of an individual (i.e., continues to either increase or decline
over the entire life span), the value of K_1 will take the value of the factor score at
birth or death (for a decrease or increase, respectively). The curve segment K_1-K_2
indicates the rate of developmental change during childhood, adolescence, and
early adulthood.

The parameter K_3 represents the factor score at the onset of senescence (or
death if there is no senescent period). It is to be expected that factor scores will
always decline in any post-senescence measurement. The segment of development
represented by the K_2-K_3 portion of the curve is, of course, factor change over the
major part of the life span of the individual.

While Figure 3-4 shows the prototypic factor as a function of age, the relationship between actual performance level and performance level limit is brought
out in Figure 3-5. Here we see a difference between actual and potential performance level for a given factor, where actual performance level refers to the observed score on a given factor, and potential performance level refers to a
theoretical upper limit determined by heredity and environment.

A similar set of concepts is called for when we focus on age of maturity, the
age at which maximum performance occurs. However, in this case (see Figure
3-6) the difference between actual (M_a) and potential (M_t) performance is a matter of timing rather than level of performance per se. M_t denotes the earliest possible age of maturity as determined by heredity and environment.

Representation of qualitative changes   Buss and Royce (1975) have
analyzed the developmental processes of differentiation and consolidation as they
relate to individuality in terms of factor divergence, convergence, and parallelism.
The last of these three refers to the changing of one factor into another in a one-to-
one fashion. These three relations were shown to be prototypic inasmuch as more
complex relations could be conceived as concatenations of various combinations of

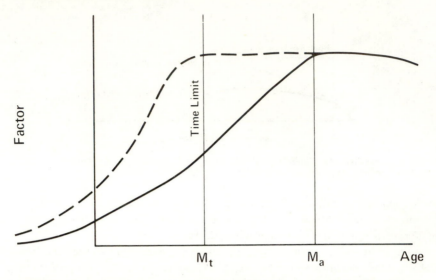

FIGURE 3-6 The relationship between performance and age of maturity. (From Royce, 1973)

divergence, convergence, and parallelism. The three prototypic relations discussed by Buss and Royce are shown in Figure 3-7.

Hypothetical examples of each of the prototypic relations are straightforward. For example, convergence (B) could involve increases in the correlation between cognitive *memorization* and *verbal* factors over selected time intervals. Such a change would result in a new pattern of factor loadings and the possible emergence of a single factor of "verbal memorization." Divergence (A) represents the opposite and, in such a case, a *conceptualizing* factor might divide into, say, a *verbal* and a *reasoning* factor. Parallelism (C) would mean that two factors maintain a relatively constant covariation over time but, also, change their separate factor loadings at about the same point in time.

The evolution of higher-order factors and the increasing hierarchicalization of personality can be represented as involving these same basic relations (cf. Buss & Royce, 1975). Two possibilities are represented in Figure 3-8. In A, the initial six individual factors eventually give rise to a single fourth-order factor. This occurs largely through recurrent convergences, though it should be noted that divergence is also implicated at the center of the second-order level. In B, a single higher-order factor gives rise to four primary factors. While divergence is primarily implicated, convergence is also represented at the center of the second- and first-order levels.

With respect to the evolution of goals, the fourth kind of transformation identified in our model, it is important to realize that all of the other transformations are, in part, responsible. For example, with increasing hierarchicalization and given the integrative role of higher-order factors and systems of the hierarchy, changes in integrative goals should follow. But other relationships are also in-

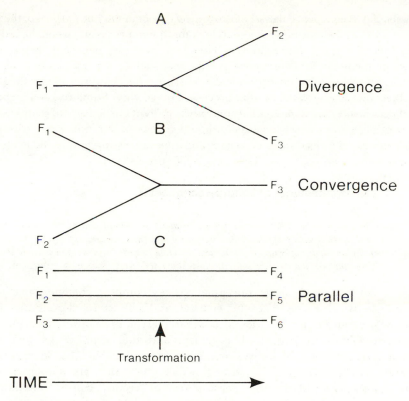

FIGURE 3-7   The three ideal factor-relation types of divergence, convergence, and parallelism. (From Buss & Royce, 1975, Fig. 1, p. 89)

FIGURE 3-8   Abstract model of the hierarchical development of factor structures, showing convergence (A) toward higher-order factors and divergence (B) yielding lower-order factors. (Based on Fig. 4 of Buss & Royce, 1975)

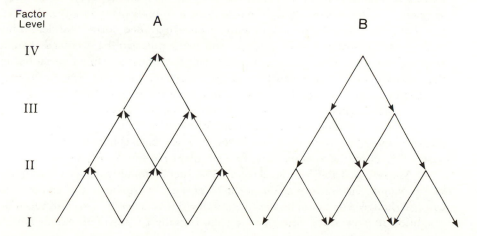

volved. Given a particular set of processing components, the outputs of these components can provide norms or goals for subsequent processing when the individual is functioning accommodatively. Thus, for example, particular percepts often define the norm for subsequent perceptions, such as when an individual finds it difficult to find a lost object in some new context because prior perceptions of that object interfere with the current process of perceiving. Similarly, at a higher level of personality, information that contradicts individuals' images of themselves may be difficult to process. Eventually, however, continued interaction with the environment can lead to more accommodative processing and to the evolution of new norms and goals (see, for example, Figure 3-3).

The Determinants of Metamorphogenesis

The transformations that occur in personality and its component systems over the life span are the result of: (a) genetic programs, (b) cultural programs, (c) self-generated programs, (d) fluctuations in the functioning of genetic, cultural, and individual structures, and (e) interactions among these three structures and their characteristic fluctuations. (Powell, Royce, & Voorhees, in press)

An individual can be conceptualized as a complex, changing structure, the plans for which reside in genetic, cultural, and self-generated programs. Each of these programs is, in turn, viewed as a characteristic of an open system that evokes increasingly more organized structures and that exploits the low entropy energy/information of its environment (Prigogine, Allen, & Herman, 1977; Brent, 1978a, 1978b). As illustrated in Table 3-2, there are characteristic functions associated with the principal structures of heredity, culture, and individual. Furthermore, distinctive fluctuations can occur within each of these functions. In the case of *genetic structures*, the characteristic function is maintenance of biological adaptability or reproduction and the other functions of life. The fluctuations that occur in the functioning of such structures include meiotic reproduction, assortative mating, mutations, and chromosomal breakage. By identifying *cultural programs* in this same context we mean to convey the idea that a particular culture's symbols, customs, norms, institutions, and so on embody plans for any individual member's life. For example, every culture has age-graded norms that determine when formal education begins, when adult work roles can be occupied, and at what age sexual intercourse is permissible. But fluctuations or blind variations in the functions of a culture can lead to cultural change and, in turn, to further changes in the functions of the culture. The human rights movement that began in the United States in the late 1950s and peaked in the late 1960s provides a good example of how small fluctuations can be amplified and eventually lead to changes in the social integration of the culture. In the long run, such changes will have a pervasive impact on the total pattern of social integration in North America.

As noted in Table 3-2, local conditions, such as family size, local resources, and economic factors, are a few of the important fluctuations that can lead to cultural change. For example, the changes that have occurred (and continue to be amplified) in a few small oil-exporting nations in the 1970s will ultimately have a

TABLE 3-2 Overview of the Structures, Functions, and Fluctuations of Heredity, Culture, and Individual

	STRUCTURE	FUNCTION	SAMPLE FLUCTUATIONS
Heredity	Genetic programs (genotype and phenotype)	Biological adaptation (maintenance of reproduction, metabolism, and other aspects of life)	Mutations, meiotic reproduction, assortative mating, genetic drift, changing environmental (ecological) pressures, catastrophies
Culture	Cultural programs (symbols and norms)	Social integration (adaptation, cultural survival and continuity)	Cultural and individual innovations and importation, local conditions (resources, family size, etc.), immigration, wars, natural disasters
Individual	Personality and its component systems (source traits and behavior)	Personality integration (e.g., emotional balance, sensory-motor integration, world view, life style, self-image)	Idiosyncratic experiences, curiosity, creativity, divergent thinking, regulation of uncertainty and risk

very important impact on the course of cultural evolution in the world as a whole. One point we want to make with regard to this aspect of Table 3-2 is that cultural institutions and symbols, and the fluctuations in the functions of these structures, have an important determining influence on the course of individual human development.

The portion of Table 3-2 that is most directly relevant (although not always the most important!) to understanding *individual* psychological development is the last row. In Chapter 1 we presented a brief description of the basic factor-system structures of personality. We also alluded to some of the characteristic functions of these structures. For example, the total personality is viewed as a composite of sensory, motor, cognitive, affective, style, and value systems, and each of these systems is characterized as a hierarchy of information-processing components identified via factor analysis. Furthermore, there are distinctive functions associated with these various structures: Cognition and affect transform information in order to discover ecological invariants or to maintain optimal internal arousal; style and value function as personality integrators; and the sensory and motor systems are information transducers. A major function of the integrative suprasystem is to design and organize (i.e., self-generate) plans that lead to changes in its own structure and functioning. Furthermore, as suggested in Table 3-2, the idiosyncratic experiences of an individual represent fluctuations in the functioning of personality structures, and these fluctuations also lead to the evolution of more complicated personality structures. That is, the specific accommodative interchanges that an individual has with the environment in pursuing specific goals lead to internal changes in the functioning of the various structures of personality.

Another point to consider in understanding changes in the structure of personality is that individuals, like all complex adaptive systems, engage in the *regulation* of uncertainty and risk (R. Jung, 1965), as we discussed above. Humans and other living systems do not simply reduce uncertainty and risk to an absolute minimum. Rather, such systems frequently increase uncertainty or risk in order to eventually reduce it. Consider, for example, that an individual must be exposed to uncertainty and risk of varying degrees in order to gain a greater knowledge of the surrounding environment. By taking a different route home from work one day, one may be exposed to uncertainties and, possibly, greater risks (particularly in a high-crime district), but it is precisely because such uncertainties and risks occur that one can gain a greater knowledge of the world. To express this another way, unplanned, idiosyncratic experiences represent fluctuations in personality functioning, and such fluctuations are amplified according to individuals' tendencies or propensities to expose themselves to risk or uncertainty. Some organisms (e.g., humans) have a greater propensity for and capability of manipulating risk and uncertainty than do other organisms (e.g., paramecia toward the other extreme) and, hence, greater capability of discovering information and finding optimal arousal states. Similarly, individual humans vary in their propensity or ability to engage in the manipulation of risk and uncertainty.

Heredity, culture, and self can be described as imposing successively more restricted limits on individual psychological development. This is illustrated in Figure 3-9, where heredity is depicted as determining the range of values for a particular psychological process. We conceptualize the role of culture in a similar manner. That is, culture can restrict or extend the expression of various psychological factors, but it cannot exceed the limits set by heredity. Consider, for example, the expression of genius. Given that an individual inherits all the necessary genes for a high-level development on all the factors of cognition, the actual level of intelligence attained throughout the course of the life span will be influenced by culture. Thus, because of heredity–environment interaction, such an individual is unlikely to grow up retarded, regardless of the cultural conditions in which development occurs.[13] Similarly, although individuals with more modest genetic endowments would not be expected to reach the same level as that of a genius, culture can have an important determining impact within the limits established by heredity. The individual choices and plans that an individual generates over the life span can act as further restrictions on the course of development. Career choices, as well as career changes later in life, for example, usually have a pervasive impact on all aspects of psychological development. In addition,

[13]It is interesting to note that when geniuses of great stature are identified, their family and cultural conditions are frequently not so unusual as to suggest that environment was the cause of the person's genius.

FIGURE 3-9   An expansion of the basic life-span development curve, illustrating the relationships among heredity, culture, and individual.

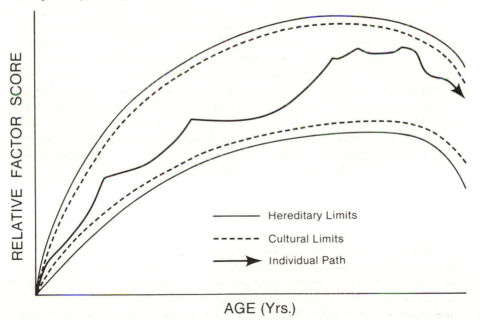

RELATIVE FACTOR SCORE

——————— Hereditary Limits

- - - - - - Cultural Limits

———▶ Individual Path

AGE (Yrs.)

the fluctuations introduced by an individual's idiosyncratic experiences, as well as the local conditions and other fluctuations in the surrounding culture, can take an individual outside what would otherwise be the boundaries of development as specified by cultural programs. Thus, individuals can become innovators and rebels who can either produce changes (e.g., Martin Luther King, Jr., Mahatma Ghandi) or be ostracized, depending on the individual, his or her heredity, and the culture and its local conditions.

Uncertainties and fluctuations in development   A number of constraints seriously limit the predictability of human development and the possibility of highly "deterministic" models of the developmental process. For example, *fluctuations* are identified in the *metamorphogenetic* principle as important determinants of structural change in personality. Just as biological or hereditary structures experiment with blind variations in their functions and selectively retain those structures with successful outcomes (via biological evolution), cultures and individuals also engage in a variety of "experiments," with results that are unpredictable beforehand. Just as rats or cats in a Thorndikian instrumental learning task would never discover the solution to their problem without "experimentation," humans would never have discovered relativity, thermodynamics, or any of the other explanatory principles of science if they had not engaged in activities with uncertain outcomes. Fluctuations can also increase an organism's survival value by making behavior unpredictable to predators, as a fleeing rabbit does. If a running back's behavior is unpredictable to himself, it most likely will be unpredictable to a pursuing defensive player (e.g., O. J. Simpson insisted that he did not know which way he would move).

A number of psychological theories have incorporated this uncertainty into their basic explanatory framework. The Thorndikian (1898) notion of trial-and-error learning is one example. Much later Hull (1952) explored the possibility of quantifying his various theoretical constructs in terms of the momentary *oscillations* of behavioral tendencies (reflected in the standard deviation of the distribution of paired comparisons of various response measures taken over trials), using one of L. L. Thurstone's (1927) scaling procedures. Still later, Estes (e.g., 1959) investigated mathematical models of learning using stochastic models and opened a major field of psychological research based on a fundamental premise of randomness in behavioral processes. Analogously, modern research design (as in analysis of variance) is based on knowledge of the "organized," but stochastic, characteristics of sampling distributions when samples are taken at random. D. T. Campbell's (1960, 1974) evolutionary epistemology is another important example of this attempt to understand complex behavior by recognizing the importance of uncertainty, or "blindness," at the molecular level. A variety of frameworks take uncertainty of particular events as axiomatic in any further understanding of the phenomena of interest. We also think that fluctuations are basic in any theory of human development. The point is that such processes should be taken into consideration in understanding human development, rather than hoping that future research will reveal that it really is not so "blind" after all.

There is still another way of thinking about the role attributed to fluctuations in determining the course of development—namely, that it is the divergent, "creative" aspects of various functions that lie at the core of individual, cultural, and biological development. The accommodative interactions of organisms with the world sometimes lead to regression, death, or other negative outcomes, but in all three types of development greater differentiation and organization emerge as the overall adaptive mechanism. The cultures of native Indians in North America several centuries ago provide a good example of this. The whole range of possible cultural organizations was represented at the time Europeans began to explore and settle the continent (Farb, 1978). The cultures in North America at that time ranged from the relatively undifferentiated and simply organized Utes of the western deserts to the complex and hierarchically organized Aztecs and Mayan civilizations of Mexico and Central and South America. The development of modern science provides another example of the trend toward greater differentiation and greater integration. Individual psychological development displays analogous trends over the life span. That is, humans begin life with relatively undifferentiated perceptual, conceptual, and symbolizing abilities, emotions, values, and so on, but they rapidly evolve complex structures for analyzing and reacting to the world in which they are embedded. Such changes are possible because the individual ventures out, explores, and remodels the world in ways that are essentially unpredictable beforehand.

A number of the above points are illustrated in Figure 3–10, an abstract depiction of goal-directed behavior. As shown at the top of Figure 3–10, individual A is motivated to attain a particular goal. However, as shown in panel B, unpredictable experiences are encountered in pursuit of this goal. Such fluctuations could be unique learning experiences, unusual or unexpected local conditions—in short, any of a variety of conditions that are unpredictable. Once such a fluctuation is encountered, a number of possible alternative directions emerge (X, Y, or Z), partly because of hereditary, environmental, and self determinants. Those alternatives that increase the individual's adaptability (i.e., make goal attainment more likely or make possible higher-level goals) are selectively retained. And, as shown in panel C, by recognizing that goals can be ordered according to their "level," the process of development can be described by a pathway through a series of fluctuations. That segment of the pathway labeled 1 characterizes a period of accommodation, segment 2 a period of assimilation, and segment 3 a period of regression or decline.

Such considerations pose some important questions concerning the "emergence of order out of chaos." When one considers very complex events such as cultural history, there seems to be a fundamental unpredictability that limits our ability to predict their future course. It is our view that a similar situation exists at the level of personal history—i.e., that life-span development has a fundamental unpredictability associated with it. On the other hand, there is sufficient order in human affairs that we can make gross predictions about the course of life. Just as Toynbee (1962) can discern something of the molar patterns in cultural history, it is possible to discern something of the molar patterns of individual development.

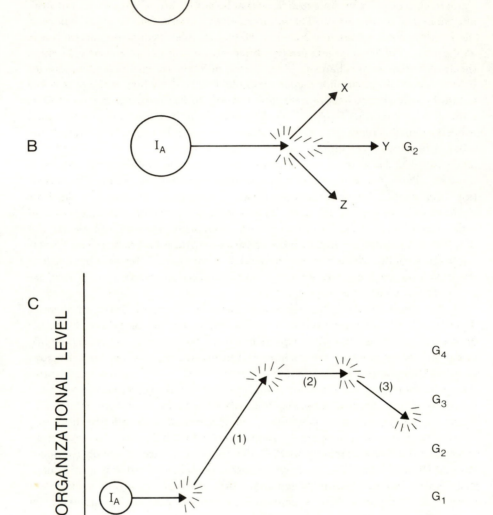

FIGURE 3–10   Goal direction over the life span. This is an abstract depiction that takes fluctuations into account.

One of the important keys to understanding the more molar patterns in both cultural and individual development lies in styles and values. That is, styles and values are both personality and cultural integrators. This means they are simultaneously the major determinants of stability and change in both personality and society. It also means—and this is the main point—that the emergence of new styles and values is largely a creative, unpredictable process!

Another important point is that, given the fluctuations and uncertainties involved in psychological development, even simple quantitative changes cannot be adequately represented by smooth mathematical functions (as in Figures 3-4, 3-5, and 3-6). Instead, when we summarize the empirical findings regarding factor change in Chapter 7, we will make use of broad bands to describe life-span quantitative changes.

THE FACTOR-GENE MODEL[14]

Since the assessment of gene effects can only occur via observable phenotypes, the identification of reliable and valid phenotypes is clearly a crucial prerequisite to genetic analysis. This is a relatively minor problem in studying physical characteristics, such as height and eye color, but it has been a major stumbling block in research on behavior genetics, particularly when dealing with complex behaviors such as intelligence and emotionality. And although the power of factor analysis lies in its ability to identify components of behavioral complexes, relatively little effort has been devoted to replicating factor-identified components.

The point is that invariant factors provide the behavior geneticist with a convincing basis for the identification of stable behavioral phenotypes. Failure to take this step, particularly when dealing with complex behavior, constitutes a serious methodological deficiency (Royce, 1979a; Royce & Mos, 1979). In particular, it leads to contradictory data and conceptual confusion. The major reason is that the same concept (e.g., emotionality) is used for different subsets of variables that implicitly reflect unknown but different underlying dimensions of complex behaviors. Since such a situation involves different dimensions masquerading under the same, apparently univariate, dimension, investigators cannot help but (unknowingly) report apparently contradictory findings. Unless bivariate studies are preceded by multivariate studies that get at the dimensionality issue (Royce, 1950, 1977b), investigators will continue to be harassed in this way. The factor-gene model was developed as one way to deal with the issue of identifying stable behavioral phenotypes.

The Relationship
between Factors and Genes

It will be recalled that the factor-gene model involves an elaboration of the first term of equation 3.6. The key terms for our immediate purposes are F and H′, where F refers to a matrix of factor scores and H′ is based on the underlying genotype. A visual version of the proposed model, which is exemplified by in-

[14]The factor-gene basis of individuality is discussed more thoroughly in Royce (1977d, 1979a).

telligence and its components, is depicted in Figure 3-11. The key concept is that there are multiple factors at both the behavioral and genetic levels, and that they are linked via a variety of unspecified, intervening, psychobiological mechanisms (labeled psychophysiological genetics). Note that in both the behavioral and genetic domains, many elemental factors account for a complex. On the behavioral side many different factors (both first-order factors such as space and memory, and higher-order factors such as g_1 and g_2) or behavioral phenotypes account for the complex we call intelligence. On the genetic side, various combinations of many genes account for a particular behavior phenotype such as S or M. Thus, a person may inherit all of the capital letter forms of the gene pairs of the space factor (i.e., AA, BB, CC, DD, EE, FF, GG). Since this means that the individual has the maximum number (seven chosen arbitrarily) of capital letter genes for this particular genotype, and assuming optimal environmental conditions, performance should be at the highest possible level in tasks involving the perception of spatial relationships. If another person inherited genes f, g, h, i, j, k, l and m from the available gene pairs of the M factor, a minimal performance on pure memory tasks should occur.

Such profile differences are brought out most dramatically when the element or component aspect of factor analysis is contrasted with the results of more traditional psychometric approaches that obscure the underlying components. For example, if we average the two profiles depicted in Figure 3-12, we get exactly the same value, 50, or an IQ of 100. If the IQ was the only information available, we would conclude that these individuals are intellectually identical. It is obvious, however, that they are identical only in their performance on the perception factor. Otherwise person A (solid line) is essentially verbal in his intellectual strength whereas person B (broken line) is essentially quantitative. These high and low peaks of mental ability profiles are, of course, a major aspect of individuality theory.

Note that the hereditary correlate for *each factor* is polygenic and that the usual genetic mechanisms, such as dominance, epistasis, pleiotropy, and sex linkage, are operative, depending on the factor in question. It is important to note that the factor-gene model does *not* imply a one factor–one gene linkage, as erroneously claimed by Fuller and Thompson (1960). Nor does the model imply that there are mutually exclusive blocks of genes with corresponding uncorrelated factorial phenotypes. Rather, it implies that specifiable subsets of the gene pool account for the hereditary variation and covariation of factors. For example, gene pairs Aa through Gg combine, via biological phenotypes 1 and 2, to account for hereditary variation on the space factor, and gene pairs Ff through Ll combine, via biological phenotypes 3 and 4, to account for hereditary variations on the memory factor. Covariation of phenotypes, however, is attributed to gene subsets which are common to two or more phenotypes. These include gene pairs Cc, Dd, Ff, Gg, Ii, Jj, Ll, and Mm. However, only four gene pairs are relevant to correlated behavior phenotypes—namely Ff and Gg, as the hereditary basis for the correlation between the memory and space factors, and Ll and Mm, as the hereditary

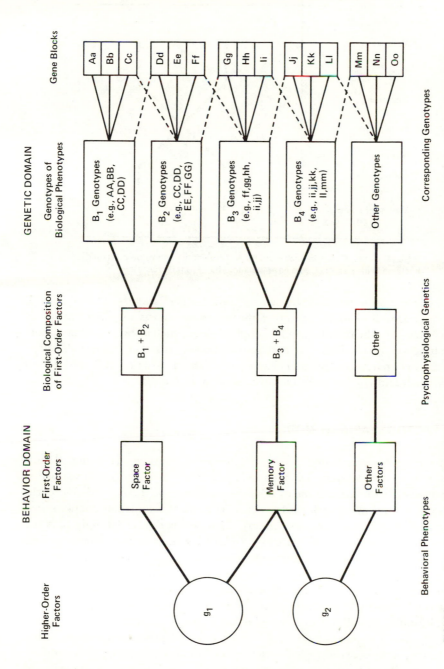

FIGURE 3-11 The most probable linkage between the multifactor theory of psychology and the multifactor theory of genetics. The capital letters signify the presence of the trait or phenotype and the small letters mean the absence of the characteristic. (A modified version of Royce, 1957, Fig. 5, p. 370)

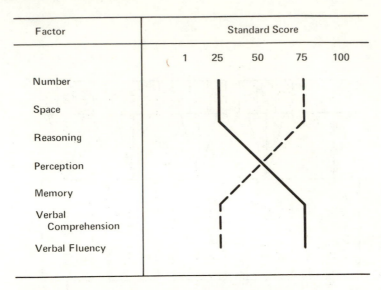

Factor	Standard Score

FIGURE 3-12 Opposite mental ability profiles for two individuals, A (solid line) and B (broken line), who have the same IQ. (From Royce, 1964)

source of correlation between the memory and "other" factors. The other gene pairs, Cc, Dd, Ii, and Jj, constitute the hereditary basis for those biological phenotypes (i.e., the full range of psychophysiology, such as brain function, hormone function, and biochemical mechanisms) that are relevant to specifiable first-order factors (gene pairs Cc and Dd account for the covariation of B_1 and B_2 and gene pairs Ii and Jj account for the covariation of B_3 and B_4).

THE FACTOR-LEARNING MODEL

The key to how learning affects factors lies in how we conceive of learning. Traditional treatments of learning will not be adequate since they were not developed in the context of factor analysis and do not focus on structure. Thus, we define learning as any change in psychological structure (i.e., factors and their relationships) due to experience (e.g., practice effects). This conception of learning puts the focus on the psychological structure that underlies change in performance per se, and it applies to all structural levels and facets, such as cognitive structure and affective structure, and all of their individual components. Thus, changes at the higher-order levels of psychological structure would represent shifts in style or world view, changes in cognitive structure relate to the usual school learning or general fund of knowledge an individual has acquired, and changes in affective structure refer to temperament and value shifts. All are manifestations of acculturation, shifts in psychological structure due to cultural learning. The implication is that different cultures or environments will maximize different combinations of structural components. For example, the environmental-cultural forces of relatively "primitive" societies will reinforce those cognitive and affective components that are consistent with such activities as hunting, fishing, agriculture, and other basic survival behavior. Similarly, so-called "developed"cultures will require that their participants learn a great deal about numbers and words, in some cases to the extent of developing "expertise" in one of the knowledge specialties such as the arts or the sciences. In short, differential reinforcement is probably the learning mechanism that can best account for the acculturation process. But note one important difference between the present account and the traditional socialization account. The standard view reinforces responses; in our view, it is the change in underlying psychological structure that is important.

When we talk of factor learning we are really referring to two different, though interrelated, categories of phenomena. On the one hand, *factor learning* refers to learning processes that may be influenced by factors in the various domains of individuality. In this case we will refer to *factor involvement* in learning processes, or some similar phrase. On the other hand, *factor learning* also refers to how factors are acquired; that is, to those processes that influence the quantitative and qualitative changes that can occur in factors. In this case, we use *learning of factors*, or a similar phrase.

Factor Involvement in the Learning Process

The first aspect of factor learning, factor involvement in various learning processes, is reflected in the changes in weights of various factors in the basic factor equation (see equation 3.1). There are several general determinants of which subset of factors will be involved in any learning situation. Actually, this point is discussed in a number of different contexts throughout the book, but for now it will suffice to indicate that factor involvement relates to: (1) the specific task demands, (2) the dimensional characteristics (i.e., the personality type) of a given individual, and (3) the overall goals of the individual.

The essence of what is involved can be captured by reference to Figure 3–13, where we see a progressive change in the contributions of various factors to total variance in a task involving the acquisition of a complex motor skill. Fleishman reports a systematic decrease in the contribution of nonmotor factors, with an attendant systematic increase in the motor factors. Thus, we are dealing with a special case of equation 3.4, a case where the change in factor weights is due to practice effects.

Individuality theory provides a general context for describing and categorizing the variety of learning processes in which factors can be involved and, as a result, undergo changes in their relative weighting. In Table 3–3 we present an overall summary of how various learning processes are related to the systems of integrative personality. As can be seen in the table, the sensory and motor systems are thought to be most directly relevant to a process we call sensory-motor pro-

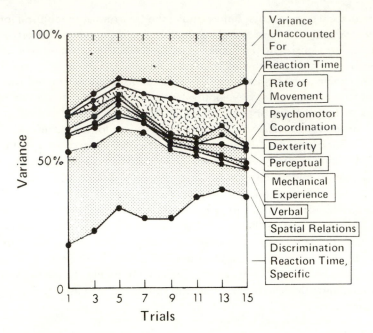

FIGURE 3-13 Percentage of variance represented by each factor at different stages of practice on a discrimination reaction time task (percentage of variance is represented by the area shaded in for each factor). (After Fleishman & Hempel, 1955)

gramming. Although described in greater detail in Chapter 4, sensory-motor programming can be described as the *spatial and temporal organization of sensory and motor processes to obtain relevant sensory inputs and to coordinate motor outputs*. In new situations, or in situations where positive transfer is unlikely, the initial stages of sensory-motor programming are apt to involve cognitive factors to a larger extent than during subsequent stages. In general, as sensory-motor programming proceeds, the functioning of the sensory and motor systems becomes more automatized and, thus, more directly related to just sensory and motor factors.

At the next level of Table 3–3 we have the cognitive and affective systems, which we have identified as more directly involved in *constructional* and *connectional*

TABLE 3-3   Overview of the Various Learning Processes in Which Factors Are Involved

LEVEL OF PERSONALITY	TYPE OF LEARNING FOR EACH SYSTEM	
Integrative–Self-Organizing	Decision-Making	
	(Style)	(Value)
Transformational-Adaptive	Constructional	Connectional
	(Cognition)	(Affect)
Transductional-Controlled Process	Sensory-Motor Programming	
	(Sensory)	(Motor)

learning processes, respectively. Constructional processes concern the creation of percepts, concepts, and symbols. Perceptual learning is primarily a matter of increasing the sharpness of existing perceptions, moving increasingly in the direction of finer and finer discriminations. Conceptual learning involves the formation of new concepts as well as the extension and finer delineation of familiar ones. Since concepts constitute the key terms of disciplines of knowledge, conceptual learning is of particular importance in gaining knowledge—that is, in getting a technical awareness of a discipline such as one of the arts or sciences. Symbolic learning is focused on the formation of new symbols and increasing one's insights concerning the meanings of old ones. The formation of symbols is the key to involvement in the arts: visual symbols are involved in painting, sculpture, and photography; auditory symbols in music; and the various literary forms in creative writing.

Connectional learning as it relates to the affective system involves the association of events (or their cognitive representation in the form of percepts, symbols, or concepts) that are affectively or emotionally arousing. In general, instrumental conditioning is more aligned with the cognitive system, and the affective system is more involved in classical conditioning processes. However, it should be noted that there is a great deal of overlap. For example, as we will show in Chapter 5, some of the lower-level cognitive processes (e.g., memorization) are more connectional in the sense that otherwise unrelated bits of information become connected together mentally. And some affective activities have constructional characteristics (e.g., self-sentiment; see Chapter 5).

Finally, the process at the highest level in Table 3–3, which we consider to involve most directly styles and values, is that of decision making. The point is that *which* goals are to be pursued most persistently and *how* they are to be pursued, are problems that are more directly under the control of values and styles, respectively. While the decision-making process per se is ostensibly a cognitive activity, the implementation of this activity is coordinated and integrated at the level of styles and values.

Processes Influencing
the Learning of Factors

As indicated above, factor changes can be quantitative and qualitative. Quantitative change is reflected in changes in the factor scores of an individual (F_{ij} in equation 3.1); qualitative change is reflected in changes in the pattern of correlations among factors (and thus also in the emergence, convergence, and divergence of particular factor dimensions). Figure 3–14, which parallels Table 3–3, presents an overview of the various processes considered to influence qualitative and quantitative changes in the factor dimensions of individuality. At the lowest level we see the process of tuning as being most critical in the sensory and motor domains. For example, exposure to a rich visual environment leads to greater efficiency and sensitivity of various sensory systems, as evidenced by the

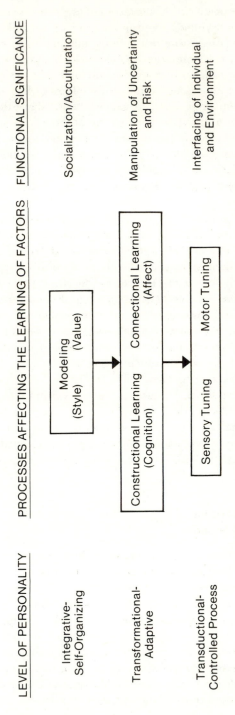

FIGURE 3-14 Overview of the various learning processes that influence changes in factor scores and factor structure.

voluminous literature on enriched versus deprived environments. However, the dimensional *processors* of the sensory system are not greatly affected by experience. Rather, experience probably operates more as a threshold effect, in which a minimum of experience is necessary for the system to function properly. Additional experience beyond this minimum may have a graded effect on sensory factors, but the overall effect is expected to be slight. Similarly, we view the effects of learning on the quantitative and qualitative characteristics in the motor domain to be rather small. Although experience does contribute to the efficiency and other characteristics of motor processing, most of the changes that can be observed are probably more attributable to the whole of sensory-motor programming whereby the various motor processes become better *organized* in motor programs for complex behavior.

The next level in Figure 3–14, where we have cognition and affect, has the same entries as Table 3–3. The implication is that quantitative and qualitative changes in the factors in these domains are brought about by their involvement in various learning situations requiring constructional and connectional processes. The changes that occur in cognitive and affective structure are probably much smaller than normally thought. That is, learning has its greatest impact on *what* is learned, rather than on the factors and systems involved in the processing of what is learned.

We can now elaborate on this point in the context of Figure 3–15, where the abstract relations among *factor involvement*, *content learning*, and the *learning of factors* are shown. The general idea is that various goals, or needs, and environmental demands lead to the involvement of factors from the relevant domains in the processing of information. This leads to the learning of particular contents (ideas, percepts, emotions, etc.), and the accompanying use of factors leads to quantitative and qualitative changes in the factor dimensions. It is our view that the latter effect is relatively small in the case of the sensory and motor systems, a little larger in the case of cognition and affect, and very robust in the case of styles and values. Finally, the acquired changes in the processing dimensions feed back into the first step.

The top level of Figure 3–14 indicates that styles and values are acquired through a process of *modeling*. We intend this term as a short-hand reference for the various ways that individuals become socialized or acculturated by the surrounding society and culture. An abstract view of this process is shown in Figure 3–16. This figure focuses on how we might relate the social institutions and social norms of collective humankind to the styles and values of individuals via complex systems of transformation. This involves systems of interaction, communication, and influence that transform social norms and institutions into psychological events and vice versa. We think the process of modeling significant others (parents, teachers, shamans, etc.) in the environment is the most significant process involved in the acquisition of styles and values. But individuals can also engage in "self-modeling" wherein one's actions in earlier situations can be reconstructed and modeled in subsequent situations. The downward-pointing ar-

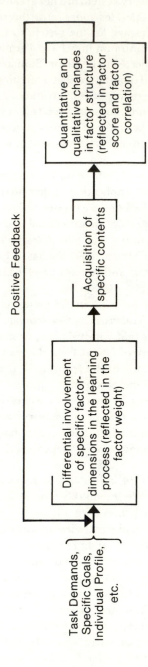

FIGURE 3–15 Interrelationship among factor learning, content learning, and environmental demands.

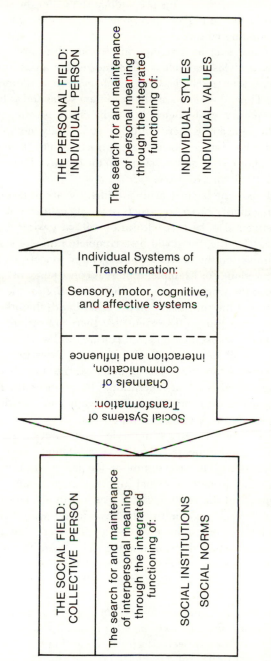

FIGURE 3–16 The interactive relationships between individual and social-cultural environment. (From Royce & Powell, 1978)

rows in Figure 3–14 are meant to represent the prepotency of higher-level processes over lower-level processes. This prepotency stems, on the one hand, from
the coordinating influence of higher-level goals and, on the other, from the influence of the surrounding culture.

A complex culture, such as contemporary world culture, is a weighted composite of several major styles and values. This means that a particular culture or
subculture can be characterized as a style and value type in a manner comparable
to personality type. Thus, if we focus on the dominant styles and values, we would
characterize contemporary technological Western culture as rational-empirical in
style and intrinsic in value and Eastern culture as stylistically metaphoric and self-
oriented in terms of value. Other subcultural contrasts include the commitment in
the arts to the metaphoric style and in science to the empirical and rational styles
(see Royce & Mos, 1980; and Royce, 1977c).

Thus, according to the factor-learning model, the acculturation process occurs primarily via the higher-order constructs of the style and value systems. Furthermore, the effectiveness of such acculturation will vary widely, depending on
many circumstances. That is, there will be a complete range of learning effects,
depending, for example, on the degree of homogeneity concerning the dominant
style and value in question. For example, if there is consistency in commitment to
a given style between the world culture and the subculture on the one hand and
between the parents and the subculture on the other hand, then the socialization
effects will be maximized. But to the extent that there are discrepancies in style
and value commitments between parents, subculture, and world culture, the consequent socialization will be reduced. For example, because of the relative
heterogeneity of contemporary life in North America, traditional values have not
been effectively transmitted in recent generations. This state of affairs has been accompanied by the generation of a profusion of new values and a wide range of subcultures with complex and mixed value components.

To summarize, when investigating styles and values, one learns about
"how" and "what" commitments. "How" commitments have to do with a
general way of doing things, a preferred mode for processing information. The
empiricist learns a commitment to factual inputs, the rationalist's priority concerns logical thought, and the metaphorist learns a commitment to meaningful
symbol formation. "What" commitments have to do with "what is worth
doing." Thus, one learns a hierarchy of values, a priority of values that constitute
the basis for value-consequent decision making. The "significant other" value
commitment says that "serving others" is the most significant commitment one
can make, whereas the value commitment to self says that self-development
should be the focus of one's efforts.

Although the affective dimensions are not highly trainable, *learning about
situations that result in affectivity does appear to be trainable.* Furthermore, various
aspects of affectivity have clearly been affected by conditioning. The most obvious
examples of this are culturally conditioned fears, such as the fear of snakes in
modern cultures and the fear of God during the Middle Ages. Early childhood

traumatic conditioning would also account for a range of special phobias, such as a fear of anybody dressed in a certain color or a generalized fear of the dark.

Although sensory and motor functioning has a heavy genetic component, it is equally clear that sensory-motor skills are highly trainable. If this were not the case, athletes would not train as intensively and effectively as they do. All motor components are probably trainable, but some, such as endurance and speed, clearly involve limits. Such limits are tied to the structural limitations of the body. It would be impossible for a human, for example, to achieve the locomotor speed of a horse or a cheetah. A major aspect of motor learning involves learning new techniques or motor programs. A new technique provides a new approach to an old skill demand, and when it works, it constitutes a better answer than the old technique. Examples include the new styles of high-jumping and pole-vaulting. To the extent that new athletic techniques reflect style rather than motor skill per se, we are actually describing stylistic learning rather than just motor learning. As with other complex phenomena, it is probably a matter of cooperative style-cognitive-motor functioning—that is, a mixture of style, cognition, and motor learning.

II

THE STRUCTURE, FUNCTION, AND DEVELOPMENT OF THE BASIC SYSTEMS OF PERSONALITY

In this section of the book we present the details of each of the six systems of personality. In Chapter 4 we describe the basic structures and functions of the transductive sensory and motor systems. Chapter 5 considers the transformational level of personality and describes the structures and functions of cognition and affect. The structure of the integrative style and value systems is described in Chapter 6. While we also allude to the functional significance of styles and values, their integrative role is considered in greater detail in Part III of the book. In Chapter 7 we present the quantitative changes that occur at the system and subsystem levels over the life span and consider the effects of heredity and environment in such changes. In general, these four chapters present the empirical basis for our overall theory, although empirical considerations are brought out in other sections as well.

4

The Sensory and Motor
Transduction Systems

The sensory system[1] is primarily responsible for the transduction of energy from the environment and its transmission through the nervous system. Sensory functions are interwoven with perceptual functions, but we can distinguish sensation from perception in accordance with Gibson's (1966) distinction between the two meanings of *to sense*: to feel, and to detect. Thus, sensory and perceiving functions can be distinguished in the following ways:

1. Sensation mainly involves the input transduction of energy and the transmission of decoded information, whereas perception involves the construction of percepts.[2]
2. Sensation depends primarily on sense organ or peripheral function; perception depends mostly on cortical brain function.
3. Sensation leads to a diffuse awareness of the input; perception results in the specific meaning of the input. That is, sensation is not selectively focused, whereas perception is selective and involves attentional mechanisms (Kearsley & Royce, 1977, pp. 1300–1301).

Sensory input that leads to feelings involves energy transduction and is properly within the domain of the sensory system. Sensory input that involves the transfor-

---

[1] For more details on the structure of the sensory system, see Kearsley and Royce (1977). Greg Kearsley's important contribution to our understanding of the sensory system is gratefully acknowledged.

[2] This distinction is related to our distinction between energy and information processing discussed in Chapter 2, and is discussed further in Royce and Buss (1976).

mation of information and results in meaningful percepts is considered to be part of the perceiving subsystem of the cognitive system. For example, sensation arising from lights and sounds may be viewed at the level of energy transduction (brightness, loudness qualities) or as the construction of percepts (recognition of specific patterns). The first depends mainly on the operating characteristics of the receptors and leads to awareness of the stimulation; the second depends on cognitive reconstructive operations and leads to cognitive representations of the stimulus.

These distinctions provide a general outline of what we consider to be within the boundaries of the sensory domain. We wish to emphasize that this is a tactic that allows us to work with a homogeneous subset of factor dimensions—we do not believe that a sensory system can be totally isolated from perceptual or even motor functions. However, the exact specification of the sensory system follows from the factor dimensions that describe sensory structure and processing (Kearsley & Royce, 1977, p. 1301).

SENSORY STRUCTURE
AND PROCESSES

In comparison to the number of factor-analytic studies in domains such as cognition and affect, sensation has been only sparsely explored in multivariate investigations. Insofar as individual differences in sensation are related to the integrative functioning of overall personality (see Figure 1-1), an understanding of sensory individuality would seem rather fundamental to a comprehensive model of personality. However, the sensory system seems far removed from the "core," or central processing aspects, of personality, and the expense involved in administering large batteries of sensory tests has probably deterred many researchers from exploring this area further.

Our synthesis of the literature on sensory structure is shown in Figure 4-1. As can be seen, we have postulated a multilevel, hierarchical structure composed of various factorially identified dimensions. Beginning at the top of the hierarchy, we have the highest-order construct, sensory type. This construct represents the profile for a particular individual on all the dimensions of the sensory system. If two individuals possess a similar profile of factor scores on all dimensions, they would be characterized as the same sensory "type." In general, each individual possesses a unique pattern of scores on the sensory dimensions. For example, one possible sensory type would be an individual with poor visual acuity but good color discrimination, high musical ability (rhythm, pitch), low pain sensitivity, good tactile sensitivity, dull palate, and so on. A difference in any one of these dimensions would describe a different (but similar) sensory type. Since it is at the apex of the hierarchy, sensory type is the major integrative construct of the sensory system.

The two third-order factors of spatiality and temporality are the fundamen-

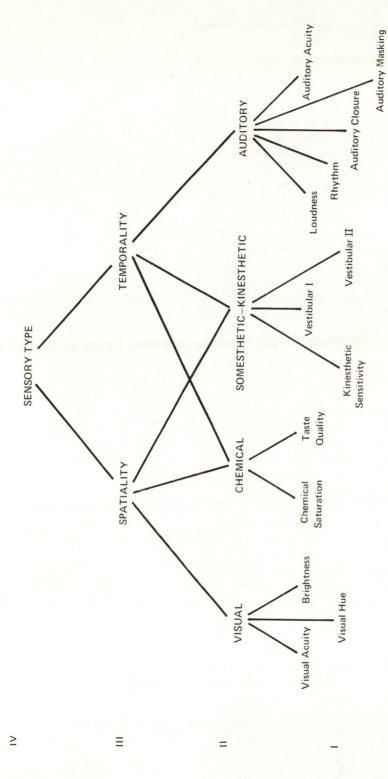

FIGURE 4-1 The hierarchical structure of the sensory system. (Modified from Kearsley & Royce, 1977)

87

tal cross-modality dimensions of the sensory system since each reflects individual differences in the integrative transduction of input from the various modalities. Spatiality is related to the transduction of a sensory pattern at many receptors simultaneously, as in the case of spatial summation in vision, taste, smell, and most forms of tactile stimulation. Thus, spatiality is a higher-order factor for the second-order visual, chemical, and somesthetic-kinesthetic dimensions. Temporality relates to the transduction of a sensory pattern from sequential stimuli separated in time (e.g., speech and certain aspects of tactile stimulation). Thus, temporality is the higher-order factor for the second-order chemical, somesthetic-kinesthetic, and auditory dimensions.[3] The visual modality is not confined to spatial processing, nor does the auditory modality involve *only* temporal processing. For example, there is sequential processing in vision (e.g., the phi phenomenon) and simultaneous processing in audition (e.g., sound localization), as well as both within a particular modality (e.g., taste). The point is that in *relative* terms, the visual modality transduces mostly spatial, simultaneous stimulation, whereas the auditory modality transduces mainly temporal, sequential stimulation, and the chemical and kinesthetic-somesthetic modalities transduce equally via both modes.

As far as individuality is concerned, we would expect individuals to show a particular pattern of integrating temporal and spatial stimulation, which would have a major overall effect on sensory processing. What we are suggesting is that a high score on the spatiality or temporality dimension would denote a disposition toward that particular mode of sensory processing. A person may prefer auditory stimulation to visual, or characteristically respond to the temporal aspects of somesthetic stimulation rather than the spatial. Moreover, as high-level dimensions, we would expect spatiality and temporality to have major interaction effects with the higher-order dimensions of the other personality systems (such as the motor system). Kearsley and Royce (1977) have also suggested that these two dimensions may be thought of as corresponding to different rates of sensory processing, or that the mode of sensory processing (i.e., simultaneous or sequential) determines the adaptation rate for a particular sensory modality. Thus, it has been suggested that these dimensions reflect the pattern of individual differences in adaptation rates across different modalities.

There are four suggested second-order dimensions: *visual, chemical, somesthetic-kinesthetic*, and *auditory*. Each of these second-order factors subsumes a number of modality-specific first-order factors that are differentially sensitive to ambient energy. *Visual* describes receptors optimally sensitive to light energy; *chemical* describes chemoreceptors sensitive to certain simple and complex chemical patterns; *somesthetic-kinesthetic* describes receptors sensitive to a variety of intrinsic and extrinsic mechanical, thermal, and electrical energy; and *auditory* indicates the

---

[3]We would like to draw attention to the proposal of Das, Kirby, and Jarman (1975) that dimensions of sequential and simultaneous processing are the major processing modes of cognition. We think these two modes are much too primary to be cognitive dimensions and that they more rightly belong as basic modes of sensory processing.

transduction of sound energy. Within the broad ranges in which these transducers operate, each individual has a particular set of sensitivities and ranges. These sensitivities and ranges may be tapped by measurements of absolute and relative thresholds for each modality. We are proposing that these idiosyncratic sensitivities are reflected in the individual power exponents found in psychophysical investigations of the various senses (see Kearsley & Royce, 1977). Although each modality will have a characteristic exponent,[4] these will differ for particular individuals. This allows for differential sensitivities across modalities for an individual, and it also describes the modality-specific dimensions on which they may differ. The important theoretical proposal being suggested here is that dimensions of sensory differences as described by factor scores should correspond to the values obtained for individual power exponents in the same modality for a particular individual.

Finally, we come to the first-order dimensions, which are the primary sensory factors. Beginning with those dimensions integrated by the visual dimension, *visual acuity* is indicated by various measures of spatial discrimination (detection, resolution, localization), *visual hue* is measured by tests of color discrimination or recognition, and *brightness* by the absolute sensitivity to light intensity. The chemical dimension includes the two factors of *chemical saturation*, which indicates differential sensitivity to the chemical properties of odors, and *taste quality*, which reflects the sensitivity to gustatory quality (sweet, sour, etc.). Of the three factors dominated by *somesthetic-kinesthetic*, *kinesthetic sensitivity* refers to awareness of muscular and body movement or position and is indicated by tests of postural discrimination. *Vestibular I* refers to sense of direction, and *vestibular II* reflects sense of motion. In the case of the *auditory* factors, *auditory acuity* refers to temporal discrimination, *auditory masking* indicates the ability to recognize or discriminate auditory patterns in distracting noise, *auditory closure* is indicated by the ability to discriminate auditory forms, *rhythm* (pitch) involves the discrimination or judgment of auditory patterns, and *loudness* reflects sensitivity to absolute sound intensity.

The structure of the sensory system as outlined above must be viewed as quite tentative in nature. There is almost certainly a more complex structure to the sensory system than has been described here. But, as we suggested above, sensory structures have not been extensively explored by factor analysts. It should be noted that there is some empirical evidence for each of the second-order factors. For example, Horn's (1973) higher-order analysis includes a general auditory factor, and Juurmaa (1967) found evidence for a general cutaneous tactile factor. The visual dimension is suggested by Cattell's (1971) broad second-order visualization factor in his abilities model. And we take the work of Pfaffmann (1959) as suggesting a relatively broad olfactory dimension. Also, we should fur-

---

[4]Of course, we mean here the characteristic *range* of exponents since there is sampling variability and there are differences due to the particular psychophysical technique employed and the stimulus conditions used. For example, the loudness exponent ranges from .15 to .85 with a modal value of .55 (Marks, 1974).

ther note that the empirical evidence for the second-order factors is weak and that the three postulated constructs at the third and fourth orders have no direct empirical support at present. Thus, we anticipate the necessity for changes in the details of the hierarchical structure (Kearsley & Royce, 1977, pp. 1304–8).

Sensory Processing

A general model of sensory processing involves indicating how the structural dimensions already discussed interact over time. As discussed in Chapter 3, factors can be viewed as process dimensions that reflect the predominant functions in the tests or tasks (variables) from which the factors are derived. It seems important, then, to describe the manner in which stimulation in various energy forms is transduced into either perceptual information for the cognitive system, or feeling information in the affective system, or both. Energy impinging on sensory receptors may be acoustic, chemical, electromagnetic, gravitational, mechanical, or thermal. Corresponding to each of these energy forms are certain modalities: audition, taste and olfaction, vision, kinesthesis, and somesthesis. These different energy forms impinge on all receptors at once; however, by virtue of particular sensitivities, nerve pathways, and fairly specific cortical innervation, different sensations arise. But none of these components is in a one-to-one relationship with a specific sensory modality (Melzack & Wall, 1962). Furthermore, although it may be commonly thought that each sensory quality maps onto a specific stimulus dimension, it is well known that some sensations are not stimulus-specific (e.g., Marks, 1975). What is needed, therefore, is a process model that allows for the particular range of sensitivity of the various modalities and, at the same time, for cross-modal interactions.

Our general model of the functional sequence of sensory processing is given in Figure 4–2. At the left side of the figure are the "inputs" to the sensory system—the major forms of ambient energy. Each kind and range of energy stimulates particular receptor cells, which correspond to the different sensory modalities. Receptor thresholds determine when the stimulation is sufficient to cause afferent transmission. This is where the characteristic value of the psychophysically identified sensory exponent plays a role. If the exponent is considered to relate to the basic operating characteristic of the receptor, then the exponents indicate quantitative differences in the type of stimulation necessary for suprathreshold activity. Such exponents also reflect a qualitative distinction between receptors characterized by exponents less than one, which indicate the compression of physical intensity, and those characterized by exponents greater than one, which reflect the expansion or amplification of physical energy. For example, the power exponents for brightness and loudness are both below one; therefore, the receptor function of these two sensory dimensions is to compress acoustic and light energy, respectively. Whether one considers the quantitative or qualitative aspects of power exponents, the important point is the relationship between the threshold for a particular type of receptor function and the characteristic expo-

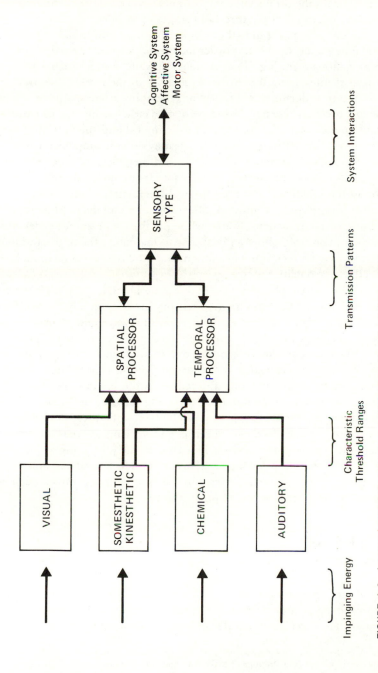

FIGURE 4-2 A general model of sensory processing. (From Kearsley & Royce, 1977)

nent. Moreover, since we have theoretically linked individual differences in sensory exponents with the primary sensory dimensions, we think these dimensions are functionally operative at the threshold stages of sensory processing.

The receptor types (and their corresponding threshold ranges) are represented functionally by the first-order factors, which describe particular kinds of within-modality processing. The modality-specific second-order dimensions serve the role of integrating the threshold activity of their respective first-order dimensions and transducing this activity into the appropriate spatial or temporal transmission pattern. These patterns may involve either sequential or simultaneous neural impulses that may correspond to temporal and spatial summation at the synaptic level. Furthermore, such patterns may differ in amplitude (intensity), frequency, periodicity, duration, and so on, and they probably code the quality of sensation (e.g., hot–cold; sweet–sour). Sensory type controls the overall sensory integration of the individual and the top-level interaction of the sensory system with the other systems (e.g., cognition, affect, motor), and the production of percepts, feelings, or motor actions. Thus, while the first- and second-order dimensions play their major role within a given sensory modality, the third- and fourth-order dimensions exert their influence on sensory qualities across all modalities as well as on other personality systems.

Despite the oversimplified nature of this general model, it is sufficient to indicate how individual differences arise in sensory processing. The first-order factors account for modality-specific differences in the range and intensities of the various types of energy that will be required for suprathreshold stimulation. The second-order factors reflect more general (but still modality-specific) parameters —the type of sensory transduction that characterizes four modalities. The third-order factors relate to the potential differences in the integration of sequential temporality and spatial simultaneity processing across all modalities. The general argument we are making is that modality-specific individual differences are more evident in the early stages of sensory processing whereas the modality-independent differences play a greater role later in the processing sequence. Finally, we should note that Kearsley and Royce provide several examples of how first-order factor processes might interact in the execution of complex behavioral sequences (Kearsley & Royce, 1977, pp. 1308–10).

MOTOR STRUCTURE
AND PROCESSES[5]

The study of human motor functions has been generally relegated to applied differential psychology, particularly in recreation, human engineering, industry, and education. However, in recent decades the factor-analytic research on motor

[5]For more details on the motor system, see Powell, Katzko, and Royce (1978). We wish to acknowledge the important contributions of Mike Katzko to our understanding of the motor system and sensory-motor integration.

abilities conducted by Fleishman (1975) and his associates, and the experimental-theoretic research on various aspects of motor control conducted by Adams (1968) and many others, have been significant in reestablishing the importance of studying human motor functions. For example, Fleishman's work, having focused on individual differences in motor functioning, served to emphasize the importance of the structure of complex *abilities*. The research by Adams and others, on the other hand, has emphasized the importance of process and the nature of complex motor *functions*. Because of the renewed interest in motor functions brought about by these developments in the study of motor skills, as well as advances in mainstream experimental psychology, it has become increasingly clear that an understanding of integrated human functioning requires an understanding of motor functions. Furthermore, since it is through the behavioral output of individuals that it is possible to learn anything about personality organization, it can be argued that motor functions are more relevant than sensory functions to the central aspects of personality.

Structure of the Motor System

The factor-analytic literature is so rich in such areas as cognition and affect that it has been possible to impose quite restrictive criteria (such as factor invariance) on the selection of factors to be included in our inventory. Unfortunately, this was not the case with regard to the motor domain. The only reliable investigations of motor factors have centered around Fleishman's (1964; 1972b; 1975) factorially identified motor abilities. Furthermore, there have been no higher-order factor analytic investigations, and many important areas of motor performance have not been subjected to factor-analytic investigation. Motor speech, for example, clearly falls within the domain of motor skills (e.g., MacNeilage, 1974) and, while there is a great deal of relevant experimental research, there still have been no appropriate factor-analytic investigations.[6] Because of the general importance of motor functions within our theoretical scheme, it was necessary to develop a set of specific criteria to guide the synthesis of a hierarchy of motor skills that extends well beyond the current areas of investigation. The criteria that guided this synthesis of the dimensions of the motor hierarchy are as follows:

1. The dimension had been reliably identified in factor-analytic investigations. Unfortunately, this criterion applied only in the case of first-order factors.
2. Higher-order dimensions were inductively generated from the identified first-order factors. This was done on the basis of judged similarities among the various tasks subsumed by these factors.
3. All of the higher-order factors were identified as the underlying construct of experimental (non-factor-analytic) research where functional interrelationships among neuromuscular processes have been found.

[6]But there is at least one factor-analytic investigation of speech articulation available (Wood, 1974).

4. The fourth criterion was directly related to our theoretical conception of the nature of the motor system. That is, we proposed dimensions that could be described as hierarchically decomposable classes of motor programs or classes of parameters of motor performance.

The multilevel hierarchy that we synthesized using the above criteria is shown in Figure 4–3 (Powell, Katzko, & Royce, 1978, p. 193). Fleishman's motor abilities are considered to be first-order factors, but there are several second-order factors for which no first-order factors have been identified.[7] This is most obvious in the case of the second-order factors underlying *bodily orchestration* (nonverbal or gestural communication) and *vocalization* (motor speech). The fourth-order factors of *spatiality* and *temporality* are the most abstract dimensions of motor functions along which individuals can vary, and they allude to the following notions: (1) motor programs specify the spatiotemporal patterning of behavior; (2) some aspects of motor functioning can be characterized primarily in terms of sequential processing (temporality), and others can be characterized primarily in terms of simultaneous processing (spatiality); and (3) a close alignment can be found between the sensory and motor systems.

Higher-order Factors

Spatiality and *temporality* describe the most abstract dimensions of individual differences in motor functioning. *Spatiality* characterizes a broad class of motor functions that relate principally to the organization of behavior through space. The processing involved in the programming of spatially oriented motor functions involves relatively greater simultaneous processing and the right hemisphere of the cerebral (associative) cortex. *Temporality*, on the other hand, characterizes the broad class of motor functions that relate to the organization of behavior through time. The processing involved in temporally oriented behaviors involves relatively greater emphasis on sequential processing and the left hemisphere of the cerebral (associative) cortex. It is important to note that these are both relative concepts, as are the analogous constructs in the sensory domain. That is, ostensibly spatial behaviors obviously have a temporal component as well, and individuals who are considered to be relatively high on spatiality must also possess a certain degree of temporality. Even so, the distinction is an important one, as exemplified by contrasting the motor functions entailed by *transport* through space and *vocalization*. While bodily transport, or the movement of the body from one point to another in three-dimensional space, cannot take place in either infinite or zero amount of time, it can be programmed relatively independently of time constraints. Vocalization, as exemplified by communicative speech, certainly involves changes in

---

[7]It is important to note that the motor system is the only one of the six systems that has required *five* levels. With the exception of styles, which has three levels, the other systems have been hypothesized to have four levels. We think the difference has to do with the specificity of the Fleishman factors at the primary level. The need for five levels may also be due to the hierarchical complexity of motor functions.

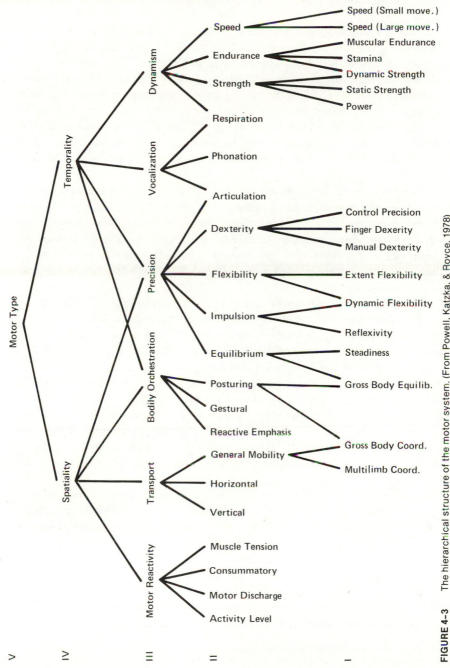

FIGURE 4-3   The hierarchical structure of the motor system. (From Powell, Katzka, & Royce, 1978)

95

the spatial configuration of small muscle groups, but speech is comprehensible precisely because of the temporal relations among its sequentially organized elements.

Motor reactivity has been suggested from the results of factor analytic investigations of emotionality (Royce, 1977b; Royce & McDermott, 1977). It and a variety of second-order factors appear as nonautonomic accompaniments, or "spill over" from emotional arousal. With the exception of the *consummatory* factor at the second-order level, all of the other factors dominated by motor reactivity have been reliably identified (though, in some cases, the "level" may be variable). Although factors subsumed by motor reactivity are closely related to autonomic processes, it should be emphasized that they reference the purely motoric components that accompany autonomic arousal (see Royce & McDermott, 1977).

Transport refers to the general movement of the body, or parts of the body, through three-dimensional space. Transport is postulated to be decomposable into the three components of *horizontal* movement (movement with respect to the median plane of the body), *vertical* movement (movement of the body with respect to the substrate), and *general mobility* (gross coordination of bodily transport). The last of these is further decomposable into two dimensions: *multilimb coordination* and *gross body coordination.*

Bodily orchestration refers to the dimensions underlying the bodily movements typically involved in nonverbal communication. As such, it refers to the integrative organization of the body with respect to its general orientation (i.e., *posturing*) and emphatic movements (i.e., *reactive emphasis* and *gestural*). Although there have been a few structural analyses of *bodily orchestration*, most such analyses have focused on the emotional factors hypothesized to underlie the observable organized patterns of behavior (e.g., van Hoof, 1973). However, some of the experimental literature has focused on the purely motoric aspects of nonverbal communications. *Posturing* (e.g., Mehrabian, 1972), *gesturing* (Schefflin, 1968), and *reactive emphasis* (e.g., Ekman, 1972) have emerged from a variety of studies as important and relatively independent neuromuscular systems for nonverbal communication.[8]

Precision could probably be described as the "coordination" of movements, or by K. V. Smith's (1972) term "articulation." However, coordination is involved in all integrated movements, and *articulation* is more appropriately reserved for characterizing an important dimension of motor speech. Precision subsumes the second-order factors of equilibrium (ability to maintain balance and steadiness), *impulsion* (general reactivity of the body to changing conditions), *flexibility* (the ability to make adjustments and modifications in graded or discrete movements), *dexterity* (the precision of small movements), and *articulation* (the precision of the movements of the lips, tongue, mouth cavity, in enunciation).

---

[8]From the results of a variety of investigations it is possible to speculate that *lower facial, medial facial,* and *upper facial* represent three of the first-order factors underlying reactive emphasis (see Izard, 1971; Exline, 1972).

Vocalization refers specifically to motor speech and has probably been the subject of more *experimental* investigations than any of the other factors of the motor hierarchy. And it is interesting to note that a great deal of the motor cortex in humans is devoted to control of the organs of motor speech. Of course, vocalization is not generally dealt with under the rubric of motor skills, but this is due more to the extant divisions of academic disciplines than to any meaningful characteristics of the structure of the motor system.[9]

Dynamism characterizes the common aspects of the physical proficiency dimensions related to the energetic components of skilled sequences. With the exception of *respiration*, the second-order factors subsumed by *dynamism* represent abstractions of the commonalities among the physical proficiency abilities isolated by Fleishman (1975) and Rimoldi (1951) (Powell, Katzko, & Royce, 1978, pp. 197–99).

First-order factors

Fleishman's systematic research on the structure of motor abilities at the first-order level has been relied on in the construction of the motor hierarchy shown in Figure 4–3. We refer you to Fleishman's various reviews of his research (1964, 1966, 1972a, 1972b, 1975) and to Powell, Katzko, and Royce (1978) for a more thorough review of the research in this area.[10]

Reading from left to right in Figure 4–3, the first-order motor abilities are defined as follows:

> *Multilimb coordination* is the movement of more than one limb simultaneously in a smooth, coordinated fashion, while seated or standing.
> *Gross body coordination* represents simultaneous movement of various body parts while in motion.
> *Gross body equilibrium* includes the maintenance of bodily position (balance) in spite of forces acting against it.
> *Steadiness* refers to the balance of precise movements where speed and strength are minimized as requirements.
> *Reflexivity* reflects the speed with which a movement can be made in a series of rapid repetitions.

[9] The results of the factor-analytic investigation of articulation errors conducted by Wood (1974) can be used to suggest the following first-order factors underlying (motor speech) *articulation*: *phonemic integration* (the ability to articulate phonemes and blends, without distortion, in the initial, final, and medial positions); *articulatory distinctiveness* (the ability to maintain distinction, in all positions, among the various speech sounds); and *speech blending* (the ability to pronounce blends without misarticulation). Furthermore, Fleishman's (1964) *articulation speed* is probably a first-order factor under motor speech *articulation*.

[10] The first-order factors in our hierarchy do not always correspond exactly with either Fleishman's labels or interpretations. We do not mean to imply, however, that the original factors are invalid. Rather, our theoretical perspective represents an attempt to identify *general* motor capacities. Essentially, a person's factor score is considered to be indicative of a maximum performance level with respect to an underlying component whose value can fluctuate—depending on the particular task and also depending on which muscle group is operating. We have tried to interpret anatomically specific motor factors as being clues to the nature of more general motor capacities.

Dynamic flexibility is the rapid and repeated flexing and stretching movements of the body under circumstances where the recovery from strain is an important demand.

Extent flexibility is measured by stretching (forward, backward, or laterally) as far as possible.

Manual dexterity is the manipulation of large objects in a skillful manner and under speed constraints.

Finger dexterity relates to movement of fairly small objects primarily using the fingers.

Control precision is reflected in adjustments of large muscle groups in a highly controlled and rapid manner.

Power is the exertion of strength against large objects and gravity—in general, it relates to the overall strength of the body.

Static strength reflects exertion of maximum force against external objects for brief periods of time, best exemplified by lifting weights or pulling against a dynamometer.

Dynamic strength is measured by the exertion of continuous or repeated forceful movements of the limbs over relatively long periods of time, without experiencing fatigue and with continued strength.

Stamina is exertion of maximum effort over relatively long periods of time.

Muscular endurance is the capacity of large-muscle groups to perform over extended periods of time without experiencing fatigue.

Speed (large movements) is reflected in rapid movements of gross body parts without an accuracy constraint.

Speed (small movements) is the rapid movements of distal muscular groups (Powell, Katzko, & Royce, 1978, pp. 194–95).

Processing Dynamics in Skilled Motor Functioning

The concepts of *motor programs* and *motor schema* have come to occupy a central role in theories of motor performance (e.g., Marteniuk, 1976; Pew, 1974; Schmidt, 1975). Some of the reasons for abandoning the closed-loop, or "simple," feedback models of performance are: (a) skilled sequences typically begin from unique starting points each time they are executed; (b) skilled sequences do not necessarily require feedback or knowledge of results for acquisition or performance, (c) the temporal constraints involved in many tasks are too great to allow feedback processes to control the overall organization of behavior, and (d) there is equifinality, or motor equivalence (as, for example, when one can write with the pen held between the teeth) . . . The critical idea behind the concept of motor program is that there exists, or is reconstructed, some central representation of the movements to be made in either complex or simple behavioral sequences. This does not mean that feedback is not part of the central representation, nor does it mean that feedback is unimportant in controlling sequences of movements, for clearly feedback does play a critical role in most situations. The important point is that priority of control-decision is given over to the central processes which, in effect, determine the role that peripheral feedback is to play. (Powell, Katzko, & Royce, 1978, pp. 199–200)

We have diagramed the overall relationships among the cognitive, affective, and motor systems in Figure 4–4, where it can be seen that the principal role of the cognitive system with respect to motor functioning is in the organization of motor programs. The role of the affective system in motor functioning is elaborated on later in this chapter.

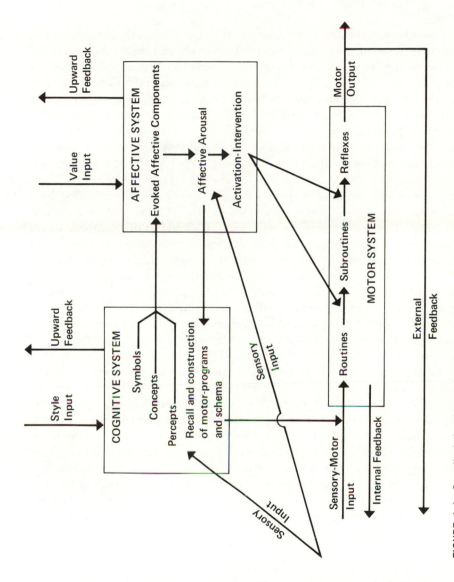

FIGURE 4-4 Overall relationships among the cognitive, affective, and motor systems, illustrating both direct and indirect channels of communication. (From Powell, Katzko, & Royce, 1978)

Four global aspects are involved in the dynamics of motor performance: (1) the control-decision processes that lie within the cognitive and affective systems; (2) motor programs that are constructed or reconstructed; (3) regulatory processes within the motor system itself, which basically entail factors above the first-order level; and (4) the elements of general classes of motor programs (i.e., the factors at all levels).

Consider handwriting as an example of the processing dynamics of motor functioning. A motor program for handwriting would be composed of two major components: the first would be a dictionary of elemental strokes; and the second a set of rules for combining these elements to form letters, words, and such. Through repeated performance and overlearning, the dictionary elements become organized into larger units or chunks, and as in any sequence of skilled movements, programming becomes increasingly automatized as learning proceeds. The principal mechanism underlying this automatization is "chunking" and the creation of higher-order rules that apply to the higher-order units or components.

Suppose that the task involves writing a word. There would first be a specification that an *equilibrium* parameter is required, as well as a *dexterity* parameter and, perhaps, *speed* (*small movements*). It should be stressed that a motor program specifies the sequential organization (temporality) of movements through space (spatiality) in accordance with the behavioral task requirements. A particular *body part* does not necessarily have to be specified as a component of the motor program unless the task environment is appropriately restricted. [11] There is generally a trade-off in performance efficiency among factor components, as, for example, when performance incorporates *dexterity*, but only at the sacrifice of *speed*. An example of these constraints is provided by writing with one's nonpreferred hand while equalizing output performance. If the criterion performance is to be maintained, then speed must be sacrificed, and if the writing instrument is held between the teeth, speed is decreased even further.

The above points are illustrated in Figure 4–5 where the word "pencil" has been written with the preferred and nonpreferred hands, and with the writing instrument held in the mouth. The fact that such different muscle groups are equifinal with respect to the general task requirements illustrates that motor programs can be constructed relatively independently of particular muscle groups; in other words, there is cross-motor generalization. [12] Furthermore, the words shown in the first column of Figure 4–5 were written with a *precision* (*dexterity*) constraint; those shown in the second column were written with a *speed* (*small movements*) constraint. A comparison of the two columns illustrates the functional inter-

----

[11]Of course, motor speech is an obvious exception to this. But again, there is some flexibility. For example, people who have had the larynx removed can learn to communicate via what can be described as "articulated belching."

[12]We mean to imply that there is a direct analogy between the phenomenon of cross-model generalization on the sensory side and what we are calling cross-motor generalization on the motor side.

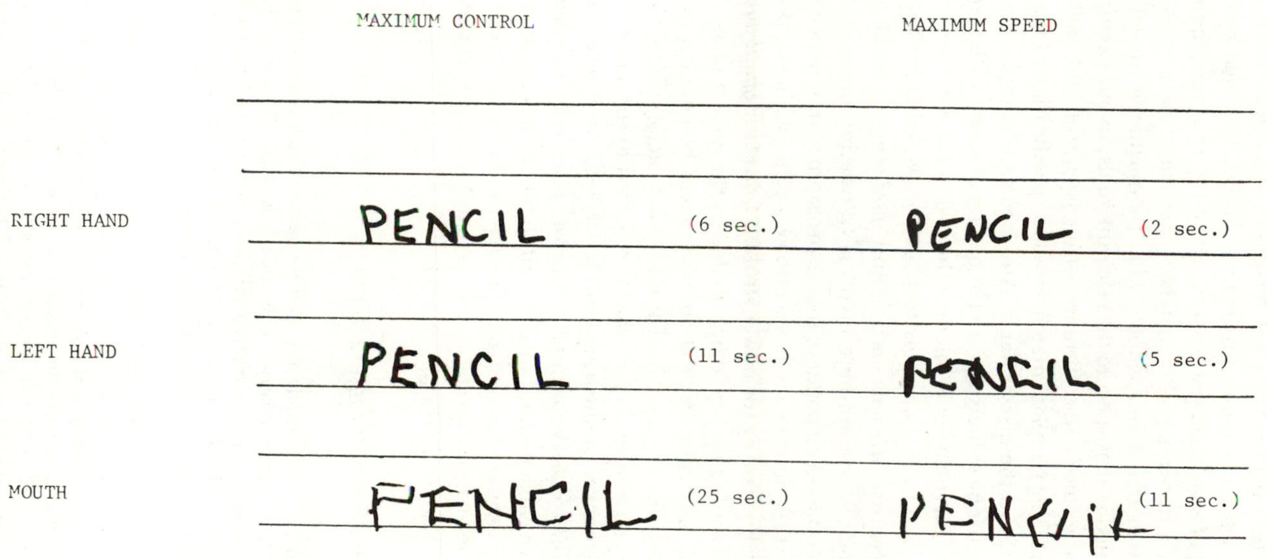

MAXIMUM CONTROL

MAXIMUM SPEED

RIGHT HAND

PENCIL (6 sec.)

PENCIL (2 sec.)

LEFT HAND

PENCIL (11 sec.)

PENCIL (5 sec.)

MOUTH

PENCIL (25 sec.)

PENCiL (11 sec.)

FIGURE 4-5 An illustration of muscular equivalence and speed-accuracy trade-off in a handwriting task. (From Powell, Katzko, & Royce, 1978)

relatedness of the various factors in speed–accuracy trade-offs, and a comparison of the rows illustrates cross-motor equivalence in motor programming. Obviously, such trade-offs in performance are related to individual differences.

Some further aspects of motor processing can be illustrated by taking as an example the hitting of a golf ball toward a target. First, the task requirements are analyzed with respect to two possible matches—*normative* and *template* (these concepts are discussed in detail in Chapter 11). In normative matches the task demands are evaluated with respect to the relevant goals; in our example the goals would involve both accuracy and distance—that is, hitting the ball as close as possible to the target. The template match entails a specification of the factors that are necessary to perform the task at hand. An important point here is that, in all cases, the analysis must be exhaustive; all factors are assessed with respect to their possible utility in the successful enactment of the task. We have assumed in our example that the relevant factors are *gross body equilibrium*, *extent flexibility*, *multilimb coordination*, *control precision*, *dynamic strength*, and *speed (large movements)*.

A second stage of programming involves translating the task into a list of behaviors along with the corresponding motor programs (and, hence, factors). In the golf example the task must be analyzed into two general phases: posturing and backswing, and the downswing (or power stroke). *Gross body equilibrium*, *extent flexibility*, and *multilimb coordination* would be entailed by the former phase, *control precision*, *dynamic strength*, and *speed (large movements)* would be entailed by the second phase. A performance level on each of the relevant factors must also be established, based on a prior conception of what is required to complete the task or on relevant past performance, as illustrated in Figure 4–6. An interesting feature of this stage involves the capacity to transfer control of behavior to other routines if existing performance capacities are insufficient to attain the end state of the task. For example, the performer may return to the driving range to improve the power of the swing or engage in other special activities to develop the performance factors (Powell, Katzko, & Royce, 1978, pp. 202–4).

Cognitive-affective-motor interactions

There are a variety of situations and task demands which require specific affective processes in an integrated way. This point is well illustrated by expressive movements, dramatic acting, normal social interaction and communication, nonverbal communication—indeed, most of the important integrated sequences of behavior in which individuals engage require that affective processes be reflected in the general flow of behavior.

As illustrated in Figure 4-4, the cognitive system interacts indirectly with the motor system when particular percepts, concepts, or symbols evoke specific affective processes. The affective components produce affective arousal or inhibition which, in turn, activate or disengage specific motor processes. This indirect mode of interaction between the cognitive and motor systems is quite typical of everyday interaction and can also be illustrated by dramatic acting. The first (rehearsal) stage of dramatic performances is totally cognitive: movements through space and time (blocking), gestures, and vocalizations (lines) are slowly organized into an overall gestalt (role),

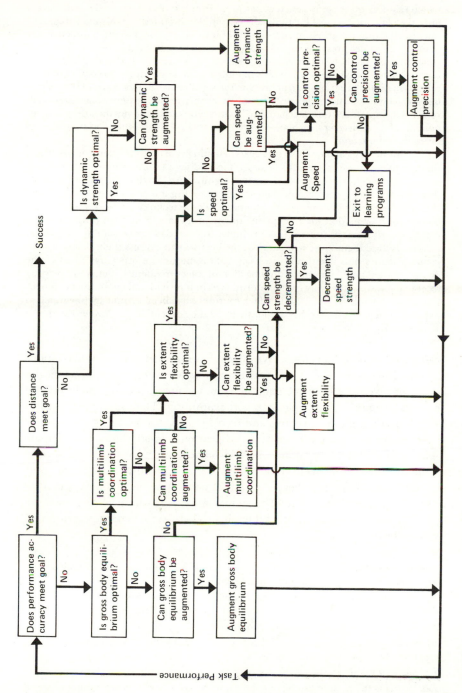

FIGURE 4-6 Processing analysis of the task of hitting a golf ball toward the green. (From Powell, Katzko, & Royce, 1978)

103

which requires quite complicated motor programming. But the actual performance, once the play opens, must be minimally cognitively-oriented. At this later stage, the integrated motor programs must be highly automatized, with attention directed only at the specific cues presented by other actors and the cognitive significance (percepts, concepts, and symbols) of their action. The percepts, etc., evoked in this manner, in turn, evoke affective processes which modulate and augment the execution of well-rehearsed motor programs. To appreciate the significance of this mode of interaction between cognitive and motor systems one need only recall the performances of well-rehearsed, but otherwise ''mechanical,'' actors who fail to convey the affective components of the character they play—or the ''insincerity'' that sometimes stands out in everyday interaction.

The dramaturgical model can also be used to illustrate indirect interaction between the affective and motor systems. During the middle and later phases of rehearsal, character development takes on greater significance as the specific movements through time and space become increasingly more organized and well-learned, and then the focus turns to the specific emotions. These feelings, in turn, motivate the construction or modification of specific motor programs so that the proper feelings can be clearly communicated. [For example, in everyday conversation] individuals frequently find themselves searching for the best way to express their feelings, some aspiring actors find it difficult to clearly communicate the inner dynamics of the character they play, and miscommunication of affect frequently occurs in everyday interactions. Also, the truly great performances in international gymnastics competition are as notable for the ways in which routines have been complexly integrated to express a range of affect as they are for their ''skilled execution.'' (Powell, Katzko, & Royce, 1978, p. 205)

Sensory-motor integration   We have diagrammed the overall relationships among the sensory, cognitive, and motor systems in Figure 4–7. Technically speaking, what we have been referring to as motor programming might best be referred to as ''cognitive-sensory motor'' programming. That is, motor programming requires cognitive constructive and reconstructive processes, but it also involves the sensory system inasmuch as motor programs are designed to anticipate particular ranges of sensory inputs. In this regard, we have identified several sensory-motor factors that seem to be involved in monitoring a variety of other motor factors and linking together sensory and motor functions. The factor structure of sensory-motor integration is shown in Figure 4–8, where we also show the linkages with the sensory and motor domains. These sensory-motor factors are defined as follows.

Audiogenic reactivity relates to motor reactions to loud auditory stimuli. It may appear as tremors or, in extreme instances, as seizures.

Response orientation is the ability to make rapid and accurate selection of controls and direction of movements in response to single or multiple stimuli.

Ambidexterity is the ability to use the nonpreferred hand.

Eye-hand coordination refers to the ability to execute quick and precise movements with emphasis on good, accurate aiming.

Reaction time relates to the speed of simple reactions to auditory or visual stimuli.

Rate control is the precise timing of continuous responses to stimuli varying in speed and direction.

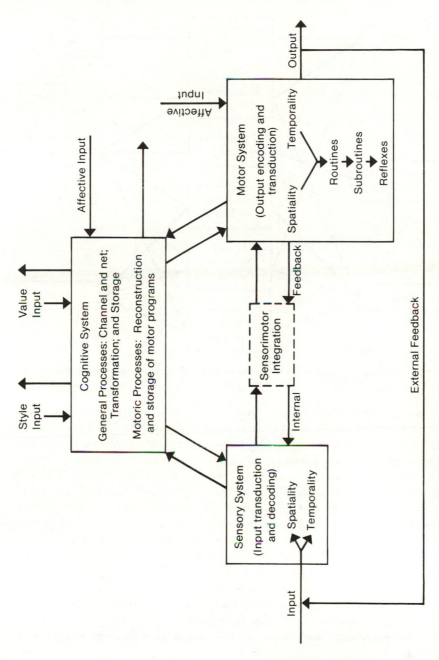

FIGURE 4-7 Overall relationships among the sensory, motor, and cognitive systems.

105

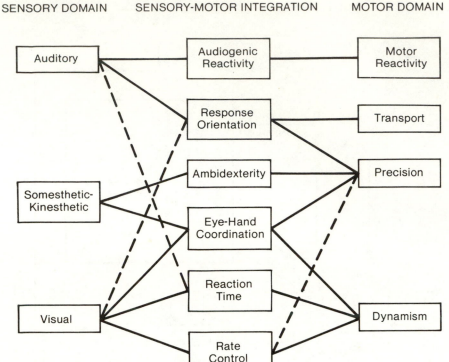

FIGURE 4-8 Overall structure of sensory-motor integration and the interrelations with sensory and motor factors.

Some of these sensory-motor factors are actually motor factors that always function under the constraints of external stimulation and, therefore, they may reflect a neural wiring system linking sensory and motor factors, but remaining autonomous of both. For example, reaction time correlates with *impulsion*, but it is not merely the speed of onset (as in the case with impulsion), it is speed of onset with respect to an *external cue*. Similarly, eye-hand coordination is limited by the existing performance level of *dexterity* factors, or the *multilimb coordination* (depending on the nature of the task). *Ambidexterity* indicates the extent to which the *dexterity* factors manifested in each hand are equal. In the extreme it would indicate the extent to which dexterity is manifested equally in all body parts. Perhaps, also, it reflects the overall adaptability and flexibility of motor programs that are maximally independent of specific muscle groups.

Our more general proposal is that each of the principal motor factors should have a corresponding sensory-motor factor that monitors output performance, though current research has not revealed the full range of possibilities concerning this issue.

5

The Cognitive and Affective Transformation Systems

One feature that distinguishes our theory from many other theories of personality is the inclusion of cognition as a central aspect of overall personality organization. Affective processes have been the focal point of many theoretical analyses of personality, but it is really the combination of cognition and affect that is at the core of integrated human functioning and individual differences in behavior, thought, emotion, arousal, and so forth. Thus, both should be given appropriate consideration in any general theory of personality and individual differences.

THE COGNITIVE SYSTEM[1]

The starting point for our analysis of cognition is a postulated hierarchy of cognitive abilities based on Royce's (1964) model of three ways of knowing. There have been a variety of recent attempts to integrate individual difference variables into information-processing models (e.g., Carroll, 1976; M. W. Eysenck, 1977; Hunt, Lunneborg, & Lewis, 1975; Snow, 1976a, 1976b). In our model we em-

[1]For a more complete discussion of the literature related to cognitive structure, see Diamond and Royce (1980). We wish to acknowledge Steve Diamond's important contributions to our model of the cognitive system. For a more thorough presentation of the issues relevant to cognitive processing, see Powell and Royce (1982).

phasize the search for *invariants* as a major goal of human cognition. *Invariants* have been considered to be of central importance in Gibson's (1966, 1972) theory of perception, in Piaget's (e.g., 1976, 1977) research, and in the recent attempts by Shaw and his associates (e.g., Shaw & Bransford, 1977) to develop a general model of cognition.

The empirical bases for our structural model are the 32 factors of the cognitive hierarchy. This includes the 23 first-order cognitive factors that may be considered invariant (as established by their appearance in at least two of the following major reviews: French (1965), Guilford (1967), Ahmavaara (1957), and Pawlik (1966). As shown in Figure 5-1, there are six factors that are invariant at the second order: *verbal, reasoning, spatiovisual, memorization, fluency,* and *imaginativeness.* And finally, there are three third-order factors: *perceiving, conceptualizing,* and *symbolizing.* These three factors also identify the three subsystems of the cognitive domain.

Cognitive abilities typically manifest a strong degree of interrelationship, or what factor analysts have called *positive manifold.* Some investigators have interpreted this as reflecting Spearman's general factor (''g''). However, we think the positive manifold can be attributed to cooperative functioning among all the cognitive abilities rather than general intelligence. However, it should be noted that the cognitive factors that cross over the subhierarchies of perceiving, conceptualizing, and symbolizing are not shown in Figure 5-1 for the sake of simplifying exposition.

Higher-order Factors

Perceiving refers to abilities involved in cognitive ability to manipulate the directly perceptible qualities of things, although the object does not have to be present in the perceptual field in order for its qualities to be mentally manipulated. The second-order factor of spatiovisual ability shows up most clearly in tests that require the subject to recognize the appearance of a three-dimensional figure that is rotated in space (*visualization*). It also shows up in tests requiring visual arrangement of parts that are out of their customary place (*spatial relations*), holding in mind a visual configuration (*flexibility of closure*), coalescing visual parts into a whole (*speed of closure*), maintaining flexibility with respect to possible organization of figural material (*figural adaptive flexibility*), solving spatial mazes (*spatial scanning*), and speed in identifying visual elements (*perceptual speed*). The second-order factor of *memorization* is expressed in measures of rote commitment to memory, including *memory span* (the number of elements that can be held in immediate memory), *memory for designs* (the ability to reproduce a design), and *associative memory* (paired associates or serial learning). A *spatiovisual* factor has been found repeatedly in second-order analyses (e.g., Horn & Cattell, 1966) and a *memorization* factor has been found in one full-scale second-order analysis (Horn & Bramble, 1967). The reason that memorization emerges as a perceptual activity is most clearly illustrated by the case of *memory span.* In visual digit-span tasks a subject's score is

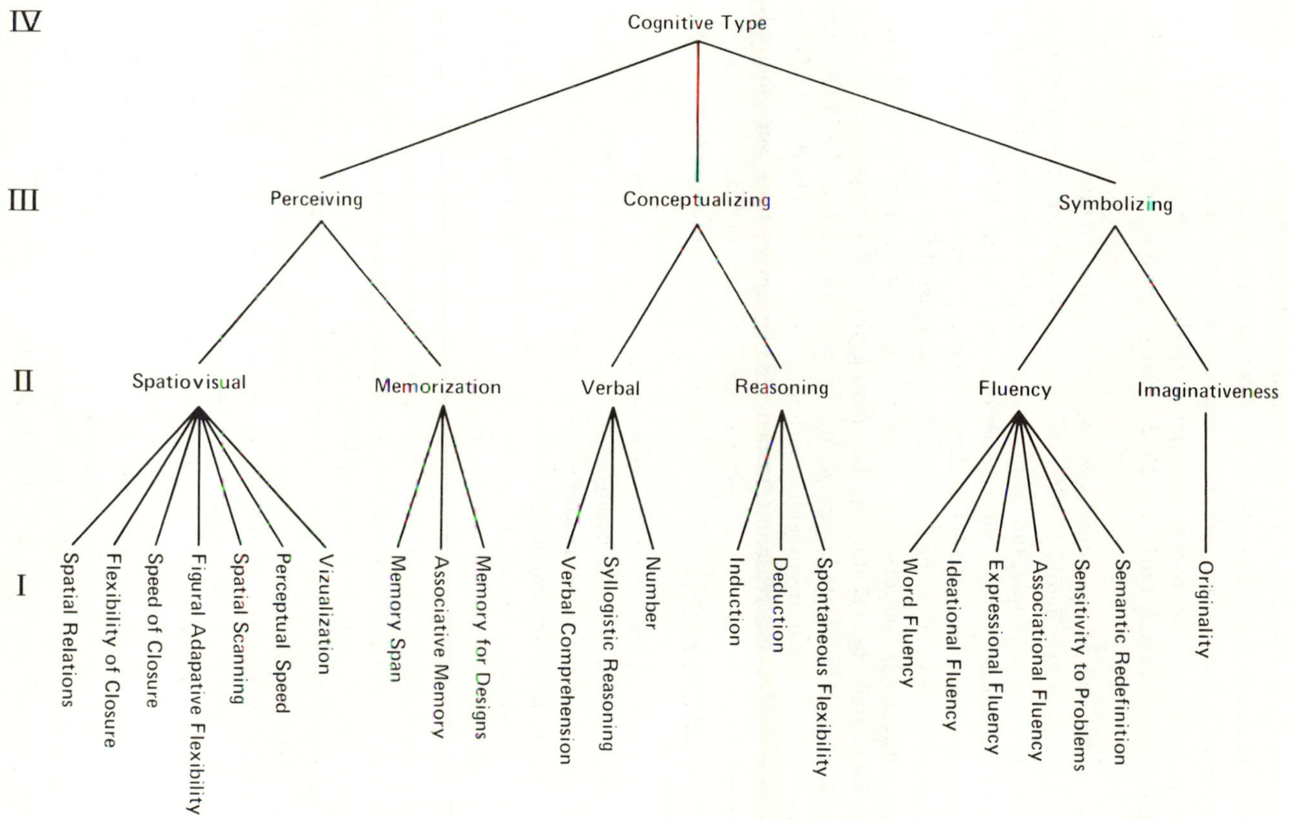

FIGURE 5-1 The hierarchical structure of the cognitive system. (Modified from Diamond & Royce, 1980)

IV — Cognitive Type

III — Symbolizing, Conceptualizing, Perceiving

II — Imaginativeness, Fluency, Reasoning, Verbal, Memorization, Spatiovisual

I — Originality, Semantic Redefinition, Sensitivity to Problems, Associational Fluency, Expressional Fluency, Ideational Fluency, Word Fluency, Spontaneous Flexibility, Deduction, Induction, Number, Syllogistic Reasoning, Verbal Comprehension, Memory for Designs, Associative Memory, Memory Span, Vizualization, Perceptual Speed, Spatial Scanning, Figural Adapative Flexibility, Speed of Closure, Flexibility of Closure, Spatial Relations

the number of simultaneously presented digits that can be apprehended. The span of apprehension appears as a perceptual phenomenon because individuals must "image" the relative locations of the several digits to be recalled. When digits are presented auditorally, the span is about the same length and may also be construed as a perceptual activity. Applying the same reasoning to *associative memory*, we think it is based on the purely perceptual qualities of the material to be remembered (see Craik & Lockhart, 1972, on depth of processing for a similar view).

As in the case of the motor system, our theoretical interpretation of a number of the cognitive factors goes beyond the current empirical manifestations of those factors. For example, the factor representing the quantity of perceptual schemata is named *spatiovisual*, but only because the *visual* modality has been the main object to study. Horn (1977) has begun to study auditory abilities, and we expect these to be related to the second-order spatiovisual factor.

Conceptualizing is supported as a third-order factor in three factor analyses reported by Cattell (1971), although he offers a different interpretation. All of these analyses were conducted using young subjects, and all found a third-order factor with strong saturations in both *verbal* and *reasoning*. Verbal loaded this factor .54 on the average, and reasoning loaded .78. However, they were the only second-order factors employed in these analyses. A third-order factor has also appeared in the hierarchical analyses of the British, despite differences in factoring techniques.

The strongest correlate of the second-order factor of verbal is *verbal comprehension* (knowledge of the meaning of words). Verbal also correlates strongly with *syllogistic reasoning* (formal reasoning from stated premises) and *number* (speed and accuracy in basic arithmetic operations).

The second-order factor of *reasoning* (Horn & Cattell, 1966) relates most closely to *inductive reasoning* (discovery of a rule that characterizes some sequence) and *deductive reasoning* (application of an abstract rule to solve a problem). Reasoning is also implicated in *spontaneous flexibility* (the formation of a multiplicity of logical groupings). In the Cattell and Horn second-order analyses, *verbal* is labeled *crystallized intelligence* and reasoning is labeled *fluid intelligence*, although Horn (1976) has suggested that these factors resemble expanded verbal and reasoning primaries. We have used Horn's suggestion in labeling these two factors.

Verbal and reasoning factors are clearly conceptual in nature—verbal is dependent on the number of concepts in the person's repertoire, and a high score on reasoning indicates a capacity to generate abstract concepts. This inference is based on an assessment of the apparent demands of the corresponding cognitive tests. Verbal tests employ questions that individuals can answer only if they have the appropriate concepts (as in vocabulary tests), but reasoning tests, such as letter series or Raven's Progressive Matrices, require the subject to generate a concept that ideally all subjects possess. The difficulty with reasoning tests comes from requiring a clear understanding of the concept at an abstract level. Even vocabulary tests can be made to load on reasoning if the words employed are in everyone's repertoire and subtle discriminations of meaning are required (Cattell, 1971). This interpretation allows for the resolution of some apparent paradoxes concerning the primaries that load verbal and reasoning. Number loads on verbal because, although concepts are primarily verbal, individuals also have numerical concepts. Syllogistic reasoning loads verbal more strongly than it does reasoning because it depends on particular conceptual knowledge about logical relations rather than the exercise of abstract logic.

Symbolizing refers to the representing of a number of objects or ideas with a single form, and to cultural forms articulated in artistic or literary productions (Royce, 1964b). Symbolizing includes *fluency* and *imaginativeness*, both of which have appeared in second-order analyses (e.g., Horn & Cattell, 1966). Fluency consists primarily of various divergent productive abilities studied in Guilford's laboratory. These fluencies include the ability to produce ideas quickly about an object or condition (*ideational fluency*), the ability to find quickly an expression fitting some structural constraint (*expressional fluency*), facility in producing words with a certain meaning (*associational fluency*), and facility in producing words that fit certain structural restrictions (*word fluency*).

Imaginativeness, which has been extracted by Rossman and Horn (1972), shows up on tasks that require truly clever responses. The fluencies are related to symbolism in their divergent character since the relevant tests require the subject to rely on suggestive rather than denotative aspects of concepts. *Originality* is the only primary factor clearly associated with imaginativeness, and it is measured by tests that require the production of clever plot titles and remote consequences of hypotheses. The lack of primary factors underlying imaginativeness emphasizes that the symbolic capacities have not been investigated adequately (Diamond & Royce, 1980, pp. 37–42).

First-order Factors

Spatial scanning (the ability to integrate isolated aspects of the visual field) and *flexibility of closure* (or the ability to locate specific patterns in a complex configuration) relate directly to the more general process of perceptual decoding. These two factors can be interpreted as tapping into processes oriented toward identifying meaningful structures in complex stimulus arrays. On the other hand, the factors of *spatial relations* (the ability to put together isolated parts into a recognizable whole) and *spatial orientation* (the ability to visualize how things appear under altered conditions) relate more closely to the interaction between processes invoked in decoding and the perceptual structures that the individual already possesses. *Memory span* represents the ability to find structural patterns among the elements of complex arrays; *associative memory* (or the ability to memorize semantically unrelated material) and *memory for designs* (the ability to recognize complex designs that have been experienced before) both relate to the interaction of current processing activities with existing perceptual structures.

It should be emphasized that all of these primary factors reflect the various ways in which perceptual information can be transformed. This is aptly illustrated in the case of *spatial orientation*, which loads heaviest on tests requiring subjects to identify rotated transforms of complex figures like those investigated in the Shepard and Metzler (1971) experiments. Shepard has found that the speed of recognition of such rotated figures varies inversely as a linear function of the number of degrees of rotation. The important point in the present context is that there are reliable individual differences in the underlying processes involved in such mental rotations.

Similarly, the conceptualizing primaries relate to the ways in which individuals mentally manipulate conceptual information. For example, *number* taps the ability of an individual to manipulate the abstract, numerical characteristics of information in the process of conceptual decoding and encoding. *Verbal* ability taps skills in transforming surface structures into conceptual deep structures (and vice versa). *Syllogistic reasoning* relates to the ability to transform conceptual material into constituent propositions. *Induction* and *deduction* concern the ability to relate current propositions to existing propositional structures, and *spontaneous flexibility* concerns the ability to transform propositional structures into alternative forms (i.e., finding the consequences of reclassification).

Symbolizing abilities are particularly difficult to characterize. However, we think they relate to the ability to mentally manipulate and transform information relevant to *contextual dependencies*. For example, consider the factor of *semantic redefinition*, which relates to the ability to imagine different functions for objects or parts of objects and thus to use them in novel ways. The abstract properties or conceptual aspects of any object—say, a "coat hanger"—are unrelated to the particular context in which the object appears. Whether it hangs in a closet or lies on the floor beside the bed, it remains a coat hanger. The same applies whether it actually has a coat on it at the time or whether it has ever held a real coat. But a more creative or symbolic interpretation of a "coat hanger" requires identification of the dependencies among the conceptual or perceptual qualities of it and the context in which those properties appear. Its use in actually holding coats is related in part to *its shape in a particular context*. For example, "coat hanger" would probably be a different sort of entity in an igloo. Analogously, recognizing that a "coat hanger" can help extricate keys from a locked car requires that the properties of the actual object be mentally transformed in relation to the new situation.

We view the symbolizing abilities as being particularly focused on the identification of *metaphoric invariants*. The invariants identified are metaphoric because there must be a transformation of both content and context in order to find an invariant according to some particular constraint. Thus, most of the fluency factors are related to information encoding, and the differences among these various fluency factors are critically related to the types of constraints imposed (or the types of invariants being sought). *Semantic redefinition* and *word fluency* (the ability to produce words in accordance with restrictions other than meaning) are related to the ability to generate symbolic variations on conceptual material, but variations that are independent of the specific concepts involved. *Associational fluency* (the ability to produce large numbers of words with similar meaning) relates to the interaction of existing symbolic and conceptual structures with currently available information. *Expressional fluency* refers to the ability to construct appropriate expressions and, thus, taps the ability to transform symbolic relationships into interpretable forms of communication. *Ideational fluency* concerns the ability to produce ideas quickly about a stated condition or object, *sensitivity to problems* taps the ability to imagine problems associated with a change in some object, and *originality* is the ability to construct unusual or clever conceptualizations.

In considering the symbolizing aspects of cognition, some attention should be given to the existential and emotional aspects of symbols. This is clear even from the factor-analytic evidence because, for example, many of the symbolizing factors also load on affective variables (see Diamond & Royce, 1980, and Wardell & Royce, 1978), which is not as true of the perceiving and conceptualizing factors. It might be said in ordinary language that particular concepts are accurate or, perhaps, even that they are insightful, but it is not as typical to say that they "affect us deeply" as it is in the case of symbols. Conceptual analogies may facilitate understanding and provide a basis for reasoning, but great metaphors "illuminate reality," create new understanding, and produce changes in our perceptions of how we relate to reality. While scientific theories and analogies provide new ways of reasoning about the nature of reality, powerful metaphors in art, religion, and mythology provide new images of humankind in relation to reality. However, it should be noted that revolutionary science does have a symbolic aspect. For example, the Copernican, Darwinian, Einsteinian, and Freudian revolutions were *revolutionary* precisely because they employed powerful metaphors that resulted in humans seeing themselves in a new relationship to the rest of the universe.

The Functional Role of the Cognitive System

As we have alluded to or discussed in several places, we think the primary function of the cognitive system is the detection or construction of invariants. Thus we begin our discussion of the functional role of the cognitive system with a discussion of different types of invariants.

If the physical properties of the ecological environment in which all organisms have evolved were highly pliable and altered erratically and unpredictably from moment to moment, it is unlikely that organismic evolution could have occurred. Certainly, environments change, but the changes that occur are often sufficiently prolonged or predictable (as in seasonable variations) that organisms have time to adapt to such changing conditions. And, even though there are obvious changes in ecological niches over eons of time, it is also clear that other aspects of the environment do not change. For example, the information that is provided by the ambient optic array or by sound waves has not changed since terrestrial organisms began to evolve, and the regular change of seasons has become an environmental invariant. As a result of such ecological stabilities and the adaptive significance of sensitivity to them, organisms have evolved that are differentially sensitive to the physical characteristics of the information available in the environment. These and related points have been developed extensively by Gibson (e.g., 1966). For example, with regard to the invariant information in an ambient optic array, Gibson notes:

> The *contours* in an array are invariant with most of the changes in illumination. The *textures* of an array are reliably invariant with change of observation point. The property of a contour being *closed* or *unclosed* is always invariant. The *form* of a closed contour in the array is independent of lighting but highly variant with change of observation point. A great many properties of the array are *lawfully* or *regularly* variant with change of observation point, and this means that in each case a property defined by the law is *invariant.* (1972, p. 221, emphasis in the original)

One thrust of Gibson's theorizing is to force a closer look at the importance of environmental invariants in order to understand human perception. This perspective also suggests the importance of identifying cognitive processes that enable such invariants to be detected.

With regard to *conceptual invariants*, the centuries of searching for appropriate or acceptable conceptualizations of the nature of the physical universe has taught physicists many lessons—one of the most important relates to the concept of invariance. Blanpied has expressed the point eloquently:

> The human mind derives undoubted satisfaction in contemplating a principle or principles of order underlying the seemingly constant change that manifests itself throughout the universe, of believing that some things are constant, unchanging, incorruptible. Indeed, the very concept of constancy has been used to suggest perfection itself. When Plato wedded the philosophical contemplation of perfection with the idea of geometric perfection, he arrived at his doctrine of planetary spheres, and thus laid the basis for a system of mathematical physics whose intrinsic appeal exerted a sufficient grip upon the human imagination to hold it in thrall for almost two thousand years, despite the considerable evidence that the imagined perfection of the heavens could not be interpreted in so simple and obvious a manner. . . . But Plato did not originate the idea that symmetry implies perfection, nor was he by any means the last to use it. In art, in music, in poetry, the relationship between symmetry, constancy, and perfection is encountered so frequently that it has become commonplace. Examples abound in other fields as well, as in the use of the balance to symbolize justice for example. Whenever it is encountered, the idea usually carries the additional implication that an object or concept which is symmetric is somehow understood and requires no further explanation. (1969, p. 174)

The concepts of symmetry, invariance, and constancy are important in the conceptualizations of modern physics (see Wigner, 1967). For example, the invariant relationships implied by physical equations frequently lead to the discovery of new phenomena at the subatomic level.

Actually, invariance plays an important role in the direction of all scientific activity. Whether couched in terms of the "search for laws," the "discovery of principles," or "the discovery of functional relationships," scientific explorations are motivated by the desire to find *invariants* in the environment. Laws, principles, functional relationships, functional unities, and such are alternative ways of expressing the concepts of symmetry or invariance that underlie a wide range of surface manifestations. Scientific methodology (including statistical techniques) is oriented toward the evaluation of reliability—that is, toward the determination of the extent to which relationships may be considered invariant. In summary, invariance has been formalized and developed to the extent that it lies at the heart of modern thinking and research, and theoretical physics is the example par excellence of the identification of conceptual invariants.

At the core of symbols and metaphors, whether in science, religion, or art, is the representation of some invariant. Typically the invariant has to do with individuals and their relation to existence. For a work of art to have an emotional or intellectual impact, whether the form is a play, a poem, a concerto, a novel, or a photograph, it must express insights that transcend the idiosyncratic experiences of any particular symbolizer. The day-to-day trials and tribulations of a salesman would ordinarily make for a boring and uninsightful story or play—unless there are aspects of his relationship to himself, to other people, or to nature that tap the variety of human experiences. For example, Arthur Miller (1951) achieves this via the character of Willy Loman in his play *The Death of a Salesman*. As a symbol, Willy Loman transcends any particular "individuality," thereby expressing an invariant in the nature of human existence, and it is because of this transcendence and the communication of invariance that the symbol is comprehensible and "moving" in the emotional sense.

There is a seemingly contradictory aspect of symbols that should be considered. Religious symbols, such as the Christ or Buddha, are presented and understood in great detail—they are not merely abstract ideas or icons, but *specific individuals* who led special lives. This also happens in various forms of art. The characters in plays, whether a Hamlet or a Willy Loman, are specific individuals who have their own individual lives as well as their symbolic existences. The problem with all this is that, while a symbol must be transcendent, it must also be very specific—in the case of religion, so specific that it often becomes concretized. This contradictory aspect emerges, in part, because it is necessary for other individuals to have something "concrete" to relate to and to identify with. But it also emerges because specific *contexts* identify the contextual dependencies (e.g., relation between humankind and "meaning," humankind and emotions, humankind and nature) that are the focus of symbols and metaphors.

Cognitive Processing

Figure 5-2 provides a model of cognition as an information-processing system. The concept of invariants and the roles of individual differences have been incorporated, and there is a multilevel, hierarchical organization where the decision-control processes are conceived as coordinating the activity of the three

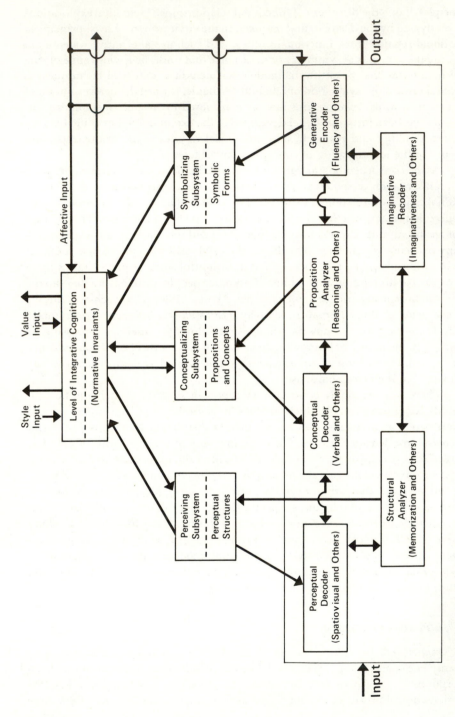

FIGURE 5-2 A multifactor-systems model of cognition as an information-processing system. (From Powell & Royce, 1982)

ity. That is, the probability that a particular pathway will be followed must include the individual's profile of cognitive styles. For example, individuals who are higher on metaphoric styles will rely more on generative encoding and imaginative recoding in finding solutions to decision problems, even though the experimenter may intend for the task to be ostensibly a conceptualizing type of task.

The principal function of second-order processes relates to the coordination of the multifaceted activities of lower-order processes in the construction of meaningful and integrated information. For example, a first-order process such as *flexibility of closure* locates specific patterns in a complex configuration, whereas perceptual decoding relates more to the general problem of locating things in space. And, while *spatial scanning* finds pathways through a complex array, perceptual decoding is more directly concerned with organized percepts of the field. Analogously, with the conceptualizing subsystem, *verbal* abilities relate to the size of an individual's vocabulary, but conceptual decoding relates to the general problem of transforming verbal stimuli into meaningful concepts.

A comparison of the major characteristics of perceiving, conceptualizing, and symbolizing as knowledge-seeking cognitive activities is provided in Table 5-1. As described in Chapter 9, each of these cognitive processes can give rise to a particular epistemology when uncertainty is recognized and a specific criterion is invoked. The relevant epistemologies associated with each way of knowing are shown in row 5 of Table 5-1; the relevant truth criteria are indicated in row 4. As noted in row 3 of the table, processing within the perceiving subsystem tends to be more in parallel; in the conceptualizing subsystem it tends to be more sequential, and in the symbolizing subsystem it tends to be a combination of parallel and sequential. As described above, context is of central importance in symbolizing but of relative unimportance in perceiving and conceptualizing. And, as discussed in Chapter 10, symbolizing has a central role in an individual's search for self-knowledge. Finally, the role of affect in cognitive processing is to activate a given cognitive subsystem and, particularly in the case of the symbolizing subsystem, to generate emotive states. Thus, symbols are the most affect-laden of the three classes of cognition, followed by percepts; concepts are the least affect-laden. The complex interactions between cognition and affect are addressed in Chapter 9.

THE AFFECTIVE SYSTEM[4]

As in the case of cognition, the affective domain has been investigated thoroughly enough so that it was possible to invoke the "strong invariance" criterion in constructing the affective hierarchy.[5] The affective hierarchy is presented in Figure

[4] For a more thorough discussion of the relevant research literature, see Royce and McDermott (1977). We wish to acknowledge John McDermott's important contribution to our model of the affective system.

[5] In the case of the affective system, by "strong invariance" we mean demonstrated replicability involving some combination of the following: (1) factor identification by two or more investigations (i.e., in two or more different laboratories), (2) repeated replication as part of a massive research program, (3) experimental manipulation of a factorially identified construct.

principal subsystems. In turn, these subsystems coordinate the activity of the various transformational processes of the lowest layer. Percepts, concepts and propositions, and symbols are considered to have a coordinating impact on the lower-level processes (transformations, encodings, etc.), and the ongoing processing activities of lower-level components also modify perceptual, conceptual, and symbolic structures. This is analogous to the notion that information can be "stored" in long-term memory. But, as in Neisser's more recent model (1976; see also Bransford, Franks, McCarrell, & Nitsch, 1977), we think memory can be viewed as a problem of "modification of existing schemata" rather than as a problem in "storage."[2]

Cognition is goal-directed and "knowledge of the world" can be described as a cognitive goal, but knowledge involves the discovery of invariants. As discussed in several places above, the principal goal of cognition can be described as the regulation or *management of uncertainty*. But, in order to discover what is invariant, it is necessary to expose oneself to uncertainty (perform transformations whose results are uncertain beforehand) in available information and relationships to the environment.[3] What this means is that in order to find out what is *invariant* an individual must change or transform the information in some fashion. The implication here is that the management of uncertainty and the search for invariants are different ways of describing the same underlying process.

A variety of factors influence the amount of uncertainty an individual will tolerate and the specific transformations produced. In addition to cognitive abilities, for example, the individual's profile of styles and values affect the management of uncertainty. Furthermore, the various effects of affective arousal must also be considered.

A Test–Operate–Test–Exit (TOTE) hierarchy for describing the decision-control processes of cognition is presented in Figure 5-3. The important normative match here relates to the extent that perceptual, conceptual, and symbolic schemata express sufficient invariance about the environment for the current adaptive requirements to be met. Whether a given discrepancy between current norms and existing cognitive schemata can be ignored is related to the affective and evaluative characteristics of the individual. Affective characteristics should also influence the extent to which individuals will increase uncertainty in order to reduce that uncertainty (*emotional stability* might be critical here). Values are also relevant, because, for example, an individual who is higher on an *intrinsic*

[2] It is often forgotten within the information-processing literature that the notion of "storage" is really a metaphor. It is not at all apparent, for example, that memory should be "something that is filed away" for future reference or that the mammalian nervous system has evolved separate, localizable structures that represent the "storage" or "memory" devices of the organism. Nor is it even clear that such a possibility would have any particular adaptive advantage.

[3] If the results of knowledge-seeking activities did not produce *uncertain* results, we would not engage in them. For example, experimental results that were assured beyond doubt before being collected would be uninteresting, unnecessary, and uninformative. As another example, perceptual exploration of the environment will cease when we have exhausted all of the possible uncertainties that it affords. Total predictability is monotonous and thereby reduces perceptual (or other) exploration.

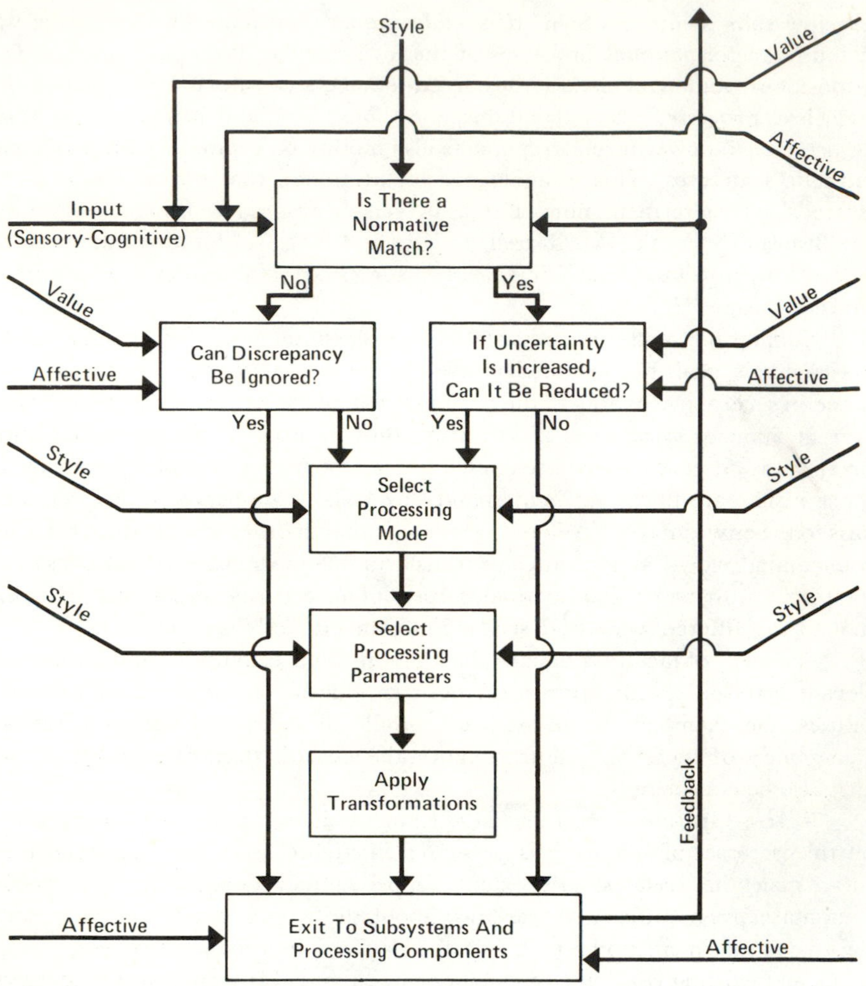

FIGURE 5-3   A TOTE-hierarchy model of cognitive decision-control processes. (From Powell & Royce, 1982)

evaluative orientation will be more likely to engage in the manipulation of conceptual uncertainty and less likely to ignore conceptual discrepancies, whereas an individual with a *social* value orientation would be more likely to focus on perceptual invariants. Cognitive styles, on the other hand, influence the selection of processing modes and parameters. For example, individuals who are higher on empirical style give greater emphasis to perceiving as a mode of processing, whereas individuals higher on rational style emphasize conceptualizing as a mode of processing.

The higher levels of the cognitive system impose general limits on the particular cognitions that are processed and coordinate the goal-seeking activities of lower-level components. For example, the perceiving subsystem, and individual's

percepts, have a directive influence on the information about the phy characteristics of the environment that are actually processed at any partic time. Similarly, an individual's repertoire of propositions and concepts coordir the conceptual decoding and propositional analysis of currently available r tional information. In general, the third-order processes coordinate the process of particular percepts, concepts, and symbols.

It is important to emphasize that our model is drawn from *both* factor ar systems theory. One advantage to this synthesis is that, in areas where informa tion is lacking from one perspective, the other perspective may provide helpfu clues. Thus, for example, although *visual* perceiving abilities have been studied ir great detail, little information is available concerning perceiving in other sense modalities. To presume, then, that the *spatiovisual* and *memorization* factors (Figure 5–1) exhaust the perceiving domain at the second order would be premature. Systems analysis can be helpful in constructing a general model of the perceiving subsystem in spite of such deficiencies in the factor-analytic literature by pointing toward the general processes of information-processing systems. The processes diagrammed in Figure 5–2 were arrived at in this manner. While other factors may be discovered at the second-order level, it is our hypothesis that they will represent different aspects of these general processes. For example, should extensive factor analysis in the auditory domain yield a new factor at the second order, this will probably still reflect the process of perceptual decoding. Similarly, future investigations of *reasoning* abilities may identify additional second-order factors, but we expect that they would still reflect some aspect of propositional analysis.

The lower-order components identified in Figure 5–2 are intended to represent systems or information-processing approximations to the second-order factors identified in Figure 5–1. They are defined as follows:

1. *Perceptual decoder* transforms information transduced by the sensory system into meaningful perceptual structures.
2. *Structural analyzer* extracts information about the physical properties of large sets of interrelated events processed by the sensory system.
3. *Conceptual decoder* converts either perceptual or conceptual information into abstract concepts and systems of interrelated concepts.
4. *Proposition analyzer* extracts information about relations among concepts and expresses it in propositional form.
5. *Imaginative recoder* analyzes the divergent qualities of concepts and percepts.
6. *Generative encoder* is a creative processor for expressing contextual relations among percepts and concepts and feelings.

The successive pairs of these relate to the lower-level functioning of the perceiving, conceptualizing, and symbolizing subsystems respectively.

Considering equifinality, there are a variety of specific pathways through this system for processing information, and only severe task restrictions will lead to a high degree of predictability with regard to the sequential characteristics of processing. On the other hand, a better understanding and appreciation of the role of individual differences in cognitive processing can also increase predictabil-

TABLE 5-1 A Comparison of the Epistemic Characteristics of the Three Higher-order Factors of Perceiving, Conceptualizing, and Symbolizing

CHARACTERISTICS	FACTORS		
	PERCEIVING	CONCEPTUALIZING	SYMBOLIZING
Primary focus of processing activities	Physical properties	Relations among physical and conceptual properties	Contextual dependencies
Processing activities tend to be conducted	In parallel	Sequentially	In parallel and sequentially
The primary objective of processing activities	Perceptual structures	Concepts and propositions	Symbolic forms
The truth criterion that is invoked	Veridical–nonveridical	Logical–illogical	Universal–idiosyncratic
Epistemology that arises	Empiricism	Rationalism	Metaphorism
Human existence, as a potential context	Of no special importance	Of no special importance	Often of central importance
Role in the search for self-knowledge	Of no special importance	Of no special importance	Probably of central importance
The principal role of affect in cognitive processing	To activate perceptual activity and be activated by perceptual structures	To activate conceptual activity and be activated by concepts	To provide an emotional context and activate symbolic activity

5–4.[6] Each of the factors in this hierarchy is described in the following pages. As in previous discussions, our descriptions are presented in two parts. This first is concerned with the higher-order factors and the second with the lower-order factors.

Higher-order Factors

Emotional stability corresponds closely to H. J. Eysenck's third-order "neuroticism," and is related to energy mobilization positively and anxiety and excitability negatively. This factor is possibly close to Cattell's third-order factor "maladaptation" (representing the opposite pole of the stability label) and perhaps Guilford's postulated third-order "emotional health" factor.

Emotional independence refers to Eysenck's "psychoticism" factor, but we did not use his label since its pathological overtones can be misleading. H. J. Eysenck and S. B. G. Eysenck (1976) suggest that there is a continuum from normal to psychotic, and that this continuum describes the predisposition to psychotic breakdown. Individuals high on psychoticism have been described as follows: solitary, not caring for other people; troublesome, not fitting in; cruel, inhumane; lacking feeling, insensitive; sensation-seeking, avid for strong stimuli; hostile to others, aggressive; liking odd, unusual things; having a disregard for danger, foolhardy; and as making fools of other people, upsetting them (H. J. Eysenck, 1964, p. 98). Cattell (1973) found several third-order factors empirically, two of which he called "anti-social, unconcern" and "readiness." We have interpreted these two as "social adaptability" and "emotional detachedness," respectively. Emotional independence may represent a combination of these two Cattellian factors, as H. J. Eysenck has suggested. As shown in Figure 5–4, independence is thought to associate positively with autonomy and cortertia.

Introversion-extraversion corresponds to Eysenck's third-order "extraversion," and it is proposed that the introversion pole of this factor is related positively to Cattell's "social inhibition" and "general inhibition." Cattell (1973) found social inhibition related to a third-order factor he called "strength of contact," which might correspond to our introversion–extraversion.

Energy mobilization is a conceptual amalgamation of Poley and Royce's (1976b) second-order dimensions identified as "motor reactivity" and "active avoidance II." This factor reflects a primitive survival mechanism whereby aroused energy is optimally mobilized for fight or flight.

Anxiety is Cattell's T-data factor of "anxiety" versus "good adjustment," which he has also found closely aligned to his Q-data anxiety factor. Low anxiety

---

[6]In order to interpret cross-level relationships in Figure 5–4, begin with the appropriate pole of each *third*-order dimension. The positive and negative signs shown will then describe the relationships between third-order and second-order, between second-order and primary, and between third-order and primary factors. For example, begin with a hypothetical individual who is high in emotional stability. The negative sign between that third-order factor and *anxiety* implies that he will tend to be low in anxiety. The negative sign between *anxiety* and *ergic tension* implies, in turn, that this person low in anxiety will also be low in ergic tension. And moving directly from third- to first-order, the emotionally stable person is low in ergic tension. In short, when determining cross-level relationships, Figure 5–4 should be viewed from top down.

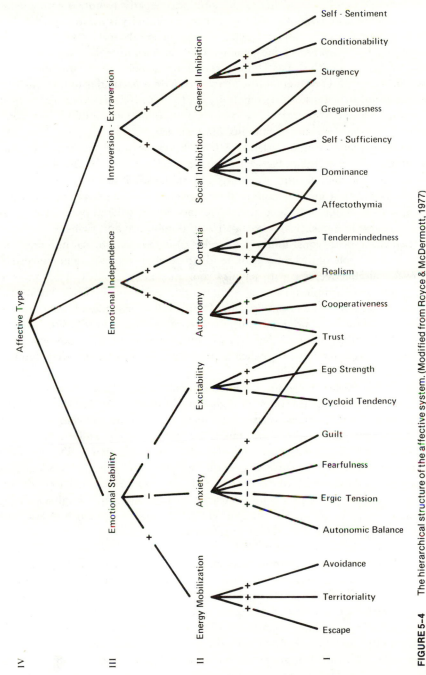

FIGURE 5-4 The hierarchical structure of the affective system. (Modified from Royce & McDermott, 1977)

123

is positively linked with autonomic balance (in the direction of sympathetic imbalance), ergic tension, fearfulness, and guilt and negatively linked with trust.

Excitability is an hypothesized factor. Low excitability is positively related to cycloid tendency and negatively related to ego strength and trust. Cattell described something similar at the primary level in his rating and questionnaire work: "... a cognitive excitability, restlessness, and often anti-social expressiveness ... Environmental insecurity acting on a particular temperamental substrate seems to be the key to (excitability)" (1973, p. 162). It would also appear that Guilford's (1975) postulated second-order "emotional stability" is a combination of our anxiety and excitability dimensions.

Autonomy, labeled independence by Cattell, has been well replicated in Cattell's laboratory. His Q-data factor "independence" versus "subduedness" has been described in the following way: "Its general nature is clearly a pristine self-will as opposed to a general taming by experience and deprivation" (Cattell, 1973, p. 187). High independence is negatively associated with trust and cooperativeness and positively associated with dominance and realism.

Cortertia appears consistently in Cattell's Q-data research. An individual at the "cortertia" pole of this dimension tends to be alert, realistic, and concerned with practical effectiveness, with feelings cool and under control. The opposite pole, "pathemia," implies a warm, sentimental, melancholy, daydreaming individual who tends to like art and drama. Cattell (1973) speculated that cortertia represents "a functional predominance of cerebral cortical action" as opposed to pathemia, which represents "living at the hypothalamic level." Low cortertia is negatively associated with realism and positively associated with tender-mindedness and affectothymia.

Social inhibition corresponds to Cattell's second-order Q-data "exvia–invia" factor, where the invia pole represents high social inhibition. At the other pole, exvia represents "a willingness to risk decisions on vague data, quicker social and other judgements, higher optimism, more disregard for rules, and freedom from depressive inhibition over mistakes" (Cattell, 1973). Cattell (1965, p. 124) discussed the distinction between general inhibition (which is neurologically determined) and this social inhibition, which gives "more role to early childhood experience with *people* in producing a strictly social inhibition." High social inhibition is negatively related to affectothymia, dominance, gregariousness, and surgency and positively related to self-sufficiency.

General inhibition is closest to Cattell's T-data "inhibition" factor, which he described as "... a largely constitutional cortical capacity to inhibit, partially based on hypothalamic reactivity to threat, and opposed to impulsiveness and to the tendency easily to dissociate unpleasant or threatening memories" (Cattell, 1957, p. 240). There may also be some correspondence between this and Guilford's (1975) postulated second-order factor of "introversion–extraversion." General inhibition is positively identified by conditionability and self-sentiment and negatively identified by surgency (Royce & McDermott, 1977, pp. 219–22).

First-order Factors

Escape emerged from research concerning mouse emotionality (e.g., Royce, Poley, & Yeudall, 1973) as an "underwater swimming factor." Poley and Royce (1976b) thought that a general escape process was involved and did find an "escape" factor at the second-order.

Territoriality was discovered in the mouse emotionality research and was "defined primarily by various urination indices as measures of territorial marking" (Poley & Royce, 1976b).

Avoidance was found at the second and third orders with mice and was distinguished from escape in the following way:

> High activity (lower latencies) corresponds to better active avoidance. It is reasonable to hypothesize that an animal's behavior in a stressful situation is guided both by escape tendencies ... and tendencies to actively avoid the situation in response to cues (CS's) which the animal has learned to avoid through past experience. (Royce & Poley, 1976b, p. 72)

Autonomic balance has been identified in a wide range of human and animal studies, including the research on mouse emotionality cited above. This factor is considered to reflect an internal mode of energy release, and there is strong evidence of invariance across genotype and species (Royce, 1966b).

Ergic tension is Cattell's label for a factor that represents "the total aroused unexpressed drive tension (from ergic sources)" covering "tense, driven, overactive behavior" (Cattell, 1973). He describes it as "relaxed, tranquil, torpid, unfrustrated, composed" versus "tense, frustrated, driven, overwrought."

Fearfulness represents a broadening of the "acrophobia" factor found in research on mouse emotionality. In humans this factor may be similar to French's (1973) Factor II, "poise, sociability versus self-consciousness."

Guilt stems from Cattell's Q-data research. Non-guilt-proneness is described as "untroubled adequacy (self-assured, placid, secure, complacent, serene)" versus "guilt proneness (apprehensive, self-reproaching, insecure, worrying, troubled)" (Cattell, 1973).

Cycloid tendency is closest to Guilford's "cycloid disposition," which he contrasts with "emotional stability" (Guilford, 1975).

Ego strength comes from Cattell's Q-data wherein lower ego strength (at mercy of feelings, emotionally less stable, easily upset, changeable) is contrasted with higher ego strength (emotionally stable, mature, faces reality, calm, capacity to cope with emotional difficulties (from Cattell, 1973).

Trust corresponds to Cattell's Q-data factor "alaxia" (trusting, accepting conditions) versus "protension," or "paranoid tendency" (suspicious, hard to fool). Protension, or lack of trust, is described as "self-opinionated, sceptical, jealous, and suspicious behavior ... essentially an inner tension accompanied by strong tendencies to projection" (Cattell, 1973).

Cooperativeness is closest to Guilford's "personal relations." The uncooperative, intolerant individual is "given to critical fault-finding generally; has little confidence or trust in others; is self-centered and self-pitying" (Guilford & Zimmerman, 1956).

Realism is our label for Cattell's Q-data "praxernia" (having practical, down-to-earth concerns) versus "autio" (imaginative, bohemian, absentminded), which he has also described as "practical concernedness" versus "hysteric unconcernedness" (Cattell, 1973).

Tendermindedness, originally suggested by William James, appears in Cattell's Q-data research as "harria" (tough-minded, self-reliant, realistic) versus "premsia" (tenderminded, sensitive, clinging, dependent, overprotected) (Cattell, 1973).

Affectothymia comes from Cattell's Q-data research where he refers to "sizia" (reserved, detached, critical, aloof, stiff) in contrast to "affectia" (outgoing, warmhearted, easygoing, participating) (Cattell, 1973).

Dominance is closest to Cattell's Q-data factor "submissiveness" (humble, mild, easily led, docile, accommodating) versus "dominance" (assertive, aggressive, competitive, stubborn) (Cattell, 1973) and Guilford's "ascendance" (Guilford, 1975).

Self-sufficiency is Cattell's Q-data factor "group adherence" (group-dependent, a "joiner" and sound follower) in contrast to "self-sufficiency" (self-sufficient, resourceful, prefers own decisions) (Cattell, 1973).

Gregariousness appears consistently across laboratories. Cattell in his Q-data has "threctia" (shy, timid, threat-sensitive) versus "parmia" (venturesome, uninhibited, socially bold) (Cattell, 1973); Guilford has a "sociability" factor (Guilford, 1975); and French (1973) hypothesized "gregariousness."

Conditionability is hypothesized as a result of H. J. Eysenck's work on the differential conditionability of extraverts and introverts and his finding that extraverts, in certain situations, condition less well than introverts.

Surgency is Cattell's Q-data factor "desurgency" (sober, taciturn, serious) versus "surgency" (happy-go-lucky, heedless, gay, uninhibited, enthusiastic) (Cattell, 1973).

Self-sentiment has been revealed in Cattell's (1973) Q-data research. "Low self-sentiment integration" (undisciplined self-conflict, lax, follows own urges, careless of social rules) is contrasted with "high strength of self-sentiment" (controlled, exacting will power, socially precise, compulsive, following self-image) (Royce & McDermott, 1977, pp. 222–24).

The Functional Role
of the Affective System

The concept of arousal is the key to the functioning of the affective system. And since arousal effects are typically generated at the apex of a given hierarchy, we begin our discussion of the affective system with a description of the functional significance of the three subhierarchies of Figure 5–4.

Introversion–extraversion   In general, introverts can be characterized as having an excess of cortical excitation (via the reticular activating system), whereas extraverts are dominated by cortical inhibition (H. J. Eysenck, 1957; H. J. Eysenck & S. B. G. Eysenck, 1969). Thus, under identical stimulating conditions, introverts are operating in a relatively higher state of (cortical-reticular) arousal than extraverts. This excitatory imbalance produces constraints on overt behavior, such that extraverts tend to seek out additional external stimulation whereas introverts, already in a high state of arousal, do not. Eysenck and his associates have made extensive observations of the behavioral consequences of this hypothesized state of affairs. For example, it has been found that extraverts (high inhibition or low arousal) are more difficult to condition, have less tolerance for sensory deprivation, manifest large figural aftereffects and a high degree of perceptual constancy, and are low in level of aspiration (H. J. Eysenck, 1970, provides a summary of the early research findings related to introversion–extraversion). We have expanded on these basic views in suggesting that each of the seven primaries under introversion–extraversion is differentially activated in the further processing of information via this particular subhierarchy of the affective system. More specifically, an affective-introverted type reflects high conditionability, high self-sentiment, low surgency, high self-sufficiency, low affectothymia, low dominance, and low gregariousness, whereas the typical extraverted profile reflects an opposite pattern.

Emotional stability   Although the evidence in support of a higher-order construct of emotional stability is as strong as the case for introversion–extraversion, the quantity of empirical research is not as great. However, the evidence in support of first-order factors, as well as linkages to the second-order factors, is more convincing than in the case of introversion–extraversion. This is partly due to the more behaviorally oriented investigations that have been brought to bear in this subdomain (e.g., more experimentally controllable animal populations have been used rather than humans and questionnaires).

Broadhurst and his associates (Broadhurst, 1975; Wilcock & Broadhurst, 1967) provide convincing experimental evidence for a general construct of emotional reactivity in the rat. They show, for example, that open field measures are related to a wide range of emotional behavior and their physiological correlates. Furthermore, in a detailed analysis of open field constructs, Royce (1977a) presents the case for the linkage between the research of Broadhurst and others on "emotionality" and the construct of emotional stability. It can be seen from Figure 5–4 that escape and avoidance factors are included as first-order factors and that we have specified the second-order factors as energy mobilization and excitability. Although there is some empirical basis for the latter two factors, they must be viewed as hypothesized constructs.

The rationale for the factors of this subhierarchy presupposes that limbic system arousal constitutes a relatively primitive biological subsystem that is primarily concerned with maximizing the immediate availability of energy in the service of organismic survival. For example, the fight or flight release of aroused energy, well-documented in the early literature on emotionality theory (e.g., see Cannon, 1927), is consistent with such a perspective. That is, survival is a primary goal of living organisms, and energy that can be optimally mobilized is required in situations where either intense fight or flight is required. And the three first-order factors of territoriality, escape, and avoidance that are subsumed under energy mobilization in Figure 5-4 are clearly survival-oriented dimensions. The most obvious case in point is the escape factor identified in Royce's mouse research (Royce, Poley, & Yeudall, 1973) by an underwater swimming task—a situation where failure to swim the length of the tank in time results in drowning. The survival value of avoidance is equally obvious and, because of the extensive research on avoidance conditioning, a great deal is known about this component. However, the finding which is most relevant in this context is that under optimal conditions avoidance behavior leads to survival, but that too much avoiding under non-optimal conditions is maladaptive (e.g., see Royce, Yeudall, & Poley, 1971).

There is also extensive research on territoriality involving both animals (e.g., Calhoun, 1962; Egan & Royce, 1973; Tinbergen, 1951; Thorpe, 1956) and humans (e.g., Esser, 1972; Freedman, 1971; Gillis, 1973; Schmitt, 1966; Wallis & Maliphant, 1967) indicating that there is an increase in aggression and social pathology in high-density populations. In the case of the anxiety factor the rationale is that internal release of aroused energy is what is common to such first-order factors as autonomic balance, fearfulness, and ergic tension. Activation of the autonomic balance and fearfulness factors, for example, would result in massive energy increments internally released via such mechanisms as the autonomic nervous system and hormone secretions. Examples of such effects in the case of the autonomic balance factor are legion, as they include the well-understood physiological effects of the autonomic nervous system. The behavioral effects, however, are not as well understood, although there are some relevant findings. Wenger (1948), for example, has demonstrated that sympathetic autonomic imbalance is characteristic of neurotics and combat fatigue cases.

The functional significance of transforming energy potential into kinetic energy via such factors as autonomic balance and fearfulness is in the service of increased work demands placed on the organism. Thus, when additional work is in fact required, the availability of the extra energy will answer an immediate organismic demand. On the other hand, should the extra energy become available when there are no extra work demands on the organism, it is hypothesized that the availability of surplus internal energy is frequently converted to organismic stress, psychosomatic manifestations, and other manifestations of anxiety, such as guilt and suspiciousness (distrust).

What about the remaining second-order factor of this subhierarchy, excitability? In this case we depart from the simple survival principle to one where information processing and energy processing are more equally involved. The implication is that high levels of arousal in these cases involve a greater proportion of information processing, and that this results in increments in conflict, which, in turn, become differentially manifested via the emotional stability factors of moodiness (i.e., cycloid tendency), ego strength, and degree of trust.

Emotional independence   Emotional independence differs from emotional stability and introversion–extraversion in that little theory or empirical evidence exists to assist in determining its functional role. The descriptions represent a mixture of Eysenck, Cattell, and Guilford factors; therefore, cross-level linkages remain largely hypothetical. *Emotional independence* represents our relabeling of Eysenck's "psychoticism" dimension in his three-factor personality system. We have adopted the term *emotional independence* rather than psychoticism because of the pathological connotation of Eysenck's label. A lack of "socialization" is implied by emotional independence. But high emotional insensitivity and hostility are also implied—so that no one of these labels entirely suffices. We have conceptualized this factor in terms of the primaries and secondaries that (hypothetically) identify it. For example, Eysenck (H. J. Eysenck & S. B. G. Eysenck, 1976) has suggested that emotional independence may be a combination of two Cattellian third-order factors that Cattell (1973) tentatively called "antisocial unconcern" and "readiness." Cattell's second-order factors of autonomy and cortertia loaded on antisocial unconcern and readiness, respectively. Substituting emotional independence for these latter two, it is proposed that, proceeding from the third-order to the second-order, an individual high on emotional independence will be high on autonomy and high on cortertia. And proceeding to the primaries, high autonomy implies a lack of trust and cooperativeness, as well as high dominance and realism; high cortertia implies low tendermindedness and affectothymia, and high realism. In short, the individual who scores high on cortertia tends to be realistic, tough-minded, and detached or aloof (i.e., scores low on the affectothymia dimension) (Royce & McDermott, 1977, pp. 199–206).

Affective Processing

In an attempt to describe the information-processing significance of the affective dimensions introduced in Figure 5–4, we make use of a variety of system properties and principles (Chapter 3). Processes are interpreted as information-energetic in a sense similar to that proposed by systems-information theorists (Bertalanffy, 1955; J. G. Miller, 1978). As we have noted, cybernetic processes among hierarchically organized feedback units have been proposed by a number of theorists, and as with our analysis of the other domains of personality, such hierarchical organization is fundamental to our analysis of affective processing.

No attempt is made here, however, to spell out or speculate about exact mechanisms, temporal sequences, or such that might be involved, since the affective system has not traditionally been explored in terms of information processing, and little support could be mustered for such explication at this time. It is also recognized that any description of affective processing must necessarily remain incomplete until interactions between affect and cognition (see Chapter 8) have been taken into consideration (i.e., it is clear that cognitive processes are involved in affect). Further, in order to study ongoing information-energy processing and arrive at some overall picture, one would have to move beyond the affective system (or the cognitive system, or any one system for that matter), since affective processes represent only one part of the total picture. In other words, it is impossible to trace the flow of information-energy completely from stimulus input to response output by analyzing any one of the six systems. Concern here, then, is with the direction and pervasiveness of influences whenever the affective system is activated. The proposed functional interrelationships among affective factors are put forward in the context of feedback and other system control mechanisms.

Figure 5-5 presents an overall model of affect as a complex hierarchical information-processing system in which the concepts of optimal arousal level and the management of risk have been incorporated. Such a model of the affective system follows from our general systems information-processing model. However, it should be noted such a general model of affective processing is entirely speculative in the case of the affective system since affective processing has been investigated very little empirically and theoretically. We mean for this model to be suggestive of the direction that integrative investigation of affective processing might take. As noted in the figure, the primary goal at the level of integrative affect is to maintain an optimal level of internal arousal, where the norm is specified by the cognitive system (and its appraisal of task demands), styles, and values. The three higher-order factors of introversion–extraversion, emotional stability, and emotional independence correspond to three subsystems of arousal.[7] The lower-level system functions are related to the second-order factors. For example, factors related to introversion–extraversion are more relevant to the processing of affective *inputs*. At the other extreme, factors related to emotional stability seem more relevant to the processing of affective *outputs*, such as in the mobilization of flight–fight reactions and the evoking of specific motoric processes. Finally, factors under emotional stabililty appear to be more relevant to the central processing activities of affect (e.g., decider, channel and net, association, etc.; see Table 3-1).

In Figure 5-6, the high-level decision-control processes of the affective system are modeled in the form of a TOTE hierarchy. In the attempt to maintain optimal internal arousal, the affective system must engage in the manipulation of risk. That is, information is transformed in order to maintain or achieve the level of arousal that is necessary for any particular task or goal. Throughout, the process is regulated by styles and values. As discussed in the next chapter, styles are related primarily to the regulation of attention, and values are thought to determine the optimality of particular risks. There is always risk involved because under specifiable circumstances (e.g., J. G. Miller, 1978) the system can be understimulated or overwhelmed by too little or too much arousal. Both of these

---

[7]The best available evidence (H. J. Eysenck & S. B. G. Eysenck, 1976) is that the arousal correlate of emotional independence is hormonal (i.e., testosterene) rather than neural. This difference is critical in our later elaboration of emotion (see Chapter 8).

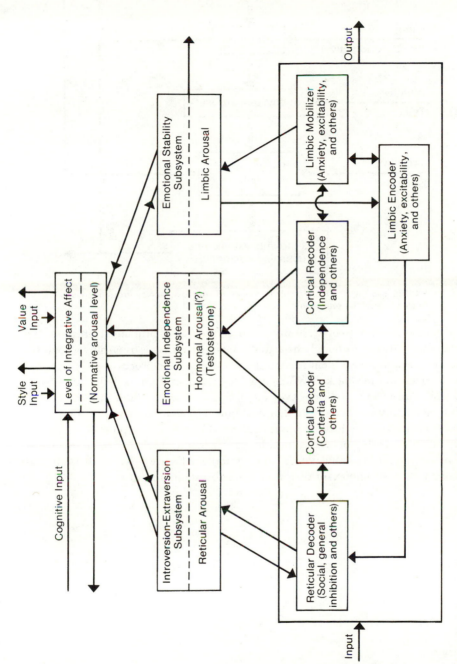

FIGURE 5-5 A multifactor-systems model of affect as an information-processing system.

131

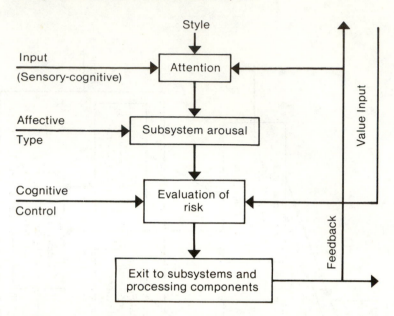

FIGURE 5-6 A TOTE-hierarchical model of the decision-control processes related to affective processing.

possibilities can lead to internal stress and, in the case of prolonged stress, even to system breakdown. Although the actual assessment of risk is ostensibly a cognitive activity, the affective system is centrally involved in the process.

Given the feedback relationships illustrated in Figures 5-5 and 5-6, the possibility of vicious circles of ever-increasing arousal are built into the system. Thus, for example, the arousal that is output by the affective system may evoke processes that provide further inputs to affect. These further inputs, depending on attentional and other processes, may lead to further arousal, and so on in an ever-increasing spiral. As a final note, near the middle of Figure 5-6 we indicate that affective type is an important determiner of subsystem arousal.

6

The Style and Value
Integrative Systems

We now turn our attention to the integrative, self-organizing layer of personality and to the structure of styles and values. As described in Chapter 1, as one ascends the hierarchy of systems depicted in Figure 1–1 the focus is increasingly on systems that: (1) have a higher priority of action; (2) can input control information to other systems; (3) are concerned with longer units of time; and (4) are deeper (in the sense of significance) than other systems. One way of thinking of this kind of organization is to consider the complexity that characterizes the systems already described. For example, the sensory system is sensitive to an incredible array of stimulus events, and the motor system controls the execution of infinitely variable behaviors that are subtly organized through time and space. At the next level we have cognition, which transforms information in order to discover invariants in the environment, and affect, which controls an extremely complex array of internal arousal effects. The general point is that such complex activities have to be coordinated, directed, and focused. Otherwise individuals would become lost in the sea of immediate experiences that impinges on the senses and challenges cognitive and affective processes.

We think styles and values provide the direction and attentional focus required by the lower-level systems of sensory, motor, cognition, and affect. Styles and values are similar inasmuch as they both provide conceptual linkages between cognition and affect. However, the critical difference is that styles provide directional focus by selecting for particular *modes* of cognitive and affective processing,

133

whereas values select for informational *content*. Informational content refers to the enormous range of items in the world to which one can become committed. The major point is that *what* one can value constitutes a very large set of alternatives, whereas *how* one does things constitutes a relatively small set of alternatives. This difference in the what and how of commitments is also reflected in the structure of the two systems. In particular, the value system is composed of 60 dimensions organized at four levels, in contrast to the style system, which is composed of only 15 dimensions organized at three levels—that is, without a primary level. Future research may uncover more specific style commitments, but we do not think this is likely because the style dimensions represent such broad strategies for selecting abilities and arousal mechanisms. In this chapter we present the structure of these two integrative systems. Although some comments are included concerning the functional significance of styles and values, this topic is more fully developed in Part III of the book where a variety of integrative processes are considered. For example, in these later chapters styles are shown to provide a basis for world view, values are presented as a basis for life style, and styles and values together determine self-image.

THE STYLE SYSTEM[1]

The analysis that follows distinguishes between three major style constructs: cognitive style, affective style, and cognitive-affective styles. The first two are concerned with fundamental consistencies in relationships among styles and cognitive abilities and affective traits, respectively. Cognitive-affective styles are concerned with consistent ways in which styles simultaneously integrate both cognition *and* affect.

Styles "recruit" abilities and affective traits that are involved in a specifiable situation. Styles, then, determine the combinations of traits that are activated when alternative possibilities exist—for example, when a person has a wide potential array of relevant traits or when the situation is sufficiently complex that multiple modes of response are feasible. In an object-sorting task, for example, a cognitive style might give more weight to perceptual and inductive reasoning abilities than to conceptual and deductive reasoning abilities. Similarly, an affective style might moderate between the expression of anxiety or impulsivity in sorting. Given the integrative nature of styles and the hypothesis that they link to both cognition and affect, it is not possible to present style structure in terms of a single hierarchy, as we were able to do for other systems of personality.

The Structure of Cognitive-affective Styles

Since the available evidence is too sparse, it is not possible at this time to spell out a taxonomy of style constructs based only on factor-analytic research.

---

[1] For more details regarding the structure of styles, see Wardell and Royce (1978). We wish to acknowledge Doug Wardell's important contribution to our understanding of the structure of styles.

However, we can identify a number of styles that reflect some degree of construct validity based on extensive empirical (although usually non-factor-analytic) research. As a result of an extensive series of theoretical-empirical studies on epistemic styles, we have identified three higher-order constructs that we have hypothesized to be near the apex of the style hierarchy. These three general styles, identified as empirical, rational, and metaphoric, are presumed to reflect three different ways in which cognition and affect are integrated. Our present understanding of these styles is limited largely to the context of psychological epistemology and world view (see Chapter 9).

Empirical styles involve a commitment to relating to the world through one's senses and to testing one's ideas about reality in terms of reliability and validity of observations. Affectively, there is a commitment to the arousal that comes via immediate experience. We think this third-order cognitive-affective style is equivalent to *extensiveness of scanning*, which has been described as " . . . a relatively stable disposition to attend to tasks intensively and in a focused manner, yet with extensive coverage of relatively incidental aspects of the field" (Holtzman, 1966, p. 835).

Rational styles involve a commitment to relating to the world through one's rational/analytic skills and to testing one's ideas about reality in terms of logical consistency. Affectively, there is a commitment to remaining aloof from the arousal effects of the immediate environment. We think this third-order style construct is equivalent to an analytic versus global style, known originally as field independence and later as psychological differentiation. Witkin, Dyk, Faterson, Goodenough, and Karp have described this style as " . . . an analytic, in contrast to a global, way of perceiving; [it] entails a tendency to experience items as discrete from their backgrounds, and reflects ability to overcome the influence of an embedding context (1962, pp. 57–58).

Metaphoric styles involve a commitment to symbolic-metaphoric experience and to testing one's ideas or awareness about reality in terms of their universality (i.e., to constructing cognitive representations of experience that have the greatest degree of generality). Although no stylistic construct that can be equated to the metaphoric style has appeared in the empirical literature, there is some evidence (Wardell & Royce, 1975), particularly in research on creativity, that correlations between symbolizing cognitive abilities such as ideational fluency and surgency in the introversion–extraversion affective domain reflect a stylistic consistency (Wardell & Royce, 1978, pp. 485–86).

The Structure of Cognitive Styles

Our hypotheses as to which cognitive styles ought to cluster with each of the higher-order styles are summarized in Figure 6-1. The analytic ("reflective") and abstract cognitive styles are linked to the rational style, while the relational ("impulsive") and concrete styles are linked to the empirical style. Narrow category width, high conceptual differentiation, and cognitive complexity are linked to rationalism. The "sharpening" extreme of leveling versus sharpening

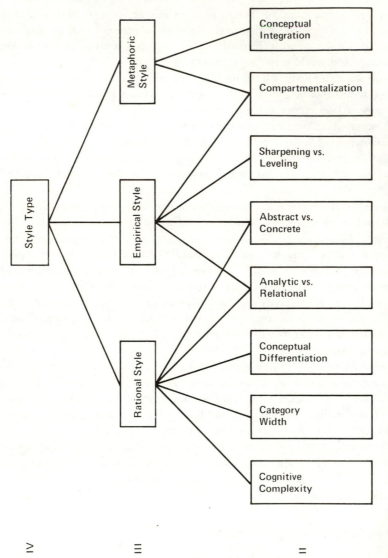

FIGURE 6-1 Hierarchical structure of cognitive styles. (Modified from Wardell & Royce, 1978)

styles is linked to the empirical style, high conceptual integration is linked to the metaphoric style, and compartmentalization is related to both empiricism (high) and metaphorism (low).

Although it seems likely that the organization at the second order will be modified by future research, it is not unreasonable to anticipate that a hierarchical structure such as we have indicated in Figure 6–1 will accommodate future empirical data. This includes the three cognitive-affective styles as higher-order personality integrators and the designation of the lowest level of style constructs as second-order factors. The empirical basis for all the second-order style constructs is extensive; the relevant literature is discussed at length in Wardell and Royce (1978). In the following we provide brief descriptions of the second-order factors depicted in Figure 6–1.

Cognitive complexity refers to the extent to which an individual makes use of available cognitive structure whenever information is being processed. Gardner and Schoen suggest that "persons of great 'cognitive complexity' presumably make more, and more complex, distinctions between persons and events—conceptual differentiation in categorizing can be conceived of as an aspect of cognitive complexity" (1962, p. 5). In reading or in conversation, for example, more effort is put into applying and referring new inputs to one's preexisting understanding, to differentiating and integrating one's personal constructs with respect to the environment, and to maintaining consistency and coherence. The processes of analyzing, making conceptual distinctions, abstracting, constructing, and integrating new concepts are important to the cognitively complex person.

Category width, or broad versus narrow categorizing, has also been called equivalence range (Sloane, Gorlow, & Jackson, 1963), and refers to differentiations within the range of a single concept. Gardner, Holzman, Klein, Linton, and Spence have referred to this style as:

> the degree to which subjects are impelled to act on or ignore an awareness of differences. A narrow equivalence range seemed to imply detailed categorization of certain aspects of experience. "Narrow-range" subjects had relatively exact standards for judging similarlity. "Broad-range" subjects, on the other hand, were less finicky about fine stimulus differences, and grouped stimuli into broader categories. (1959, p. 39)

Conceptual differentiation refers to the process of bringing a large number of concepts to bear on cognitive tasks. It is reflected in object-sorting tasks, in which some people consistently make more and smaller differentiations among dissimilar particulars. As Gardner and Schoen point out, "In contrast to category-width tests, in which each item assesses the limits of one conceptual realm, free-sorting tests require the spontaneous differentiation of heterogeneous items into a complex of more or less related groups" (1962, p. 3). Thus, differentiation refers to the number of distinct conceptual discriminations made concerning a subject matter. For example, *length* and *width* are greater discriminators among objects than *size*. More differentiated people are inclined to pursue and use more detailed conceptualizations; that is, they tend to have a "conceptual" orientation. In contrast, category width (see text) refers to the degree of discrimination in the use of a single concept. *Large, huge,* and *giant-sized* are narrower categories (and shorter equivalence ranges) than *big.*

Analytical versus relational categorizing is concerned with favored types of concepts. More specifically, according to Kagan, Moss, and Sigel this style refers to

> whether one forms "analytic-descriptive" concepts (based on similarity in objective elements within a stimulus complex that was part of the total stimulus) or "inferential-categorical" concepts ("involving an inference about the stimuli grouped together") as opposed to "relational concepts" ("based on a functional relationship between or among the stimuli grouped together"). (1963, p. 76)

The implication from Kagan's research with children is that analytic concepts are favored by "reflective" children, and relational concepts by "impulsive" children.

Abstract versus concrete refers to the orientation toward, or preference for, concept formation and manipulation generally, as distinct from conceptual differentiation, which is concerned specifically with the production of concepts that serve to differentiate particulars. The abstract person, according to Schroder, Driver, and Streufert (1967), uses more information and more strategies to solve problems. It has also been suggested that different kinds of information receive attention. That is, the more concrete individual is thought to be more dependent on the physical attributes of the activating stimulus.

Leveling versus sharpening has also been identified as assimilation (Klein, 1951). Sharpening was originally hypothesized as: ". . . a tendency to be hypersensitive to minutaie, to respond excessively to the fine nuances and small differences, to exaggerate change, and to keep adjacent or successive stimuli from fusing or losing identity" (p. 332). Research has generally supported this distinction, using judgments of sequentially presented stimuli and serial reproduction of stories. Gardner and his associates (1959, p. 219), for example, found that "levelers are characterized by maximal assimilation effects, and by memory organizations in which the fine shades of distinctions among individual elements are lost."

Compartmentalization, discussed a great deal in the psychoanalytic literature, has been operationalized by Messick and Kogan (1963) when they found that the number of categories in an object-sorting task could be distinguished from the number of objects left unsorted. The number of categories is a measure of conceptual differentiation, and leaving large numbers of miscellaneous objects ungrouped after the sorting task (which was correlated with restricted productive ideation) was identified as "a tendency to compartmentalize ideas . . . in discrete categories . . . a possible limitation in the production of diverse ideas" (Messick & Kogan, 1963, p. 50).

Conceptual integration refers to the inclination to explore and develop relationships among concepts. For example, Harvey, Hunt, and Schroder define it as "the relating or hooking of parts (concepts) to each other and to previous conceptual standards" (1961, p. 18). As such, it is often considered, along with conceptual differentiation, as an aspect of cognitive complexity. That is, the "conceptually oriented" person is oriented toward both producing and combining concepts (Wardell & Royce, 1978, pp. 477–80).

The Structure of Affective Styles

The hypothesized affective style hierarchy is shown in Figure 6–2. It is proposed that the rational style is associated with the tendency to eliminate contradictory cues (i.e., constricted versus flexible control) and that the empirical style is associated with low tolerance for unrealistic experiences as well as the affective trait of general inhibition. We suggest that inhibition develops from high conditionability in conjunction with a "moral" or strict upbringing. Furthermore, the inhibited person is more reflective (i.e., reflection versus impulsivity), more extensive and intensive in scanning perceptual fields, and more concerned for empirical standards. The physiognomic versus literal style is associated with metaphoric since we presume that persons who are more concerned with symbolic aspects of experiences will also be more responsive to the emotional rather than strictly literal (i.e., logical or empirical) components of them.

Tolerance for the unconventional or for "unrealistic experiences" is defined as "acceptance of experiences which do not agree with what one knows to be true" (Gardner et al., 1959, p. 31). According to Klein, low tolerance is " . . . reflected on the Rorschach in reluctance to project or fantasize, in refusals to attribute to the blots qualities that were known not to be there, and in difficulty in adopting an 'as if' attitude . . . in the apparent movement test" (1970, p. 148). "Tolerance" may be very important in determining levels of aspiration and patience during goal-oriented activities that involve unusual or unconventional matters. For example, a person who demands perceptual verisimilitude (i.e., who is "intolerant") would perhaps be more inclined to demand explanations before accepting unconventional perceptual phenomena.

Constricted versus flexible control may be referred to by strong versus weak automatization (Broverman, 1964) and cognitive interference or interference proneness (Klein, Barr, & Wolitsky, 1967, p. 510). Gardner and his associates suggest that these are

> Terms . . . to describe differing reactions to stimulus fields containing contradictory or intrusive cues . . . constricted-control subjects resorted to counteractive measures in their attempts to overcome the disruptive effect of intrusive cues . . . Flexible-control subjects seemed relatively comfortable in situations that involved contradictory or intrusive cues. (1959, p. 53)

Theoretically, "constricted" persons should show less patience when goal-oriented activities involve intrusive cues, but higher levels of aspiration for overcoming intrusions.

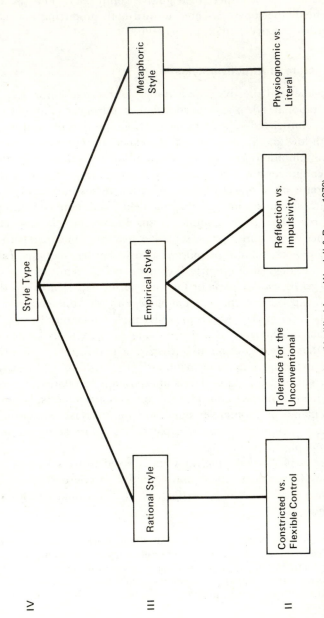

FIGURE 6-2 Hierarchical structure of affective styles. (Modified from Wardell & Royce, 1978)

Reflection versus impulsivity is, according to Kagan, "the degree to which a subject considers alternative hypotheses in contrast to reporting hypotheses with minimal consideration of their probable validity" (1965a, p. 159). For the impulsive child, emotional states and affective traits intrude to disrupt the evaluation of possible answers under conditions of response uncertainty. Responses show less scanning of alternatives and less concern for validity, probably either because intrusive emotional states are overwhelming (e.g., hyperactivity) or because concern about negative results is underdeveloped (e.g., psychopathy). Studies have shown that reflection increases with age beginning with school, and that reflective children are better at a variety of inductive-reasoning and problem-solving tasks (see Wardell & Royce, 1978). There is also some evidence that reflectives are also more attentive, less hyperactive, and less aggressive.

Physiognomic versus literal was first proposed by Klein in 1951, who, in review, states that

> [for the physiognomic person] percepts are often subtly suffused with emotional or expressive qualities. Inanimate objects or events seem to move, become motivated and assume expressive and "human" auras . . . All these experiences involved a preference for the dynamic and emotive rather than for the static and literal. (Klein, 1970, pp. 151–52)

Although little empirical work has been done with this style, we suggest that the "physiognomic" person (like the "impulsive") is disrupted by intrusive emotionality. In this instance, emotionality may be stimulated by the person's own heightened sensitivity to the emotional connotations of his activities and perceptions (Wardell & Royce, 1978, pp. 482–84).

Functional Significance
of Style Structure

We show the overall structure of the style system in Figure 6–3. The three cognitive-affective styles are represented as higher-order constructs that integrate cognitive and affective styles within a hierarchical framework. The empirical style is related to analytic versus relational, concrete thinking, sharpened and precise memories, and compartmentalization on the cognitive side, and to impulsivity and intolerance for unrealistic experiences on the affective side. Similarly, high conceptual differentiation, narrow categorizing, analysis, and abstract thinking are associated with the rational style, as is the affective style of constricted reactions to contradictory cues. All of these rational styles share an emphasis on analysis, independence, and rational control as well as an epistemic concern for logical coherence. Finally, the cognitive concern for integrating concepts (i.e., via the conceptual integration and compartmentalization styles) though their symbolic, emotive, and analogical similarities is reflected in the affective realm by a sensitivity to these aspects rather than strictly literal attributes (i.e., the physiognomic versus literal affective style). In particular, sensitivity to emotional

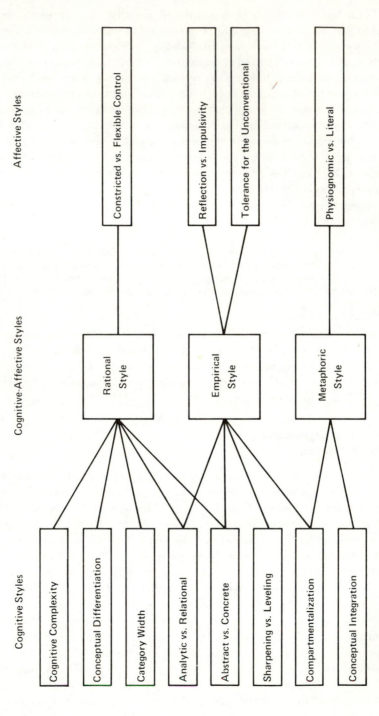

FIGURE 6-3 Relationships of cognitive-affective styles with cognitive and affective styles. (From Wardell & Royce, 1978)

cues can be disruptive to extended, sequentially planned activity, but the exuberant metaphorical style so characterized is common to much creative work in which the concern is largely in the context of discovery rather than justification.

We have taken the stance that the three higher-order styles of empirical, rational, and metaphoric can be profitably characterized in terms of attentional processes. We have already alluded to this via Figure 5-6, for example, where we suggested that affective processing is influenced by style through attentional processes. Also in Figure 5-3 our proposal is that the principal impact of styles on cognitive processing is in terms of the selection of particular processing modes, which also implicates attentional mechanisms. The following three aspects of attention have been proposed in the style literature: (1) *extensiveness* of attention over a field; (2) *selectiveness* of attention with respect to specific aspects of the field; and (3) the overall *breadth* of attention. The first of these, extensiveness, relates to the amount and the detail of the field that is explored at a given time. We think this is controlled primarily by the empirical styles. Selectiveness, on the other hand, refers to the extent to which one aspect of the field is concentrated on, which we think characterizes the rational styles. Finally, attentional breadth refers to the greater inclusiveness and integration of the objects of attention, which is the attentional role of the metaphoric styles.

The most important aspect of the functional role of styles has to do with their linkages to cognitive abilities and affective traits. Although there are linkages at all levels of the cognitive and affective hierarchies, in Figure 6-4 we show only the second-order linkages for simplicity of presentation. However, we do briefly discuss linkages at all levels in the following paragraphs (see Wardell & Royce, 1978, for more details).

Linkages to cognition   As shown by the left side of Figure 6-4, the rational style is more likely to be associated with conceptual abilities, the empirical style with perceiving abilities, and the metaphoric style with symbolizing abilities. In general, a variety of cognitive tasks that involve overcoming embeddedness have been found to be related to field articulation, or rational style. There is also a possible linkage to the second-order spatiovisual ability since field articulation has been found to be related to closure and adaptive flexibility. The empirical style has been equated to extensiveness of scanning, which in turn has been found to be correlated with spatial scanning and speed of closure. These latter factors are lower-order perceiving abilities that relate to the spatiovisual factor at the second order. There is also a connection with reasoning since inductive reasoning requires the construction of appropriate generalizations by scanning a configuration of empirical information. The connections between the metaphoric style and the cognitive symbolizing abilities are more speculative, although Wardell and Royce (1978) report some suggestive evidence. In any case, we think the metaphoric style has to do with the *breadth* of attention as reflected in the creative and synthesizing cognitive abilities.

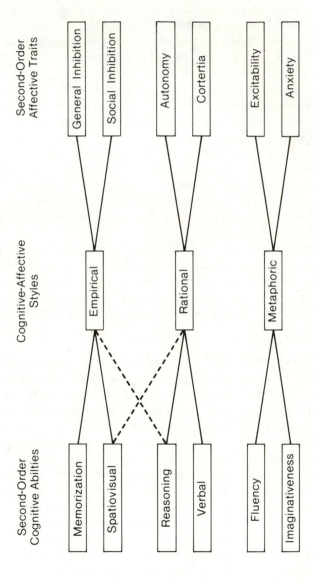

FIGURE 6-4 Style linkages to second-order cognitive abilities and affective traits.

144

Linkages to affect   The stylistic linkages to affect are shown on the right of Figure 6–4. In general, the empirical styles link to introversion–extraversion factors of general and social inhibition, rational links to the emotional independence factors of autonomy and cortertia, and metaphoric relates to the emotional stability factors of excitability and anxiety. With regard to the empirical style, extensive scanners can be described as "preoccupied with veridicality, exactness, and the adequacy of their response, and perhaps control over impulses" (Royce, 1973b, p. 334). These characteristics are associated with affective introversion and inhibition. Similarly, individuals who are low on extensive scanning or empirical style can be described as sociable, self-confident, and emotionally reactive—traits that are associated with extraversion. Field-articulate individuals (i.e., high on rational style) can be described as "highly autonomous individuals with a stable self-view; socially, they show little interest in and need for people, and they manifest a relatively intellectual and impersonal approach to problems" (Royce, 1973b, p. 334). These are descriptions that also apply to individuals high on emotional independence and the second-order factors of autonomy and cortertia. The linkage of metaphoric style to emotional stability is an inference based on the correlations among fluency measures and such ratings as impulsive, expansive, talkative, friendly, independent-minded, unruly, playful, unconventional, emotional, and volatile—ratings that also correlate with creativity.

This completes our discussion of the basic structure of styles and their functional linkages to cognition and affect. We now turn our attention to the basic structure of values.

THE VALUE SYSTEM[2]

Any theoretical project with the scope of the individuality project is apt to encounter many areas where *any* theoretical idea will generate controversy because the problem is difficult. For example, given the extensiveness of research in cognition over the past two decades, any model of cognition is apt to be controversial. But the area of values in human behavior is more apt to generate controversy than any other. Thus, we want to be clear at the outset that we are not proposing a "value theory," nor do we think "human values" can be understood outside the context of human cultural and historical development. Also, we do not want to psychologize morals, although the psychological processes we consider are relevant to individual moral behavior. We are focused on values as those aspects of the total personality that give direction to an individual's thoughts and feelings. More specifically, we conceptualize values as having linkages to cognition and affect in a manner that is formally parallel to styles. However, cognitive values reflect *interests* and affective values reflect *needs*. The role of these needs and interests is to coor-

[2]We wish to express our appreciation to Don Schopflocher, Frederick Bell, and Ken Meehan for their assistance in reviewing the empirical literature relevant to the construction of Figures 6–5 and 6–6.

dinate and integrate the information-processing activities of lower-level systems. We begin by discussing cognitive-affective values, which are concerned with ways in which values simultaneously integrate both cognitive and affective traits.

Cognitive-affective Values

We have hypothesized that there are three factors at the third order of the value domain: intrinsic, self, and social. These three higher-order values reflect basic orientations toward what is important to understand cognitively and react to emotionally in the world. The emphasis here is on specific informational *content* (styles emphasize processing *mode*). As such, these basic value orientations select for specific kinds of percepts, concepts, and symbols, as well as specific affective reactions. In other words, individuals have basic value commitments that specify *what* is worth knowing about the world, and which aspects of the world one should react to with feeling. To understand the world requires considerable effort, and given the vast range of possibilities available, some way of narrowing and focusing cognitive activity is necessary. Similarly, the infinite array of events that individuals are potentially sensitive to, and that can possibly be internally arousing must also be narrowed and focused. The three cognitive-affective values described in the following paragraphs provide the starting point for such a narrowing and focusing of reactions to the world. They provide basic orientations that allow general classes of information to be ignored and other classes to be focused on, enhanced, searched out, and even pursued with determination.

Intrinsic   With an intrinsic value orientation, an individual puts emphasis on excelling at particular tasks and achieving goals. Emphasis is not only given to mastering tasks that are particularly challenging to one's intellect, but also to mastering tasks that are physically challenging. Accomplishments that involve one's thought processes and being able to develop elegant mental solutions to problems are prized over all other possible accomplishments. Affectively, an intrinsic orientation places value on not being affectively changed by the environment. The important point is that one must prevent emotional reactions from coloring the external world as it "really is" to an uninvolved observer.

Self   A self value commitment is characterized by an emphasis on being a unique individual, maintaining one's independence regardless of the consequences that follow, and behaving according to one's own standards of conduct. Since there is a strong emphasis on what happens outside and inside one's own body, there is also a strong emphasis on affective reactions. The characteristics of the external world are not important in themselves but for the internal reactions or the cognitive creativity that they can stimulate.

Social   The social value commitment orients an individual to attend to movements toward and away from other people. Being helpful and praised and comforted by others and accomplishing "good" are the most desirable ends. The external world is appreciated in terms of what it can do to or for people in general.

Movements away from and toward other people are important in terms of one's own affective reactions.

These three basic values are third-order factors in the hierarchies of both cognitive and affective values, which we describe in the next sections.

The Structure of Affective Values (Needs)

We interpret affective values as psychological needs that direct, coordinate, and arouse affective processes in goal-directed activities. Such needs are evoked by a wide range of external and internal events. Once evoked, specific affective reactions are also made more likely. The hierarchical structure of needs is shown in Figure 6–5, where it can be seen that needs are dominated at the third order by intrinsic, self, and social value orientations.

Second-order Factors

Most of the factors at the second order in Figure 6–5 have been discovered in a variety of factor-analytic investigations of psychological needs. We will not provide an exhaustive review of this empirical literature, but exemplary references are provided in the following paragraphs.

Organization refers to the need to maintain order and reasonable structure in one's life and is characterized by strong positive loadings on order and cognitive structure and a strong negative loading on impulsivity. Support for this factor comes from Edwards and Abbott (1973), Nesselroade and Baltes (1975), and Seidman, Goldings, Hogan, and LeBow (1974).

General achievement is the general need to accomplish goals according to standards and to endure in spite of adversity. Edwards and Abbott (1973) and Huba, Segal, and Singer (1977), have reported such a need with loadings on achievement and endurance.

Meaning refers to the need to maintain a sense of understanding and coherence in one's life, although this factor is only moderately well established in empirical research. The intraception scale on the Edwards' Personal Preference Schedule has similar content. The meaning factor has been reported by Skinner, Jackson, and Rampton (1976), Siess and Jackson (1970), and Stricker (1974).

Self-protection refers to the need to protect oneself from external harm, whether through aggression, withdrawal, or maintenance of domination over others. It has strong positive loadings on aggression and defendence and negative loadings on affiliation, nurturance, and abasement (Huber et al., 1977; Seidman et al., 1974; Stricker, 1974).

Ascendance is the need to stand out, to show off, and be dominant over others or events outside oneself. It shows strong positive loadings on dominance and exhibition and a moderate positive loading on aggression (Huba et al., 1977; Nesselroade & Baltes, 1975; Stricker, 1974).

Contact, referring to the need for direct contact and interaction with other people, is only moderately well established and is characterized by positive

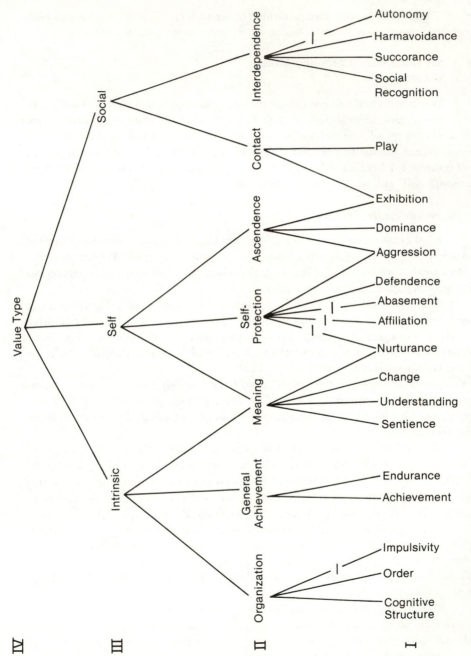

FIGURE 6-5 The hierarchical structure of affective values (needs).

loadings for play, affiliation, and exhibition (Huba et al., 1977; Nesselroade & Baltes, 1975; Siess & Jackson, 1970).

Interdependence is the need to relate interactively with other people in a safe, dependent way. It is characterized by positive loadings on social recognition, succorance, and "harmavoidance," and by a negative loading on autonomy (Nesselroade & Baltes, 1975; Skinner et al., 1976; Stricker, 1974).

First-order Factors

In an analysis of twelve of Murray's need variables that employed four separate measurement techniques, Huba and Hamilton (1976) have demonstrated that convergent and discriminant validity exists for the first-order constructs of Figure 6-5. However, the most potent findings have accrued in the development of the Personality Research Form (PRF; D. N. Jackson, 1967). The reasons for this include: (1) the PRF was developed using a rigorous and psychometrically advanced sequential strategy (A. S. Jackson, 1971); (2) all twenty of the PRF scales have been factorially confirmed in an item factor analysis (Helms & Jackson, 1977); (3) of all the available scales, the PRF uses the largest number of needs from Murray's (1938) original taxonomy; and, most important, (4) of the existing assessment techniques for measuring needs the PRF scales have been studied factor analytically more often. Thus, for a variety of reasons we have selected the PRF variables as the first-order factors in our need hierarchy. The following descriptions have been paraphrased from D. N. Jackson (1967, pp. 6–7).

Cognitive structure refers to the need to reduce ambiguity and uncertainty and to make decisions on the basis of certain knowledge rather than guesses or probabilities.

Order relates to keeping one's surroundings neat and organized, and avoiding clutter, confusion, and disorganization.

Impulsivity involves action without deliberation and the free expression of feelings, wishes, and emotions.

Achievement entails the accomplishment of difficult tasks while maintaining high standards and the willingness to work toward distant goals.

Endurance is the need to persevere even in the face of difficulty and to be patient in various work habits.

Sentience involves being sensitive to many forms of experience and incorporating these into one's mode of living.

Understanding refers to intellectual curiosity about matters involving knowledge.

Change entails the liking of new and different experiences and readily adapting to changes in the environment.

Nurturance is the need to give sympathy and comfort to others.

Affiliation involves the need to be with friends and people in general and to maintain associations with others.

Abasement involves showing a high degree of humility and even self-effacement.

Defendence is the need to protect oneself from the criticism and attacks by others.

Aggression brings the individual into combat and argument in order to do harm or "get even" with someone else.

Dominance is the attempt to control the environment, or to influence, lead, direct, or control other people.

Exhibition is the need to be the center of attention or to gain notice from others.

Play relates to doing things simply for fun and maintaining a light-hearted and easy-going attitude.

Social recognition is the desire to be held in high esteem by acquaintances and to receive approval and recognition.

Succorance is the need for sympathy, protection, love, advice, and reassurance from other people.

Harmavoidance relates to avoiding activities involving danger and maximizing personal safety.

Autonomy is the desire for lack of confinement or restrictions of any kind.

The Structure of Cognitive Values (Interests)

We interpret cognitive values to be psychological interests that direct, coordinate, and evoke cognitive activities in the pursuit of high-level goals. Such interests can be aroused by a variety of external situations, and once aroused they direct cognition toward processing activities that are consistent with the individual's goals. The hierarchical structure of interests is shown in Figure 6-6, where it can be seen that interests, like needs, are dominated at the third-order by the three value orientations of intrinsic, self, and social.

Second-order Factors

Although the major interest inventories range widely in the number of constructs used to cover the first-order, they converge to the same six constructs at the second-order. The number of first-order constructs range from nine for the Minnesota Vocational Interest Scales to 22 basic scales for the Strong Vocational Interest Schedule and 23 for the Kuder Core Interest Scales. Separate factor analyses of all four of these indicate that they reduce to six factors or clusters (Cole & Hanson, 1971). Furthermore, despite large differences in the way in which these scales cover the terrain at the first order, when fitted to a hexagonal configuration, which was used as the standard, all four scales converged on the same six constructs. The convergence includes interrelationships as well as the number six. This degree of convergence is so rare that it suggests that the six dimensions

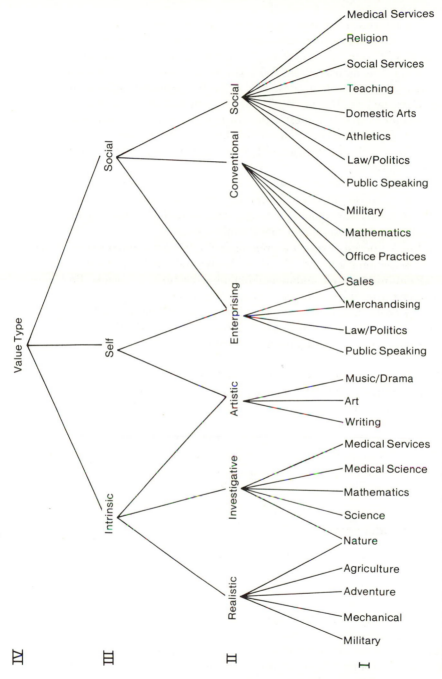

FIGURE 6-6 The hierarchical structure of cognitive values (interests).

151

and their relationships constitute an accurate portrayal of interests at the second order.

The six constructs that constituted the standard for comparison form the Holland Vocational Preference Inventory (Holland, 1965) and are also the core of Holland's (1973) theory of careers. There has been a close liaison between Holland and D. P. Campbell in mapping out the interest domain and, although the six constructs are thoroughly described by Holland, our descriptions are based on D. P. Campbell's (1977, pp. 31–32) briefer summaries.

Realistic expresses interest in the practical and physical and concern for conventional political and economic goals. There is a strong preference for concrete over abstract goals and individuals high on realism show interest in athletic and technical skills.

Investigative individuals usually show a great deal of concern for scientific aspects of the world. The focus is on problem solving, particularly as it might involve abstract and ambiguous problems. Correspondingly, there is a deemphasis of social skills, leadership, and conventional attitudes.

Artistic interests express a preference for free and unstructured situations and for self-expression and creativity. Individuals high on artistic tend to be asocial and introspective and to avoid highly structured problems. Problems are approached from the standpoint of self-expression.

Enterprising interests are directed toward power, status, leadership, and the attainment of organizational goals or economic aims. Individuals high on enterprising tend to be more aggressive and outgoing and also more cheerful and sociable.

Conventional expresses interest in well-ordered environments and varied but systematic activities of a conventional nature. There is an emphasis on being practical, efficient, and orderly. Problematic situations and interpersonal relationships are avoided.

Social interests reflect a concern for the social, humanistic, and religious aspects of life. Emphasis is placed on responsibility as well as on solving problems through feelings and the interpersonal manipulations of others. An important theme involves being helpful to other people and making "the world a better place to live in."

First-order Factors

Despite the large number of factor-analytic investigations in this domain, a set of invariant factors has yet to be identified. Therefore, we have turned to Campbell's identification of 22 basic scales from research on the Strong Vocational Interest Blank. Although D. P. Campbell did not employ factor analysis, he did obtain homogeneous scales by identifying clusters of correlated items. He then inspected these scales and identified them on the basis of content. This procedure resulted in 22 basic interest scales, which we have adopted as the basis for our first-order factors in Figure 6–6. Thus the following descriptions are based on D. P. Campbell's (1977, pp. 37–38) summaries of the relevant items for each of the scales. However, we have provided broader descriptions of the factors than what might be applicable to *only* occupational pursuits. The point is that while we think an individual's work life is probably the most important aspect of interests, interests should also include other aspects of a person's life. Thus, we want to suggest that the interests that have been the focus of empirical research should be conceptualized from a broader perspective than *only* items on a vocational interest inventory.

Military relates to activities involved in warfare or planning for combat situations.

Mechanical involves interest in working with tools and one's hands and, in general, perceptual-motor problem-solving tasks.

Adventure entails taking chances in order to accomplish particular goals or for the excitement of taking risks.

Agriculture expresses concern for activities involved in raising crops, caring for domesticated animals, and outdoor activities.

Nature entails activities related to wildlife and the outdoors.

Science reflects interest in varied aspects of laboratory investigations and scientific inference.

Mathematics involves a focus on mathematical expressions and calculations and on the manipulation of abstract symbols according to rules.

Medical science expresses concern for the scientific basis and activities related to bodily health and care.

Medical service expresses concern for the technical aspects of examining and facilitating bodily health.

Writing reflects interest in written communication and the media that convey the written word.

Art represents interest in the visual communication of ideas and symbols.

Music/drama refers to interest in the performing arts and stage productions of various kinds.

Public speaking describes interest in various aspects of oral communication and related media.

Law/politics involves focusing on governmental institutions and practices.

Merchandizing expresses interest in marketing and distribution of goods and services.

Sales relates to persuasive selling of goods and services to consumers.

Office practices relates to a focus on organization of clerical activities.

Athletics entails a focus on various aspects of recreational sports.

Domestic arts involves concern for the structure and functions of household activities.

Teaching represents interest in instructional activities and the administration of such activities.

Social services reflects concern for social welfare and activities of a charitable nature.

Religious represents concern for religious education and practice.

Functional Significance
of Value Structure

The overall structure of values at the second- and third-order levels is diagramed in Figure 6-7. The cognitive-affective values are shown in the middle of the figure. The intrinsic value orientation relates to interest in the investigation of the "realistic" aspects of the external world (on the cognitive side) and to the need to maintain organized cognitive schemes and achieve meaningful solutions to puzzles presented by the world (on the affective side). Cognitively, the self value orientation relates to interest in the artistic and enterprising aspects of the environment; affectively, it relates to the need for self-protection and self-enhancement or ascendence. Finally, the social value orientation reflects cognitive interest in the conventional aspects of society and in accomplishing social good, and it reflects the affective need to maintain social contact and to be an interdependent part of a network of social relations. In short, the intrinsic value focuses on achieving organized concepts of external reality, self focuses more on self-preservation and the expression of internal feelings, and social is concerned with creating and maintaining the social embeddedness of the individual.

Throughout the first two parts of the book we have alluded to the functional role of values in personality integration and have described their involvement in selecting particular contents of information-processing activities. In the paragraphs below we summarize the role of values in information processing and comment briefly on their possible linkages to cognition and affect. And in Part III of the book we consider the integrative role of values in greater detail.

As we have indicated, interests and needs determine the *content* focus of cognition and affect. They express an individual's commitments as to *what* is worth taking risks for. On the cognitive side, interests provide a basis for selecting (from the myriad of possibilities) those contents that are worth pursuing further. In effect, they propel the individual to regulate particular kinds of uncertainties. And on the affective side, needs express the kinds of goals that are worth taking risks for by determining which classes of external events will be internally arousing. In providing internal needs, values determine what the individual will consider to be noxious or appealing, what should be avoided and what should be searched out, what will be affectively arousing and what will be inhibiting to future exploration. In short, interests direct attention toward particular aspects of the external world; needs determine the role of affect in relating to those aspects of the world.

Linkages to cognition   Because there has not been sufficient research on this question, our theoretical ideas about how interests link to cognitive abilities and to affective traits are speculative at this point. Our hypotheses are illustrated in Figure 6-8. Our theoretical analysis suggests that *intrinsic* interests and needs link with the conceptual cognitive abilities, *self* interests and needs link with symbolizing abilities, and *social* interests and needs link with perceiving abilities. That is, *intrinsic* focuses on the solvable aspects of problems presented by the world.

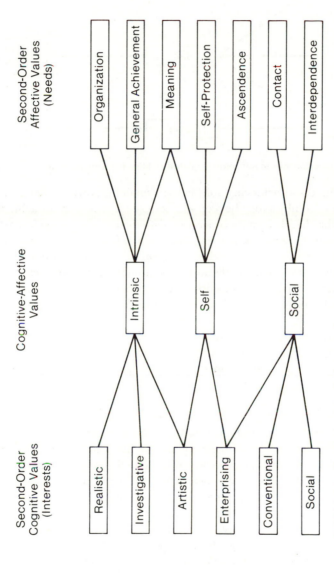

FIGURE 6-7 Overall structure of values showing the hierarchical relations of cognitive-affective values to cognitive and affective values.

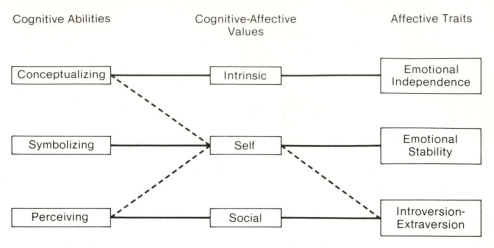

Cognitive Abilities   Cognitive-Affective Values   Affective Traits

FIGURE 6-8   Value linkages to third-order cognitive abilities and affective traits.

Emphasis is given to achieving solutions to unambiguous problems, in which these solutions can ultimately be seen as a series of logical steps or achievements. *Self*, on the other hand, is more concerned with the artistic-symbolic significance of one's emotions in relationship to external events. Finally, the *social* value orientation focuses one's attention on the condition of the surrounding world. That world is largely composed of people and other animals, and of artifacts that are important because of their relationships to other people. (That is, the perceptual world that confronts most individuals is a world composed of humans and their artifacts.)

In Figure 6-8 we have also drawn some secondary linkages between *self* and conceptualizing and perceiving. This was done because we think a *self* value orientation can also give importance to the perceptual and conceptual aspects of one's self.

Linkages to affect   We have also shown the possible linkages of the three value orientations to affect in Figure 6-8. We think *intrinsic* needs link with emotional independence, *self* links to emotional stability, and *social* links to the extraversion pole of introversion–extraversion. The focus that results from an *intrinsic* need has to do with the characteristics and manipulations of the external world without the interfering or coloring aspects of internal arousal. Thus, the ''emotional remoteness'' of the independence trait is implicated. *Self*, on the other hand, links to emotional stability because of the importance given to internal affective reactions in determining what is important about the external world. *Self* also relates secondarily to the introversion pole of introversion–extraversion. This is due primarily to the importance of internal events as sources of arousal. Finally, the *social* need links to affective extraversion, since other people in the external environment provide important sources for internal activation.

7

Life Span Development and the Heredity-environment Issue

Having described the basic structures and processes associated with each of the systems of personality, it is now possible to discuss the developmental changes that occur in each of these systems over the life span as well as the hereditary and environmental bases of the factors. For the sake of organization and simplicity, we present an overall view of the developmental trends at the level of systems and subsystems. The empirical basis for our model is discussed in Powell, Holt, and Royce (1982), and the empirical basis for our claims about the role of heredity is discussed at length in Royce (1979a).

QUANTITATIVE SUBSYSTEM AND SYSTEM CHANGES[1]

An organized view of quantitative changes in the development of individual differences is made possible by focusing on the higher-order factors of each of the six domains of personality. By averaging the curves for the lower-order dimensions (Powell, Holt, & Royce, 1982) in each of the domains, it is possible to develop

[1] We wish to express our appreciation to Peter Holt for his valuable assistance in reviewing the empirical literature on factor development.

hypotheses regarding the overall trends in development. Figure 7-1 presents an overall model of quantitative changes at the higher order for the sensory, motor, cognitive, affective, style, and value systems. In each case bands of varying widths have been drawn to reflect the most likely course of development. The reason for such bands is that the available empirical evidence does not allow us to be more precise. In addition, the *metamorphogenetic* model (see Chapter 3) leads to the expectation that there are varying degrees of hereditary, environmental, and fluctuational restrictions imposed on these developmental functions over the life span. For example, sensory and motor functioning are more genetically determined than styles and values, and styles and values are more subject to unpredictable influences. Thus, the wider the band width of these curves (i.e., as we ascend in Figure 7-1), the greater the degree of uncertainty associated with development.

The third-order factors in both the sensory and motor domains are thought to reach a maximum very early in life and to undergo subsequent decline throughout the rest of life. One implication of this is that individuals become increasingly "cut off" or isolated from the world in very old age (i.e., the period of greatest decline in sensory and motor functions). This implies increasing difficulty for the aging individual to process the information that the surrounding culture presents. It should also become increasingly more difficult to respond according to society's standards whenever those standards are judged against more youthful norms. However, because of the principle of equifinality of compensatory functioning, the changes that accompany aging are not necessarily detrimental to competent functioning. For example, declining sensory and motor skills do not constitute declining intellectual skills. [2]

As illustrated via the next level of Figure 7-1, developmental changes in the higher-order factors of cognition and affect are more complicated than in the cases of the sensory and motor systems. In the case of cognition, perceiving is thought to begin earlier than conceptualizing and symbolizing, to peak earlier (in the twenties), and to decline more rapidly. Conceptualizing is expected to decline slightly during the last portion of the life span. Finally, as can be seen, symbolizing shows an increase over the last portion of the life span. Thus, in the case of cognition, compensatory functioning would seem to be important in life-span development since, as an individual's perceiving and reasoning skills decline, symbolizing skills are on the increase and can, therefore, partially compensate for these losses.

The developmental trends in affect are not so monotonic as in the other systems. There appear to be cyclical functions for the third-order factors of *emotional dependence*, *introversion*, and *emotional instability*. We think this relationship reflects, in part, the problems of growth, independence, and integration that an individual faces during adolescence (at least in Western society) as well as the increasing stress that accompanies the aging process.

---

[2] It should also be noted that there is no reason to expect that older individuals will want to perform complex information processing in the same manner as their youthful counterparts. Goals do evolve and change over the course of an individual's life, most frequently to the benefit of the individual's psychological adaptability.

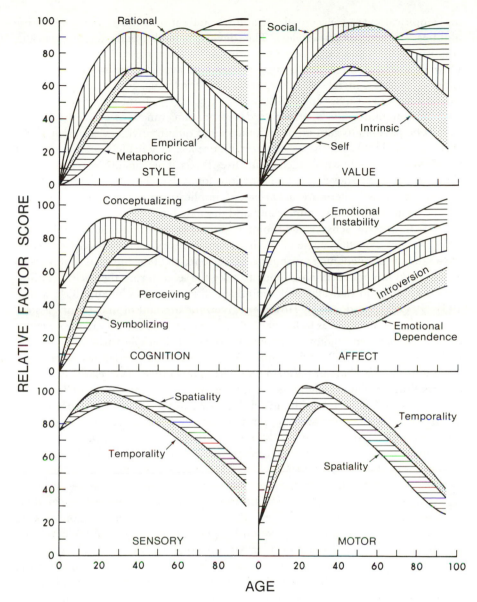

FIGURE 7-1   A general model of quantitative development of each of the third-order factors in the six domains of individuality.

Finally, we come to the integrative level of styles and values. Due to their integrative roles in personality organization, the development of styles and values is strongly influenced by particular cognitive abilities and affective dimensions. For example, because of the functional linkages between styles and abilities, there should be some similarities in the developmental curves for perceiving abilities and empirical styles, conceptualizing abilities and rational styles, and symbolizing abilities and metaphoric styles. The developmental trends for the various cognitive abilities and the cognitive styles are consistent with this hypothesis.[3] However, we do not mean to suggest that changes in cognitive abilities *cause* changes in styles, merely that there should be similarities in the development of functionally linked styles and abilities.

By combining the appropriate developmental functions of Figure 7–1, it should be possible to gain an overall picture of quantitative development at the system level. This has been carried out in Figure 7–2, where life-span functions for the six systems are shown for each of the three levels of personality. As can be seen, there are distinctive developmental functions for each of these levels and for the individual systems. There are a variety of implications relevant to this overall model. Some of these are enumerated and discussed in the following paragraphs.

1. In general, sensory and motor functions change more radically than the other systems over the course of the life span. Sensory functioning is somewhat ahead of motor functioning during the earlier portion of the life span, but it peaks earlier, and motor functioning tends to take the lead during the early twenties. And both drop off radically after the middle thirties (see Lehman, 1951; Miles, 1931, 1933; Welford, 1977). However, given the amount of uncertainty associated with such functions as well as the role that experience can play in the development of sensory and motor functions, there is considerable variability possible within the age range of 20 to 50. Thus, we hypothesize a low relationship between age and sensory and motor performance within this range. The relatively greater general fitness of younger subjects can inflate the relationship with age (Botwinick & Thompson, 1968), as can the general slowing of the decision-making process (Welford, 1978) and increased competition, as in professional sports. Regarding the slowing of decision-making, it should be noted that older age groups have been observed to improve on tasks when time restrictions are lifted, although older subjects generally take longer on such tasks. These various relationships suggest that physical activities requiring split-second timing or extreme physical strength (football, boxing, tennis, etc.) will be performed best by individuals in their twenties or early thirties at the latest. Sports requiring careful decision-making strategy and integrated motor functioning (e.g., golf, billiards, etc.) should be best performed by individuals in their early thirties and later.

2. One of the more interesting implications to come out of this overall analysis is the suggestion that affect is dominant during the first portion of the life span (along with the very last portion), whereas cognition is dominant during most of adulthood. Affect peaks during adolescence and declines until about mid-

---

[3]We also expect the life-span development course of metaphoric styles and symbolizing abilities to be more influenced by affective development than is true of perceiving and conceptualizing. That is, symbolizing cognitive skills and metaphoric styles are more related to affect than are the other abilities and styles. Therefore, the curves for symbolizing and for metaphoric styles have been drawn so as to reflect this hypothesized relationship. As can be seen in Figure 7–1, there is a small rise in these curves during adolescence that corresponds to the peaking of emotionality during this period.

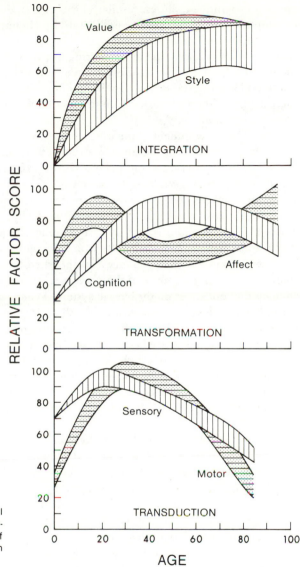

FIGURE 7-2 A general model of quantitative system development, arrived at by averaging of the subsystem functions shown in Figure 7-1.

dle adulthood, when it begins to rise again. Cognition, on the other hand, continues to increase monotonically until the age range of 50 to 60, reaching a peak during the forties and fifties, and then declining slightly over the remainder of the life span. These relationships are consistent with a variety of findings in the life-span developmental literature. For example, young adulthood is cited by older people as being the "happiest" period of their lives (Hurlock, 1958)—a period that corresponds to the decline of various affective functions and the increase in cognitive abilities. Similarly, this corresponds to the period of greatest accomplishment, productivity, and creativity (Lehman, 1951). With the subsequent decline in intelligence that begins in the late fifties and early sixties, and with the other changes that are occurring in personality and society (e.g., retirement), the gradual rise in the affective dimensions over the last portion of adulthood is understandable. Another point to consider in this regard is that with increasing age there is an increase in loss of friends and family and, hence, increasing isolation.

3. The development of the integrative level of personality is potentially the most interesting and important for a detailed understanding of personality integration, but it is also the most clouded and probably the most problematic for empirical research. While styles and values are influenced the most by environmental effects and thus allow for greater variation across individuals and age groups, they also tend to be stable over time (Kelly, 1955; Mischel, 1968, 1969; Troll, 1975). The point is that styles and values are personality integrators, and they are apt to change only when there are changes in the integrative problems an individual faces—such as changes in the surrounding environment, internal changes within one or more of the other systems of personality, or physiological changes that put stress on the overall system. When change has been found to occur in basic values (e.g., as measured by the Allport-Vernon Study of Values; see Hoge & Bender, 1974) identifiable social, cultural, or other aspects of an individual's personality have been found to be responsible for the changes. For example, the rise and fall of religious values, observed longitudinally by Hoge and Bender (1974) over the period from 1933 to 1969, reflected general trends in the culture and the college subculture (e.g., social conservatism that peaked during the McCarthy era of the 1950s, followed by increasing social criticism throughout the 1960s).

It was also found that those individuals who had undergone greater value change from 1955 to 1969 also showed greater anxiety and frustration. Neugarten's comprehensive study of personality (Neugarten and others, 1964) also found that the "content" areas of personality, such as self-image (which we consider to be an output of style and value interaction), were relatively stable over the age range of 40 to 90. Furthermore, Neugarten and her associates found increasing "interiorization" over this same age span, which is consistent with our view that increasing emphasis is placed on self value orientations and that individuals become increasingly introverted. Neugarten concludes, "Older people seem to move toward more eccentric, self-preoccupied positions and to attend increasingly to the control and satisfaction of needs" (1964, p. 190). As a final comment here, periods of rapid social change should give rise to more self-alienation and anomie (Durkheim, 1951). That is, changing social conditions should give rise to changing styles and values, which in turn should give rise to changes in one's integrative self-images.

4. Infancy, childhood, and adolescence represent accommodative phases in development during which time the individual is adapting to the surrounding en-

vironment by making internal changes in cognitive, affective, and other structures. Most of adulthood can be described as being assimilative —a time when internal structures remain fairly stable and the individual adapts by gaining new information about old things or by making changes in the environment. The approach of old age brings on another phase of accommodation; the individual must adapt to a changing internal milieu and sometimes to dramatic changes in the external environment (death of loved ones, retirement, etc.). Emotionality is greater during both the earlier and later accommodative phases; intellectual, cognitive functions dominate over the middle, assimilative phase.

5. Transductional processes, which are most important in the direct acquisition of information about the surrounding environment, are maximally developed during infancy, childhood, and adolescence but then decline over the remainder of the life span. Transformational processes, on the other hand, are organized for maximum flexibility in adapting over the widest possible ecological variation. Within cognition, for example, there is always a subsystem at its peak level; this means compensatory cognitive functioning occurs throughout the life span. And the cyclicity of affect ties in with organismic development—arousal is available during maturationally critical periods (i.e., adolescence and old age). Stylistic integration, although primarily learned, is closely tied to the development of the cognitive system (and secondarily to the affective system), such that style developmental peaks occur after those of cognition. Again, this asynchronous development means that some subsystem will always be available for dealing with ecological invariants. Looking at the other integrative system, value development is more tied to affective development (and secondarily to cognitive development, via interests), and hence, to particular developmental difficulties that an individual faces. That is, values serve to direct attention to the most salient problems an individual faces at any particular phase of life. In adolescence, for example, an important task is to build relationships outside the nuclear family and to take steps toward identifying a mate. Adulthood is a time of providing for oneself and one's family and securing one's resources for the future. Finally, in old age the individual is confronted more with the task of making sense of one's own life and death.

HEREDITARY DIFFERENCES
IN PERSONALITY

In order to deal with the broad range of findings in this area we have evolved a three-category scheme for assessing the strength of the evidence for claims of a hereditary effect. We use the terms *strong*, *moderate*, and *minimal* as arbitrary, qualitative distinctions. For example, a laboratory investigation involving a highly replicable behavioral phenotype (such as avoidance conditioning), highly inbred mouse strains, and a diallel cross-mating design would be evaluated as a strong test of a hereditary effect. Heritability coefficients obtained on human populations, on the other hand, will usually be evaluated as weaker tests of a hereditary effect. However, in spite of the confounding effects of the heritability coefficient, it would also be inappropriate to ignore these findings, particularly when accompanied by careful investigation. Our discussion is presented in terms of the six basic systems.

Sensory and Motor Systems

No research on the sensory system has been directed at factor-gene relationships. On the other hand there is an extensive non-factor-analytic literature. Vision is probably the most thoroughly investigated of the sense modalities. The most obvious example is color blindness, which is due to a recessive, sex-linked gene, and expresses itself in males (Pickford, 1951; Thiessen, 1972). A high degree of genetic determination has also been reported for accommodative convergence and extreme myopia (Hofstetter, 1948; Hofstetter & Rife, 1953), and Eysenck and Prell (1951) report a hereditary effect for performance on the critical flicker-fusion task.

Fuller and Thompson (1960) report that hereditary deafness of various sorts has been identified in humans and dogs. For example, MZ twins are distinguishable from less closely related subjects on tune deafness as measured by the Seashore (auditory) tests. However, it is probable that the most extensive research related to audition has been conducted on audiogenic seizures. This research, which was initiated by Hall (1947), has since proliferated to include a wide range of biochemical findings associated with the seizure phenomenon.

Although taste has not been extensively investigated, the data available on this sensory modality are highly convincing. A case in point is the early finding (Snyder, 1931) that individuals with a specifiable recessive allele are unable to detect PTC (phenylthiocarbomide). Other compounds that are associated with genetically determined taste sensitivities include diphenyl guanedine, brucine, and propylthiouracil. Strain differences in sensitivity to cyclohexamide have also been identified in rat populations (Tobach, Bellin, & Das, 1974).

Although there is evidence of hereditary effects in the remaining sense modalities (olfaction, proprioception, thermal, etc.), the findings are fragmentary. However, the overall impression that emerges from reviewing the research in the sensory domain is that a large genetic component is involved. The most convincing basis for this conclusion is the research on color and taste blindness, hereditary deafness, and susceptibility to audiogenic seizures.

There are also no data on the genetic correlates of factors in the motor system. However, an educated guess is that heredity accounts for a significant portion of motor performance. The basis for such a statement comes from several sources. First, there is the fact that various species of animals can be bred for specifiable motor characteristics. On the basis of the phylogeny of motor behavior, there is little reason to suppose that humans would be much different. Second, it is well established that human stature and weight have a large hereditary component

(Mueller, 1976), and it is obvious that stature and weight at least delimit the development of certain motor abilities. Third, the mildly mentally retarded can be differentiated from normals on a number of motor abilities, many of which share variables with the motor system factors (Eckert & Rarick, 1976; Dobbins, 1976). There is evidence that at least a portion of such differences involve a genetic component. Fourth, Ahe and Perez de Francisco (1974) argue cogently for a significant genetic component of cardiovascular and neurocirculatory individual differences that would obviously delimit the development of endurance factors. Fifth, there are a number of studies demonstrating a significant genetic component in such motor variables as reaction time (Surwillo, 1977), tapping speed (Eysenck & Prell, 1951), pursuit rotor and steadiness (McNemar, 1933; Vandenberg, 1962), and hand speed and dexterity (McNemar, 1933). Although the evidence from any one of these studies is not particularly strong, the combined findings support the contention of a significant genetic component in individual differences involving the motor system (Royce, 1979a, pp.631-32).

Cognitive and Affective Systems

The generally held view is that intelligence is among the most heritable of the various facets of personality. In fact, it has been estimated that 60 percent to 80 percent of the observed variation in general intelligence (as measured by the IQ or its equivalent) is due to genetic variation. Estimates of this kind are typically based on heritability coefficients, twin studies, and global measures of intelligence such as the Binet or the Wechsler. Despite the limitations inherent in human studies (e.g., see Kamin, 1974), the impact of the cumulative evidence—namely, that there is strong evidence for hereditary sources of intellectual variability—is impressive. The data summarized by Erlenmeyer-Kimling & Jarvik (1963) are particularly impressive because of the consistency of the findings over such a wide range of observations (i.e., 56 studies involving 99 groups, covering a period of 50 years of investigation). The data involve correlations between paired individuals of varying degrees of genetic relationships (e.g., unrelated individuals reared apart at one extreme and identical twins reared together or apart at the other extreme). The overall conclusion is that intellectual similarity varies with genetic similarity.

Turning our attention to factorially identified components of intelligence, on the other hand, it is surprising how few investigations have been carried out in the cognitive domain. In fact, direct evidence on the genetic correlates of cognitive factors is limited to the Primary Mental Abilities and a handful of studies. Even so, there is direct evidence of a significant hereditary effect for seven (e.g., Thurstone's Primary Mental Abilities) of the thirty-two factors of the cognitive hierarchy and indirect evidence for three additional cognitive factors (i.e., a total of around 31 percent of the cognitive system). The combination of high replicability and high magnitudes of heritability estimates indicates that a hereditary effect is particularly strong for three factors—verbal comprehension, spatial relations, and word fluency. However, the evidence is only moderately strong in the case of the memorization, perceptual speed, inductive reasoning, and number factors, and the evidence is weakest in the case of the associative memory, associational fluency, and ideational fluency dimensions. (Royce, 1979a, pp. 614, 619)

Research on the hereditary basis of factors in the affective domain is extensive. Furthermore, it includes investigations at all levels of the affective hierarchy.

> There is evidence for a significant hereditary effect for twenty-five of the thirty factors (i.e., 83%) of the affective system. The strong evidence factors include all three third-order factors and six primaries (surgency, fearfulness, escape, territoriality, avoidance, and autonomic balance). The moderate evidence factors include three second-order factors (social inhibition, cortertia, and anxiety) and eight primaries. And the minimal evidence factors include two second-order factors (autonomy and excitability) and three primaries. (Royce, 1979a, p. 627)

Style and Value Systems

> There is hereditary evidence for only one of the factor-identified styles in the style system, the rational or field articulation style. Because of the persistent finding that males are more field independent than females, Goodenough et al. (1977) tested the hypothesis that field articulation is an x chromosome (i.e., sex) linked characteristic. This investigation involved a sample of 67 three-son families. G. R. Goodenough, E. Gandini, E. Olkin, L. Pizzamiglio, D. Thayer, and H. Witkin tested for the possibility of x-chromosome linkage via two markers, red-green color blindness and x_g (a) blood groupings, and they tested for field articulation via nine measures of cognitive style and ability. They found that brothers who are identical in the x_g (a) phenotype are more like each other on the embedded figures and the rod and frame tests than brothers who are different in the x_g (a) phenotype. No significant findings were reported for the other field articulation marker variables, nor did a significant difference appear for brothers who differed in the red-green color blindness marker. This constitutes evidence that an x-chromosome gene contributes to variation on the field articulation, or rational style.
>
> This finding raises many questions in a domain where the notion of a hereditary source of phenotypic variation appears to be highly counterintuitive. Specifically, the view is that it makes good sense to argue that genes contribute to *what* organisms can do (i.e., abilities) but not to *how* they do things (i.e., styles). Furthermore, there are a multitude of questions concerning the nature of Witkin's concept of field articulation. For example, although it was originally called a cognitive style, it has gone through several terminological shifts (e.g., see Witkin, 1974), and it has been identified via both ability and affective markers (Wardell & Royce, 1978). (Royce, 1979a, pp. 627–28)

In general, there has been a conceptual confounding of field articulation as a style construct on the one hand and as a spatiovisual cognitive ability on the other hand. This confounding raises difficult questions concerning exactly what aspect of personality (e.g., style per se, cognitive ability, or affect) is affected by heredity in the Goodenough and associates investigation. The Wardell-Royce (1978) analysis constitutes a significant step in the direction of teasing out the intricate relationships that hold between cognitive-affective styles (such as field articulation, or rational style) and the cognitive and affective systems. These points suggest that the Goodenough et al. hereditary effect is probably due to the cognitive ability of spatial relations.

> To our knowledge there have been no attempts to investigate the hereditary basis of factor-identified values. This includes both the affective (i.e., needs) and the cognitive (i.e., interests) aspects of the value hierarchy.
>
> There have been weak hints that the interest patterns of twins are more similar than sibs (e.g., Helen Koch, 1966) but these studies typically involved psychometrically inadequate measures (e.g., a simple biographical rating sheet rather than the Strong or the Kuder). However, a study by Grotevant, Scarr, and Weinburg (1978) appears to measure up to contemporary standards. However, the genetic aspect merely involves the interest patterns between parents, natural siblings, and adopted siblings. Because of the genetic weakness of such studies, the finding that the interests among parents and their biological offspring are more similar than the interests of nonbiologically related individuals must be regarded as merely suggestive.
>
> Furthermore, even if these findings are confirmed, it will still be necessary to determine just what it is about interest patterns that is gene determined. Our analysis above of the style system strongly suggests that its heritability is traceable to the cognitive and affective dimensions to which it is linked. Because cognitive values (i.e., interests) are also cognitive-affective linkage constructs we think that such heritability claims may also be related to the linked cognitive and affective dimensions. (Royce, 1979a, pp. 630–31)

ENVIRONMENTAL EFFECTS ON PERSONALITY[4]

The available evidence on hereditary and environmental effects on the dimensions of personality does not support the widely held view that environmental effects are greater. In fact, the quantity of research on environmental effects is surprisingly small, and the evidence for such effects is even smaller. Because of the meager evidence, our summary of factor-learning effects is not as clear and informative as our summary of factor-gene effects. We will, therefore, present a sampling of the available findings rather than an exhaustive summary of the empirical literature. We will also offer suggestions for further empirical research.

Factor Involvement in Learning

As described in Chapter 3, we make a distinction between the involvement of *factors in learning* and the *learning of factors*. The latter relates to environmental learning effects on changes in factor scores and structure; the former relates to the

---

[4]We wish to express our appreciation to Mike Katzko and Frederick Bell for their assistance in reviewing the empirical literature on factor learning.

role of existing factors in determining performance on learning tasks. We provide a sampling of research findings in the present section with regard to factor involvement in learning.

Sensory and motor   Overall, there have been relatively few investigations of the role of sensory and motor skills in performance on learning tasks. The work by Fleishman and Hempel (1955) is the most pertinent. As we noted in Chapter 3, in a study of discrimination reaction time, motor and sensory-motor factors (reaction time, rate of movement, etc.) accounted for an increasing proportion of the total variance in performance as trials increased. Correspondingly, there was a decrease in the proportion of variance accounted for by such cognitive factors as spatial relations and verbal abilities. Fleishman and Hempel also found that such factors as visual reaction time consistently discriminated between individuals in terms of their performance across trials. In a subsequent investigation, Fleishman and Fruchter (1960) found that different skills were involved at different stages of Morse code learning. For example, auditory-perceptual factors were involved during the earlier stages, and the cognitive speed of closure factor was involved during the later stages.

Although the Fleishman studies are the only investigations in the sensory-motor domain that are directly focused on factors, there are a wide range of non-factor-analytic studies on the effects of cognitive and affective variables on sensory-motor performance. Hollingsworth (1975) found that anxiety related to performance on a gross motor task. And Ismail, Kephart, and Cowell (1963) found relationships between academic achievement (which presumably involves cognitive abilities) and performance on tests of coordination and static balance. A comprehensive study by T. G. Thurstone (1959) found that low IQ subjects (range 50 to 70) performed poorly on a variety of motor tasks when compared with the normal population.

Cognition and affect   In contrast to the sensory and motor domain, a wide variety of experiments have investigated the role of cognitive and affective factors in learning processes. For example, several studies have shown relationships between factors in Guilford's "structure of intellect" model and learning in academic school situations (e.g., Guilford, 1978). And a large number of recent studies have explored the relationships between cognitive factors and aspects of performance on cognitive information-processing tasks. The work by Snow is exemplary of this research. For example, Snow, Marshalik, and Lohman (1976) found that verbal ability correlated with the slope parameters in a memory search task, which partially replicated similar findings by Hunt, Frost, and Lunneborg (1973). One general point we wish to make regarding this growing literature on the relationships between cognitive abilities and information-processing tasks relates to the role of basic factors. That is, there has been a tendency to rely on available test data (such as SAT scores for college students employed as subjects; e.g., Hunt, Lunneborg, & Lewis, 1975) rather than selecting specific measures that are relatively factor pure and are selected for specific theoretical reasons. We think the latter procedure will be more productive in terms of yielding results that are more clearly interpretable than has been the case in the past.

In the area of affect, a variety of recent studies have related variables such as anxiety to learning tasks; some of this literature has been reviewed by Schaie and Goulet (1977). The general conclusion is that individuals high on trait anxiety tend to perform better on simpler tasks than do individuals of low anxiety. However, the reverse holds for more complex tasks (e.g., Spielberger, 1973), though these relationships may be complicated by intelligence (e.g., Gaudrey & Spielberger, 1970). And in a large number of investigations (H. J. Eysenck, 1976) introversion has been shown to be associated with better performance than has extraversion. Introverts have also been found to exhibit longer habituation rates in orienting responses to visual stimulation (R. M. Stelmach, Bourgeois, Chian, & Pickard, 1979).

Style and value   Field independence (interpreted as rational cognitive style) has been related to better memory in a variety of situations (see M. W. Eysenck, 1977). For example, Davis and Frank (1979) suggest that high information load, greater interference potential, and less subjective organization are factors that account for the poorer memory performance of field-dependent individuals. In a review of field independence, Goodenough (1976) concludes that this style relates to various aspects of memory and learning. Cognitive flexibility, another cognitive style, is also associated with better memory performance, which Cosden, Ellis, and Feeney (1979) attribute to more efficient strategies. Although values have not been as carefully studied in relation to cognitive task performance, Staats, Gross, Guay, and Carlson (1973) have shown that interests (as measured by the Strong test) are related to attitude conditioning. Also, Strong interest scales correlate with academic performance and the PRF needs of autonomy and endurance were related to performance in self-paced instruction (e.g., Lindgren, 1973).

Learning of Factors

There has been very little research on the effects of learning on factor level or factor structure. We are not sure why, but we think it may be attributed in part to the inherent difficulty as well as the possibility that sensory, motor, cognitive, and affective factors are so strongly influenced by heredity (as discussed earlier in this chapter). The ideal experiment would involve testing subjects on a particular battery of tests prior to exposure to selected learning procedures. After learning the subjects would be administered parallel tests that measure the same factors, and factor analyses would then be performed on the pretest and posttest results separately. A comparison of pretest and posttest factor-analytic results would reveal any changes in factor structure as due to learning (in comparison with a control group). Comparisons with norm groups could be used to detect changes in performance levels on the relevant factors. Such an experiment would be difficult, time consuming, and expensive to conduct! Furthermore, in order to detect changes in the factor level or factor structure, one would have to have very powerful learning experiences—that is, given the relatively important role of heredity.

A few of the available studies will be cursorily described. In the motor area it is surprising that physical fitness programs or special physical education classes have little effect on motor factors. However, large changes have been found showing the influence of affective factors on intellectual functioning (Ismail & Young, 1976; Oliver, 1958). A variety of studies attempting to reduce an individual's anxiety have found that, while a variety of procedures reduce *state* anxiety, they fail to produce changes in *trait* anxiety (e.g., Stoulenmire, 1972). And several investigators (e.g., Burger & Blackman, 1976; Butterfield, Warbold, & Belmont, 1973) report evidence of changes in cognitive memory span among retarded people by teaching them organizational strategies. A variety of social or background variables including social background (Gunderson, 1969), ethnic background (Bachman, Lynch, & Loeding, 1979), recalled early parent-child relations (Byers, Forrest, & Zaccaria, 1968), and social class (Pettit, Pettit, & Welhowitz, 1974) have been found to be related to needs or interests.

In conclusion, we wish to emphasize again that research on the effects of learning on factors and factor structure is very meager. This represents a very important area for future empirical research, and we think the models presented in Chapter 3 can serve as important schema for organizing such efforts.

HEREDITY, ENVIRONMENT, AND INDIVIDUALITY

What conclusions can be drawn concerning the relative roles of heredity and environment as sources of psychological variation? On the basis of the available empirical evidence plus evolutionary theory, the following conclusions seem to be justified:

1. The information processing of the sensory and motor transductive systems occurs at the interface between the organism and the environment and is, therefore, critical to species survival. That is, organismic survival is presumed to be impossible without an effective input-output structure (J. G. Miller, 1978), meaning that species with ineffective input and output transducers are weeded out via natural selection. The point is that, on theoretical grounds, the sensory and motor systems, which are the most biologically primitive of the six systems, should be more influenced by heredity than environment. Furthermore, the empirical evidence is consistent with this view. In short, the sensory and motor systems are heredity-dominant systems, meaning that hereditary influences are greater than environmental influences in the functioning of these two systems.

2. The two transformation systems, cognition and affect, are partially

heredity-dominant systems. This means that although heredity is more important than environment, it is not as important as in a heredity-dominant system—perhaps in the neighborhood of 60 percent of the variance is attributable to heredity and the remainder is attributable to environment. How does this conform with the evolutionary-adaptive functioning of the organism? As information transformers, cognition and affect take the transduced information provided by the sensory system and change it into some other psychologically meaningful form, such as cognitions (i.e., percepts, concepts, and symbols) and affects (i.e., arousal and emotions). The major role of the cognitive system is to interpret or understand the environment by identifying environmental invariants—that is, perceptual, conceptual, and symbolic invariants. Since such invariants constitute human constructions of "the way things are," they are also critical components of world view. The affective system plays a similar role, but the transformational process is focused on preparing the organism for action via a variety of arousal mechanisms. The affective system is organized for coping with the daily stresses of life as well as providing a basis for life style. In short, the argument is that the cognitive and affective systems have been evolutionarily selected for adaptive flexibility. Biological flexibility implies the capacity to adapt to the widest possible range of ecologies. Thus, such reactions as fixed action patterns and rigid perceptions would be inconsistent with optimizing flexibility. The implication is that behavior dependent on the cognitive and affective systems would be too rigid in the case of extreme genetic determination, too flexible in the case of extreme environmental determination, but optimally flexible in the case of nearly equivalent genetic-environment determination.

3. We hypothesize that the functioning of the style and value systems is environment-dominant. This means that environment is more important than heredity in such cases. Why should this be the case? As discussed in Chapter 6, these two systems are primarily concerned with integration—that is, the coordination and synthesis of information and personality. However, integration clearly requires prior informational inputs and transformations. But it seems equally clear that there will be a wide range of possible syntheses, depending on what information has been processed, how it has been transformed, and the particular styles and values that have guided the synthesizing process. The point is that nature has not evolved a genetic-evolutionary mechanism for transmitting informational content (an acquired characteristic) from one generation to the next. Thus, biological evolution appears to be irrelevant in the case of styles and values. But cultural evolution is critical, for cultural evolution concerns those styles and values that have been institutionalized. The institutionalization of styles and values refers to "how" and "what" commitments that were so adaptive in a given time and place that it was thought they might be equally adaptive in another time and place. Thus, styles and values are passed on from one generation to the next via the culture. Furthermore, they constitute the major building blocks for such molar behavioral complexities as world view, life style, and self-image. In short,

styles and values are relevant to the big questions of existence—the nature of reality, the key to one's self-identity, and the way in which we should live our daily lives. Psychological questions of this magnitude are clearly beyond the realm of genes. The genes have enough burden to bear in accounting for variations in the sensory, motor, cognitive, and affective systems. (Royce, 1979a, pp. 632–35)

INTEGRATIVE PROCESSES

Given the combination of individual differences, the structure, processes, and development of personality systems, and the complex interactions among these systems, individuality theory provides a rich framework for dealing with the more molar and complex aspects of human personality. This is illustrated in the next few chapters, wherein we attempt to "put humpty-dumpty together again." The concepts introduced thus far enable us to deal with the higher-level processes that can be characterized as constituting the core of integrative personality. Thus, after we present the basic principles of system interactions in Chapter 8, we subsequently demonstrate how the six systems interact to produce the major integrative constructions of belief system, emotion, world view, life style, self-image, and personal meaning.

8

Systems Interactions, and Individual Differences in Belief Systems and Emotion

It is important to emphasize at the outset that we think complex functioning always involves interactions among the six basic systems. This is illustrated by Figures 5–3 and 5–6 in our chapter on the cognitive and affective systems. The general point is that whenever any one of the six systems is attempting to attain a goal, all the others also have their input into the problem. For example, the goal of cognition is to discover ecological invariants, and the process of striving for this goal is influenced at each stage by affect, style, value, and sensory inputs, and even feedback relations with the motor system. As a further example of the interdependence among the various systems, our discussion of the motor system in Chapter 4 emphasized the interacting relations among sensory, cognition, affect, and motor processes. In the present chapter we present the basic aspects of system interactions and integrations and consider belief systems and emotions as the outcomes of such system interactions.

BASIC ASPECTS OF SYSTEM INTERACTIONS

Our overall figure (Figure 1–1) of integrative personality includes interactions among the component systems. For example, there are direct inputs from the cognitive system to the total system and direct outputs from the total system to the affective system. Other interactions include the mutual relationships between cognition and affect, and between cognition and values, and a one-way linkage between cognition and motor. In other words, there is considerable variety in the way the six systems interact with each other. One way of characterizing such interactions is in terms of *cooperative functioning*, by which we mean simultaneous activation of two or more systems toward a common goal. Although such cooperation varies with task requirements, we think cooperation among systems also reflects the natural organization of mental processes.

Some system interrelations can be described as *highly cooperative*, whereas others are best described as *weakly cooperative*. For example, interactions among systems on the same level reflect highly cooperative relationships. These interactions include style and value, cognition and affect, and sensory and motor. We attribute this high degree of cooperation in the interaction of the paired systems to serving a common function—integration, transformation, or transduction, respectively. And since style and value have been hypothesized to have an integrative role, there should be highly cooperative relations involved in all paired combinations of style or value and cognition or affect. For the remaining interactive combinations, the weakest cooperation occurs between those system pairs that are the most disparate in their functioning—namely, combinations involving style or value and sensory or motor. There are also moderate levels of cooperation reflected in the combinations of sensory-cognitive, sensory-affective, cognitive-motor, and affective-motor.

The various pairwise comparisons among all six systems are shown in Table 8–1. The various entries in the table refer to the constructive outputs of system interactions, except for the main diagonal, which refers to the output of a given system independent of the outputs of the other systems.

TABLE 8-1   System Interactions and Integrations

	SENSORY	MOTOR	COGNITION	AFFECT	STYLE	VALUE
Sensory	Transduced information					
Motor	Sensory motor integration	Motor programs				
Cognition	Meaningful information	Motor schema	Environmental invariants			
Affect	Feelings	Affect-laden movement	Emotion	Internal arousal		
Style	Sensory style	Motor style	World view	Affective style	Modes of processing	
Value	Value-laden information	Value-laden movement	Belief system	Life style	Self-image	Needs and interests

Consider the main diagonal of Table 8-1. As discussed in Chapter 4, the outputs of sensory and motor are transduced patterns of information and motor programs respectively. On the input side of things, very complex space-time events in the environment are transduced into sensory information (sights, sounds, tastes, smells, etc.). On the output side, complex ideas about events in the environment are translated into complex movements (tapping, writing, dancing, singing, etc.) through space and time. Cognition and affect are oriented toward the construction of environmental invariants and the creation of internal arousal, as we discussed in Chapter 5. Cognitions are interpretations of the surrounding environment in the form of percepts, concepts, and symbols. Affect relates to preparing individuals for action by evoking processes related to internal arousal. Finally, style and value integrate information by determining the "how" and "what" of information processing. Styles express preferences for ways of doing or feeling about things. Values, on the other hand, select what is important to be uncertain about or what is worth taking risks for. In short, styles and values are involved in determining important aspects of personal meaning for individuals.

The pairwise system interaction effects shown in the off-diagonal entries of Table 8-1 describe constructions of varying degrees of psychological importance. For example, entries toward the bottom right refer to outputs that are relatively important in individuals' attempts to create personal meaning. But entries toward the left side tend to reflect lower-level sensory and motor activities. There are a variety of interactive combinations in Table 8-1 in which there seems to be a *suffusion* of activities (e.g., sensory-value, motor-value, and affect-motor). Also, there are a variety of *dominance* effects involving the style system in the sensory-style, motor-style, cognitive-style, and affect-style interactions where the style system assumes a dominant, integrative role. The remaining nine combinations all reflect a high degree of *fused* output and come closer to the core aspects of integrative personality. Sensory-motor interaction has already been described in Chapter 4, and the remaining chapters of Part III will deal with interactions involving style, value, cognition, and affect.

Subsystem Alignments

Table 8-2 shows the third-order dimensions for each of the six systems aligned in terms of the strongest intersystem interactions. Thus, sensory and motor spatiality are aligned with introversion–extraversion, social orientation, and empiricism. In the middle row sensory and motor temporality are aligned with conceptualizing, emotional independence, intrinsic, and rationalism. And sensory-motor temporality-spatiality is aligned with symbolizing, emotional stability, self-orientation, and metaphorism.

The alignments of the subsystems shown in Table 8-2 are based primarily on our analysis of high-level interactions, which are discussed throughout the remaining chapters. The most obvious consistencies in alignment are the temporality and spatiality dimensions of both the sensory and motor systems. The cogni-

TABLE 8-2   Cross-System Alignment of Third-Order Dimensions

	SENSORY	COGNITION	AFFECT	VALUE	STYLE	MOTOR
Third-order Factors	Spatiality	Perceiving	Introversion–extraversion	Social	Empiricism	Spatiality
	Temporality	Conceptualizing	Emotional independence	Intrinsic	Rationalism	Temporality
	Temporality-spatiality	Symbolizing	Emotional stability	Self	Metaphorism	Temporality-spatiality

tive and style dimensions also constitute tight alignments—symbolizing paired with metaphorism, conceptualizing with rationalism, and perceiving with empiricism. Furthermore, the alignment of spatiality with perceiving and empiricism, temporality with conceptualizing and with rationalism, and temporality-spatiality with symbolizing and metaphorism are also conceptually consistent. The remaining alignments, involving the affective and value domains, are less clear. Nevertheless, the rationale is that emotional independence and intrinsic value are consistent with conceptualizing-rationalism in the middle row, and that introversion–extraversion and social orientation are critically tuned in to perceiving and empiricism. The remaining entries are probably the weakest—namely, the introversion–extraversion and self value aligning with symbolizing and metaphorism.

What can account for this alignment of third-order dimensions? In a subsequent chapter (Chapter 11) on personality type we put forward the hypothesis that each of the three rows of Table 8-2 constitutes a suprasystem personality type, characterized by the six third-order dimensions. The rationale is that each of these alignments constitutes a basic psychological adaptation to the demands of the environment.

In general, we think cooperative functioning among various systems occurs primarily at the subsystem and system levels rather than at lower levels. The interactions between style and cognition provide an example of a high degree of cooperative functioning. Figure 8-1 provides an overview of the cross-system linkages. The strongest linkages are evident at the third-order (see dotted lines in Figure 8-1); we will provide a more detailed discussion of the significance of these linkages in Chapter 9. The conceptual linkages are striking—they involve the pairing of conceptualizing abilities with rational style, perceiving abilities with empirical style, and symbolizing abilities with metaphoric style. The theoretical basis for these relationships is extensive and convincing (e.g., see Royce, 1974, 1975; Royce, Coward, Egan, Kessel, & Mos, 1978) and there is some empirical evidence as well (e.g., Royce & Mos, 1980).

The most convincing of the second-order interactions involves three styles—cognitive complexity, analytic versus relational, and abstract versus concrete—and the second-order cognitive reasoning factor. The implication is that these three rational styles are more critically involved in the formation and use of concepts than other cognitive styles. Two other second-order linkages involve the

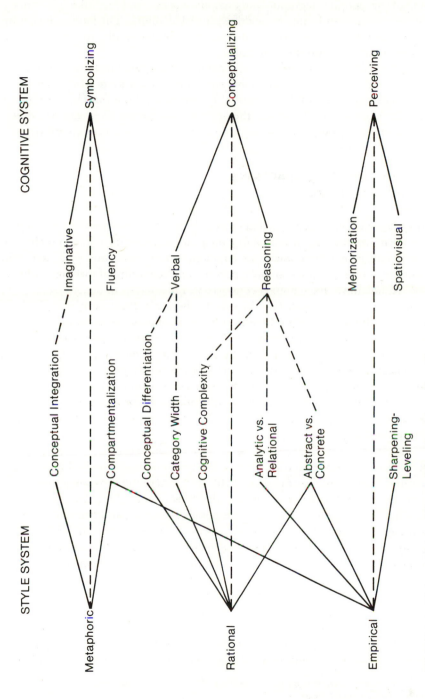

FIGURE 8-1 Higher-order interactions between the style and cognitive systems.

pairing of conceptual integration and imaginativeness, and the linking of conceptual differentiation and category width with verbal ability. The latter linkages involve making fine-grained verbal-conceptual distinctions, and the former involves the ability to provide holistic syntheses.

In the following sections of this chapter we illustrate our basic approach to system interactions via two interactive constructs: belief systems and emotion. Our analysis of the first of these is not well developed; the second has been more thoroughly worked out. Together, they provide comprehensive examples of our approach to dealing with the problem of system interactions and integrations.

COGNITION-VALUE INTERACTIONS
AND BELIEF SYSTEMS

The psychological constructions that emerge from system interactions are important in the understanding of personality integration since they relate to such complex and integrative phenomena as emotion, world view, life style, and self-concept. Such interactions also make possible an accounting of ideology or belief system. Although we have not yet conducted a full analysis of belief systems, our preliminary analysis suggests that they can be viewed as the output of the interaction between the cognitive and value systems.[1] That is, values imply commitment, and cognition produces ideas. Beliefs can be viewed as "valued cognitions," or cognitions that are retained because of their "meaning" potential (i.e., significance) rather than their truth. Such cognitions can be retained and taught by an entire culture or civilization for generations or even an "epoch" or a "period" of history, if sufficiently valued. While *knowledge* is arrived at by applying specific truth criteria (Chapter 9), *beliefs* are arrived at by selecting ideas that are need-satisfying.

Although a great variety of belief systems are possible, the most easily describable ones arise from the possible alignments of cognition and value at the third-order. These are illustrated via Table 8-3, where the three major cognitive subsystems are indicated by the rows and the three major value subsystems are indicated by the columns. There are nine possible pairings and consequent belief systems, as summarized by the cells of Table 8-3. Proceeding from left to right in the table, the first and third columns express ideas about ultimate relationships between the individual and society, while the middle column relates to the "ideal" society. All of the entries in the first column give society a priority over the individual in one way or another: *pragmatism* focuses on social structures that work; *socialism* is focused on the ideal society, whether it works or not; and *statism* places so much value on society that the individual may be sacrificed if necessary. In contrast, all the entries in the third column describe belief systems that place the individual over society. *Anarchism* is the belief that, no matter what else, individual

---

[1]Belief systems and ideologies differ in terms of the motor component; that is, ideologies are "action-oriented" belief systems.

TABLE 8–3 The Belief Systems Resulting from the Major Cognition-value Linkages

COGNITIVE ABILITIES	VALUES		
	SOCIAL	INTRINSIC	SELF
Perceiving	Pragmatism (whatever works is desirable)	Scientism (factually derived ideas are more important than any others)	Anarchism (the individual has priority over everything else)
Conceptualizing	Socialism (individual needs can be satisfied, given the right circumstances)	Idealism (what can be conceived can be achieved)	Utopianism (there are ways in which society and individual can achieve ultimate integration)
Symbolizing	Statism (institutionalized beliefs about societal symbols are most important)	Personalism (individual achievement occurs in the context of societal symbols)	Humanism (individual human dignity is of supreme importance)

needs should rule supreme; *utopianism* sets up an impossible ideal for individual and society; and *humanism* claims that societies should exist to advance the human condition. Finally, entries in the middle column are generally more abstract and not as related to the issue of individual versus society. *Scientism*, which is very prominent in twentieth-century Western civilization, expresses the belief that the only meaningful interpretation of the "way things are" is what can be experienced via the senses. *Idealism* puts emphasis on social structures that are possible only in the context of a logically coherent system. *Personalism* maintains that societal symbols have personal reference to how individuals should lead their lives.

As suggested by the alignments described in Table 8–2 and our subsequent discussion, the closest alignments should occur between perceiving and social, conceptual and intrinsic, and symbolizing and self. Thus, the main diagonal of Table 8–3 describes belief systems that are the most "cohesive" and have a more central role in adaptation.

COGNITION–AFFECT INTERACTION AND EMOTION[2]

A general understanding of the relationships between cognition and affect is central to a variety of psychological phenomena, but surprisingly little has been written on this subject. One of the major reasons for this is that research on "thought" and "feeling" have progressed relatively independently of each other. This situation has made progress difficult in the empirical and theoretical study of emotion. Another difficulty here is sheer complexity, since emotion simultaneously involves subjective thoughts and feelings, physiological reactions, behavior, and individual differences. What seems to be required is an approach that considers all facets of emotional phenomena. While our approach does not deal sufficiently with the physiological aspects, we do offer an analysis of the relevant cognitive-affective interaction effects, and, of course, we deal explicitly with individual differences.

Although it seems reasonable to initiate theoretical investigation with a definition of the phenomenon under consideration, in the case of "emotion" there simply is no concensus as to what it should denote. Plutchik (1962), for example, lists 21 definitions, and Strongman (1978) concludes that "emotion defies definition." Because of ignorance in this domain, the best we can hope to achieve at this stage is a satisfactory *working* definition of emotion. From our perspective such a definition should allude to: (1) all the relevant aspects of emotion; (2) the differentiation of emotions, both psychologically and physiologically; and (3) the multidimensional and multisystemic aspects of personality. Thus, we begin with the following working definition: *Emotions are differentially patterned states of cognition and affect that involve specifiable deviations from the steady state of the total psychological and physiological system* (revised from Royce & Diamond, 1980, p. 267).

[2]For a more thorough discussion of our model of emotion, see Royce and Diamond (1980). We wish to acknowledge Steve Diamond's important contribution to our model of emotion.

Cognition-affect Interaction

The hypothesized role of cognition is in processing the experiential and behavioral aspects of emotion. Affect, on the other hand, is thought to share in the determination of behavioral outputs as well as to be directly involved in the physiological manifestations of emotion. For example, consider anxiety as one form of emotional reaction. The relevant affective components are part of the emotional stability subsystem (see Figure 5–4). They include a second-order anxiety factor, and autonomic balance, ergic tension, fear, and guilt components at the first order. All of these factors relate to limbic arousal, since all are dominated by emotional stability at the third order. Furthermore, arousal will evoke a variety of behavioral processes. Cognitive evaluation would presumably involve the entire cognitive system, but symbolizing and perceiving seem to carry more weight than conceptualizing. During an aroused state of anxiety, the relevant cognitive processes will be involved in interpreting the internal and external events. Although we cannot be certain about the details, especially temporal ones, both cognitive and affective processes interact during such an emotional state.

Since knowledge of the details of emotive states is so limited, it is not possible to provide a moment-to-moment account of the state of the cognitive and affective systems. However, an analysis for larger time frames is possible, as shown in Table 8–4. An emotional state is viewed as composed of three phases—the critical phase, or the time span of the emotion per se, and the time spans before and after the critical phase. Of course, each of these time periods will vary, depending on the emotion in question and its intensity, chronic character, etc.

The first row indicates the interpretive role of the cognitive system before, during, and after the critical period. The second row summarizes the coping role of the affective system, which involves alerting the organism during the precritical phase; reaching a critical arousal level during the second phase; and recovering from arousal peak during the third phase. The interaction between the two systems is indicated in the third row. The key to this interaction is shown in the middle cell, the critical phase, which refers to the "fused" subjective experience or reaction. This is the time

TABLE 8–4   Cognition-affect Activation for Three Phases of an Emotional State (Royce & Diamond, 1980)

SYSTEMS ACTIVATED	PHASES OF AN EMOTIONAL STATE		
	PRECRITICAL PHASE	CRITICAL PHASE	POSTCRITICAL PHASE
Cognition	Interpretation of the situation	The quality of the experience/reaction	Evaluation of the experience/reaction
Affect	Alerting signal	Intensity of the experience/reaction	Preservation or recovery of normal arousal level
Cognition-affect interaction	Readiness to react	Subjective experience/reaction	Meaning analysis (assimilation/accommodation)

period which is most clearly describable as the emotional state, whether it be anger, fear, or joy. (Royce & Diamond, 1980, p. 285)

There is also an aspect that is phenomenological or experiential in nature. That is, the meaning for the individual is determined as a postcritical event that is manifested via either assimilating the emotive sequence or rendering an appropriate accommodation. Similarly, the organismic readiness to react to the situation at hand is indicated in the precritical phase.

The dimensional aspect of individuality theory allows us to probe more deeply into the issue of emotional states. More specifically, different subsets and weights of cognitive and affective factors combine to account for different emotional states of the organism. The details of system and dimensional activation can be illustrated via Figure 8–2, which describes reactions in a fear-provoking situation (e.g., the sudden appearance of a dangerous animal or a person with a machine gun).

The hierarchical-structural-functional relationships of each of the four relevant subsystems (i.e., perceiving, conceptualizing, introversion–extraversion, and emotional stability) are indicated via solid connecting lines. Third-order factors are represented via squares, second-order factors are indicated by rectangles, and the first-order factors are indicated by the oval figures. Sequencing is indicated via numbers and broken-line connections. The cognitive system is shown on the left side of the diagram and the affective system is shown on the right.

The first step (see the upper left corner of Figure 8–2) involves the perception of the fear provoking stimulus. This involves activation of the spatio-visual factor at the second-order and spatial scanning and visualization of the stimulus at the first-order. Activation of the spatio-visual factor subsequently leads to activation of memorization processes (step 2). This is followed by a general mental alertness via the introversion–extraversion dimension (step 3) and the rapid elicitation of associations to the stimulus situation through associative memory and conditionability factors (step 4). The critical associations are triggered via affective reaction through the emotional stability factor, leading ultimately to activation of the avoidance, escape, and fearfulness components (step 5). Activation of associative memory also leads to simultaneous activation of conceptualizing, in particular the induction factor, which involves extracting the essentials of the situation (step 6). It should be noted that cognitive processing at this point involves a continual interaction between the inductive and deductive components (step 7), and that there is also a continual interaction between conceptualizing and emotional stability (step 8). The remaining sequence involves coding by the verbal and verbal comprehension factors (step 9), and subsequent routing to associative memory (step 10), thereby providing a loop to the reactivation of the two arousal systems (via emotional stability and the conditionability component of introversion–extraversion).[3] (Royce & Diamond, 1980, pp. 286–88)

The major inadequacy of Figure 8–2 lies in the inability to spell out the details of timing. However, we have provided a crude first step toward resolving this problem by indicating (on the left margin of Figure 8–2) the three time periods specified in Table 8–4. Thus, the information processing that is critical for Phase One can be seen to involve the factor components of the perceiving and introversion–extraversion

[3]It should be emphasized that the memorization factors under discussion are viewed as reconstructive *processes* of cognition rather than *storage* concepts (see Chapter 5).

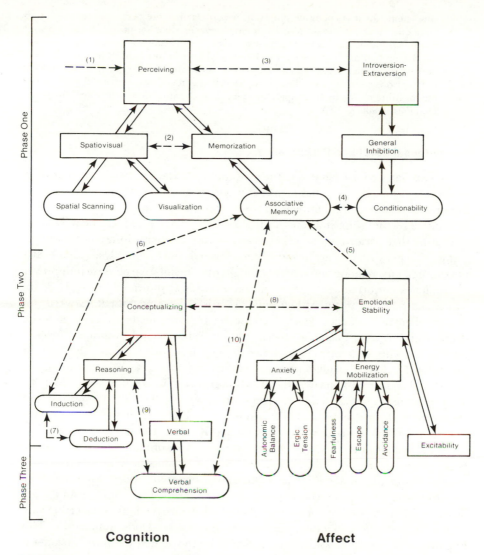

Cognition   **Affect**

FIGURE 8-2 Information flow diagram showing cognitive and affective coactivation in a fear-arousing situation. (From Royce & Diamond, 1980)

subhierarchies. The key processing during this precritical phase has to do with cognitive interpretation (via perception) combined with an affective alert (via introversion–extraversion). On the other hand, it is the coactivation of the conceptualizing and emotional stability subsystems that constitutes the key processing during Phase Two (see the middle segment of Figure 8–2), the critical phase. Affective intensity occurs via the massive effects of limbic arousal (i.e., via the emotional stability subsystem), and the subjective experience of fear is a cognitive output of perceptual-conceptual-memorial interaction. The final phase (postcritical or Phase Three; see the bottom segment of Figure 8–2) primarily involves the conceptualizing subsystem, for it is cognitive reflection which clarifies the personal meaning of an emotional state. It should also be noted, however, that secondary reactivation of emotional stability and introversion–extraversion can occur via the loop between verbal comprehension and associative memory. This can also lead to further reactivation of conceptualizing. Feedback loops of this type are necessary in order to allow for the vicarious recurrence of Phase Two, as well as extended cognitive reevaluations of the meaning of an emotive experience and their eventual desensitization. (Royce & Diamond, 1980, p. 289)

Arousal Level and Performance

Thus far we have alluded to the concept of arousal level as being important in the complex interactions between cognition and affect. We think there are three important relationships between arousal and performance. First there is a facilitative relationship, indicated in Figure 8–3a. This is an incremental curve, indicating that performance level increases with increments in arousal level, increments in performance are negatively accelerated, and eventually asymptote at a maximum. This relationship may be thought of as facilitative because it improves or facilitates performance. The second relationship is indicated in Figure 8–3b, which is a reflected image of Figure 8–3a. It is a decremental curve, which indicates that performance level decreases with increments in arousal level, decrements in performance are positively accelerated, and eventually reach a minimum. This decremental relationship may be thought of as inhibitory or disruptive because it results in a lower performance level. Combining these two curves yields the well-known Yerkes-Dodson inverted-U function shown in 8–3c. This relationship indicates that increments in arousal will result in improved performance levels up to a specifiable maximum, beyond which further increments in arousal will result in performance decrements (Royce & Diamond, 1980, p. 276).

Individual differences in emotion are seen as a product of the interaction between the cognitive and affective systems. And since arousability is also a critical aspect of our theory, the relationships between arousal level and both cognitive and affective functioning is of special interest. Proceeding from the top down in Figure 5–4 we hypothesize that the entire introversion–extraversion subsystem follows the facilitative segment of the Yerkes-Dodson function. This hypothesis is consistent with the long-established view that the introversion–extraversion dimension and arousal level covary. What is new in our hypothesis is the extension of this relationship to the entire introversion-extraversion subhierarchy. A similar analysis of emotional stability leads to the hypothesis that this subsystem follows the disruptive segment of the Yerkes-Dodson relationship (see Figure 8–3b). This means that emotional stability declines as arousal level increases. It also means that all the other dimensions of the emotional stability subhierarchy covary in a disruptive fashion with arousal level.

There is less firm evidence concerning the physiological basis of emotional independence than there is for either of the other third-order dimensions of affect. Royce and Diamond (1980) suggest that emotional independence is related to the

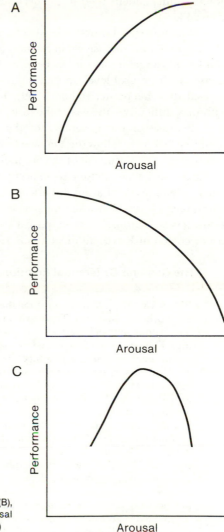

FIGURE 8-3 The incremental (A), decremental (B), and inverted-U (C) relationships between arousal and performance. (From Royce & Diamond, 1980)

above arousal effects in an indirect manner. By introducing Routtenberg's (1968) idea that the two arousal systems are mutually inhibitory, they interpret the independence factor as inversely representing the strength of this inhibitory tendency. This means that the domination of either reticular or limbic arousal, which is typical of low-independence subjects, does not hold for high-independence subjects. It implies, for example, that, with high independence, a high level of limbic arousal is compatible with either a high or a low level of reticular arousal. In short, Royce and Diamond suggest that persons who are emotionally dependent are subject to the standard arousal effects indicated above, whereas persons who are emotionally independent tend to intellectualize about their emotions, regardless of arousal level.

The inverted-U, or Yerkes-Dodson, relationship has been experimentally investigated most intensively in relation to cognitive task performance. In studies of a broad range of tasks it has been uniformly found that task performance increases with arousal level up to a point and decreases with further elevation of arousal after that point (Malmo, 1959). The placement of the optimal point varies with task difficulty—the easier the task, the higher the optimal arousal level.

Because of the generality of the empirical findings, we expect all the cognitive factors to follow the Yerkes-Dodson curve. We would expect differences, however, in the placement of the optimal point for different factors. Considering the three third-order factors, we expect performance on perceiving tasks to be optimal at high levels of arousal, performance on conceptual tasks to be optimal at intermediate levels of arousal, and performance on symbolizing tasks to be optimal at low levels of arousal. The empirical and theoretical bases for these conjectures are discussed in Royce and Diamond (1980, pp. 281–84).

The Case for Differential Emotions

Plutchik (1962; 1980) accounts for the full range of emotions via combinations of eight primary emotions. These primaries are indicated in the first column of Table 8–5. Although the primary emotions are initially defined in terms of subjective feelings, they are also differentiated in terms of specifiable behavior patterns as well as evolutionary-adaptive significance. Fear, for example, is described introspectively as "unpleasant, tense, excited, and constricted" (Plutchik, 1962, p. 45), behaviorally in terms of escape or withdrawal, and functionally in terms of fulfilling a protective role. In Plutchik's view emotions function in terms of organismic survival in one way or another—directly in the case of the protective–destructive emotions of fear and anger, and less directly for the remaining emotions.

Although we see a compatibility between Plutchik's views and individuality theory, it should be noted that he does not consider physiology, and his treatment of cognition is implicit rather than explicit. Furthermore, Plutchik was not primarily concerned with individual differences. Because of the apparent complementarity, however, we [have explored] the possibility of combining the Plutchik model with the individuality model, as is shown in Table 8–5. The link-up between the two models is provided via the eight emotions listed in the first column. Cognitive and affective subsystem involvements, along with their correlated arousal systems, are indicated in the columns to the right. . . .

We begin with the fear/anger and expectancy/surprise emotions. According to the first two rows of Table 8–5, fear and anger states are mediated via the emotional stability subsystem, and expectancy and surprise states are mediated via the introversion–extraversion subsystem. While these two cases are similar in that they involve specifiable subsets of affective dimensions, the dimensions which comprise the relevant sets are essentially non-overlapping (see Figure 5-4).[4] [That is,] emotional stability includes energy mobilization, anxiety, and excitability at the secondary

[4]There is actually some overlap due to secondary relationships not shown in Figure 5-4. Thus, there would be overlap whenever a lower-order factor loads on two or more higher-order factors (e.g., see the dominance and trust factors in Figure 5-4).

TABLE 8-5   The Individuality Model in Terms of Plutchik's Eight Primary Emotions (from Royce & Diamond, 1980)

PLUTCHIK'S EMOTIONS	INDIVIDUALITY MODEL		
	AFFECTIVE SUBSYSTEM	AROUSAL SUBSYSTEM	COGNITIVE SUBSYSTEM
Fear/anger	Emotional stability	Limbic	Symbolizing/perceiving
Expectancy/ surprise	Introversion– extraversion	Reticular	Perceiving/symbolizing
Joy/sadness	Emotional dependence/ introversion– extraversion	Reticular	Conceptualizing/ perceiving
Acceptance/disgust	Emotional independence/ emotional stability	Limbic	Conceptualizing/ symbolizing

level, and such primaries as escape, avoidance, autonomic balance, ergic tension, and fearfulness. [And] introversion–extraversion, on the other hand, subsumes general and social inhibition at the second order, and such first-order factors as gregariousness, dominance, surgency, and affectothymia. But the recruitment of these affective subsystems also implies activation of the limbic system in the case of the fear/anger emotions, and activation of the reticular system in the case of the expectancy/surprise emotions. While this state of affairs involves arousal in both cases, it should be clear that the accompanying physiological patterns are quite different in the two cases. In the fear/anger case the physiological pattern is one of massive energy mobilization via the autonomic and hormone systems, whereas the expectancy/surprise emotions imply a generally aroused or alert state of the cerebral cortex via reticular arousal.

[Turning to the last column of Table 8-5,] the entries indicate still further discriminations of emotional states, depending upon the cognitive subsystems activated. Thus, symbolizing and perceiving are activated in the case of the fear/anger and expectancy/surprise emotions, with symbolizing more heavily weighted for the expectancy/surprise emotions. This means that the symbolizing components of fluency and imaginativeness are also more heavily activated during fear/anger, whereas the spatio-visual and memorization components of the perceiving subsystem are more relevant to expectancy/surprise emotive states.

All the remaining emotional states involve conceptualizing in a dominant role. This implies a high degree of ''emotive intellectualizing'' via lower-order verbal and reasoning components. However, the components of the perceiving subsystem are also involved in the case of the joy/sadness emotions whereas the symbolizing subsystem is secondarily involved in the case of the acceptance/disgust emotions. In all four cases the dominance of the emotional independence affective subsystem implies that there are no primary effects on cognitive-affective functioning due to arousal level. There are such effects, on the other hand, because of the secondary activation of introversion–extraversion in the case of joy/sadness and emotional stability in the case of acceptance/disgust. However, there is an implication that arousal effects due to secondary activation are not as pronounced as primary activation arousal effects. Thus, the reticular arousal associated with joy/sadness would be dampened in comparison with the reticular arousal associated with expectancy and surprise, and the limbic arousal associated with acceptance/disgust would be at a lower level than that associated with fear and anger.

The implications of Table 8-5 can now be made clear—emotional states are differentiable provided all facets of emotional expression are taken into account, and providing the different facets are properly aligned. What we are suggesting is that emotions can be initially placed into four categories on the basis of the cross alignments of introspective, behavioral, functional, and physiological patterns. Furthermore, finer discriminations of emotional states are accounted for on the basis of differential involvements of the cognitive and affective systems. (Royce & Diamond, 1980, pp. 292-94)

9

Individual Differences
in World View and Life Style

COGNITIVE-VALUE INTERACTION AND WORLD VIEW

Over the past 20 years Royce (1964b, 1974, 1975, 1978b; Royce & Mos, 1980) has developed a psychophilosophical theory of knowledge that posits three basic ways of knowing—rationalism, empiricism, and metaphorism. These three "isms" are regarded as basic because of their dependence on various cognitive processes on the one hand and their epistemological justifiability on the other. This view is summarized briefly in Table 9-1, where the major implication is that different criteria for knowing are involved. The empirical style of knowing (top row) depends on the extent to which perception is accurate. The rational style (middle row) is viewed as being primarily dependent on logical consistency, and the metaphoric style (bottom row) says that knowledge is dependent on the degree to which symbolic cognitions lead to universal rather than idiosyncratic awareness.

TABLE 9-1 The Style-cognition Interaction for Three Ways of Knowing

EPISTEMIC STYLES	RELEVANT COGNITIVE ABILITIES	TRUTH CRITERIA
Empirical	Perceiving	Perception–misperception
Rational	Conceptualizing	Logical–illogical
Metaphoric	Symbolizing	Universal–idiosyncratic

Although each of these processes may lead to truth, it is important to note that each knowledge process also involves uncertainty and the possibility of error. The explicit recognition of uncertainty is an important feature that distinguishes epistemology from belief. The possibilities of perceptual-empirical error are readily apparent. The errors of the conceptual-rational approach are probably more subtle, but we have been led to believe that they have plagued the efforts of the logicians and mathematicians. And the errors of the symbolizing-metaphoric combination are even more elusive, primarily because of the sheer difficulty of providing an adequate articulation of metaphoric knowing (the problem of what symbols ''mean''; what qualifies as ''universal,'' etc.) Furthermore, we realize that none of these psychological processes operates independently of the others. That is, one does not conceptualize independently of sensory inputs and the process of symbol formation, nor do we perceive independently of concepts. In short, although the correspondences indicated in Table 9–1 are oversimplified for purposes of analysis and exposition, they represent the best fit between a given cognitive class and its parallel epistemological criterion.

In Table 9–1 we are particularly interested in showing the cooperative functioning of the style and cognitive systems. In the first row, for example, we indicate that the perceiving cognitive subsystem functions cooperatively with the empirical style subsystem. In rows two and three the conceptual cognitive abilities are indicated as functioning cooperatively with the rational style subsystem, and the symbolizing cognitive abilities are considered to be activated when the metaphoric style subsystem is functioning.

In Figure 9–1 we focus on the relationships between the human knower and the nature of reality via the three ways of knowing. The two columns to the extreme right are separated from the other three columns by a barrier between the individual and ultimate reality. That which is epistemologically untestable lies to the right of this barrier and constitutes unknowable ultimate reality. That which is testable by some criterion for knowing lies to the left of the epistemological barrier and leads to ''reality images'' that are ''true'' or ''real.'' Despite the efforts of great thinkers to somehow circumvent the epistemological limits involved, the only valid assessments open to finite humans necessarily lie to the left of the barrier. These three ways of knowing are both necessary and sufficient to account for how humans know. The basis for such a claim is our view that these three ways of knowing are basic, with the term *basic* requiring that both the psychological processes and the truth criterion involved be specifiable and primary, and that uncertainty be clearly recognized. This means that such epistemologies as authoritarianism and intuitionism cannot qualify. Intuitionism, for example, fails to qualify because it does not have a valid truth criterion, whereas authoritarianism fails because both its psychological processes and its truth criterion are based on some other (i.e., an authority) epistemic approach—i.e., authoritarianism is a *derived* way of knowing, not a basic way of knowing. Furthermore, both of these systems of thought fail to explicitly recognize the importance of uncertainty.

Although all three ways of knowing are derived from antiquity, they have

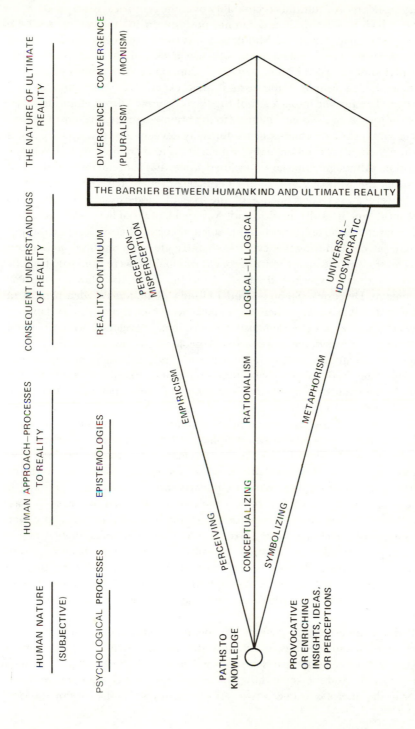

FIGURE 9-1 The basic paths to knowledge. (Modified from Royce, 1964)

193

had varying degrees of cultural acceptability over the centuries. Metaphorism, for example, which was clearly in a dominant position during the earliest period of recorded history and during the Middle Ages, is currently in a very inferior position. Empiricism, on the other hand, which was essentially nonexistent in the earliest period of recorded history, currently dominates the Western world. The most general idea behind empiricism is that experience is the source of all knowledge. The further implication of the term *experience* is that all inputs to the mind occur by way of the input channels to the brain—namely, the senses. Aristotle was probably the first philosopher to formally develop the epistemology of empiricism, although his contemporary, Epicurus, is also credited with developing this position. Although empiricism declined somewhat subsequently, it was kept alive during the Middle Ages by St. Thomas Aquinas. It received its biggest boost, however, as a consequence of the rise of modern science during the Renaissance. But it is the British and American philosophers who have contributed most to the advancement of this epistemology. The British contributions were made primarily during the seventeenth and eighteenth centuries, and in contrast to empiricism, the major contributors to rationalism were primarily from the European continent, especially the French and the Germans. They include such proponents as Descartes, Spinoza, and Leibnitz. The general idea behind rationalism is that it is reason rather than experience which is the primary source of knowledge. Thus, although rationalism was originally developed primarily in opposition to the revelational approach of theology, it has subsequently been developed primarily in contrast to empiricism. And, although empiricism currently dominates, rationalism is very much alive in contemporary thought, particularly in the context of the theory-laden view of contemporary philosophy of science (Royce, 1978a).

Although contributions to empiricism and rationalism have dominated epistemology for the past 500 years, metaphorism has not died out. The best guess as to why it has declined is the fact that science and its epistemology have dominated this period of cultural life. Even so, metaphorism has held on during this period as the critical epistemology for the arts and the humanities. Perhaps the most complete statement of this view is the one put forward by Ernst Cassirer (1953, 1955, 1957) in his three-volume work on symbolic forms. There were earlier statements, of course, by the Greeks (e.g., Aristotle) on aesthetics, and by the medieval philosopher St. Thomas Aquinas. And there have been important statements put forward by other contemporaries as well, including those of Susanne Langer (1948), and those of the philosopher Philip Wheelwright (1968), the psychologist Carl Jung (1964), and the theologian-philosopher Paul Tillich (1957).

Perhaps the important general idea behind metaphorism is that there are two forms of language—the literal and the metaphorical. And the key to understanding the metaphorical is the notion of analogy—the idea that x is like y in specifiable ways. And the key to how one might specify such connotative meanings lies in the interplay between two sets of meanings: (1) the core or standard meanings of the metaphor, and (2) the "marginal" meanings suggested by the metaphor. It is out of the interplay between the standard and "marginal" meanings that the metaphor is able to provide new vistas, thereby extending knowledge into domains not heretofore explored in sufficient detail.

As shown in Figure 9-1, each of the three ways of knowing leads to an image of reality that is projected across the epistemological barrier. Reality image refers to a person's organized set of cognitions concerning "how things are." The cognitive system produces these cognitions in the form of percepts, concepts, and symbols. As a result of the interaction between the cognitive and style systems, these percepts, concepts, and symbols are organized in a "meaningful way," and this meaningful interpretation of "the way things are" is what we mean by world view, or reality image.

However, such images of reality tend to be only partial views of the totality of reality for two major reasons—one of a philosophical nature, and the other of a psychological nature. The philosophical reason that world views are limited is that there is no way to encompass the totality of reality. One would have to be on the right-hand side of the epistemological barrier in Figure 9-1—i.e., one would have to be all-knowing—as a basis for judging how close one's current world view is to a total world view. Thus, the philosophical argument is the sceptical one that knowledge of ultimate reality simply is not possible. The psychological argument is similar—but in this case the argument concerns the psychological limitations of the knower. Since the human organism is limited in its ability to sense and to cognize, it follows that one can only know in terms of specifiable style and cognitive ranges. And, if we now add the fact of individuality (i.e., that each individual is limited by his or her particular personality type), it follows that any one individual necessarily has a limited image of reality. Elsewhere, Royce (1964b) has developed the theme that all individuals are encapsulated to varying degrees. That is, because of their particular personality profile, individuals tend to depend on one of the three ways of knowing to the exclusion of the other two.

Efforts to find truth have presumably been going on since humans first made their appearance in the universe, and these efforts have slowly evolved to the current special disciplines of knowledge such as history, literature, and biology. By definition, such specialties provide a highly selective view of reality and lead to divergent world views. The epistemological basis for this state of affairs is depicted in Figure 9-2. Focusing on the left side of the figure, it is to be understood that all three epistemologies are involved in each of the three representative disciplines of knowledge, but it is also clear that each discipline gives greater credence to one or two of them. The scientist, for example, "conceptualizes," "symbolizes," and "perceives," but minimizes metaphoric symbolizing as final judge. Conversely, the artist, who also invokes the entire cognitive repertoire, maximizes the symbolizing process at the expense of the conceptualizing and perceptual processes. There are, of course, wide variations in the possible combinations of epistemological profiles; this brief exposition should be taken as relative and typical rather than as absolute and general.

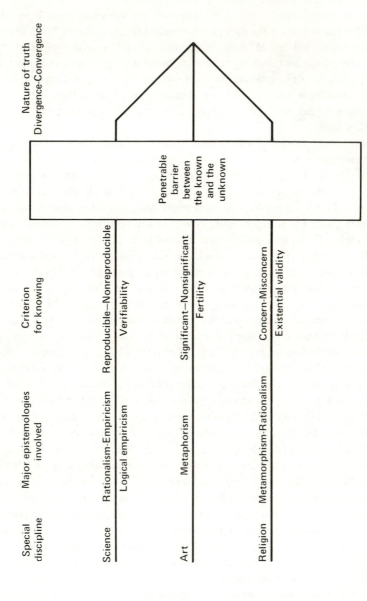

FIGURE 9-2 Representative special disciplines of knowledge. (Modified from Royce, 1964)

Epistemic Styles, Individuality, and World View

Our problem is to account for differences in world view, where *world view* is defined as *an individual's organized set of personal cognitions that constitute a model or image of reality*. Our answer is implicit in the left-hand column of Figure 9–1 under the label *Psychological Processes*. The processes in question are the cooperative functioning of the cognitive and style systems. Thus, Figure 9–1 depicts the three major epistemic styles or types—the empiricist along the top line, the rationalist along the middle line, and the metaphorist along the bottom line. In all three cases it is the cooperative functioning of the style and cognitive systems that is critical in the adaptive significance of these two systems. As noted in Chapter 5, the adaptive role of cognition is to interpret the environment by trying to identify ecological invariants. These interpretations of ''the way things are'' take the form of percepts, concepts, and symbols and, when organized, they constitute a representation of reality, or a world view. Similarly, the adaptive significance of the style system is of an integrative nature. Style functioning concerns commitments of ''how to do things.'' And, when the two systems function together, we are focused on cognitive styles or how one cognizes. And how one cognizes critically determines reality image. Thus, a reality image that is primarily perceptual in nature will be fact-oriented, whereas a reality image based on metaphors will contain more of the reality provided by ''meaningful'' symbols. The reality image of the theorist, on the other hand, will be composed of a network of concepts.

An important concept in the present context is epistemic type, which is a profile of style and cognitive dimensions, and which is defined as a style construct that simultaneously involves a valid truth criterion (i.e., leads to a justifiable knowledge claim in addition to being a characteristic mode or way of interacting with informational inputs). If we now oversimplify by confining ourselves to the third-order cognitive constructs, we can exemplify the kind of epistemic variation we have in mind. Thus, the typical scientific experimentalist, being primarily a perceiver, might have a profile such as that represented in Equation 9.1.

$$T = .5P + .3C + .2S \qquad (9.1)$$

Here T refers to type, P refers to perceiving, C refers to conceptualizing, and S refers to symbolizing.

The prototypic theoretician, on the other hand, would be characterized as:

$$T = .3P + .5C + .2S \qquad (9.2)$$

and the metaphoric type as

$$T = .3P + .2C + .5S. \qquad (9.3)$$

The major point is that the empiricist is primarily a perceiver, the rationalist is primarily a conceptualizer, and the metaphorist is primarily a symbolizer. The letters *P, C,* and *S* actually refer to the subhierarchies of cognitive and style dimensions depicted in Figure 5–1. For example, the cognitive-style profile of the conceptualizer involves a weight for each of the dimensions of the conceptualizing subhierarchy, and it will be quite different from the profile of the "perceiver" or the "symbolizer." Thus, not only are there different weights as indicated in Equations 9.1 to 9.3, but different subsets of abilities and styles are involved in these contrasting epistemic types. And, consequently, different knowledge claims and world views are generated.

There is some empirical evidence available on this point in addition to the theoretical analyses we have provided. The full range of the relevant empirical findings is summarized in a recent monograph, along with a summary of thirteen epistemological issues (Royce, Coward, Egan, Kessel, & Mos, 1978). In addition, the psychoepistemological profile has been developed as a way to empirically assess a person's epistemological hierarchy (Royce, 1970a; Royce & Smith, 1964; Smith, Royce, Ayers, & Jones, 1967). This inventory has now been through five revisions, several administrations to selected and unselected samples, and several item analyses and weighting schemes (Royce & Mos, 1980). A partial summary of findings to date is as follows:

1.   It is possible to assess a person's epistemological hierarchy by way of an inventory known as the psychoepistemological profile (PEP).
2.   It is estimated that the test-retest reliability coefficients of the three scales of the PEP are around .80–.90.
3.   There is evidence that the inventory is valid in the sense that it can discriminate between contrasting groups. For example, the data summarized in Table 9–2 show that empiricism is the dominant characteristic of the chemistry-biology group, that metaphorism is the highest in the music-drama sample, and that rationalism is highest for the mathematics-theoretical physics group. This empirical confirmation of theoretical expectations is most encouraging because of the overall consistency of the data. Furthermore, normative comparisons (i.e., when one compares scale performance *within* groups) turn out as predicted in all cases except one (i.e., the chemistry-biology group, which should have scored highest on the empirical scale, scored 1.337 on the rational scale and 1.223 on the empirical scale). And all but one

TABLE 9–2 Group Means on Empirical, Metaphoric, and Rational Scales of the Psycho-epistemological Profile (Revised Experimental Form II) (from Royce, 1974)

GROUPS	EMPIRICAL SCALE	METAPHORIC SCALE	RATIONAL SCALE
Chem–bio $N = 48$	1.223	1.141	1.337
Mu–drama $N = 50$	1.102	1.489	1.203
Math–phy $N = 44$	1.162	1.142	1.452

(mathematics-physics = 1.142 *versus* chemistry-biology = 1.141 on the metaphoric scale) of the nine possible "t" tests are significant beyond the 5 percent level. However, this finding means that there is no significant difference in metaphorism between the chemistry-biology and the mathematics-physics samples, a finding which is consistent with the theory. The higher performance of the music-drama group (at 1.489) than either of the chemistry-biology (1.141) or the mathematics-physics (1.142) groups is also consistent with the theory.

VALUE-AFFECT INTERACTION
AND LIFE STYLES[1]

The higher-order value orientations discussed in Chapter 6 constitute the basis for different paths to being or the construction of distinctive life styles. Each value orientation and its consequent path to being is directed toward the instantiation of the good life, or a meaningful existence, but the nature of the ultimate goal is distinctively defined for each path to being. Thus far in our analysis we have identified three distinctive ways of being, which we have labeled *altruism*, *individualism*, and *icarism*. These are indicated in the center of Figure 9-3 as different philosophies of life. Each of the paths to being originates in a particular value orientation that is directed toward a specifiable existential goal. Furthermore, each value orientation leads to a valid philosophy of life when (1) there is an implication of existential risk or the possibility of failure, and (2) a criterion is available for evaluating the existential validity (significance, meaningfulness) of any particular pattern in living.

The basic value orientations that correspond to the three philosophies of life are shown on the left side of Figure 9-3.[2] The *episodical* nature of the different patterns in living to which these value orientations are directed emphasizes that individuals temporally organize their lives around major themes that give them continuity (e.g., Goffman, 1961; Harré, 1974).[3] An *intrinsic* value orientation entails life episodes that are structured around themes involving perfection of knowledge, skills, professional careers, and so on, but, ultimately, the existential goals can be described in terms of *mastery*. Mastery–nonmastery, therefore, provides the existential criterion for a mode of being that is intrinsically oriented and dominated by the philosophy of life we have labeled *icarism*. In a similar way, a *self* value orientation entails life episodes structured around themes of independence and

[1]See Powell and Royce (1978) for a more thorough discussion of various life styles. We wish to express our appreciation to Don Schopflocher and Paul Enabnit for their suggestions and criticisms during the early stages of our thinking about the nature of life styles.

[2]The most obvious value orientation that has been suggested to us by numerous readers was "power," but it should be clear from the value hierarchy of Chapter 6 that this is encompassed by the broader "self" orientation.

[3]Harré (1974), for example, has suggested that the unit of analysis in the field of social psychology should be the *episode*. What we do in interacting with other humans has a beginning, a dominant theme, and an end. We think greater progress in understanding the social psychology of behavior will develop with closer attention to the larger units (i.e., episodes) that are the real building blocks of interactive behavior.

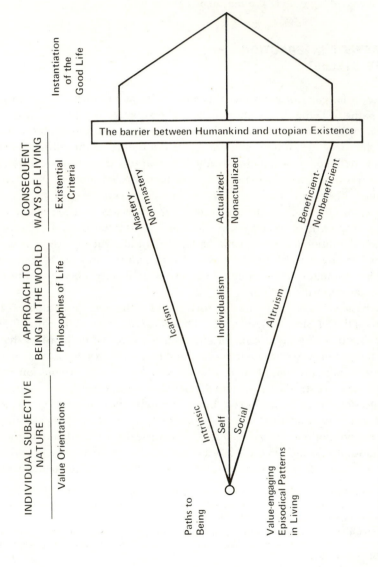

FIGURE 9-3 The basic paths to being. (From Powell & Royce, 1978)

realization of individual characteristics and uniqueness that are ultimately describable as *self-actualization*. And a *social* value-orientation motivates themes of devotion, giving, and even self-sacrifice, but ultimately, existential validation comes in terms of *beneficence* for other humans.

As we noted, in addition to the requirement that there must be an existential criterion, a valid philosophy of life also implies a degree of existential risk. As emphasized by many existentialist writers, in order to know what is worth living for, one must identify what is worth dying for. Quite literally, hundreds of volumes have been written in the fields of psychology, philosophy, sociology, and theology regarding the validity of altruism (e.g., Matter, 1974) and individualism (e.g., D. L. Miller, 1967) as alternative philosophies of life. These philosophic commitments clearly imply existential risk. The altruist, for example, who wishes to better the plight of other people in various parts of the world, may face poverty, disease, death, and alienation from the main thrust of Western society. Analogously, the individualist faces ever-increasing dangers in an age of mass society and bureaucracy, perhaps symbolized best by Kesey's fictional hero McMurphy (Kesey, 1962), who flirted with death and received much worse—a lobotomy.

On the other hand, it has been difficult to identify an appropriate synoptic term for describing a philosophy of life based on an intrinsic value orientation and validated by an existential criterion of mastery–nonmastery. Moreover, the terms that do come close (e.g., expertism, perfectionism), fail to convey a clear implication of risk. That risks are involved in such a philosophy of life should be clear: Creative writers may be haunted by eager critics and blank pages; great gymnasts may reach their peak before they are out of their teens; and scientists may discover that a lifetime of work has been totally misguided. More exotic feats such as moon walks, polar and deep sea explorations, motorcycle riding, and bronco busting quite obviously present physical risks to the individuals who find meaning in attempting them. Because the Greek myth of Icarus has long been a symbol of human ambitions, and because the myth also embodies the idea of risk, we chose icarism as the label for the philosophy of life characteristic of the intrinsically oriented path to being in the world (Powell & Royce, 1978, pp. 989–90).

Value-affect Integrations

Life style is considered to be the result, or a systems output, of the linkages between the value and affective systems. As in the case of style-cognitive integration, value-affective integration is *coordinated* from the integrative level of personality and is constrained by the overall system goal of optimizing personal meaning. In this context, the concept of life style represents a strategy for instantiating the individual's values and feelings in the world in which one must live so as to optimize personal meaning. While a world view commits individuals to particular images of reality, a life style commits them to particular modes of existence. In the case of world view, the problem of *coordination* is related to the management of information uncertainty; in the case of life styles, *coordination* is related to the management of existential risks. Life styles, then, are strategic solutions to the individual's overall plans for optimizing personal meaning, these solutions being in the form of episodical patterns in living.

The integration of values and affect in order to produce life styles as outputs from system interactions involves *coordination* from the higher, integrative level of the overall system. One way to view the problem of coordination and integration is from the standpoint of multilevel decision problems, such as, in the case of personality, maximizing personal meaning. This overall decision problem can be hierarchically decomposed into increasingly smaller decision problems, as, for example, when plans can be decomposed into strategies, tactics, and so on. Thus, life styles can be conceptualized as strategies for instantiating values and affect, as solutions (however tentative) to the decision problems entailed by the overall system goals and purposes.

A more thorough understanding of life styles requires that the roles of affect or feelings be considered. For example, an individual who is socially motivated but high on introversion could encounter many problems in working out a satisfying life style. Affect can be easily brought into the analysis by representing it at the lowest level of the hierarchy of decision structures. That is, integrative personality represents the highest level, and the goals and purposes of this level are viewed as *plans*. Values are at the next level, and their goals and purposes (decision problems) are viewed as *strategies*. Finally, at the next level is affect, with goals and purposes viewed as *tactics*, although, of course, there still may be interlevel conflicts related to the problem of system coordination. We have illustrated this conceptualization of the integration of values and affect in the production of distinctive life styles in Figure 9-4. In Figures 9-4A and 9-4B, examples are presented of two different life styles that are differentiated by the specific decision problems at *both* the level of values and the level of affect. In the case of individual A on the left-hand side of the figure, an *individualist* life style can be seen to involve maximizing unique qualities of self at the level of value orientations and emotional independence at the affective level. Similarly, individual B must maximize beneficence at the value orientation level and minimize social inhibition at the affective level in order to attain an *altruistic* life style. On the right-hand side of the figure, we have life styles that are primarily a function of affective integration (see Figures 9-4C and 9-4D).

Whether such typological distinctions are fruitful depends on the extent to which specific classes of decision problems contribute to a general understanding of individual differences. The concept of distinctive life styles links an existential analysis of being in the world with individual differences in value-affect integration. From the viewpoint of the former, life styles reflect distinctive modes of being in the world—commitment to particular paths to being, certain risks, and the attainment of the good life. From the viewpoint of the latter, life styles represent the outcomes of the interactions between the affective and the value systems (Powell & Royce, 1978, p. 1001).

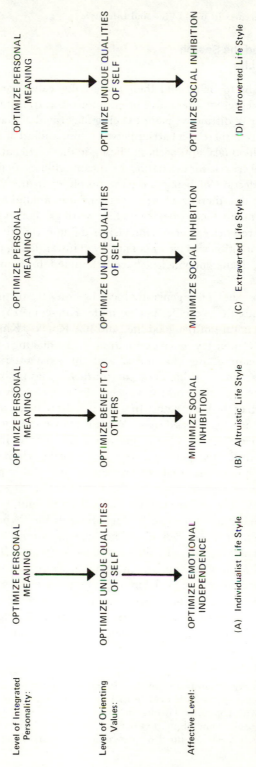

FIGURE 9–4 Multilevel decision structures as a possible basis for classifying existential hierarchies. (From Powell & Royce, 1978)

Life Styles and the Search
for the Good Life

The basic paths to being and their underlying value commitments and philosophies of life represent alternative orientations toward instantiations of the good life. The notion of distinctive paths to being illustrated in Figure 9–3 also incorporates the idea that there is a barrier between humankind and Utopian existence. Although individuals' approaches to being in the world entail philosophies of life and existential criteria for evaluating the meaningfulness of life patterns, the achievement of perfection of being (i.e., the absolute) in the world is an impossibility. The fact that there is a barrier between humankind and Utopian existence has been a major focus of existentialist writings: For example, Sartre's phrase ''existence precedes essence'' emphasizes the uncertainties and risks that attend the human condition and the impossibility of instantiating the good life. At the other extreme, transcendentalists have attempted to ignore this barrier altogether.

Humanistic psychologists generally have been aware of the problems involved in instantiating the good life. For example, Kinget (1975) has offered her own analysis of the nature of the good life, and like Rogers, Kinget emphasizes that the good life is a ''journey, not a destination.'' The making of commitments, the striving for meaning, the challenges, and the existential risks are what ultimately determine the good life. The commitments that individuals make in choosing a path to being in the world and the existential risks they must encounter are different for each of the basic paths. In a sense paths to being and philosophies of life define distinctive *psychological niches*. What is relevant or meaningful in one niche may actually conflict with what is relevant or meaningful in another niche. This implication of distinctive paths to being can be further clarified by exploring the ways in which individuals attempt to reconcile their philosophies of life and their work lives.

Work is inextricably tied to what it means to be alive and, hence, becomes a focal point for humans attempting to find meaning in life. Whether a laborer, teacher, philosopher, or clerk, individuals become economically, ideologically, socially, and personally identified by the kind of work they do. This becomes all too apparent when a physical impairment may cut short an individual's work career or creative individuals are forced into premature retirement. Furthermore, the alienation characteristic of modern technological societies is often attributed to the inability to find meaning in one's work on an assembly line. For example, Mike LeFevre would purposefully put occasional dents in the sheets of steel he was producing:

> . . . yes, I want my signature on 'em, too. Sometimes, out of pure meanness, when I make something, I put a little dent in it. I like to do something to make it really unique. Hit it with a hammer. I deliberately fuck it up to see if it'll get by, just so I can say I did it. It could be anything. Let me put it this way: I think God invented the dodo bird so when we get up there we could tell Him, 'Don't you ever make

mistakes?' and He'd say, 'Sure, look' . . . I'd like to make my imprint. My dodo bird. A mistake, *mine*. Let's say the whole building is nothing but red bricks. I'd like to have just the black one or the white one or the purple one. Deliberately fuck up. (Terkel, 1974, p. 10)

The point is that many individuals for whom work is not meaningful still try to leave their signature.

In Figure 9–5 we have shown how three sample occupational careers can be viewed in terms of the philosophies of life that they satisfy, and how careers can be viewed as different ways of being in the world.[4] The life of the artisan, for example, requires a commitment to mastery of particular tasks and the expression of individual uniqueness. Thus, icarism and individualism are implicated as the most relevant philosophies of life. Analogously, professional careers are seen to entail icarism and altruism as the relevant philosophies of life. The occupational career of a scientist, for example, entails not only an intrinsic value orientation and attempts to produce insightful theories, experiments, and images of reality, but also a concern for the contribution that one's work makes to the scientific or broader community. A scientist's feeling of fulfillment may well come from attempts to correct the existing world views of those communities—as illustrated by the careers of scientists such as Galileo, Darwin, and Freud.

Human services, the third example in Figure 9–5, exemplifies individuals with occupational careers that entail the expression of social value orientations and altruism as the dominant philosophy of life. The criterion for self-validation for an individual who pursues an occupational career in human services is dependent on the extent to which such efforts prove to be helpful to others. It is interesting to note that human services have become increasingly organized under government bureaucracies in recent times. Individuals entering human service careers under such circumstances frequently find that the bureaucratic "red-tape" frustrates their attempts to be helpful. Highly motivated teachers, juvenile workers, clinicians, and medical doctors, for example, are often thwarted by institutionalized modes of operation. Many such people leave for other, less rewarding careers; others direct their efforts toward humanizing the system; and still others find that it is easier to pursue such careers in underdeveloped nations.

Examples of Specific Life Styles

In the following pages we consider examples of specific individuals who pursued the life styles diagramed in Figure 9–3. Case studies can always be risky, but we are concerned with how specific individuals live their lives; therefore, such examples are important in enriching the concepts we have introduced.

[4]We do not intend to imply that the motives for work cannot be purely "economic," for, clearly, they can be. In fact, the point is that most people "work" for "economic" reasons and, because they spend most of their lives, thoughts, dreams, and interactions with others, with the kind of work they actually do lingering always in the background, they must rationalize their work lives with their philosophies of life.

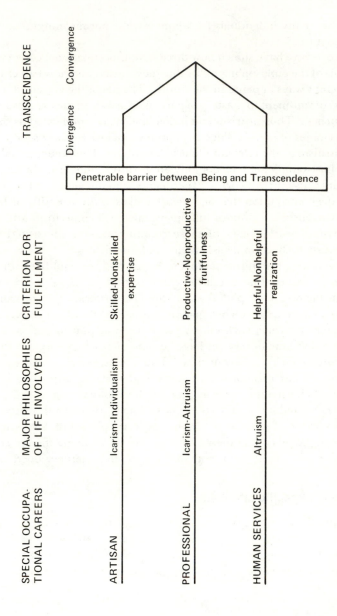

FIGURE 9-5 Sample types of occupational careers providing ways of being in the world. (From Powell & Royce, 1978)

Icarism   The lives of many creative individuals, including architects, artisans, artists, astronauts, aviators, and so on throughout the alphabet, illustrate the point that what is worth dying for (and, thus, what is worth living for) can be mastery. Clark L. Hull, for example, was a dominant figure in American psychology for more than two decades of this century (ca. 1929–1952). He applied a great intellect to the insurmountable problems involved in constructing a general theory of mammalian behavior, and willfully lost himself and his personal uniqueness as an "individual" in the process. Hull could not have been less concerned about "self-actualization," and those who knew Hull personally would doubtless agree that his life was very far from being motivated by altruism.

Death was a constant concern to Hull—not because it would end his "life"—but because it would end his attempts at mastery of a scientific understanding of behavior and, thus, his meaningful existence in the world.[5] This point is richly illustrated by numerous entries throughout his life in his personal diary notes, or what he called his "Idea Books" (see Ammons & Ammons, 1962; Hull, 1962). More than fifteen years before his major contribution to psychology Hull noted that "I am now 43 years old. I assume that after fifty years a man's creative potentialities are practically exhausted. Therefore whatever really creative work I must do must be done before that time" (January, 1928—Hull, 1962, p. 824). The following passage was part of his entry on the anniversary of his sixty-first birthday:

> I have been working along for the last two or three years with the expectation that any day I may have a cerebral hemorrhage which will put a permanent stop to any more creative work. I hurry along as fast as I can, getting my work out bit by bit. . . . And so I go on. *I seem to have no fear of death, but only anxiety to salvage as much from life in the way of systematic science as possible.* I often wonder whether I am not pretty hypochondriacal about my mental condition . . . But it doesn't matter much whether I am or not. It spurs me on to get the most out of my failing body. . . . (May 24, 1945; Hull, 1962, p. 872, emphasis added)

Individualism   As a philosophy of life, individualism involves value commitments to self-actualization rather than mastery or beneficence. Riesman's concept of the "nerve of failure" expresses much of the essence of individualism, inasmuch as it is " . . . simply the nerve to be one's self when that self is not approved of by the dominant ethic of a society" (1954, p. 48). It involves more than being willing to risk failure, as failure is defined by the dominant ethics of society: The "nerve of failure" requires defining success and failure for oneself without regard to society's norms.

[5]Hull's autobiography (Hull, 1952a, 1952b), as well as the excerpts from his Idea Books, which have been reprinted by Ammons and Ammons (1962; also see Hull, 1962), should be consulted for further information regarding Hull's constant concern over the possibility of an early death. For example, it is important to note that he was first trained in engineering and pursued training in psychology only after he had been afflicted by poliomyelitis. He was afflicted by numerous other illnesses (including psychosomatic) throughout the remainder of his life.

Leeteg, the Legend, a person described by Michener and Day (1957), seems like some fictional character glamorized by a popular movie, but he actually lived on the island of Tahiti. Leeteg's life provides an idealization of the individualist philosophy, since he risked truly heretical conduct—the possibility of never rejoining the company or the dominant ethic. He was well known throughout the island of Tahiti, not for the black felt oil paintings he did for six days a week, but for how he spent the other one: tearing old Papeete apart, chasing half-naked girls down the street, punching policemen, knocking Chinese down, cursing sailors, etc., and, finally, sleeping it off in jail. Leeteg:

> vowed that he would build the most expensive, luxurious, and altogether resplendent privy in the Southern Hemisphere, and not since the days of the Roman emperors has anyone enjoyed such a toilet. It was built like a low Polynesian temple, with thick, masonry walls and massive buttresses. An enormous grill of metal was set on one side, across which swam twenty-six metal fish painted seven different colors. The interior was imported Italian marble with a seating arrangement that would have satisfied Caligula. . . . From its commodious throne one could gaze on Paopao Bay and the softly swaying coconut palms. . . . Spacious enough to serve a platoon of men, it was Leeteg's noblest architectural creation and stands today to confound his enemies. They tried to prevent its building and claimed it showed the crazy American had really gone mad, but Leeteg countered that a man ought to enjoy the kind of privy that suited his personality, and he won. (Michener & Day, 1957, pp. 358–59)

Whenever Riesman's "nerve of failure" is relevant to a person's life, the life of a poet, a bar fighter, or a hermit might all be equally valid existences—depending on the particular individual. The successes of the individualist, whether it's erecting the most luxurious privy or finding one's way "back to nature," are all personally defined and do not make the individual's life any more meaningful when society either praises or sanctions those successes.

Altruism   To discuss the concept of an altruistic philosophy of life without discussing the life and work of Albert Schweitzer would be an injustice to both the concept and the man. Although he did not die of an assassin's bullet, as did Martin Luther King, Jr. and Mahatma Gandhi, his value commitments and his very being were openly criticized the world over. Schweitzer earned doctoral degrees in philosophy, theology, music, and medicine, three of the four while he was still in his twenties (Seaver, 1947). To leave the securities of a comfortable upper-class existence, a professorship, or a medical practice, and devote his life to service, to bettering the human condition, seemed contrary to the dominant value commitments of Western civilization. To many people Schweitzer's behavior would appear counter to "common sense." But, then, as Seaver (1947) suggested it takes more than "common sense" to create meaning out of human existence. Albert Schweitzer wrote eloquently and prolifically about his motives, his personal philosophy of life, and his views on what life and death meant to him. The following comes from his Goethe Prize Address, delivered in Frankfurt, 1928:

A spirit like Goethe's lays upon us three obligations. We have to wrestle with conditions so as to secure that men who are imprisoned in work and being worn out by it may nevertheless preserve the possibility of a spiritual existence. We have to wrestle with men, so that in spite of being continually drawn aside to the external things which are provided so abundantly for our age, they may find the road to inwardness and keep in it. We have to wrestle with ourselves and with all and everything around us, so that in times of confused ideals which ignore all the claims of humanity, we may remain faithful to the great humane ideals. . . . (Seaver, 1947, p. 334)

Schweitzer admitted in a number of places (see Seaver, 1947) that he was pessimistic about the future of civilization and its ability to provide a world truly adapted to humanity and the need for a spiritual existence. But for him to have built his own philosophy of life on that pessimism would have made his life and death intolerably meaningless (Powell & Royce, 1978, pp. 991–95).[6]

[6]It should also be noted that the three individuals described in Chapter 1, Einstein, Thoreau, and Gandhi, provide examples of icarism, individualism, and altruism, respectively.

10

Individual Differences
in the Role of the Self
in Integrative Personality

We think self-image is involved in our conception of integrative personality in two different ways. The first relates to the self-referential aspect of many factors at all levels, particularly in the factor hierarchies of the value and affective domains. The more emergent and centrally important way relates to complex activities at the level of integrative personality. We present a taxonomy that provides a schema for discussing these various processes related to self. The first way in which self enters the picture can be dealt with in a more cursory fashion.

In considering the first way in which self is involved in integrative personality it is instructive to examine certain factors that have emerged in the study of affective phenomena. At the first-order level of the affective hierarchy (see Figure 5–4) there are several factors, such as *self-sentiment*, *self-sufficiency*, and *ego strength*, with an obvious self-referent content, and several others, such as *tendermindedness*, *affectothymia*, and *realism* whose self-referent content is not so obvious. Consider, for example, the factor of *self-sentiment*, which refers to the extent to which one is controlled, exhibits will power, is socially precise, is compulsive, and follows one's self-image (see Cattell, 1973). The primary involvement of self in this and the other affective factors arises from the cross-situational consistency of emotional reactions and the capability of identifying those reactions as being one's own emotional reactions. Considered as affective phenomena, such feelings are only incidentally related to self as it will be dealt with below. It is only to the extent that such reactions can be consistently identified by the individual *as being one's own reactions* that the affective factors take on a self-referential content. However, self-referential content may be seen to take on greater importance when contrasted with the results from animal investigations (Royce, 1977b). There are a variety of affective factor dimensions that have emerged in both animal and human investigations, such as *autonomic balance*, *fearfulness*, and *emotional stability* (a third-order construct). Not surprisingly, these factors lack the self-referent content of the others we have noted, and it would be rather surprising to find that factors with such content could be demonstrated in nonhuman animals. This would be surprising, first, because it is doubtful that such animals as mice and rats can possess the kind of self-identity that is required to recognize subtle consistency in emotional reactions across a variety of situations. It would also be surprising on phylogenetic grounds—that is, the affective system of subhuman organisms should be less differentiated and more "stimulus-bound" than that of human organisms.

The whole problem of self-reference in integrative personality suggests two important points. First, much (though not nearly all) of the information about the structure of the affective system has come from results of investigations using questionnaires. Second, there is the critical involvement of self-identity in the emergence of a strong self-referential content which also involves an individual's interpretation of memories for past events and feelings in a variety of situations. Thus, the common thread underlying the self-referential content in the affective and other domains is the unique way in which an individual's memories for past events are tapped.

We now turn our attention to the processes related to self that we think are centrally related to integrative personality. Our discussion is oriented around a taxonomy of basic processes.

A TAXONOMY OF SELF-REFERENT TERMINOLOGY AND PROCESSES[1]

Wylie (1968) has proposed an abbreviated hierarchical taxonomy of self-referent terminology in order to categorize extant *empirical investigations* of self-image. Wylie suggested that the generic-self concept could be divided into two major subdivisions, *actual-self concept* and *ideal-self concept*. Each of these categories was further divided into two conceptual subdivisions: *actual self* was divided into the concepts of *social self* and *private self*; *ideal self* was divided into concepts of one's *own ideal self* and *other's ideals for one*. While this taxonomy may be adequate for dealing with a review of the empirical literature, we do not think it is sufficiently comprehensive to cover the full range of processes considered in psychological theory and research.

[1]We owe a great deal to Don Schopflocher for his contributions, suggestions, advice, and criticisms regarding this overall model of self.

Figure 10–1 presents a taxonomy in which we distinguish five major categories of processes relevant to self, each of which is further divided into two subprocesses. For example, decision-control processes have been subdivided into processes related to one's overt behaviors and processes related to one's inner thoughts, feelings, and such. In finding synoptic terms to apply to each of the major categories of processes and their subprocesses, we tried to avoid hyphenated expressions that include the term "self." The subsections that follow provide an overview of these categories and an elaboration of the role of each of the five processes in the integrative functioning of the self.

Decision-control Processes

A variety of self theorists and other general personality theorists have focused on the "executive," or controlling, aspects of integrative personality. Self-as-agent (see Hall & Lindzey, 1970; Wylie, 1968, 1974) is a synoptic term to refer to the ability of the individual to make complex decisions and to exercise control over thoughts and feelings and observable actions. In this vein, S. Freud's (1949; A. Freud, 1946) concept of ego was introduced in order to characterize those processes that enable the organism to take into account the contingencies of objective reality and to have some modicum of control over internal events. James (1890, 1961) and Mead (1934) spoke of the "I" as the knowing self; that is, the "I" was considered to be the thinker or the doer, or that aspect of the person that does the experiencing or deciding. Additional conceptualizations introduced to deal with decision-control processes in personality include Murray's (1938) notion of regnancy, Allport's (1961) proprium, and Snygg and Combs's (1949) phenomenal self.

Although decision and control processes have been of concern to personality theorists, there has been little viable research on such processes. For example, much of the psychological research explicitly concerned with decision making has been preoccupied with decisions and performances in laboratory tasks, where the subject has little or no personal stake in the outcomes. Of greater relevance to personality theory and research should be the kinds of decision processes that influence individuals in their career choices, selection of spouses, reactions to developmental changes (as in aging), and so on. While the counseling research and psychological testing literature has directed considerable attention to such situations, the absence of a general theoretical perspective makes it difficult to provide a coherent interpretation of such findings.[2] In our conceptual model of personality (Chapter 3), we described feedback processes that function both assimilatively and accommodatively in dealing with environmental inputs. In this context self-image may be considered a molar norm. For example, if there is a

[2]Cohen's (1964; see also Janis & Mann, 1977) studies of behavior in uncertainty come close to what we consider to be more ideal investigations of the decision processes in which humans actually engage. For example, he reported investigations of behavior in lotteries, suicides, sports, driving, divination, etc.

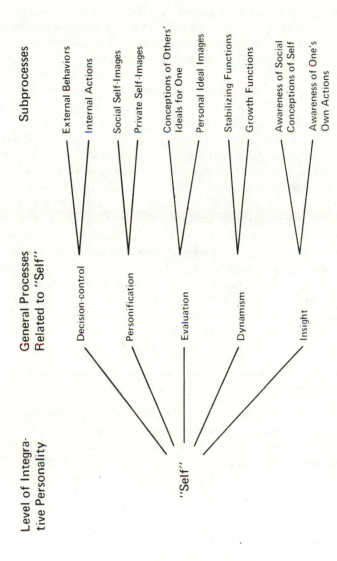

FIGURE 10–1 A taxonomy of integrative processes related to self.

213

match, the self-image is functioning assimilatively, and we are describing periods of self-acceptance and relative personal stability. If there is a mismatch of a specifiable self-image, then accommodations of the self-image are called for, and we are describing periods of self-rejection and personality change.

We have also employed TOTE hierarchies as models for representing various control processes (e.g., Chapter 5). The processing carried out by a TOTE hierarchy actually is quite simple as long as a match is obtained—only when a match is not found is its operation of wider theoretical interest. That is, as long as the system finds a match (assimilation) between current inputs and existing norms, the information-processing activities of the lower-level systems and components can continue. But a mismatch in terms of a higher-level norm signals that "all is not right" at the lower level. Therefore, given that a mismatch occurs (accommodation), decision-control processes must be brought to bear in such a way as to effect a change in lower-level processing. For example, in the day-to-day functioning of most individuals there are few or no challenges to their world views, self-images, and life styles; consequently, the lower-level processes are not disrupted. One particularly strong challenge to an individual's self-image, however, can have all the following disruptive effects: interfering with cognitive performances that normally run smoothly, heightening affective arousal, inhibiting normal social interactions, and so on. The effects are the same with challenges to an individual's world view (though, perhaps, with less affective involvement) and life style (though, perhaps, with less cognitive involvement). This whole process is analogous to the disruptive effects of any event that runs counter to expectation—that is, ongoing activity is interrupted, and there is an attempt to find out "What happened" and what can be done in order for the ongoing activity to continue. The general point is that the interesting control activities are brought out in situations where there is a failure to obtain a normative match.

Personification

A second major category of processes to which self-theorists have directed attention is the internal representation of one's own actions—that is, to the self as an object of awareness. The term *personification* was used by Sullivan (1953) to refer to the images that one has of oneself or others. It referred to the investment of objects with human characteristics (including oneself), and we mean to use the term in the same general way.[3] *Self-concept* is the term most frequently used to refer to the personification of one's own actions—to the specific images that individuals have of themselves (e.g., Thomas, 1973; Wylie, 1968, 1974). But other terms, such as *self-image, self-identity* (Erikson, 1959; James, 1890), *objective self-awareness* (Duval &

---

[3]While we consider *self-image* and *personification* to be roughly synonymous, the latter is preferred for several reasons. *Personification* has been little used, and thus, it does not have a variety of connotative meanings. Further, it is the only synoptic term that is not too abstruse and that does not involve a hyphenated expression. Finally, *personification* can refer to both a process and the end result of a process, whereas *self-image* refers only to the latter.

Wickland, 1972), and *phenomenal self-awareness* (Rogers, 1951), have all been used more or less with the same intent. The process of personification is closely related to the *me* of James (1890) and Mead (1934).

As indicated in a variety of places, style-value integration is primarily responsible for one's self-image. Table 10-1 presents the primary linkages between style and value systems, as well as a brief description of the self-images that result from such linkages. While our analysis suggests that there is a greater probability of observing the three linkages described by the main diagonal, there are nine possible pairings and resulting self-images. The empirical-social combination gives rise to a phenomenal-interactive image, rational-intrinsic gives rise to a conceptual-achieving self-image, and metaphoric-self gives rise to a transcendental-ascendant image. The other set of diagonal entries (i.e., from the upper right corner to the lower left corner) constitutes another frequently occurring continuum, ranging from a phenomenal-transcendent image (where "here-now" experience is critical) to a transcendent-interactive image (where the social myth is critical). There are six remaining continuua, involving the three *value* columns and the three *style* rows. Finally, it should be pointed out that, because of the hierarchical structure of the style and value systems (involving a total of 15 styles and 43 values), there are actually a much larger number of possible style-value pairings. The point is that our analysis is confined to the highest stratum of the style and value hierarchies—consideration of the lower levels of these hierarchies would add a large number of variations within each of the nine cells—hence, the heading "core images." But we presume our major point is now obvious—namely, that individuals can construct a wide range of self-images, and that these images depend on specific style and value commitments.

From an information-processing standpoint, these images of self result from cognitive processing of self-referent information. That is, they are *integrations of information expressed in various classes of percepts, concepts, and symbols that have a self-referent component.* For example, individuals construct and process self-referent propositions of the sort "I did such and such," "I am such and such," "I am the kind of person who . . . ," etc. The information expressed in such propositions is integrated into general themes, with the particular themes that emerge being guided by the styles and values of the individual. For example, an individual who is higher on the *empirical* styles and *social* values is more prone to attend to and integrate information concerning the veridicality of perceptions and the reactions of the social environment. On the other hand, the individual who is higher with respect to *rational* styles and *intrinsic* values is more prone to process self-referent information with respect to the consistency of personal conceptions and the achievement effects of particular actions. Finally, the individual higher on the *metaphoric* styles and the self value orientations is more apt to attend to information related to the symbolic and individualistic aspects of one's actions. Because of the central role of values in these psychological constructions, they are dynamic rather than static reflections of particular aspects of an individual's feelings or actions.

Generalized self-images can be described as abstractions across very many

TABLE 10-1   The Core Images of Self Resulting from Various Style-value Linkages

STYLES	VALUES		
	SOCIAL	INTRINSIC	SELF
Empirical	Self is viewed as an integral part of the surrounding, or immediately present, society and culture. Individuality emerges out of the experience of self in society.	Self is appreciated for the immediate effects or achievements that one has in the social context. Immediate, as opposed to long-range, achievements are most essential to one's individuality.	Self is valued for immediate experiences through all the various senses that one has. Individuality emerges out of one's here-and-now sensations and experiences.
Rational	Self is subjugated to and dominated by the social order and social dogma. Individuality of one's self or of others is valued only to the extent that they are socially understood and tolerated.	Self is appreciated and understood through one's long-term achievements in manipulating the world. Achievements set one apart from the world and others in it. Individuality is valued for its material or abstract achievements.	One understands one's self through deep and educated thought. The highest goal in life is to follow the Socratic maxim of "know thyself." Individuality is understood for its own sake.
Metaphoric	Self is considered to be a specific, concrete manifestation of social myth. Social and religious institutions provide the framework for one's knowledge and experience of one's individuality.	Self is valued and understood for its ethical and spiritual achievements. Self-insight is an achievement that one aspires to, and individuality is a product, in part, of that aspiration.	One is simultaneously a part of the world and apart from the world. Self and individuality are established by reaching beyond the material world in order to attain a deeper, transcendental meaning.

"local" situations. The relative importance of any local situation will be a function not only of an individual's particular values and affect but also of the cross-situational consistency of abstracted information. In other words individuals who image themselves as being rather *generally* competent will be less affected by any particular local discrepancy than if the cross-situational generality of their self-assessment was more restricted. What happens is analogous to calculating an arithmetic mean across situations. The greater the range of experience, and the greater the cross-situational consistency, then the less will be the effect of any particular local situation. Another consequence of this general view of self-images as integrations of information related to self-referential propositions is that, as an individual's experiences increase, the self-image should become increasingly more stable. Thus, if only adults are considered, self-images should be relatively stable over long periods of time, and it should become increasingly more difficult with advancing age to produce changes in an individual's self-image. For example, W. Mischel (1976) reports that individuals' self-reports are strongly correlated over long periods of time (e.g., ten years) in spite of significant changes in the subjects' behaviors, and in spite of the low predictability of self-report measures with respect to specific behaviors in particular situations during that time span. Conversely, a good developmental period of the study of change in self-image should be adolescence, since these individuals are actively searching for an identity.

Evaluation

Individuals differentially evaluate their actions according to internal (or internalized) norms, an aspect of self that has been the object of more empirical research than any of the other processes identified in our taxonomy. Evaluation has been investigated under such rubrics as self-acceptance, self-esteem (Coopersmith, 1967; Rogers & Dymond, 1954), and positive-self (Thomas, 1973). The salient point is that most self theorists and researchers have posited that internal norms exist for evaluating the acceptability of particular perceptions of one's self in relation to one's actions. These *evaluations* (whether made by the self or accepted as presented by others) exert a controlling influence over an individual's subsequent actions and self-perceptions. For example, positive regard and self-regard were posited by Rogers (1961; Rogers & Dymond, 1954) to have central roles in controlling the adjustive reactions of individuals.

Evaluation has been examined as an important determinant of functioning in a variety of situations, including academic achievement (e.g., Coopersmith, 1967; Everett, 1971) and general adjustment (e.g., Rogers, 1951; Thomas, 1973). In general, it is believed that a negative evaluation of self leads to behavioral inhibition—or a self-fulfilling prophesy of failure—in which individuals fail to bring all of their potential resources to bear on the problems that confront them. Analogously, the individual who has a positive evaluation of self should be more apt to recruit resources in problematic situations—thus leading to better adjustment. In this respect the various constructs related to evaluation of self are functionally similar to Rotter's construct of internal-external control of reinforcements (Phares, 1976).

As discussed above, self-image (personification) has been postulated to be the result of style-value integration. An elaboration of the postulated relationships among styles and values is shown in Figure 10–2, where we have summarized the three validation criteria related to self-acceptance. This figure shows how the different style-value linkages give rise to different images of self and criteria of self-acceptance. The combination of a *rational* style and an *intrinsic* value orientation (see the middle row of the figure) results in a conceptual-achieving personality type (column 3) and an accomplished-unaccomplished criterion for self-acceptance (column 4). We can relate this state of affairs to the earlier discussion of decision-control processes in terms of our basic system circuit (see, for example, Figure 3–3). In the case of an assimilative match, there is a confirmation of the self-image—the confirmation in this case of the person as one who is highly competent (i.e., a high achiever). A mismatch means the self has not yet been validated, and the individual must search further for an identity. Thus, a mismatch in this case would indicate that, whatever might be an appropriate im-

FIGURE 10–2 Overall relationships among styles, values, qualities of self-images, and criteria for self-evaluation.

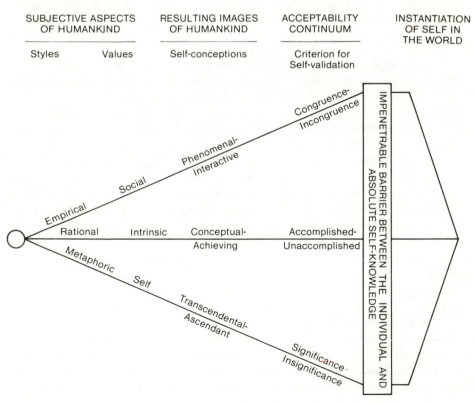

SUBJECTIVE ASPECTS OF HUMANKIND		RESULTING IMAGES OF HUMANKIND	ACCEPTABILITY CONTINUUM	INSTANTIATION OF SELF IN THE WORLD
Styles	Values	Self-conceptions	Criterion for Self-validation	

age, the concept of ''achieving'' is not it, and that further search for an appropriate self-identity is called for. This may lead to an alternative criterion, such as ''congruence'' (row 1) or ''significance'' (row 3), where *congruence* refers to giving greater importance to the opinions and needs of others and *significance* refers to an individualistic form of self-actualization. Of course, which path is chosen—or, indeed, whether such a shift is made at all—will depend on the trait characteristics (i.e., factor profile) of the individual and the critical feedback from the lower-level systems.

The images that one develops of one's self play a crucial role in subsequent thought and actions. If an individual maintains, say, a conceptual-achieving image of self and judges self-acceptance according to the acceptability continuum of accomplished-unaccomplished, then one is apt to engage in behaviors and plans that reach toward greater accomplishment. Similarly, if self-acceptability is based more on the continuum of significant-nonsignificant, then one would be more apt to engage in a greater variety of creative-artistic endeavors that bring one into closer contact with the symbolic significance of one's self.

Dynamisms

The fourth category of processes related to self is the most heterogenous, and thus the most complex, in the taxonomy presented in Figure 10–1. With the minor modification of replacing the term *energy* with *energy/information*, our usage of the term *dynamism* follows Sullivan, who defined a dynamism as a ''relatively enduring pattern of energy transformations which recurrently characterize the organism as an organism''(1953, p. 103). Most broadly, then, dynamisms are forms of adaptation. They are to be distinguished from other adaptation phenomena by their focus on maintaining the integrity of the self *as a self*. That is, they are explicitly psychological, and they help to shape the contents of consciousness. This description eliminates such biological mechanisms as biochemical homeostasis and reflexes from direct consideration.

The dynamisms that have been most extensively examined have several general properties. First, they distort information. Second, they operate below the level of awareness. Third, they operate in the short term without substantial personality reorganization. Any dynamism that operates predominantly to maintain the current state of psychological equilibrium in these ways is referred to as a *stabilizing* dynamism. Thus, defense mechanisms (A. Freud, 1946), perceptual defense (Klein, 1970; Wolitzky & Wachtel, 1973), coping mechanisms (Moos, 1976), cognitive consistency (Abelson, Aronson, McQuire, Newcomb, Rosenberg, & Tannenbaum, 1968), cognitive dissonance (Festinger, 1957), and distortion of attributional mechanisms (Shaver, 1970) are examples of stabilizing dynamisms.

Stabilizing dynamisms can be contrasted with *growth* dynamisms, which operate to direct change. Whereas stabilizing dynamisms operate in the short term to maintain a current equilibrium, growth dynamisms operate over longer periods of time to organize the succession of personality equilibria. In general, they are either goal-directed or retrogressive in character. Such processes as regression (A. Freud, 1946), alienation (Binswanger, 1958; May, 1969), psychosis, psychotherapy, self-actualization (Maslow, 1968; Rogers, 1961), individuation (C. G. Jung, 1959) and positive disintegration (Dabrowski, 1964) exemplify growth dynamisms.

Insight and the Search for Self-knowledge

The final category in our taxonomy deals with those processes that result in accurate or meaningful self-perception, or insight. Insight is a particularly difficult property to characterize, for problems of epistemology as well as those surrounding the nature of awareness and consciousness arise. The phenomena that constitute self-knowledge range from an awareness of the meaning of one's life, as framed in the abstractions of philosophical, psychological, or religious systems, to the explicit comparison of properties ascribed to self with properties that others ascribe to one or with the real properties one has "in fact."

As Wylie notes, research interest in this aspect of self stems from classic Freudian theory in which "lack of insight is alleged to be accompanied by defensiveness and /or an observer's diagnosis" (Wylie, 1968, p. 777). This quotation highlights several problems for the investigation of insight. First, the adjective *insightful* is often used with strong evaluative overtones. Second, it raises the question of the bases on which a psychologist can claim to know individuals more accurately than they know themselves. Finally, there is the question of how to discover the "true" properties of individuals against which their insight, or lack thereof, are to be assessed.

Self theorists have often shifted the focus of the investigation of insight to possessing accurate knowledge of what others believe one to be. Thus, "S will not become anxious (and hence defensive) unless and until he becomes at least dimly aware of the disparity between his phenomenal self and views others hold of him" (Wylie, 1968, p. 777). It becomes possible in this view to directly assess degree of insight by calculating the discrepancy between individuals' self-view (personification) and ratings of them by others. To the extent that such a view of insight seeks to retain the connotation of accurate self-knowledge, the methodology of measurement is based on the often questionable assumption that others know one more accurately than one knows oneself. This view also fails to consider the possibility of deceptive self-presentation or impression management (e.g., Goffman, 1959, 1974). To the extent that it investigates a particular form of self-knowledge, however, the approach adds valuable, if fragmentary, knowledge.

Although all three ways of knowing that we have discussed are relevant to an individual's search for knowledge, and each provides insights into the nature of the world, it is our view that the metaphoric way of knowing is particularly relevant to an individual's search for self-knowledge. This is partly because affect is more germane to the metaphoric mode of knowing. Our analysis in Chapter 5 of the functional significance of cognition indicated that the discovery and representation of some invariant lies at the core of symbols and metaphors, whether they occur in science, religion, or art. Typically, the invariant has to do with the relation between the individual and existence. For example, Ken Kesey achieved this in his novel *One Flew over the Cuckoo's Nest* (1962), in which McMurphy's struggle against the arbitrary power of Big Nurse provides a symbol that forces us to examine the generally dehumanizing aspects of modern society. As a symbol, McMurphy transcends himself, thereby expressing an invariant about the nature of human existence, and it is because of this communication of invariance that the symbol is cognitively comprehensible and simultaneously emotionally moving.

Perhaps the best documented exemplars of how the metaphoric mode of knowing illuminates reality come from C. G. Jung's research on archetypes. The earth mother, the old wise man, the eternal wonder child, and the hero are examples of these symbolic manifestations of the collective unconscious. The theory is that archetypes represent the recurrent themes or concerns of humankind, regardless of time (i.e., epoch of history) or space (i.e., across cultures). The hero is possibly the best exemplar of an archetype (J. Campbell, 1956), for it is manifest in contemporary life as well as in the myths and legends of antiquity. Its most obvious contemporary manifestations occur in the form of superstars of sports (e.g., the Olympics, hockey in Canada, football in the United States, and soccer in Europe and South America), films, and music. When accompanied by an early death, as in the case of Elvis Presley, such heroes take on the status of demigods. A similar phenomenon occurred in the cases of Marilyn Monroe, James Dean, Rudolf Valentino, and Manolete in earlier decades. Although not as well known outside Hispanic cultures, Manolete is probably the most convincing twentieth-century example of the archetypal hero. He is widely regarded as one of the greatest bullfighters in the history of tauromachy, and when he died (around the age of 30) in the bullring in 1947, Spain went into a state of national mourning! Furthermore, monuments have been erected throughout the country in honor of this man's exploits, and there is still a steady stream of visitors to the bullring in Linares, the site of Manolete's death. The best available explanation we have of these extraordinary phenomena is in terms of the torero as archetypal hero (Royce, 1964b). Why should the great torero epitomize the heroic reach of humankind? Because he stands quietly and bravely in the middle of an arena with nothing but a piece of red cloth in his hands as a thousand pounds of death comes charging at him. And because the audience knows that in a similar situation they would run. They recognize bravery, the courage to face death, that is necessary if one is a matador. In short, the point the matador is making is that facing death with dignity and grace symbolizes living with courage.

The hero, then, is a symbol of the human condition—that is, how to live and die. Such existential universals are the invariants that are captured via the metaphoric mode of knowing. While such knowing involves concept formation and perceptual processing, it is the symbolizing cognitive mode that is critical. A major reason the hero is such a powerful analogue of life (i.e., an archetype) is that the demands placed on the observer for vicariously "living through" are so great. The point is that a great tragedy (such as Hamlet) or a great bullfight is so effective in engaging the audience that the observing individuals temporarily drop the "vicarious" awareness because they feel they are, indeed, "living through" the experience. In short, a powerful symbol has the guts of life in it. Great plays, great literature, and living myths are not only rich in metaphoric meaning, they are also experientially real (despite being vicarious experiences).

The major conclusion of this analysis is that the commitment to a metaphoric style, particularly if combined with a "self-development" value orientation, constitutes the most potent style-value interaction for the development of self-knowledge. The pragmatic implication of this hypothesis is that, if greater self-knowledge is desired, individuals should make greater use of symbolizing abilities and affectivity on the one hand, and make greater commitments to the metaphoric style and the value of self-development on the other.

A SCHEMA
FOR THE SELF NEXUS

We can now present a general schema of the functional processes that constitute the nexus of the self in integrative personality. In Figure 10–3 the dynamisms are represented as input and output strategies and the decision-control function is portrayed as having a coordinating influence on those strategies. Personification and evaluation, in turn, have coordinating influences on decision-control processes. Insight emerges as an attribute of the self nexus as a whole, but it is particularly relevant to the interaction between dynamisms and aspects of personal memory. For the sake of completeness, cognition, affect, and motoric processes are represented as functional aspects of integrative personality, but they fall outside the self nexus.

Those processes shown in the upper half of the figure tend to be potentially conscious aspects of memory; those closer to the bottom of the figure tend to be unconscious and available only under special conditions. Cognitive abilities and aspects of affective processes can become subject to insight or self-knowledge only to the extent they are incorporated into dynamisms. Reasoning abilities, for example, might be relevant to an individual's strategies of adjusting to change (i.e., conscious growth dynamisms). Similarly, affective expression would be open to self-knowledge to the extent it mediates an individual's output strategies.

Various theoretical positions on the self nexus and systems of psychotherapy can be examined using Figure 10–3. For example, psychoanalytic therapy focuses explicitly on dynamisms, whereas behavior therapy concentrates on producing changes in the processes of motoric functioning and output dynamisms. Both reality therapy and rational-emotive therapy emphasize cognitive processes in conjunction with personifications.

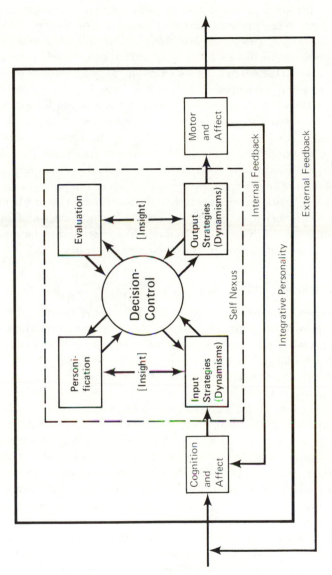

FIGURE 10-3 An overall schema for interrelating the processes that constitute the self nexus.

Regardless of where one begins an examination of the self or what tactics are used in psychotherapy, there are implications for the other aspects of the self nexus. While, for example, client-centered therapy explicitly focuses on the alignment between personification and evaluation, there is an enhancement of positive self-regard as therapy progresses, and dynamisms become progressively more subject to insight. While behavior therapies may focus on the immediate consequences of output strategies for observable behavior and emotional expression, feedback processes insure that such therapies will have profound consequences for the other processes in the self nexus—for example, an enhancement of self-regard in response to a newly developed skill (Royce & Powell, 1979, pp. 448, 450).

Although the general approach reflected by our figure focuses on the individual and the nature of internal processes underlying behavior, social field forces can easily come into consideration. Most of the significant inputs that a system such as that displayed in Figure 10-3 receives arise from a social context, and all of its expressions will be directed back at that social environment. In particular, evaluation of self is critically dependent on evaluation by others. Similarly, social role regulation provides much of the information by which individuals develop personifications, and "significant others" (particularly with family) serve as models that shape the dynamisms. In the final section of this chapter, we consider the general role of the cultural environment in greater detail.

Society and Self Image

We previously discussed a general model for interrelating the individual and society (see Figure 3-16). This analysis can now be taken a step further by noting that at the integrative level of personality the search for personal meaning critically involves self-image. The argument is that there is a similar search for social meaning that critically involves varying images of humankind in a manner that is comparable to self-image at the individual level. Thus, these images of humankind are guides to further social growth, just as self-image critically influences the individual's psychological development. Furthermore, we expect these social images of humankind to be dependent on their social counterpart—the styles and values of the group. Thus, we can generate a taxonomy of images of humankind via the collective counterpart of the individual styles and values shown in Table 10-1. Such an analysis is shown in Table 10-2. The columns of the table describe alternative values of society with respect to the nature of humankind; the rows describe alternative styles regarding how human beings are expected to pursue what is valued. Different societies at different times and places give varying emphasis to an individual's relations with others in the society, the things that an individual accomplishes, and the inner, psychic development of the individual. Modern technological societies, for example, value an individual's accomplishments most, while many Eastern societies give greater emphasis to an individual's inner, psychic development. But many North American Indian, Polynesian, and other communal societies place greater value on the social relationships among individuals within the society.

TABLE 10-2 Cultural Core Images of Human Nature

IDEAL WAYS INDIVIDUAL HUMAN BEINGS WORK TOWARD THEIR GOALS	THE MOST VALUABLE ASPECT OF INDIVIDUAL HUMAN BEINGS		
	RELATIONS WITH OTHERS IN THE WORLD	ACCOMPLISHMENTS	INNER DEVELOPMENT AND ASCENDANCY OVER THE WORLD
Interacting and being a part of the world	Individual humans are an integral part of society (Communal society)	Individual humans are achievers within the social context (Kibbutz society)	Individual humans are alienated from society and the focus is on "here-and-now" actualization (Epicurean society)
Thinking about and manipulating the world	Individual humans are replaceable parts of society (Socialistic society)	Individual humans are achievers and are set apart from each other by their achievements (Technological society)	Individual humans are contemplators of their individual nature (The Academy of Ancient Greece)
Transcending the abstract and physical world	Individual humans must always conform to the social myth of the state (Fascistic society)	Individual humans are ethical and spiritual achievers and are judged by those achievements (Protestant subculture)	Individual humans are integrated with society, but they reach beyond society for transcendental meaning (Humanistic society)

There is also a wide range of choices with respect to *how* individuals can pursue what they consider valuable. Thus, some societies (such as the kibbutz) emphasize an individual's interaction with the surrounding world, and most of the "back-to-nature" movements stress the importance of being part of the world. A similar emphasis was an important part of the Pueblo Indian cultural adaptation. On the other hand, technological societies emphasize the importance of the individual's abilities to manipulate the world mentally and physically, particularly the latter. But there are also many societies or cultures in which humans are expected to achieve what is valuable by transcending the physical world via one's inner psychic or spiritual resources. For example, many Protestant subcultures in the United States put emphasis on one's spiritual achievements, and in contemporary Islamic cultures the individual must conform to the (frequently religiously oriented) social myth of the state.

As can be seen in Table 10-2, these various combinations of societal styles and values yield a variety of images of the nature of humankind. These range from the communal image of individual humans as forming integral parts of society to the Utopian ideal in which individuals are integrated within society but can also reach beyond society for transcendental meaning. The range also includes at one extreme the Epicurean model of individual humans as experiencers who are basically alienated from social reality and emphasize limited, here-and-now experiences—such as in the hippy and drug cults that sprang up during the 1960s. At the other extreme we have the image of individual humans that is projected by contemporary Islamic Iran in which the individual is merely a concrete manifestation of the state's social myth. Between both extremes are the images of humankind offered by modern technological societies in which human beings are seen as achievers and individuals are set apart from each other by their achievements. Looking at it another way, as we move from the upper left cell of the table to the lower right cell, the individual is viewed as *a part of* society, as *apart from* society, and as *reaching beyond* society.

Table 10-2 suggests that the wide range in the images of human nature emerged out of very different adaptations to the world and represent very different ideas about the present and future course that humankind should follow. Individuals of all epochs are encapsulated by style and value commitments, which exist at both the level of society and the individual. This encapsulation separates individuals from one another and pushes societies in different directions. This can be seen by comparing the various cells of Table 10-2. Technological societies and Protestant subcultures, for example, share a common emphasis on accomplishments (which is consistent with Veblen's notion of the Protestant work ethic) and should, therefore, be able to interact with relative ease. On the other hand, our analysis indicates that there should be severe problems with any interchange between contemporary technological societies and contemporary Iran and other Islamic countries inasmuch as they do not share either style or value commitments. Even further removed from contemporary Iran would be the Epicurean image of humankind—as exemplified by the extreme repression of "pleasures of the flesh" in contemporary Iran. The long-range challenge is to break out of encapsulation without losing respect for the original style and value commitments.[4] The important things are, first, a greater awareness of the full range of possible style and value commitments; second, a willingness to scientifically study the assets and limitations of existing cultures as a basis for determining the relative viabilities of various style and value commitments; and finally, the evolution and implementation of new syntheses. Such an attempt is crucial at this point in history, for the many human images are no longer insulated from one another because of geographical, communicational, and other forms of cultural isolation. Rather, they currently stand in direct confrontation, thereby threatening world peace as well as individual stability.

[4]Twentieth-century Japan might well serve as a model of practical implementation, for Japan seems to have accommodated to the rational style and achievement value of contemporary Western culture while retaining the Eastern commitment to the metaphoric style and the intrinsic value of self-development.

11

Personality Integration, Personality Type, and Personal Meaning

In the preceding chapters we considered a variety of processes related to personality integration and personal meaning. Such constructions as world view, life style, and self-image, because of their integrative contribution to a variety of processes and because of their contribution to personal meaning, are critical in understanding personality. For example, world view reflects adaptations to external reality, and life style involves adaptations to existential reality. There are a variety of other constructions involved in adaptation and attaining personal meaning, such as ideology and emotion. Without all of these varied constructions individuals' cognitions would be chaotic juxtapositions of percepts, concepts, and symbols rather than meaningful interpretations of the world, and they would be unable to construct the life styles that provide frameworks for daily living. But, even more important, without the cohesive force of self, personality integration would be impossible. That is, everyday functioning would be fragmentary rather than coordinated, there would be little sense of inner reality, and there would be no basis on which to build a cumulative sense of personal meaning.

As we outlined in the preceding chapter, self (or the self nexus, see Figure 10–3) has multifaceted roles in personality. These roles include personifying one's self, making relevant evaluations, making adjustments via growth and stabilizing dynamisms, developing insight, and perhaps the most integrative involvement of self—its decision/control processes (which other theorists have described as the "ego" or the "I" of personality). Because of this pervasive impact of self, it is difficult to draw a distinction between the concepts of self and personality. However, we reserve the term *personality* for the total psychological system; in systems terminology, it is the *suprasystem*. There is no systems equivalent for *self*, since there are no explicit structural components like those for personality and its component systems. While the "self nexus" is composed of an individual's personal awareness and such other processes as evaluation and dynamisms, personality and self are coextensive but far from equivalent. This is further emphasized by our developmental analysis presented in the next chapter. Developmentally, the awareness of one's own personality and behavior is a life-long process. For example, while infancy is a period of "self-centeredness," it is *not* a period of self-awareness. In fact, self-awareness does not emerge as a potent force in personality integration until late childhood and, particularly, adolescence. This is followed by an increasingly conscious image of who one is throughout adulthood and old age. However, as we emphasized in Chapter 10 and as we discuss further in the present chapter, complete self-awareness, or knowledge of one's own personality, is impossible to achieve.

As with the concept of personal meaning, "self" is somewhat vague, in spite of the analysis presented in Chapter 10. As such it would seem to be of dubious empirical value to scientific psychology. Even so, it is indispensable to a theory of integrative personality.

In the present chapter we are focused at the highest level of personality, or what was identified as Level V in Table 1-2 and as the suprasystem in Figure 1-1. Thus, we are concerned with processes that integrate all the parts of personality into a unitary whole. This means we are particularly concerned with the issues related to personal meaning and person-situation interaction, and that we will also examine the concept of personality type as an indicator of differences in the way personalities are integrated.

PERSONALITY TYPE[1]

We define multivariate personality type as *the personality profile or the performance level on the total set of dimensions that constitute the suprasystem*. Similarly, we refer to type at the system level as *the system profile or the performance level on the subset of dimensions that constitute the system*. As described in Chapters 4 through 6, the construct of system type occurs at the apex of each of the six major systems (i.e., there is a sensory type, motor type, cognitive type, affective type, style type, and a value type).

---

[1] For a more thorough discussion of the concept of multivariate personality type see Diamond, Royce, and Voorhees (1981). We wish to acknowledge the important contributions of Steve Diamond and Burt Voorhees to our understanding of personality type.

What is involved here is the determination of a person's profile on all the dimensions of a given system and the subsequent empirical determination of a relatively small number of such profiles for the human population on the basis of profile or pattern analysis.

A complete personality profile based on the present version of individuality theory would involve around 185 dimensions, and it is likely that this number underestimates the number of factors required for an adequate model of personality. One way of dealing with this kind of complexity involves taking advantage of the hierarchical structure in each of the six systems. By focusing attention on the higher-order constructs in each of the six systems, system type can be estimated on the basis of two or three third-order constructs, or on the basis of eight to twelve dimensions if the analysis is extended to include the second stratum as well. At the level of the suprasystem a personality profile would consist of some 16 dimensions at the third order and around 50 dimensions if the analysis also includes constructs at the second-order level.

Two Adaptive Processes
in Personality Integration

We have proposed that linkages exist among factors in different systems, and that such factors tend to cooperate because they have analogous functions (see Table 8–2). We think the basis for such cooperation is also due to the overall search for personal meaning. That is, cooperative linkages emerge from adaptive interchanges with the environment such that consistency of processing is maintained among the interactive systems. For example, the rational style–conceptualizing ability coupling is a strong linkage and represents "natural" cooperation at the subsystem level. Similarly, the linkage between intrinsic value orientations and rational abilities also reflects a "natural" cooperative functioning. There are several reasons for all linkages such as these, including: (1) similarity of content focused on, (2) developmental relations, and (3) consistency in the relevant processing activities.

We think there are at least two different high-level adaptive strategies individuals pursue: assimilation and accommodation. Both are related to how cross-system linkages are manifested in interactions with the environment. In the *assimilative* strategy, individuals perform at roughly the same competence level on factors that are strongly linked across systems (see Table 8–2). For example, an assimilative individual might score relatively high on perceiving abilities, empirical styles, social values, and affective extraversion. What happens with such cross-system consistency is that personal meaning is constructed on the basis of information the individual is most capable of processing. This means information is assimilated in a way that is consistent with the total personality. However, an individual with such a profile will be relatively closed to rational and metaphorical kinds of information (and, thus, to accommodative interchanges). For example, this type of individual is consistently low on symbolizing, metaphoric style, self value, and affective stability; therefore, certain types of metaphoric information will be excluded. That is, symbolizing processing will be inefficient, cognitive styles will not select for this mode of processing, cognitive values will not emphasize the relevant information content, and affect will not be appropriately aroused. In short, certain types of information will be almost totally excluded, while other types will be consistently processed. Hence, assimilative individuals ignore particular classes of information in various psychological constructions.

There is a complementary tendency involving an emphasis on information that the individual is *least* able to process. This is the accommodative type, which arises from disparities in the profile on factors that align across systems. Since this type of profile results in different efficiencies on the aligned factors, individuals will be intensively exposed to their relative weaknesses in addition to their strengths. For example, if an individual is high on rational style but low on conceptualizing abilities (relative to the other styles and cognitive abilities), stylistic commitment will repeatedly expose the relative weakness of the conceptual ability factors. Since rational styles and conceptual abilities are strongly cooperative, the situations that such an individual can most effectively deal with in terms of styles are apt to be the same situations in which cognition is apt to be least effective. Stylistic commitments would thus force frequent activation of conceptualizing abilities in spite of their relative weaknesses. Such accommodative interactions are less efficient, but they are less encapsulating and can also be rewarding in terms of new ideas, feelings, values, and such (Royce, 1964b).

Integrative personality can be viewed as a complex interplay among assimilative and accommodative processes. We think the relative strength of these two tendencies differs among individuals to the extent that some individuals can be described as assimilators and others can be described as accommodators. These two types provide examples of the complex ways in which individuals adapt to environmental demands. While we cannot adequately deal with the full range of environmental demands that confront individuals, it is possible to describe the importance of the external situations that individuals must face. We do this in the next section in terms of person-situation interactions.

PERSON-SITUATION INTERACTIONS

It should be patently clear that behavior is a function of both the individual and the situation in which behavior occurs. Furthermore, it is likely that a significant proportion of the variance is attributable to person-situation interaction. The demands put on individuals in various situations can be described by the concept of *situational template*, by which we mean *the profile of psychological requirements for adapting to a specifiable situation*.

The concepts of *situational template* and *personality type* are both highly compressed conceptions of the information processing requirements for coping in the complex environments in which individuals find themselves.[2] The implication is that the degree of overlap between situational and personality profiles is crucially related to psychological functioning. For example, if the corresponding profiles are exactly the same (i.e., the same components and beta weights), performance should be perfect. If on the other hand, the profiles are totally different, then performance should be impossible. But, since neither of these two *logical* extremes are probable in real-life situations, we must look to the range of mismatches in between for relevant empirical realities. The most obvious examples of such mismatches are the masses of individuals who function below average in a given occupation or career. Such individuals possess the necessary aptitudes (e.g., sensory, cognitive, motor) and temperament (e.g., affect, style, value), but they function at a suboptimal level in a specifiable subset of the relevant dimensions. Other examples are occupational misfits—the stereotype of the square peg in a round hole. Such individuals simply do not possess the necessary aptitudes (e.g., sensory, cognitive, motor) or temperament (e.g., affect, style, value) for the task at hand.

Combining the concepts of personality type and situational template leads to the concept of *type-template match*. *This refers to the degree of alignment between the profiles of the situation and the person.* A perfect alignment would mean that a particular personality type was optimally matched to the demands of the situation. On the other hand, one consequence of a type-template mismatch is *compensatory functioning*—i.e., adapting to situational demands in terms of the available personality type. Since no single personality type can be optimal for all situations, it follows that some compensatory functioning is an inevitable characteristic of normal functioning (and the greater the type-template mismatch, the greater should be the degree of compensatory functioning). If the mismatch is primarily due to the demands of the situation, one form of adaptation is for the person to switch to a less discrepant environment. However, if the situational demands can be dealt with, adaptation will occur via some mix of assimilation and accommodation. Such adaptations can also involve changes in the external situational template, such as when individuals are able to change the surrounding social structure.

Type-template match refers to the degree of alignment between situational template and personality type, but *normative match refers to the degree of alignment between a specifiable norm (i.e., plans for achieving a goal or purpose) and feedback from the environment.* When there is a close normative match (within a specifiable tolerance), no adjustments in either the environment or the person are required. In these cases the conclusion is that the norm has assimilated the demands of the situation. However, normative adjustments are required when there is a mismatch. If the normative shift subsequently leads to a match, we have referred to such changes as accommodation.

---

[2]Despite this compression we have not elaborated further on the concept of situational template on the grounds that situational determinants go beyond the boundaries of individuality theory. However, we have elaborated on the role of multivariate personality type as a manifestation of personality integration in the context of individuality theory in Diamond, Royce, and Voorhees (1981).

The basic system circuit presented in Figure 3-3 was meant to apply to relatively simple goals or purposes as well as norms generated by higher levels of personality. Consider, for example, that a normative match can involve such molar goals or purposes as world view. This is illustrated in Figure 11-1. The idea is that, after appropriate adjustments via negative feedback, there is a match between environmental feedback and the individual's world view. This means that the extant world view is successfully projected onto the environment (this is the assimilative case accomplished via W_2. The accommodative case is also illustrated in Figure 11-1, and in this case the environment is projected onto world view. The first world view (W_1) is unable to cope with the environmental input, and adjustments are called for via positive feedback. By exploring various alternatives a new world view (W_2) is arrived at which will lead to a normative match, and the individual is described as having accommodated to the environment.[3] For example, individuals with rational views of the world sometimes find that metaphoric interpretations are more appropriate in particular situations. A radical change in world view could even involve a reordering of epistemic commitments, such as when a strongly empirical type becomes a strongly metaphoric type.

[3]These are, of course, examples of learning. Thus, the term accommodation covers an important segment of learning. The reader is referred to the factor-learning model in Chapter 3 for the details of such changes. The crucial aspect of this model is change in the underlying structure in addition to change in response. It is our view that individuality theory provides a more explanatory version of what goes on in learning. For example, if the required change in world view is primarily perceptual in nature (i.e., a question of perceptual learning), the empirical style and the perceptual cognitive subhierarchies are activated. And if the situational template calls for an accommodation in concepts (i.e., conceptual learning) or symbols (symbolic learning), then still different styles and cognitive hierarchies are activated.

FIGURE 11-1 World view depicted as a norm in the basic system circuit.

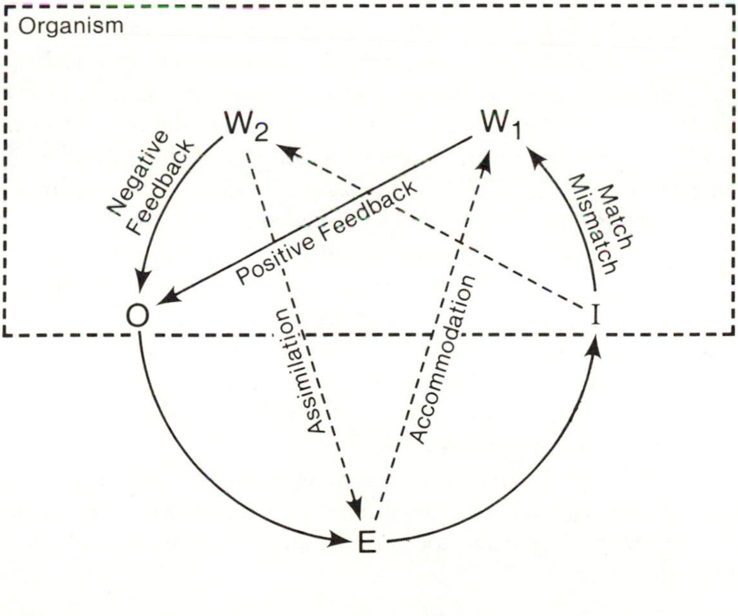

Personality integration involves a delicate balance of components at all levels of the suprasystem—interactions among elemental components, subsystems, and systems. It also involves the unifying impact of such constructions as belief systems, emotion, world view, life style, and self-image. Such interactions and integrations are, of course, enormously complex, and individuals continually attempt to find a dynamic balance between their assimilative and accommodative interchanges with the environment. The question that always underlies such interchanges is: ''Are such actions meaningful to me?'' From the standpoint of the individual, the whole point of such interchanges is to create meaningfulness. We now present some further discussion of the concept of personal meaning.

THE CONSTRUCT
OF PERSONAL MEANING

The construct of personal meaning is not only the most molar and diffuse but also the most pervasive and important construct we have considered. Consciously and unconsciously, meaning permeates everything individuals do, think, feel, and believe, and leads to an enormous range of responses. Whatever is meant by personal meaning, its core meaning concerns the significance each individual attaches to the critical aspects of living. But such terms as *life* and *significance* are so broad in reference that personal meaning is applicable to all aspects of existence. Thus, personal meaning refers to an individual's view of world, life, and self—the views one has on the big questions, such as the nature of reality and being, questions of origin and destiny, what is worth living and dying for, and who one really is.

Although this broad scope of the concept of personal meaning was intentional, this is not likely to help in giving the term useful empirical referents. Despite the difficulties in examining personal meaning from an empirical scientific standpoint, any theory of personality and individual differences that faces the full complexity of its subject cannot avoid it as an important, primitive given. By that we mean that a theory of personality should begin with the assumption that people live out their lives in terms of what they see as ''meaningful''—that is, in terms of idiosyncratic ways of approaching life. This is why we have emphasized the importance of personal meaning throughout our efforts to construct a general theory of personality and individual differences. This emphasis is consistent with the emphasis of a variety of other personality theorists (e.g., Jung, Rogers, Maslow) and with Maddi's proposal that the ''ultimate problem of motivational psychology is to understand how man searches for and finds personal meaning'' (1971, p. 137). In short, personal meaning is pervasive in terms of its influence on the behavior of individuals. In nearly everything individuals do there is always the question in the background as to whether their activities and lives are meaningful, and this should be an important focus in personality theory in spite of the empirical difficulties it poses.

The Validation Criteria
of Personal Meaning

In our attempt to explicate personal meaning we want to suggest that there are a variety of aspects to it that are of concern to each individual. As we have said, personal meaning is closely tied to an individual's world view, life style, and self-image. The relation between these three constructs and the construct of personal meaning is illustrated in Figure 11–2. As suggested by the lower segment of the figure, interactions between style and cognition account for variations in world view, affective-value interactions account for differences in life style, and variations in self-image are primarily due to style-value interactions. The important linkage to personal meaning occurs via the concept of validation criteria indicated as the top row of Figure 11–2. Epistemic validity is concerned with the validity of knowledge claims and refers to the truth criterion that underlies a specific world view. We discussed the relevance of the perception–misperception, logical–illogical, and idiosyncratic–universal criteria for different ways of knowing in Chapter 9. Existential validity, related to affect-value interaction, is focused on specifiable norms that underlie different life styles. For example, some life styles are more relevant to mastery, others are more relevant to actualization, and still others emphasize the importance of beneficence (see Chapter 9). In short, epistemic norms have to do with validating reality images and existential norms have to do with validating images of life. The third norm, indicated as the central column in Figure 11–2, has to do with validating a self-image. The key requirement in this case is acceptance, and we have suggested that some individuals consider congruence to be of greatest importance, others put emphasis on accomplishment, and still others consider symbolic significance to be the most relevant criterion (see Chapter 10).

Existential Aspects
of Personal Meaning

While we have been largely concerned with a variety of more scientific-analytic aspects of the concept of personal meaning, we are also concerned with the existential aspects of what it means to be human. The most salient existential issues concern the making of choices concerning how to do things, what is most important to do, and what kind of person one is. The climate of the contemporary world is such that individuals are confronted with a vast array of style and value systems from which they must make choices that are personally meaningful. The situation that confronts individuals in modern society is such that choices *must* be made, but there is no way to know beforehand which choices will ultimately make the most sense in terms of personal meaning. This kind of freedom requires tough shoulders, and the existential failures in Sartre's literary products such as *No Exit* and *The Flies* are potent examples of this aspect of the human condition. As we see it, these miserable creatures of Sartre's represent the struggle of individuals coming to grips with the problem of meaning. The fact that they so often end in despair is a statement about the condition of modern humankind.

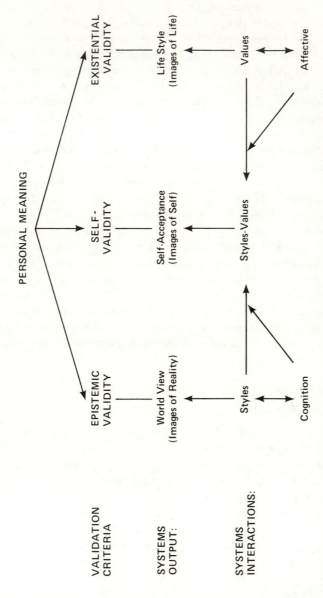

FIGURE 11-2 The decomposition of personal meaning into validation criteria, showing the relationships to the basic systems of personality.

This has been a favorite theme in literature, and it will undoubtedly continue to be in the future, for it reflects a perennial failure of man. [Good examples include] Guy de Maupassant's *The Necklace* (Maugham, 1939), where a lifetime is wasted on paying off a necklace which turns out to have been imitation; or Chekhov's *Cherry Orchard* (1920), where a group of aristocrats are identified with a clear enough value hierarchy, but the values in which they invest are no longer viable. [However, it is doubtful that the emptiness and horror of misplaced values is] more potently portrayed than in Tolstoy's *The Death of Ivan Ilytch* (Maugham, 1939). Here is a man who had been content with himself all his life. He had achieved reasonable material success and had served well as a high court judge. He is severely ill, and in fact is dying. The meaninglessness of death, and, worse yet, of his personal life, forces itself upon his last days of consciousness. He says, for example:

> "What do I want? To live and not to suffer . . . .To live? How? . . . Why, to live as I used to—well and pleasantly." "As you lived before, well and pleasantly?" the voice persisted. And in imagination he began to recall the best moments of his pleasant life. But strange to say none of those best moments of his pleasant life now seemed at all what they had then seemed. . . . And the further he departed from childhood and the nearer he came to the present the more worthless and doubtful were the joys . . . . "It is as if I had been going downhill while I imagined I was going up. And that is really what it was. I was going up in public opinion, but to the same extent life was ebbing away from me. And now it is all done and there is only death." . . . "Maybe I did not live as I ought to have done." "But how could that be, when I did everything properly?" he replied, and immediately dismissed from his mind this, the sole solution of all the riddle of life and death, as something quite impossible. . . . And whenever the thought occurred to him, as it often did, that it all resulted from his not having lived as he ought to have done, he at once recalled the correctness of his whole life and dismissed so strange an idea. (Maugham, 1939, pp. 589–90)

> Finally, Ivan Ilytch somehow gains insight into himself and faces the fact that he has invested in a value [hierarchy] which for him was essentially empty, for he says that "his professional duties and the whole arrangement of his life and his family, and all his social and official interests, might all have been false. He tried to defend all those things to himself and suddenly felt the weakness of what he was defending. There was nothing to defend. . . . All you have lived for and still live for is falsehood and deception, hiding life and death from you." (Maugham, 1939, p. 590)

Such a theme, however, is most likely to receive its best development in periods of value transition, such as the present century. . . . Take, for example, Charles Gray in J. P. Marquand's (1949) *Point of No Return*. Gray realizes a lifelong ambition, the vice-presidency of a bank, only to discover that his essentially materialistically oriented goals are not what he really wants. Through a lifetime of little choices he ends up essentially unfulfilled in any deep sense, and in the end he is forced to the conclusion that he has reached "the point of no return." John Phillips (1953) in the *Second Happiest Day*, warns us that we had best choose carefully, for we may get what we think we want. In this dramatization the hero willingly and very readily sells out for material and social advantages, even in the face of having to put up with a wife who will give him a life of hell. She is part of the deal, however, but, of course, he is under the impression that he really wants her. Both the wife and the job represent "success" of an external sort, but he is willing to sacrifice everything else for these all-important goals. An opposite kind of value confusion is brought out in *The Man in the Gray Flannel Suit* (Wilson, 1955). In this novel the hero allows his talents and abilities to lie fallow. He refuses to work at the high level of which he is capable because he does not want to risk what he's already got. In short, he sells out for security and safety, a value orientation which [characterized] the post-World War II, cold-war generation. (Royce, 1964b, pp. 108–9)

All of these literary characters are looking for the same thing—justification as a human being, the depth of meaning which follows from an investment of values which is consistent with one's individuality.

In one of his poems T. S. Eliot (1952) says we are "hollow men," and in *The Cocktail Party* (Eliot, 1952) he explores the ramifications of 20th century [emptiness]. . . . Huxley (1932) and Orwell (1949) move from meaningless, hollowness, and emptiness to thingness, or "mechanical man." That is, they take highly specialized, robotized, non-feeling, non-thinking man as we know him in our highly industrialized, Western civilization, and they fictitiously take this dehumanization process to its logical conclusion. One of their major themes is that individuality gets crushed by the state. Unfortunately, it is not necessary to turn to fiction to realize the truth of this state of affairs. We merely have to recount the recent totalitarianisms of the fascists, the Nazis, and other forms of dictatorship. Even democratic socialism runs the risk of losing the individual in one of the closets of bureaucracy. Bureaucrats in a democratic world, of course, recognize the political equality of the individual, but many [Britons] are of the opinion that the humanness of a person, both of the bureaucrat and of the member of socialist society who is being serviced, somehow gets lost in the red tape [and in services which are dictated by the outputs of a computer]. (Royce, 1964b, pp. 72–73)

The dehumanization process suggests that man is dying, and the [ever present threat of thermonuclear war] suggests that man's 'nothingness' may be closer than the existentialists think. About all that remains of humanity is an outer shell, for the inner man is on his last legs. And the twentieth century [existential dilemma] is one of purposelessness, meaninglessness, valuelessness, hollowness, emptiness. No amount of tranquilizer drugs or positive thinking can cope with a situation of this magnitude. The depth probing of the psychotherapist or the meditative life of the reflective man is necessary here in order to help man come to grips with [value commitments. The existential failure] gives up in despair in the face of freedom and responsibility to choose. The weight of the world descends upon the person with such a view, [and one] simply sinks under the impact of nothingness. Apparently what is devastating is the realization that nothingness does, in fact, exist as a legitimate choice, and the . . . existentialist failure seems drawn to such a choice by default. . . . [In summary], modern man seems to be saying something like this: "If you can't convince me that there is some kind of ultimate reality, or if you can't convince me that there are certain absolute values by which I can live my life, I'll commit psychological suicide. That is, either convince me that there is one truth or one right way of doing things or I'll conclude that everything is meaningless and I won't try anymore." (Royce, 1964b, pp. 76–77)

FINAL COMMENT
ON ENCAPSULATION

Royce (1964b) has described humans as being encapsulated in the sense that knowledge of ultimate reality is desired but is unattainable. Thus, one is encapsulated by virtue of the individual paths to knowledge that are available. While different paths to knowledge, such as rationalism or empiricism, may provide penetrating insights into reality or enriching images of the world, none (individually or in combination) can hurdle, or otherwise overcome, the barrier that stands between humankind and ultimate reality. Furthermore, to the extent that a particular way of knowing is not made use of, images of reality will be impoverished. Royce has discussed the meaning of encapsulation as:

> claiming to have all the truth when one only has part of it . . . claiming to have truth without being sufficiently aware of the limitations of one's approach to truth . . . looking at life partially, but issuing statements concerning the wholeness of living. In its most important sense the term 'encapsulation' refers to projecting a knowledge of ultimate reality from the [conceptual] framework of a limited reality image. (1964b, p. 30)

New disciplines of knowledge are being formed at an ever-increasing pace, each with an ever-decreasing range of focus on reality; hardly a day passes without the birth of a new theory, philosophy, slogan, or banner-waving spiritual revival that lays claim to ultimate truth. The nature of reality has not been probed deeply enough (nor is it likely that it ever will be) to not have new disciplines and theories. But to the extent that the restricted images of reality they offer are not recognized, or the inanity of claims to ultimate truth go uncriticized, individuals will remain ever more encapsulated.

Individuality theory, especially our analyses of ways of being in the world and self-image, suggests other aspects of encapsulation. As indicated in Chapter 9 (see Figure 9–3), there is a barrier between humankind and Utopian existence. While distinctive modes of living can lead to a meaningful existence in the world, there still remains a barrier between humankind and a sense of absolute being in the world. This Janus-faced character of encapsulation is illustrated in Figure 11–3. As shown by the left side of the figure, the search for knowledge of the world is limited by the distinctive ways of knowing that are available to humankind and by the epistemic commitments that are made. Thus, knowledge of reality is restricted to the right side of the barrier between humankind and ultimate reality. Analogously, the search for a meaningful existence in the world (see the right side of the figure) is limited by the distinctive value orientations available and the commitments that are actually made. Thus, individuals are further encapsulated by the barrier between humankind and Utopian existence. Meaningful existence is restricted to the left side of this barrier.

Just as there has been a proliferation of philosophies on world views in recent times, there has also been a surge of new philosophies for living. Some of these philosophies for living have been self-styled as new religions, others as psychologies, philosophies, or psychotherapies. All present dilemmas to humanity in this age of mass communication, where it is difficult to filter out information about competing philosophies and values. But, most importantly, all contribute to encapsulation to the extent that restricted modes of being are defended and proselytized as the ultimate in meaningful existence. Philosophies of life are based on limited value orientations and feelings about what it means to be a part of the world. If the pitfalls of encapsulated existence are to be avoided, the limitations of

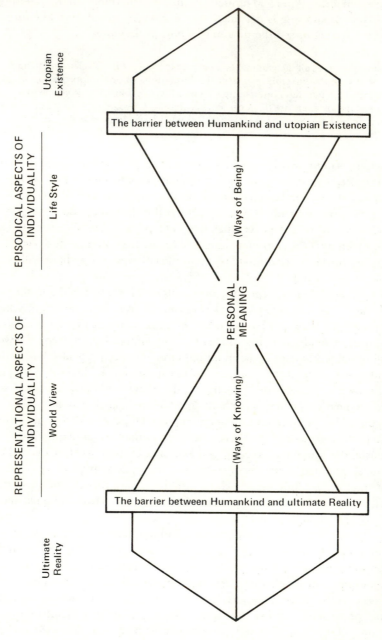

FIGURE 11-3 The double aspect of encapsulation. (From Powell & Royce, 1978)

240

the existential validity of distinctive philosophies of life must be recognized. In short, movement away from encapsulation requires considerable effort directed toward broadening value orientations so as to enrich one's existence in the world.

Finally, we should consider what, to self-conscious, reflective, choosing individuals, must be the ultimate encapsulating barrier—this is the barrier between humankind and absolute self-knowledge (see Figure 10–2), such that individuals are restricted to images of themselves based on particular style and value commitments. While many philosophies, psychologies, psychotherapies, religions, cults, and meditative systems seem to promise the key to self-insight, each offers an encapsulated pathway to the extent they are based on particular style-value commitments. The fundamental problem remains that there is no way to reach an ultimate reality about one's self. However, individuals can enrich their images of themselves by pursuing new avenues of understanding and valuing. Furthermore, in this age of empiricism, and occasional rationalism, individuals should also be encouraged to explore metaphoric ways of understanding themselves and the world around them.

12

Personality Integration
over the Life Span

In this chapter we present a summary of the qualitative changes or transformations that personality undergoes over the life span. There is considerable empirical evidence to support the notion that psychological functioning becomes increasingly differentiated over the life span. Werner (1948) summarized the earlier research that supported a similar hypothesis in the form of his *orthogenetic* principle. Witkin and his associates (1962) also present evidence for differentiation of a variety of psychological processes, and Kearsley, Buss, and Royce (1975) discuss differentiation and consolidation among the factors in the cognitive domain and present a structural model involving factor divergence, parallelism, and convergence. For example, their model suggests that higher-order factors of perceiving, conceptualizing, and symbolizing differentiate out of a more global, less articulated, and less well-developed perceiving factor. Furthermore, most of the cognitive factors are thought to emerge during childhood and adolescence and continue to develop in parallel throughout much of adulthood. In old age these differentiated structures become more consolidated and reverse the trend that was begun in infancy (and prenatally).

Other domains of personality undergo similar transformations, although the empirical evidence is too meager to propose a convincing model of the relevant convergences and divergences for each of these other areas. However, in Figure 12–1 we provide a speculative model of system and subsystem development based

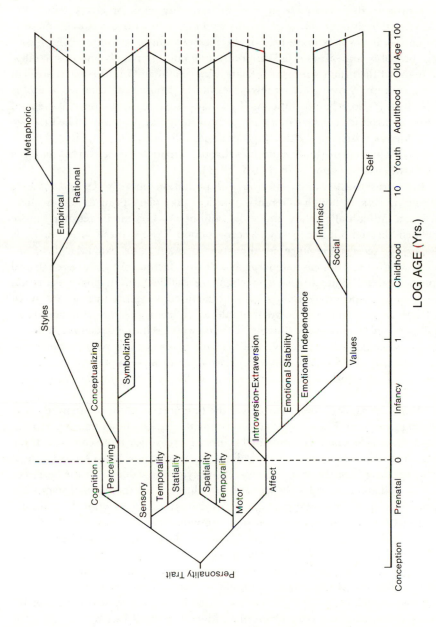

FIGURE 12-1 Model of system and subsystem differentiation and consolidation.

on the overall model of qualitative development presented in Chapter 7. As described in Chapter 3, lines that diverge from each other represent factor *divergence*, while those that run parallel reflect factor *parallelism*, and converging lines represent the *convergence* of two or more systems or subsystems. We hypothesize that differentiation of sensory and motor functions occurs prenatally, although this is perhaps more true of the former than of the latter. The motor system probably undergoes rapid differentiation both prenatally and postnatally, since many of the infant's movements are very global and unarticulated at birth but develop rapidly over the first few years of life. Many such changes in motor functions may also relate to functional changes, such as in the development of cognitive controls for constructing and monitoring motor programs. The first two years of life are critical in the development and differentiation of various factors, although this process no doubt continues throughout adolescence and beyond (see also Lewis & Rosenbaum, 1978; Izard, 1971).

In contrast to affect and cognition, differentiation among styles and values is a lifelong process, although differentiation does take place prior to adolescence. That is, an individual's values and styles continue to become increasingly more articulated throughout the postadolescent period. Along these lines, there is evidence of factor divergence in the style domain. For example, field independence does not appear to emerge as a distinct factor until about age 10, and it is probable that it is not distinct from cognitive abilities until that time. As a final comment with respect to consolidation and factor convergence that occurs in old age, these phenomena may be attributable to the compensatory functioning of overall personality and its six systems. That is, with declining sensory and motor skills, as well as declining cognitive abilities and increasing introversion and emotional instability in affect, the remaining components of the suprasystem coalesce to form integrated and compensatory structures for attaining the various goals of personality.

With increasing differentiation over the first portion of the life span, there is increasing pressure for more integration among the various functions of personality. That is, as information processing becomes increasingly more complex, there is increasing need for structures to coordinate such activities. The best example of this "integrating" process is the emergence of styles and values over the period of late childhood and early adolescence. We can illustrate the increasing integration of personality via a series of system diagrams that outline the relationships among the various systems and components of individuality. We begin with Figure 12-2a, in which integrative personality is depicted as relatively undifferentiated but nevertheless as a multilevel, hierarchical system. Such a model best describes the structure of personality in very young infancy, where the primary concern is with the adaptation of evolving perceptual structures to internal activation and to the outside world. Figure 12-2b, on the other hand, is a system model of integrative personality at a later phase of childhood, in which there is a more differentiated and hierarchical organization. There are distinct cognitive and affective systems that form a learning-adaptive level of integrative personality,

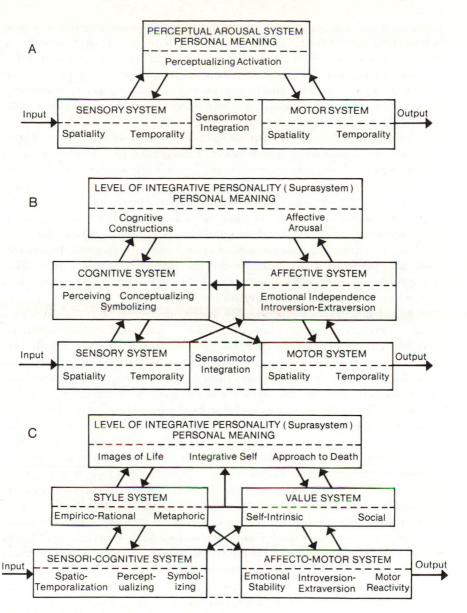

FIGURE 12-2 Hypothetical systems model of personality in (A) very young infancy, (B) late childhood and early adolescence, and (C) very old age.

although these two systems are not fully differentiated as yet. Styles and values have not yet emerged, and the integrative goals of the system can be broadly described as the maintenance of emotional balance. With increasing differentiation, however, and with increasing cultural training directed at instilling particular styles and values to guide and coordinate cognitive and affective activities, an integrative, self-organizing layer of personality emerges. Thus, personality in adulthood is represented in Figure 1-1, where all six systems have emerged as relatively independent but complexly interacting components of integrative personality. Now the integrative goal becomes one of maintaining personal meaning, and styles and values can be seen to occupy a central role in the coordination of the rest of the system to attain this goal.

To complete this overview of life-span developmental integration, Figure 12-2c provides a multilevel, system model of integrative personality in very old age. The primary feature incorporated in this figure is that much consolidation occurs over the last portion of the life span, such that there is no longer a sharp distinction between the cognitive and sensory systems on the one hand, and the affective and motor systems on the other. Accordingly, there is decreasing interchange between the individual and the outside world—one is more restricted to rational and metaphoric reconstructions of reality and to very gross, undifferentiated, affective expressions. Furthermore, the integrative goals of personality during this later stage are described in terms of constructing images of life, one's approach to death, and a general integration of self. [1]

As with other aspects of personality, goals or decision problems also undergo systematic evolution over the life span. These changes reflect the various influences of heredity, culture, and self, and the fluctuations in the functions of these structures. For example, the growing complexity of the individual over the early years of life necessitates such changes from a purely biological standpoint, and culture requires that an individual's goals change with increasing age and "maturity." This problem of goal evolution can be viewed as closely related to the perspective developed by Erikson wherein an individual is viewed as passing through a life-time sequence of identity crises and it is thought that each crisis must be successfully resolved before the next is undertaken. Analogously, we view the individual as taking up a series of decision problems that must be successfully solved before there is further growth (in the form of differentiation and integration) and new decision problems to manage. Furthermore, individuality theory conceptualizes regression as a reversion to earlier decision problems. For example, "neurotic" reactions can develop when an individual experiences a "loss of values" (which is not uncommon in modern society). Individuals so entrapped in existential crises can be viewed as temporarily integrated at an earlier phase of development (e.g., the concern is often with cognitive-affective balance) until one can develop newer, more appropriate values and decision problems. There are many similarities between this view and that expressed by Dabrowski (1964), and

[1]It should be noted that the "old age" personality structure constitutes a "reduced version" of the "adult" personality structure. Preadult personality structures are also "reduced versions." The postadult reduction is a matter of developmental regression, whereas the preadult reduction is a reflection of developmental immaturity. Thus, the adult personality structure is our norm for maturity in that it constitutes personality functioning in its most complete and differentiated form.

it is important to note that the Piagetian recognition of shifting levels of equilibration is analogous to our notion of goal evolution.

The integrative goals of personality have been described in terms of *personal meaning* in Figures 1-1 and 12-2, and in previous statements where personal meaning has been linked to world view, life style, and self-image in adulthood. But what is meaningful to the developing individual should shift with the emergence of new systems and components and with the life-span shifts in system "dominance" and "peaking." Thus, for example, in infancy "meaning" is unarticulated and unconscious, and is primarily focused around the coactivation of the sensory and motor systems, and the diffuse functioning of cognition and affect. Physiological needs, such as comfort and contact, are more dominant in the individual's actions during this phase of development. Later on, during adolescence, meaning centers around cognitive and affective functioning and the questioning of values. In terms of system interactions this means that during adolescence cognition and affect are most critical—though styles, and in particular, values, take on increasing importance. In later adolescence cognitive-value interactions become increasingly important and give rise to the development of an individual's personal beliefs, ideology, ethics, and so on. This is the time in life when the individual is most apt to become involved in cults, ideological movements, or religious revivals. Although such engagements may develop out of sincere personal convictions, they may also come about as symptoms of the desire to reorganize one's value commitments. Individuals may also become involved in cults or ideological movements during later phases of development when there is value confusion or alienation (as in old age), though again, such engagements can stem from strongly held personal beliefs and convictions.

As we suggested in the Introduction (Chapter 1), personal meaning in adulthood is primarily a matter of struggling with three questions: "What kind of world is this I live in?" "How can I live my life such that my needs and values are satisfied?" and, "Who am I?" Answers to the first question, however tentative or changing they might be, yield the individual's world view, answers to the second yield a life style, and answers to the third yield a self-image. Overall, the focus of adulthood and the second half of life shifts increasingly toward what Carl Jung called the "quest for meaning," or a living out of one's thoughts, feelings, and values, as well as a struggle with various existential crises.

With increasing age, the focus shifts toward greater emphasis on self-completion and life style. Thus, there is an increasing assertion of self, without regard for the consequences, in combination with a retrospective analysis and summing up of one's life. In short, with advancing age personal meaning becomes increasingly existentially oriented, as in the concern for the "meaning of life." This quest for life's meaning is either resolved or further revised during the last phase of life. It involves an overall integration or coalescing of self, world view, and life style. One's life is reviewed as an affirmation or failure of "life's meaning," and existential angst probably reaches a peak. And like Ivan Ilytch (from Tolstoy), each individual must face the real possibility that ''All you have lived for and still live for is falsehood and deception, hiding life and death from you'' (cited in Royce, 1964a, p. 124). As summarized in Royce:

> each of us must face death, not in the abstract, not in terms of obituary columns and vital statistics, but in terms of *my death*, and in the not too distant future. But we must also face life, not in terms of the roles we play, the money we make, or the small daily frustrations, but in terms of the long range meaning of *my* total life span and the longer range meaning of the existence of *mankind*. (1964a, p. 125)

Given the assumption that the self-concept is primarily a function of styles and values, it follows that the integrative role of the concept of self is primarily unconscious in infancy, surges into consciousness during adolescence along with the emergence of styles and values, is well-articulated in adulthood, and is dominant and assertive in old age. The direction of one's life will vary accordingly. In infancy one's life is largely programmed by heredity, as exemplified in the temperamental differences among infants that extend well beyond childhood (e.g., excitability and introversion–extraversion). Adolescence represents a time in life when one is directed more by the culture and significant others (peer groups, family, potential mates, etc.). But in adulthood, direction is a complex outcome of heredity, environment, and ''self.'' One can choose, for example, to be married, to have children, to divorce, or to do none of these things. Individuals can change careers, or decide not to pursue a career at all. However, such self-direction is not necessarily comforting, as emphasized in existential and other writings. For example, Riesman's (1950) other-directed person would prefer to follow the herd rather than the dictates of his or her underlying individuality, not because of a belief in the herd, but because there is a greater consequent feeling of security (i.e., less ambiguity). ''Fromm (1941) takes this analysis many steps further and points out that modern man prefers to be told by strong, authoritarian leaders, that he wants his values handed down to him in an absolute form, that a Hitler is a very understandable and perhaps unconsciously desired product of our times, and that we literally want to escape from freedom.'' (Royce, 1964b, p. 72)

Finally, development in old age is primarily an assertion of self, but, of course, culture can erect strong barriers to increasing self-direction and completion, such as forced retirement and the institutionalization of helplessness via old-age homes. Similarly, biological aging provides the ultimate deterrent to self-direction. Both biological and cultural processes can interact and thereby conspire to rob death totally of meaningfulness and dignity. Older people are not treated well in Western society. Furthermore, this trend seems to be getting worse just at the time that medicine and nutrition are prolonging life (and, thereby, making it possible for the aged to suffer even greater indignities). This is the plight of many of our aged, though it does not have to be this way (Seligman, 1975, gives some chilling statistics on the effects of institutionalization on the mortality rate of the aged).

OVERVIEW
OF DEVELOPMENTAL CHANGES

To summarize without qualifiers, we have put forward a multidimensional, multisystem model of personality development over the life span. Life-span development consists of increases and decreases in the factor dimensions of each domain, differentiation and consolidation of various structures and their functions, increasing hierarchicalization and integration of system structures and functions, evolution of the integrative goals of personality, and increasing self-direction or self-organization. All these transformations in personality and its component subsystems are the result of hereditary, cultural, and self-generated determinants, as well as the fluctuations in the functioning of these three sources of variation. Exploration, creativity, and blind variations in the functions of heredity, culture, and the individual introduce an essential unpredictability into developmental psychology. For example, within the limits provided by heredity and culture, an individual's idiosyncratic experiences make possible a wide range of creative courses in development; therefore, one can only project broad ''life bands'' for the course of an individual's development rather than the thin line of the typical mathematical curve.

Five phases of the life span can be characterized in terms of the above transformations (see Table 12–1). Infancy and childhood can be described as periods of rapid quantitative change and differentiation, with minimal integration and self-direction. Styles and values are not developed as distinct systems during these phases, and the greatest differentiation occurs within cognition and affect. With adolescence, however, there begins a period that is more dominated by affect and the emergence of style and value commitments. Integration occurs via cognitive and affective interactions, with the primary goal of emotional balance. Self-direction begins during this phase, paralleling style and value development. Adulthood brings on a period of relative stability which is dominated more by cognitive conceptualizing abilities and individual *intrinsic* value and *rational* style commitments. Although changes of great magnitude are possible during this period of life and self-direction is maximal, such changes are essentially unpredictable and probably lead to heightened affective involvement, at least temporarily. During the later phases of adulthood there are significant declines in sensory and motor skills and in some cognitive abilities, but there are continued increases in symbolizing abilities and increasing importance given to *self* value orientations and metaphoric styles. Finally, old age brings on a period of further decline in most sensory and motor and some cognitive abilities. *Self* value orientations are dominant, but self-direction is apt to be hampered by one's failing body and by the prejudicial reactions of society toward the aged (particularly in Western societies). The general theme of this phase of life is the approach of one's death and the ''completion'' of life.

TABLE 12-1 Summary Comparison of the Transformations of Personality during Various Phases of the Life Span

PHASE OF THE LIFE SPAN	PERSONALITY TRANSFORMATIONS				
	QUANTITATIVE	DIFFERENTIATION	INTEGRATION	INTEGRATIVE GOALS	SELF-DIRECTION
Infancy	Greatest changes in sensory and motor areas; style and value at their lowest	All systems and subsystems differentiated	Little or no personality integration	Adaptive sensory-motor integration	Minimal
Childhood	Greatest changes in the areas of cognition and affect	Subsystems and their components and higher-order factors further differentiated	Integrative action largely through affective processes	Adaptive cognitive-affective constructions	Slight
Adolescence	Greatest changes in affect, style, and value, but all are changing; sensory system at its peak	Emergence of styles and values; articulation of them increasingly important	Cognition and affect are the integrative systems	Emotional, or cognitive-affective balance; *social* value and *empirical* style dominant	Phase of initial formulation of life goals
Adulthood	Period of relative stability; some growth in styles and values, with slow decline in sensory, motor, and cognitive subdomains of perceiving and conceptualizing	Greatest differentiation in styles and values; articulation of one's life goals of central importance and a continuing process	Styles and values operate as distinct systems that organize or integrate personality	World view, life style and self-image are the focus of further growth and development; *intrinsic* value and *rational* style dominant	Phase of maximal self-direction; generally stable period, although great change is possible
Old Age	Period of even greater decline in cognitive conceptualizing and perceiving, with continued increase in symbolizing abilities; further declines in sensory and motor	A variety of functions of personality begin to consolidate in order to compensate for decline in sensory, motor, and cognitive abilities	Increasing importance given to style and value commitments and the "interiorization" of personality	Images of life, integrative self, and an approach to death; "completion" is main theme throughout; *self* value and *metaphoric* style dominant	Self-direction impaired by one's failing body and by social reactions to aging

In short, we view the life span of an individual as consisting of a period of accommodation from infancy to adulthood, followed by a period of relative assimilation throughout most of adulthood, and, finally, a period of emotional accommodation in which the individual must cope with the aging process and the resulting changes in one's body and interpersonal relationships.

IV

CONCLUSION

In this final section of the book we take the opportunity to outline what we think are the more important ideas in our overall theoretical perspective. Our intent is to provide a summary of the theory and to point to the ideas we think will be most important with respect to future advances in understanding personality and individual differences. We want to emphasize in this section that the whole process of understanding individuals is extremely complex. Even so, the complexity makes the task all the more challenging and worthwhile. Given the state of the science of psychology, the best that we can hope to accomplish is to provide a useful "map of the relevant terrain"—that is, to point toward important aspects of personality and toward their organized interrelationships. In our final chapter we review the relevant features of our map of the terrain of personality and reflect on the elements that are apt to be most important in future efforts.

13

Retrospect and Prospects

Having presented the entire theory of individual differences, it is now possible to look back at what we consider to be the more important conceptual features of our approach to understanding human personality. The elements we think will offer guidelines (or perhaps even *insights*) for future research and integrative efforts can be discussed in terms of three general topics: (1) the pervasive role of individual differences, (2) systems and information-processing conceptual models, and (3) developmental change over the life span. We will look back at the theory with respect to each of these broad topics in the sections of this chapter.

THE IMPORTANCE
OF INDIVIDUAL DIFFERENCES

As we indicated in Chapter 1, individual differences pervade all aspects of psychological functioning. Wherever one looks for them, they can be observed empirically, whether in sensory functioning, the way individuals cognize about the world, the kinds of affective reactions that are aroused in motor reactions, and so forth.

While we focused on the factor-analytic literature in Chapters 4 through 6, other sources were also examined in order to gain the most comprehensive perspective possible with respect to the multifaceted ways in which individuals differ. Whether one accepts the factor-analytic model as an appropriate research strategy, the conclusion should be the same. That is, *the variety of ways in which individuals stand apart from each other is staggering.* While the research on sensory functioning has not been as exhaustive as we would have preferred, it is still clear that the basic sensory processes studied for many decades in the psychological laboratory are subject to variation from individual to individual. The same conclusion holds for all of the other areas of personality we have surveyed. Although the motor domain was the least satisfying from the standpoint of *factor-analytic* research, it is still clear that motor processes display a wide range of variation. The areas of cognition and affect have been subject to multidimensional investigation for many decades. In fact, the basic research in these two areas has even been of practical significance in terms of application to educational and counseling situations. Again, it is very clear that these two areas of personality display a tremendous range of variation. Styles and values also display a similar range of diversity.

One of the best ways of summarizing our findings with respect to the six domains covered in Chapters 4 through 6 is in terms of higher-order factors. Sensory and motor factors are dominated at the higher levels by temporality and spatiality. That is, some sensory processes are more concerned with the temporal relations among environmental events; others are more related to spatial relationships. Auditory factors seem to fall under the first category; visual factors, under the second. Similarly, a motor factor such as dynamism seems more related to the temporal dimensions of responses, whereas motor reactivity seems to be more related to an individual's movement through space. Other sensory and motor factors involve some combination of temporality and spatiality functions. Kinesthetic-proprioceptive senses and precision motor functions provide examples of factors involving a combination of both.

The cognitive and affective domains lie closer to the core of integrative personality. On the one hand, cognitive processes involve the individual's meaningful analysis of the external world; on the other hand affective processes determine levels of internal arousal. The three third-order cognitive dimensions of perceiving, conceptualizing, and symbolizing relate to various ways of discovering invariants in the environment. Perceiving implicates the perceptible qualities of reality, conceptualizing relates to relationships among objects and concepts, and symbolizing involves an analysis of the contextual dependencies of objects and events. On the affective side we have identified three higher-order factors of emotional stability, emotional independence, and introversion–extraversion. The first of these seems to be related to limbic arousal, the last entails reticular arousal, and emotional independence is not affected by either reticular or limbic arousal.

At the highest level of personality are styles and values, which express commitments to modes of processing and to the selection of particular processing contents, respectively. We postulated three higher-order styles of empirical, rational, and metaphoric. Empirical styles relate to the extensiveness of scanning and to the selection of perceiving modes of processing; rational styles involve relating more to the abstract characteristics of things and a commitment to conceptual modes of processing; and metaphoric styles relate to breadth of attention and a commitment to symbolizing as a mode of processing. We have interpreted values as either interests (cognitive values) or needs (affective values) and have proposed a factor model in which both are dominated at the third order level by *intrinsic, self,* and *social* value orientations. *Intrinsic* needs and interests are directed toward the intrinsic worth of problems and their solutions. *Self* needs and interests relate to finding the embeddedness and intrinsic worth of one's self. Finally, *social* needs and interests entail a commitment to interactions with others and to bettering the plight of other individuals.

All the dimensions of individual differences we have described, documented, and interpreted have diverse origins. Although we have focused on environmental and hereditary sources of variation, we also think such differences arise because the human being is so *complex*. The problem of complexity cannot be overemphasized, and Koch's various writings (e.g., 1976) are important with regard to this point. Even fairly simple mechanical devices such as cars have their idiosyncratic characteristics, and the complexity of unicellular organisms is sufficient to insure that individuality is not just a characteristic of human behavior. Indeed, we have been led to expect that even biochemicals may exhibit a degree of individuality, although we think individuality should be more obvious with complex organisms.

Our general point is that individual differences can be found wherever one chooses to look for them. However, this does not mean that the final goal of psychological theory should be a description of individuals and all their various differences. Rather, we think the goal of psychology should be to understand its observables as "for instances" of general principles. But we think focusing on observable differences in the phenomena of concern is a good place to start. This is no different than the situation that confronts other sciences. For example, differences among the observable planets, stars, and other objects that punctuate the nighttime sky continue to occupy the interests, time, and imagination of astronomers and cosmologists. Similarly, chemists have long focused on differences in the chemical composition of matter, and biochemists even find that the underlying differences in structures, compounds, and bonds are important.

It might be thought that mainstream experimental (i.e., nondifferential) psychology emphasizes differences as well, since a tremendous variety of *different experimental conditions* have been compared in an equally impressive variety of empirical investigations over the past few decades. But there is an important difference here. Comparing differences among various treatment groups in an experiment is not the same as focusing on the possible differences in underlying structures among the various individuals being studied. The focus of psychological experimentation often seems to be on the differences among *tasks* that psychologists devise rather than on the characteristics, structures, and processes that compose the individuals who participate as subjects in such experiments. Of course the *end focus* of experimental investigations should be on the discovery of general principles that apply to functioning both inside and outside the laboratory. But the *beginning focus* should be on how individuals differ in terms of structure and functioning with respect to important experimental variations. In short, individuals manifest an extreme degree of individuality that can be attributed, in part, to their complexity, and such differences provide a powerful starting point for getting at an integrative understanding of psychological phenomena.

We have emphasized factor analysis as a method for exploring psychological structures that underlie individual differences. However, it should be clear from our various discussions (e.g., see Chapter 3) that we view factor analysis as an empirico-inductive technique that suffers from the same methodological difficulties (e.g., the problem of inductive inference) as other empirico-inductive approaches. Despite this, factor analysis is the best available approach for identifying underlying structures that account for the observable differences in psychological phenomena.

SYSTEMS AND INFORMATION PROCESSING

The emphasis placed on the structure of individuality brings in two important issues. First, there is the problem of how to deal with the complexity that characterizes human personality and individuality and, secondly, there is the question of how to get at process. Factor analysis and other individual-difference approaches emphasize the identification of *structure* and, as we have said in Chapter 3, one must go outside such approaches to get at process and the functional interrelations among identified structures. Furthermore, the situation is complicated by the vast range of individuality structures that can be identified. In our approach to individuality theory we have turned to systems and information-processing theory in order to deal with the problem of process and to make additional headway with the problem of complexity.[1] In Chapters 1 and 3 we intro-

---

[1]However, it should be noted in passing that there are multivariate strategies for going beyond structure to underlying causality, as exemplified by the use of *structural equation models* (see Joreskog & Sörbom, 1979; McDonald, 1979; Wold, 1980). In recent presentations, McArdle used the *Reticular Action Meta-model* (RAM) (McArdle, 1979, 1980; Horn & McArdle, 1980) to illustrate the merger of individuality theory and structural equations. In particular, McArdle demonstrated how models of multifactorial hierarchical structure could be directly specified within the confines of the RAM system of linear equations. This was also demonstrated for hierarchical models that include developmental change, reciprocal feedback, and genetic-environmental components. One immediate practical result of this specification is the ability to create a general *computer simulation model* based on individuality theory. McArdle (1980) shows that once parameter values are ascertained for all linkages in any RAM system, raw data values can be directly generated as corresponding outputs of the psychomathematical superstructure. Obviously, the formal representation of individuality theory may be further refined by the detailed study of input-output relationships.

Another, perhaps more important, empirical aspect of the RAM specification of individuality theory is that this merger of psychological and mathematical theory also permits the direct *empirical estimation and evaluation* of individuality theory in real data analysis. Unfortunately there still remain severe methodological difficulties in the actual practice of structural equation model building (see

duced a systems conception of individuality in which we view personality as composed of six interacting systems. Personality and its component systems were described as complex, hierarchical, information-processing systems with five important characteristics: (1) goal direction, (2) risk and uncertainty management, (3) interaction, (4) hierarchical structure, and (5) development. These five characteristics provide a framework for reviewing our theoretical ideas about systems and information-processing aspects of personality. We do this in the present section, except for the developmental considerations, which are taken up in the third section of the chapter.

Goal Direction

We have attributed distinctive functions or goals to each of the six systems, to each system level in the overall hierarchy of personality organization, and to the suprasystem. Beginning with the individual systems, the goal of the sensory system is to arrive at organized patterns of transduced information to provide a basis for the construction of meaningful cognitions. The motor system, on the other hand, is concerned with transducing psychological information into organized patterns of motor responses. Together these two systems form a transductive-controlled process level of personality with the overall goal of sensory-motor integration. This goal is accomplished via sensory-motor programming that involves complex feedback and feedforward processes wherein sensory inputs are anticipated (fed forward) and incorrect anticipations are corrected via positive and negative feedback.

We have described the goal of cognition (Chapter 5) as searching for ecological invariants, and we have identified three general classes of invariants: (1) perceptual, (2) relational, and (3) contextual. The identification or construction of these three types of invariants is the focus of the perceiving, conceptualizing, and symbolizing subsystems, respectively. Cognitive activity consists of *transformations* on inputs from the sensory systems, for it is in the altering of information according to set procedures that one is able to identify what is invariant, or remains the same under particular conditions. Affect also transforms information, but the goal here is to maintain optimal levels of internal arousal, and there are some well-known physiological (i.e., limbic and reticular arousal) processes that are implicated. Together, cognition and affect form the transformational, or learning-adaptive, level of overall personality with the goal of maintaining cognitive-affective balance in one's adaptations to the environment.

The two systems that are the most clearly goal-directional are styles and

---

Horn & McArdle, 1980, for a review). However, there should be no doubt that the formal aspects of psychological individuality theory and the mathematical-statistical RAM theory can benefit from a three-way interaction with real data analyses. The task at hand is still enormous, but the practical tools, such as RAM, are gradually being shaped in a way that may help shape the future of individuality theory itself.

Finally, it should also be pointed out that one of our research associates, the physicist-mathematician Voorhees, has initiated attempts to formalize individuality theory (e.g., see Voorhees, 1980, 1981a, 1981b).

values. Styles are oriented toward a general consistency in processing activities via their linkages to cognition and affect. That is, styles emphasize certain modes of processing over others. Values are even more clearly goal directional inasmuch as we view them as consisting of interests and needs. The "how" and the "what" of goal-directed activities at the level of cognition and affect (and, by implication, sensory and motor) are determined by styles and values. Together, these two systems form an integrative, self-organizing level with the overall goal of maintaining personality integration and personal meaning.

Regulation of Uncertainty and Risk

In pursuing their various goals, individuals are not simply drive–tension-reducing mechanisms. Uncertainty and risk are frequently increased in order to be reduced. To find out anything new about the world, or to satisfy one's needs in an uncertain world, individuals must venture out, explore, manipulate, and try to change the world in ways that are risky. But that is just the nature of the process. Humans are not qualitatively different in this respect from other, simpler organisms, although they can manipulate *greater amounts* of uncertainty and risk than can other organisms. Uncertainty and risk are implicated in our models of the transformational activities of cognition and affect inasmuch as transformations yield results that are essentially unpredictable. In a related manner uncertainty and risk management are implicated in constructing world views and life styles. For example, in the search for knowledge and valid images of reality one must recognize the importance of uncertainty. This is one factor that distinguishes epistemology from ideology, because the latter puts forth views of the world that make no allowance for uncertainty. And in order to evolve meaningful ways of living (i.e., life styles) in an uncertain world, there is also an implication of risk. Another way in which we have brought in this idea of uncertainty and risk management relates to our developmental model, which is discussed further in the last section of this chapter.

Interactions

We presented an overview of the variety of ways in which personality systems interact with each other (Chapter 8). An important theoretical idea in this context is that of cooperative functioning, which refers to the interaction among components from different systems or subsystems in the pursuit of a single goal (or closely interrelated goals). Examples of systems interactions include the interaction between cognition and affect in the production of emotion, style and value interactions that give rise to differences in self-image, style-cognition interactions yielding world view, and value-affect interactions giving rise to differences in life style. Cross-system cooperative functioning at the subsystem level relates to the analogous roles that higher-level factors play in the functioning of their respective systems.

Hierarchical Organization

We have posited hierarchical relations both between and within systems. The empirical evidence for the nature of the organization *within* systems seems to favor hierarchical structures overwhelmingly and we have postulated a similar structure in the motor domain. And the theoretical reasons for postulating hierarchical relations among the various systems of personality also seem compelling. For example, styles and values, cognition and affect, and sensory and motor differ among each other with respect to characteristics that lead system analysts to construct hierarchical models in a wide variety of applications. For example, differences in the range of focus, priority of actions, developmental emergence, involvement in system integrations, and so forth are consistent with the hierarchical relations among systems that we have postulated (and depicted in Figure 1-1). In general, an individual's sensory activity is coordinated by ongoing cognitive and affective activities—by what one is trying to discover about the world and by the attendant affective reactions. Also, motor activity is organized, focused, and coordinated by complex cognitive and affective processes. But cognition and affect in turn are organized, focused, and coordinated by one's stylistic and value commitments. Similarly, sensory and motor activities are directed at the immediate environment (and internal feedback), whereas cognitive and affective process relate to longer time spans, and styles and values may have a span of focus that extends over a lifetime. Such considerations as these and others all suggest that the hierarchical arrangement we have proposed is a reasonable one.

Consideration for hierarchical relationships also relates to integrative processes. The most important ones we have considered are world view, life style, self-image and the self nexus, personality type, and personal meaning. What is at issue here are the processes that make the individual an integrative whole as opposed to a loose collection of unrelated parts. Overall, the processes involved in such constructions as self-image and in the determination of personality type, world view, and so on are important molar constructions in the individual's adaptation to the environment. Each has an important role in the construction of personal meaning. For example, world view relates to epistemic validity, life style relates to existential validity, and self-image relates to self-validation. These constructions, in turn, exercise a coordinating influence on subsequent interactions with the environment via normative matching. That is, they provide norms against which subsequent interactions with the environment are compared.

To conclude our discussion on the role of systems and information-processing models, we want to emphasize the possible importance of further development of systems concepts in psychology. Systems theory has not been seriously applied in psychological research and theorizing,[2] although it has been applied in most other sciences. Our developments in individuality theory should serve to illustrate the value of such applications and provide a model for future

---

[2]One exception to this is Cattell's (1980) recent synthesis of his work on personality.

developments. We think such attempts must be made if the field is to begin building bridges across the chasms that divide and fragment psychological science. We think systems theory, with its emphasis on dealing with complexity, its cross-disciplinary history, and its sophisticated development in conjunction with computer systems are important reasons for exploring systems models further. We hope that individuality theory provides another reason for doing so.

DEVELOPMENTAL PROCESSES

The fifth characteristic of complex systems has to do with the transformations such systems undergo throughout the life span. We have described personality as undergoing a metamorphogenesis in the sense that there are a variety of structural and nonstructural changes that occur throughout an individual's life. The variety of *quantitative* changes are easier to describe by focusing on the higher-order factors in each of the systems. The spatiality and temporality factors of the sensory and motor systems follow similar courses, with the sensory factors starting out higher and peaking slightly earlier, though both reach their maximum levels during the twenties. The life span quantitative changes in cognition and affect are more complicated. The cognitive perceiving factors resemble the sensory and motor factors inasmuch as they begin at a relatively higher level, peak during the twenties and decline throughout the remainder of the life span. Conceptualizing, on the other hand, peaks during the forties or fifties and declines only slightly thereafter, and symbolizing seems to show increases throughout the life span. The affective dimensions undergo more cyclic changes, at least in Western culture with its pressures on adolescents and the aged. Emotional stability, emotional dependence, and introversion all begin at a relatively low level, peak during adolescence, decline until middle adulthood, and undergo a resurgence in old age. Finally, various styles and values increase monotonically throughout the life span, though it is important to note that a greater degree of uncertainty characterizes such functions than the other quantitative changes we have described.

With the quantitative growth in factors in all six domains, differentiation becomes manifest in the divergence of such factors and systems. Much of this differentiation occurs in the sensory and motor systems prenatally, although this continues throughout childhood. Cognitive and affective differentiation begins postnatally and occupies much of childhood and early adolescence. Styles and values begin to differentiate in late childhood and continue throughout young adulthood. With the decrease in various functions during old age, there is compensatory *consolidation* in all the systems, and particularly in sensory, motor, cognition, and affect.

With increasing differentiation there is need for increasing hierarchical organization. For example, with increasing sensory and motor integration, there is need for cognitive and affective controls to direct and coordinate sensory and motor activity. Similarly, as cognition and affect become increasingly differen-

tiated throughout childhood, there is increasing need for a focusing and directing of their activities also. Such direction is provided by styles and values, which provide an integrative, self-organizing level of personality.

As personality becomes increasingly hierarchically organized, the integrative goals also undergo evolution. For example, cognitive-affective balance provides an appropriate goal for children (and immature adults), but adulthood is more appropriately described as a search for personal meaning. And old age can be described as a summing up and assessment of the meaning of one's life. Such integrative goals underly much of an individual's behaviors, thoughts, and feelings and serve to organize such actions over long periods of time.

With the growth, differentiation, and hierarchical organization of cognition, affect, styles, and values, and with the transformation in integrative goals, there is an increasing capacity for self-direction. That is, one becomes increasingly capable of making decisions on the basis of one's own style and value commitments, and there is greater ability to react independently of environmental pressures. Although such capacities are not always made use of by individuals, there is also a greater opportunity to make changes that have a long-range impact on one's life (e.g., career changes, divorce, marriage).

All of these transformations are propelled by a variety of forces that we have described in terms of *the programs provided by, and fluctuations in, the functions of hereditary, cultural, and personality structures*. Just as mutations at the genetic level lead to alterations in hereditary structures, idiosyncratic experiences at the level of personality lead to new individuality structures. The thrust of our developmental model lies in the emphasis on idiosyncratic, creative, or uncertain experiences that individuals undergo while engaging in goal-directed activities. An important point here is that the predictability of individual human behavior over the life span is limited. That is, to the extent that idiosyncratic experiences propel development changes, developmental processes will be shrouded by uncertainty.

The roles of hereditary and environmental forces in development are described more specifically in our factor-gene and factor-learning models. We distinguish between *factor involvement* in learning processes and the *learning of factors*. We identified a range of learning processes in which the individuality factors are involved, including sensory-motor programming for the factors in the sensory and motor domains, constructional and connectional learning in the case of cognition and affect respectively, and decision-control in the case of styles and values. In turn, the factors are changed via a similar variety of learning processes. Sensory-motor tuning, cognitive constructions and affective connections, and style and value modeling account for the learning of factors in the various domains of individuality.

To conclude this review of our model of developmental changes and focuses, we want to emphasize the difficulties presented by developmental processes. That is, we want to reiterate that development represents a challenge to *any* scientific model of human personality or systems of similar complexity, since distinctive models must be introduced for each major phase of the life span. We have addressed this problem by emphasizing our systems approach (which stems from Bertalanffy's early work on embryology) and the Prigogine model of evolutionary processes. We think the end result of our effort is a theoretical model of considerable power, and one that might be useful for analyzing developmental processes other than personality development.

CONCLUDING COMMENT

The psychology of human individuality represents one of the greatest challenges to modern science. No other phenomena known in the universe can present such a strong challenge, given that individuals differ in such subtle and complex ways, engage in such marvelous but complex activities, and undergo life-span transformations that defy scientific modeling. Even so, the search for an integrative understanding of ourselves as individuals embedded in complex physical and cultural environments must be encouraged, supported, and fostered, while being criticized in detail. Our individuality theory has involved the efforts of a large number of very competent individuals working for more than a decade, with financial support from university and governmental agencies and with the advice and criticisms of many colleagues. The final product provides a map of the relevant terrain, which we hope will provide a guide for further extensions and integrations. While all of us are agreed that individuals do not function in the fragmented, isolated, and highly controlled ways that seem to be projected by modern research, little is done to overcome such images. The legitimacy, and especially the difficulty, of such integrative efforts should be recognized. Although psychology has made impressive progress in the methodological and statistical aspects of empirical research, its conceptual foundations are grossly deficient. This deficiency includes both theory and metatheory—that is, a lack of viable, substantive theory, and a lack of understanding of its philosophic foundations. Individuality theory constitutes one attempt to rectify psychology's superempiricistic bias. Although it provides a comprehensive theoretical structure in a domain that has previously been populated by a group of small, unrelated structures in a rational waste land, all such structures have their weaknesses and will, therefore, have to undergo revision in the future. It is our belief and hope that individuality theory provides a sufficiently firm foundation on which to build. Just as no one experiment or series of experiments can provide an adequate empirical foundation, no one theory is adequate for a domain as complex and broad as personality. It is to be expected, therefore, that modifications and new theory will be forthcoming in the future. Criticism and revision of a theory is, after all, an indicator of a theory's viability.

In conclusion, while the future of individuality theory is uncertain, we hope that it will provide both a challenge and encouragement for future integrative efforts.

References

ABELSON, R. P., ARONSON, E., McGUIRE, W. J., NEWCOMB, T. M., ROSENBERG, M. J., & TANNENBAUM, P. H.   *Theories of cognitive consistency: A sourcebook*. Chicago: Rand Mc-Nally, 1968.

ADAMS, J. A.   Response feedback and learning. *Psychological Bulletin*, 1968, *70*, 486–504.

AFTANAS, M. S., & ROYCE, J. R.   A factor analysis of brain damage tests administered to normal subjects with factor score comparisons across ages. *Multivariate Behavioral Research*, 1969, *4*, 459–81.

AHE, K., & PEREZ DE FRANCISCO, C.   Genetic aspects of psychophysiological variables. *Neurologia, Neurocirugia, Psiquitria*, 1974, *15*, 5–18.

AHMAVAARA, Y.   *On the unified factor theory of the mind*. Helsinki: Annals of the Finnish Academy of Science, Series 13, *106*, 1957.

ALLPORT, G. W.   *Pattern and growth in personality*. New York: Holt, Rinehart & Winston, 1961.

ALLPORT, G. W., VERNON, P. E., & LINDZEY, G.   *Study of values, Revised*. Boston: Houghton Mifflin, 1951.

AMMONS, R. B., & AMMONS, C. H.   Psychology of the scientist: I. Introduction. *Perceptual and Motor Skills*, 1962, *15*, 748–50.

ARBUS, D.   *Dianne Arbus: An aperture monograph*. New York: Millerton, 1972.

ATKINSON, R. C., & SHIFFRIN, R. M.   Human memory: A proposed system and its control processes. In K. W. Spence & J. T. Spence (Eds.), *The psychology of learning and motivation* (Vol. 2). New York: Academic Press, 1968.

BAKAN, D.   Speculation in psychology. *Journal of Humanistic Psychology*, 1975, *15*, 17–24.

BENGSTON, V. L., & LOVEJOY, M. C.   Values, personality, and social structure: An intergenerational analysis. *American Behavioral Scientist*, 1973, *16*, 880–912.

BERRIEN, F. K.   *General and social systems.* New Brunswick, N.J.: Rutgers University Press, 1968.

BERTALANFFY, L. VON.   *Modern theories of development: An introduction to theoretical biology.* London: Oxford University Press, 1933.

BERTALANFFY, L. VON.   General systems theory. *Main Currents in Modern Thought,* 1955, *11,* 75–83.

BERTALANFFY, L. VON.   General systems theory: A critical review. *General Systems,* 1962, *7,* 1–20.

BERTALANFFY, L. VON.   *Robots, men, and minds.* New York: George Braziller, 1967.

BINSWANGER, L.   The existential analysis school of thought. In R. May, E. Angel, & H. F. Ellenberger (Eds.), *Existence.* New York: Basic Books, 1958.

BLANPIED, W. A.   *Physics: Its structure and evolution.* Waltham, Mass: Blaisdell, 1969.

BLUMENTHAL, A. L.   *The process of cognition.* Englewood Cliffs, N.J.: Prentice-Hall, 1977.

BORING, E. G.   *A history of experimental psychology* (2nd ed.). Englewood Cliffs, N.J.: Prentice-Hall, 1950.

BOTWINICK, J., & THOMPSON, L. W.   Age differences in reaction time: An artifact? *Gerontologist,* 1968, *8,* 25–28.

BOWER, G. H.   Cognitive psychology: An introduction. In W. K. Estes (Ed.), *Handbook of learning and cognitive processes. Vol. 1. Introduction to concepts and issues.* Hillsdale, N.J.: Lawrence Erlbaum Associates, 1975.

BRANSFORD, J. D., FRANKS, J. J., McCARRUL, N. C., & NITSCHE, K. E.   Toward unexplaining memory. In R. Shaw & J. D. Bransford (Eds.), *Perceiving, acting, and knowing: Toward an ecological psychology.* Hillsdale, N.J.: Lawrence Erlbaum Associates, 1977.

BRENT, S. B.   Individual specialization, collective adaptation, and rate of environmental change. *Human Development,* 1978, *21,* 21–33. (a)

BRENT, S. B.   Prigogine's model for self-organization in nonequilibrium systems: Its relevance for development psychology. *Human Development,* 1978, *21,* 374–85. (b)

BRENT, S. B.   Motivation, steady-state, and structural development. *Motivation and Emotion.* 1978, *2,* 299–332. (c)

BROADHURST, P. L.   The inheritance of behavior. *Science,* 1965, *29,* 39–43.

BROADHURST, P. L.   The Maudsley reactive and nonreactive strains of rats: A survey. *Behavior Genetics,* 1975, *5,* 299–319.

BROVERMAN, D. M.   Generality and behavioral correlates of cognitive styles. *Journal of Consulting Psychology,* 1964, *28,* 487–500.

BURGER, A. L., & BLACKMAN, L. S.   Visual memory training of digit recall in L. A. Shukin, S. S. Tobin, & M. Ralk (Eds.), *Personality in middle and late life.* New York: Atherton, 1964.

BURGER, A. L., & BLACKMAN, L. S.   Visual memory training of digit recall in educable mentally retarded children. *Education and Training of the Mentally Retarded,* 1976, *11,* 5–10.

BURT, C. L.   The structure of the mind: A review of the results of factor analysis. *British Journal of Educational Psychology,* 1949, *19,* 100–11, 176–99.

BUSS, A. R.   A general developmental model for interindividual dfferences, intraindividual differences, and intraindividual changes. *Developmental Psychology,* 1974, *10,* 70–78.

BUSS, A. R., & ROYCE, J. R.   Ontogenetic changes in cognitive structure from a multivariate perspective. *Developmental Psychology,* 1975, *11,* 87–101.

BUTTERFIELD, E. C., WARBOLD, C., & BELMONT, J. M.   On the theory and practice of impairing short-term memory. *American Journal of Mental Deficiency,* 1973, *77,* 655–69.

BYERS, A. P., FORREST, G. G., & ZACCARIA, J. S.   Recalled early parent-child relation, adult needs, and occupational choice. *Journal of Counselling Psychology,* 1968, *15,* 324–28.

CALHOUN, J. B.   A behavioral sink. In E. L. Bliss (Ed.), *Roots of behavior*. New York: Harper & Row, Pub., 1962.

CAMPBELL, D. P.   *Handbook for the Strong Vocational Interest Blank*. Stanford, Calif.: Stanford University Press, 1971.

CAMPBELL, D. P.   *Manual for the SVIB-SCII Strong-Campbell Interest Inventory*. Stanford, Calif.: Stanford University Press, 1977.

CAMPBELL, D. T.   Blind variation and selective retention in creative thought as in other knowledge processes. *Psychological Review*, 1960, *67*, 380–400.

CAMPBELL, D. T.   Evolutionary epistemology. In P. A. Schilpp (Ed.), *The philosophy of Karl Popper*. Vol. 14, I & II. *The library of living philosophers*. La Salle, Ill.: Open Court Publishing Co., 1974.

CAMPBELL, D. T.   On the conflicts between biological and social evolution and between psychology and moral tradition. *American Psychologist*, 1975, *30*, 1103–26.

CAMPBELL, J.   *The hero of a thousand faces*. New York: Meridian Books, 1956.

CANNON, W. E.   The James-Lange theory of emotions: A critical examination and an alternative theory. *American Journal of Psychology*, 1927, *39*, 106–24.

CARROLL, J. B.   Psychometric tasks as cognitive tasks. In L. Resnick (Ed.), *The nature of intelligence*. Hillsdale, N.J.: Lawrence Erlbaum Associates, 1976.

CASSIRER, E.   *The philosophy of symbolic forms* (Vol. 1). New Haven, Conn.: Yale University Press, 1953.

CASSIRER, E.   *The philosophy of symbolic forms* (Vol. 2). New Haven, Conn.: Yale University Press, 1955.

CASSIRER, E.   *The philosophy of symbolic forms* (Vol. 3). New Haven, Conn.: Yale University Press, 1957.

CATTELL, R. B.   *Personality and motivation structure and measurement*. New York: World Book Co., 1957.

CATTELL, R. B.   *The scientific analysis of personality*. London: Penguin, 1965.

CATTELL, R. B. (ED.).   *Handbook of multivariate experimental psychology*. Chicago: Rand McNally, 1966. (a)

CATTELL, R. B.   Psychological theory and scientific method. In R. B. Cattell (Ed.), *Handbook of multivariate experimental psychology*. Chicago: Rand McNally, 1966. (b)

CATTELL, R. B.   *Abilities: Their structure, growth and action*. Boston: Houghton Mifflin, 1971.

CATTELL, R. B.   *Personality and mood by questionnaire*. San Francisco: Jossey-Bass, 1973.

CATTELL, R. B.   *The scientific use of factor analysis in behavioral and life sciences*. New York: Plenum Press, 1978.

CATTELL, R. B.   *Personality and learning theory*. New York: Springer, 1979 (Vol. 1), 1980 (Vol. 2).

CHEKHOV, A.   The cherry orchard. In *Plays by Anton Chekhov*. London: Duckworth, 1920.

COHEN, J.   *Behavior in uncertainty and its social implications*. New York: Basic Books, 1964.

COLE, N. S., & HANSON, G. R.   An analysis of the structure of vocational interest. *Journal of Counseling Psychology*, 1971, *18*, 478–86.

COOPERSMITH, S.   *The antecedents of self-esteem*. San Francisco: W. H. Freeman & Company, Publishers, 1967.

COSDEN, M. A., ELLIS, H. C., & FEENEY, D. M.   Cognitive flexibility-rigidity, repetition effects, and memory. *Journal of Research in Personality*, 1979, *13*, 386–95.

COULTER, N. A., JR.   Toward a theory of teleogenetic control systems. *General Systems*, 1968, *12*, 85–89.

COWARD, H., & ROYCE, J. R.   The epistemological basis for humanistic psychology. In J. R. Royce & L. P. Mos (Eds.), *Humanistic psychology: Concepts and criticisms*. New York: Plenum Press, 1981.

CRAIK, F. I. M., & LOCKHART, R. S.   Levels of processing: A framework for memory research. *Journal of Verbal Learning and Verbal Behavior*, 1972, *11*, 671–84.

CRONBACH, L. J., & SNOW, R. E.   *Aptitudes and instructional methods: A handbook for research on interactions.* New York: Irvington Publishers, 1977.

DABROWSKI, K.   *Positive disintegration.* Boston, Mass.: Little, Brown, 1964.

DAS, J. P., KIRBY, J., & JARMAN, R. F.   Simultaneous and successive syntheses: An alternative model for cognitive abilities. *Psychological Bulletin,* 1975, *82,* 87–103.

DAVIS, J. K., & FRANK, B. M.   Learning and memory of field independent-dependent individuals. *Journal of Research in Personality,* 1979, *13,* 469–79.

DAY, W.   Contemporary behaviorism and the concept of intentionality. In W. J. Arnold (Ed.), *Nebraska Symposium on Motivation 1975: The Conceptual Foundations of Psychology.* Lincoln: University of Nebraska Press, 1976.

DIAMOND, S., & ROYCE, J. R.   Cognitive abilities as expressions of three "ways of knowing." *Multivariate Behavioral Research,* 1980, *15,* 31–56.

DIAMOND, S., ROYCE, J. R., & VOORHEES, B.   The factor fulfillment model and the concept of multivariate personality type. *Personality and Individual Differences,* 1981, *2,* 181–89.

DICKENS, R.   *Thoreau: The complete individualist.* New York: Exposition Press, 1974.

DOBBINS, D. A.   Separation potential of educable and intellectually normal boys as function of motor performance. *Research Quarterly,* 1976, *47,* 346–57.

DOBBINS, D. A., & RARICK, G. L.   Structural similarity of the motor domain of normal and educable retarded boys. *Research Quarterly,* 1975, *46,* 447–56.

DURKHEIM, E.   *Suicide: A study of sociology* (J. A. Spaulding & G. Simpson, trans.). Glencoe, Ill.: Free Press, 1951.

DUVAL, S., & WICKLUND, R. A.   *A theory of objective self-awareness.* New York: Academic Press, 1972.

ECKERT, H. M., & RARICK, G. L.   Stabilometer performance of educable mentally retarded and normal children. *Research Quarterly,* 1976, *47,* 619–23.

EDWARDS, A. L.   *Manual for the Edwards Personal Preference Schedule* (rev. ed.). New York: Psychological Corporation, 1959.

EDWARDS, A. L., & ABBOTT, R. D.   Relationships among the Edwards Personality Inventory Scales, the Edwards Personality Preference Schedule, and the Personality Research Form Scales. *Journal of Consulting and Clinical Psychology,* 1973, *40,* 27–32.

EDWARDS, A. L., ABBOTT, R. D., & KLOCKARS, A. J.   A factor analysis of the EPPS and the PRF personality inventories. *Educational and Psychological Measurement,* 1972, *32,* 23–29.

EGAN, O., & ROYCE, J. R.   Litter size and emotionality in two strains of mice. *Journal of Comparative and Physiological Psychology,* 1973, *83,* 55–59.

EGAN, O., ROYCE, J. R., & POLEY, W.   Evidence for a territorial marking factor of mouse emotionality. *Psychonomic Science,* 1972, *27,* 272–74.

EINSTEIN, A.   Considerations concerning the fundaments of theoretical physics. *Science,* 1940, *91,* 487–92.

EKMAN, P.   Universal and cultural differences in facial expressions of emotions. In J. Cole (Ed.), *Nebraska Symposium on Motivation, 1971.* Lincoln: University of Nebraska Press, 1972.

ELIOT, T. S.   *The complete poems and plays.* New York: Harcourt Brace Jovanovich, 1952.

ENGELAND, W., & DAWSON, W.   Individual differences in power functions for a 1-week interval. *Perception and Psychophysics,* 1974, *15,* 349–52.

ERIKSON, E. H.   Identity and the life cycle. *Psychological Issues,* 1959, *1,* 1–171.

ERIKSON, E. H.   *Identity, youth, and crisis.* New York: W. W. Norton & Company, 1968.

ERLENMEYER-KIMLING, L., & JARVIK, L.   Genetics and intelligence: A review. *Science,* 1963, *142,* 1477–79.

ESSER, A. H.   A biosocial perspective on crowding. In J. R Wohlwill & D. H. Carson (Eds.), *Environment and the social sciences.* Washington: American Psychological Association, 1972.

ESTES, W. K.   The statistical approach to learning theory. In S. Koch (Ed.), *Psychology:*

A study of a science. Vol. 2. General systematic formulations, learning, and special processes. New York: McGraw-Hill, 1959.

EVERETT, A. V.   The self concept of high, medium, and low academic achievers. *Australian Journal of Education,* 1971, *15,* 319–23.

EXLINE, R.   Visual interaction: The glances of power and preference. In J. Cole (Ed.), *Nebraska Symposium on Motivation, 1971.* Lincoln: University of Nebraska Press, 1972.

EYSENCK, H. J.   *The dynamics of anxiety and hysteria.* London: Routledge & Kegan Paul, 1957.

EYSENCK, H. J.   *Experiments in personality* (Vol. 2). New York: Humanities Press, 1960.

EYSENCK, H. J.   *Crime and personality.* London: Routledge & Kegan Paul, 1964.

EYSENCK, H. J.   *The biological basis of personality.* Springfield, Ill.: Charles C Thomas, 1967.

EYSENCK, H. J.   *The structure of human personality.* London: Methuen, 1970.

EYSENCK, H. J.   *Eysenck on extraversion.* New York: John Wiley, 1973.

EYSENCK, H. J.   *The measurement of personality.* Baltimore: University Park Press, 1976.

EYSENCK, H. J., & EYSENCK, S. B. G.   *Personality structure and measurement.* London: Routledge & Kegan Paul, 1969.

EYSENCK, H. J., & EYSENCK, S. B. G.   *Psychoticism as a dimension of personality.* London: Hodder & Stoughton, 1976.

EYSENCK, H. J., & PRELL, D. B.   The inheritance of neuroticism: An experimental study. *Journal of Mental Science,* 1951, *97,* 411–65.

EYSENCK, M. W.   *Human memory: Theory, research, and individual differences.* Oxford: Pergamon Press, 1977.

FARB, P.   *Man's rise to civilization as shown by the Indians of North America from primeval times to the coming of the industrial state* (Rev. ed.). New York: Dutton, 1978.

FESTINGER, L.   *A theory of cognitive dissonance.* New York: Row, Peterson, & Co., 1957.

FEYERABEND, P. K.   Problems of empiricism. In R. G. Colodny (Ed.), *Beyond the edge of certainty.* Englewood Cliffs, N.J.: Prentice-Hall, 1965.

FEYERABEND, P. K.   Against method. In M. Radner & S. Winokur (Eds.), *Minnesota Studies in the Philosophy of Science* (Vol. 4). Minneapolis: University of Minnesota Press, 1970.

FITTS, W. H.   *Manual for the Tennessee Self-Concept Scale.* Nashville: Counsellor Recordings and Tests, 1965. (a)

FITTS, W. H.   The self-concept and human behavior. *Nashville Mental Health Center Research Bulletin,* No. 1, 1965. (b)

FITTS, W. H.   *The self-concept and psychopathology.* Nashville, Tenn.: Dede Wallace Center, 1972. (Monograph IV.)

FLEISHMAN, E. A.   *Structure and measurement of physical fitness.* Englewood Cliffs, N.J.: Prentice-Hall, 1964.

FLEISHMAN, E. A.   Individual differences in motor learning. In R. M. Gagné (Ed.), *Learning and individual differences.* Columbus, Ohio: Chas. E. Merrill, 1966.

FLEISHMAN, E. A.   On the relation between abilities, learning, and human performance. *American Psychologist,* 1972, *27,* 1017–32. (a)

FLEISHMAN, E. A.   Structure and measurement of psychomotor abilities. In R. N. Singer (Ed.), *The psychomotor domain: Movement behaviors.* Philadelphia: Lea & Febiger, 1972. (b)

FLEISHMAN, E. A.   Toward a taxonomy of human performance. *American Psychologist,* 1975, *30,* 1127–49.

FLEISHMAN, E. A., & FRUCHTER, B.   Factor structure and predictability of successive stages of learning Morse code. *Journal of Applied Psychology,* 1960, *44,* 97–101.

FLEISHMAN, E. A., & HEMPEL, W. E., JR.   Changes in factor structure of a complex psychomotor test as a function of practice. *Psychometrika,* 1954, *18,* 239–52.

FLEISHMAN, E. A., & HEMPEL, W. E., JR.   The relation between abilities and improvement with practice in a visual discrimination reaction task. *Journal of Experimental Psychology,* 1955, *49,* 301–12.

FRANK, P. G.   *The validation of scientific theories.* Boston: Beacon Press, 1964.

FREEDMAN, J.   Population density and human performance and aggressiveness. In A. Damon (Ed.), *Physiological anthropology.* Cambridge: Harvard University Press, 1971.

FRENCH, J. W.   The relationship of problem-solving styles to the factor composition of tests. *Educational Psychological Measurement,* 1965, *25,* 9–28.

FRENCH, J. W.   *Toward the establishment of non-cognitive factors through literature search and interpretation.* Princeton, N.J.: Educational Testing Service, 1973.

FREUD, A.   *The ego and the mechanisms of defense.* New York: International Universities Press, 1946.

FREUD, S.   *An outline of psychoanalysis.* New York: W. W. Norton & Co., 1949.

FROMM, E.   *Escape from freedom.* New York: Farrar & Rinehart, 1941.

FRUGHTER, B.   *Introduction to factor analysis.* Princeton, N.J.: Van Nostrand Co., 1954.

FULLER, J. L., & THOMPSON, W. R.   *Behavior genetics.* New York: John Wiley, 1960.

GAGE, N. L., & CRONBACH, L. J.   Conceptual and methodological problems in interpersonal perception. *Psychological Review,* 1955, *62,* 411–22.

GAGNÉ, R. M. (ED.),   *Learning and individual differences.* Columbus, Ohio: Chas. C. Merrill, 1966.

GARDNER, R. W., HOLZMAN, P. S., KLEIN, G. S., LINTON, H., & SPENCE, D. P.   Cognitive control: A study of individual consistencies in cognitive behavior. *Psychological Issues,* 1959, *1,* No. 4.

GARDNER, R. W., & LONG, R. I.   Cognitive controls of attention and inhibition: A study of individual consistencies. *British Journal of Psychology,* 1962, *53,* 381–88.

GARDNER, R. W., & SCHOEN, R. A.   Differentiation and abstraction in concept formation. *Psychological Monographs,* 1962, *76* (Whole No. 560).

GARNER, W. R.   *Uncertainty and structure as psychological constructs.* New York: John Wiley, 1962.

GAUDREY, E., & SPIELBERGER, C. D.   Anxiety and intelligence in paired-associate learning. *Journal of Educational Psychology,* 1970, *61,* 386–91.

GIBSON, J. J.   *The senses considered as perceptual systems.* Boston: Houghton Mifflin, 1966.

GIBSON, J. J.   A theory of direct visual perception. In J. R. Royce & W. W. Rozeboom (Eds.), *The psychology of knowing.* New York: Gordon & Breach, 1972.

GILLIS, A. R.   Types of human population density and social pathology. Discussion paper No. 7, Population Research Laboratory, Department of Sociology, University of Alberta, 1973.

GLASER, R.   Individuals and learning: The new aptitudes. *Educational Researcher,* June 1972, pp. 5–12.

GOFFMAN, E.   *The presentation of self in everyday life.* Garden City, N.Y.: Doubleday, 1959.

GOFFMAN, E.   *Encounters: Two studies in the sociology of interaction.* Indianapolis: Bobbs-Merrill, 1961.

GOFFMAN, E.   *Frame analysis: An essay on the organization of experience.* New York: Harper & Row, Pub., 1974.

GOODENOUGH, D. R.   The role of individual differences in field dependence as a factor in learning and memory. *Psychological Bulletin,* 1976, *83,* 675–94.

GOODENOUGH, D. R., GANDINI, E., OLKIN, E., PIZZAMIGLIO, L., THAYER, D., & WITKIN, H.   A study of x-chromosome linkage with field dependence and spatial visualization. *Behavior Genetics,* 1977, *7,* 373–87.

GORSUCH, R. L.   *Factor analysis.* Philadephia: Saunders, 1974.

GROSSMAN, P. D.   *A textbook of physiological psychology.* New York: John Wiley, 1967.

GUILFORD, J. P.   *Personality.* New York: McGraw-Hill, 1959.

GUILFORD, J. P.   *The nature of human intelligence.* New York: McGraw-Hill, 1967.

GUILFORD, J. P.   Factors and factors of personality. *Psychological Bulletin,* 1975, *82,* 802–14.

GUILFORD, J. P.   Education with an informal psychology. *Education,* 1978, *98,* 11–15.

GUILFORD, J. P., & HOEPFNER, R.   *The analysis of intelligence.* New York: McGraw-Hill, 1971.

GUILFORD, J. P., & ZIMMERMAN, W. S. Fourteen dimensions of temperament. *Psychological Monographs*, 1956, *70*, 1–26.

GUNDERSON, M. M. Relationships between expressed personality needs and social background and military status variables. *Journal of Psychology*, 1969, *31*, 217–24.

HABERMAS, J. *Knowledge and human interests*. Boston: Beacon Press, 1971.

HALL, C. S. Genetic differences in fatal audiogenic seizures between two inbred strains of house mice. *Journal of Heredity*. 1947, *38*, 2–6.

HALL, C. S., & LINDZEY, G. *Theories of personality* (2nd ed.). New York: John Wiley, 1970.

HANLEY, C. M. Factor analysis of speech perception. *Journal of Speech & Hearing Disorders*, 1956, *21*, 76–87.

HANSON, N. R. *Patterns of discovery*. Cambridge: University Press, 1961.

HARMAN, H. H. *Modern factor analysis* (Rev. ed.). Chicago: University of Chicago Press, 1976.

HARRÉ, R. Some remarks on "rule" as a scientific concept. In T. Mischel (Ed.), *Understanding other persons*. Oxford: Basil Blackwell, 1974.

HARRÉ, R. History of philosophy of science. In P. Edwards (Ed.), *The Encyclopedia of Philosophy* (Vol. 6). New York: Macmillan, 1976.

HARVEY, O. J., HUNT, D. E., & SCHRODER, H. M. *Conceptual systems and personality organization*. New York: John Wiley, 1961.

HEBB, D. O. *The organization of behavior*. New York: John Wiley, 1949.

HELMS, E., & JACKSON, D. N. The item factor structure of the Personality Research Form. *Applied Psychological Measurement*, 1977, *21*, 185–94.

HOFSTETTER, H. W. Accommodative convergence in identical twins. *American Journal of Optometry*, 1948, *25*, 480–91.

HOFSTETTER, H., & RIFE, D. Miscellaneous optometric data on twins. *American Journal of Optometry*, 1953, *30*, 139–50.

HOGE, D. R., & BENDER, I. E. Factors influencing value change among college graduates in adult life. *Journal of Personality and Social Psychology*, 1974, *29*, 572–85.

HOHN, R. L., LAVIERS, M. D., & DEATON, W. Learner characteristics and performance effects in self-paced instruction. *Psychological Reports*, 1977, *40*, 1011–12.

HOLLAND, J. L. *Manual for the Vocational Preference Inventory*. Palo Alto, Calif.: Consulting Psychologists Press, 1965.

HOLLAND, J. L. *Making vocational choices: A theory of careers*. Englewood Cliffs, N.J.: Prentice-Hall, 1973.

HOLLINGSWORTH, B. Effects of performance goals and anxiety on learning a gross motor task. *Research Quarterly*, 1975, *46*, 162–68.

HOLMES, T. M., AKSEL, R., & ROYCE, J. R. Inheritance of avoidance behavior in *mus musculus*. *Behavior Genetics*, 1974, *4*, 357–71.

HOLZMAN, P. S. Scanning: A principle of reality contact. *Perceptual Motor Skills*, 1966, *23*, 835–44.

HORN, J. L. Organization of abilities and development of abilities. *Psychological Review*, 1968, *75*, 242–59.

HORN, J. L. Theory of functions represented among auditory and visual test performances. In J. R. Royce (Ed.), *Multivariate analysis and psychological theory*. London: Academic Press, 1973.

HORN, J. L. Human abilities: A review of research and theory in the early 1970s. *Annual Review of Psychology*, 1976, pp. 437–85.

HORN, J. L. Personality and ability theory. In R. B. Cattell (Ed.), *Handbook of modern personality theory*. Washington, D.C.: Hemisphere Publishing Corporation, 1977.

HORN, J. L., & BRAMBLE, W. J. Second-order ability structure rebuilt in rights and wrongs scores. *Journal of Educational Psychology*, 1967, *58*, 115–22.

HORN, J. L., & CATTELL, R. B. Age changes in primary mental ability factors. *Journal of Gerontology*, 1966, *21*, 210–20.

HORN, J. L., & McARDLE, J. J. Perspectives on mathematical/statistical model building

(MASMOB) in research on aging. In L. W. Poon (Ed.), *Aging in the 1980's*. Washington, D.C. American Psychological Association, 1980, 503–41.

HUBA, G. T., & HAMILTON, D. L.   On the generality of trait relationships: Some analyses based on Fishe's paper. *Psychological Bulletin*, 1976, *83*, 868–76.

HUBA, C. J., SEGAL, B., & SINGER, J. L.   Organization of needs in male and female drug and alcohol users. *Journal of Consulting and Clinical Psychology*, 1977, *45*, 34–44.

HULL, C. L.   Goal attraction and directing ideas considered as habit phenomena. *Psychological Review*, 1931, *38*, 487–506.

HULL, C. L.   *Principles of behavior*. New York: Appleton-Century-Crofts, 1943.

HULL, C. L.   *A behavior system*. New Haven, Conn.: Yale University Press, 1952. (a)

HULL, C. L.   Clark L. Hull. In E. G. Boring, H. S. Langfeld, H. Werner, & R. M. Yerkes (Eds.), *A history of psychology in autobiography* (Vol. 4). Worchester: Clark University Press, 1952. (b)

HULL, C. L.   Psychology of the scientist: 4. Passages from the "Idea Books" of Clark L. Hull. *Perceptual and Motor Skills*, 1962, *15*, 807–82.

HUNT, E.   What kind of computer is man? *Cognitive Psychology*, 1971, *2*, 57–98.

HUNT, E.   The memory we must have. In R. Shank & K. Colby (Eds.), *Computer models of thought and language*. San Francisco: W. H. Freeman & Company, Publishers, 1973.

HUNT, E.   Quote the raven? Nevermore! In L. W. Gregg (Ed.), *Knowledge and cognition*. Hillsdale, N.J.: Lawrence Erlbaum Associates, 1974.

HUNT, E., FROST, N., & LUNNEBORG, C. L.   Individual differences in cognition: A new approach to intelligence. In G. Bower (Ed.), *Advances in learning and motivation* (Vol. 7). New York: Academic Press, 1973.

HUNT, E., & LANSMAN, M.   Cognitive theory applied to individual differences. In W. K. Estes (Ed.), *Handbook of learning and cognitive processes. Vol. 1. Introduction to concepts and issues*. Hillsdale, N.J.: Lawrence Erlbaum Associates, 1975.

HUNT, E., LUNNEBORG, C., & LEWIS, J.   What does it mean to be high verbal? *Cognitive Psychology*, 1975, *7*, 194–227.

HURLOCK, E. B.   *Developmental psychology* (3rd ed.). New York: McGraw-Hill, 1968.

HUXLEY, ALDOUS.   *Brave new world*. New York: Doubleday, 1932.

ISMAIL, A., KEPHART, N., & COWELL, C. C.   *Utilization of motor aptitude tests in predicting academic achievement*. Technical Report No. 1. Purdue University Research Foundation, P. U. 879-64-838, 1963.

ISMAIL, A. H., & YOUNG, R. J.   Influence of physical fitness on second- and third-order personality factors using orthogonal and oblique rotations. *Journal of Clinical Psychology*, 1976, *32*, 268–73.

IZARD, C. E.   *The face of emotion*. New York: Appleton-Century-Crofts, 1971.

JACKSON, A. S.   Factor analysis of selected muscular strength and motor performance tests. *Research Quarterly*, 1971, *42*, 164–72.

JACKSON, D. N.   *Personality research form manual*. Goshen, N.Y.: Research Psychologist Press, 1967.

JAMES, W.   *Principles of psychology*. New York: H. Holt, 1890, 2 vols.

JAMES, W.   *Psychology: The briefer course*. New York: Harper & Row, 1961 (Originally published by Henry Holt & Co., 1892).

JANIS, G. L., & MANN, L.   *Decision making: A psychological analysis of conflict, choice, and commitment*. New York: Free Press, 1977.

JÖRESKOG, K. G., & SÖRBOM, D.   *Advances in factor analysis and structural equation models*. J. D. Magidson (Ed.). Cambridge, Mass.: Abt Books, 1979.

JUNG, C. G.   *Conscious, unconscious, and individuation*. In *Collected Works* (Vol. 9, Part I). Princeton, N.J.: Princeton University Press, 1959. (Originally published in English, 1939).

JUNG, C. G.   *Man and his symbols*. London: Aldus Books, 1964.

JUNG, R.   Systems of orientation. In D. M. Kochen (Ed.), *Some problems in information science*. New York: Scarecrow Press, 1965.

JUURMAA, J.   *Ability structure and loss of vision.* American Foundation for the Blind, Research Series #18, 1967.

KAGAN, J.   Individual differences in the resolution of response uncertainty. *Journal of Personality and Social Psychology,* 1965, *2,* 154–60. (a)

KAGAN, J.   Impulsive and reflective children: Significance of conceptual tempo. In J. Krumboltz (Ed.), *Learning and the education process.* Chicago: Rand McNally, 1965. (b)

KAGAN, J., Moss, H. A., & SIGEL, I. E.   Psychological significance of styles of conceptualization. *Monographs of the Society for Research in Child Development,* 1963, *28,* 73–112.

KAMIN, L. J.   *The science and politics of IQ.* Potomac, Md.: Lawrence Erlbaum Associates, 1974.

KEARSLEY, G. P., Buss, A. R., & ROYCE, J. R.   Developmental change and the multidimentional cognitive system. *Intelligence,* 1977, *1,* 257–73.

KEARSLEY, G. P., & ROYCE, J. R.   Multifactor theory of sensation: Individuality in sensory structure and sensory processing. *Perceptual and Motor Skills,* 1977, *44,* 1299–1316.

KELLY, G. A.   *The psychology of personal constructs.* New York: W. W. Norton & Co., 1955.

KEROUAC, J.   *On the road.* New York: Viking Press, 1957.

KESEY, K.   *One flew over the cuckoo's nest.* New York: New American Library, 1962.

KINGET, G.   *On being human: A systematic view.* New York: Harcourt Brace Jovanovich, 1975.

KLEIN, G. S.   The personal world through perception. In R. R. Blake & G. V. Ramsey (Eds.), *Perception: An approach to personality.* New York: Ronald Press, 1951.

KLEIN, G. S.   Need and regulation. In M. R. Jones (Ed.), *Nebraska Symposium of Motivation.* Lincoln: University of Nebraska Press, 1954.

KLEIN, G. S.   Cognitive control and motivation. In G. Lindzey (Ed.), *Assessment of motives.* New York: Holt, Rinehart & Winston, 1958.

KLEIN, G. S.   *Perception, motives, and personality.* New York: Knopf, 1970.

KLEIN, G. S., BARR, H. C., & WOLITSKY, D.   Personality. *Annual Review of Psychology,* 1967, *18,* 467–560.

KOCH, H. L.   *Twins and twin relations.* Chicago: University of Chicago Press, 1966.

KOCH, S.   Psychology as science. In S. C. Brown (Ed.), *Philosophy of psychology.* London: Macmillan, 1974.

KOCH, S.   Language communities, search cells, and the psychological studies. In W. J. Arnold (Ed.), *The Nebraska Symposium on Motivation 1975: Conceptual foundations of psychology.* Lincoln: University of Nebraska Press, 1976.

KOESTLER, A.   Beyond atomism and holism—The concept of the holon. In A. Koestler & J. R. Smythies (Eds.), *Beyond reductionism: New perspectives in the life sciences.* London: Hutchinson, 1969.

KUDER, G. F.   *Kuder Preference Record—Vocational.* Chicago: Science Research Associates, 1948.

KUHN, T. S.   *The structure of scientific revolutions* (2nd ed.). Chicago: University of Chicago Press, 1970.

LANGER, S.   *Philosophy in a new key.* New York: Mentor, 1948.

LANGER, W. C.   *The mind of Adolf Hitler.* New York: Putnam, 1969.

LASHLEY, K. S.   Coalescence of neurology and psychology. *Proceedings of the American Philosophical Society,* 1941, *84,* 461–70.

LASZLO, E.   *Introduction to systems philosophy: Toward a new paradigm of contemporary thought.* New York: Gordon & Breach, 1972. (a)

LASZLO, E.   *The systems view of the world: The natural philosophy of the new developments in sciences.* New York: Braziller, 1972. (b)

LASZLO, E.   *A strategy for the future: The systems approach to world order.* New York: Braziller, 1974.

LECKY, P.   *Self-consistency: A theory of personality.* New York: Island Press, 1945.

Lehman, H. C.   Chronological age vs. physical proficiency in physical skills. *American Journal of Psychology,* 1951, *64,* 161–87.

Lewis, M., & Rosenbaum, L. A. (Eds.)   *The development of affect.* New York: Plenum, 1978.

Lindgren, H. C.   Strong's psychologist scale and course grades in psychology. *Perceptual and Motor Skills,* 1973, *36,* 58.

McArdle, J. J.   *A structural view of structural models.* Paper presented at the Winter Workshop on Latent Structure Models applied to Developmental Data. University of Denver, December, 1978.

McArdle, J. J.   The development of general multivariate software. *Proceedings of the Association for the Development of Computer Based Instructional Systems.* Akron, Ohio: University of Akron Press, February, 1979.

McArdle, J. J.   Causal modeling applied to psychonomic systems simulation. *Behavioral Research Methods and Instrumentation,* 1980, *12,* 193–207.

McDonald, R. P.   The structural analysis of multivariate data: A sketch of a general theory. *Multivariate Behavioral Research,* 1979, *14,* 21–28.

MacNeilage, P. F.   Speech as a motor skill. In M. G. Wade & R. Martens (Eds.), *Psychology of motor behavior and sport.* Urbana, Ill.: Human Kinetics Publishers, 1974.

Maddi, S. R.   The search for meaning. In W. J. Arnold & M. M. Page (Eds.), *The Nebraska Symposium on Motivation. 1970.* Lincoln: University of Nebraska Press, 1971.

Madsen, K. B.   *Modern theories of motivation: A comparative meta-scientific study.* New York: Halsted, 1974.

Malmo, R. B.   Activation: A neuropsychological dimension. *Psychological Review,* 1959, *66,* 367–86.

Mandler, G.   *Mind and emotion.* New York: John Wiley, 1975.

Marks, L. E.   On scales of sensation: Prolegomena to any future psychophysics that will be able to come forth as science. *Perception and Psychophysics,* 1974, *16,* 358–76.

Marks, L. E.   Synesthesia: The lucky people with mixed-up senses. *Psychology Today,* 1975, *9,* 48–52.

Marks, L. E., & Stevens, J. C.   Individual brightness functions. *Perception and Psychophysics,* 1966, *1,* 17–24.

Marquand, J. P.   *Point of no return.* Boston: Little, Brown, 1949.

Marteniuk, R. G.   *Information processing in motor skills.* New York: Holt, Rinehart, & Winston, 1976.

Martens, R., & Landers, D. M.   Effects of anxiety, competition, and failure on performance of a complex motor task. *Journal of Motor Behavior,* 1969, *1,* 1–10.

Maslow, A. H.   *Toward a psychology of being* (2nd ed.). New York: Harper & Row, 1968.

Matter, J. A.   *Love, altruism, and world crises: The challenge of Pitirim Sorokin.* Chicago: Nelson-Hall, 1974.

Maugham, W. S.   *Tellers of tales.* New York: Doubleday, 1939.

May, R. (Ed.)   *Existential psychology* (2nd ed.). New York: Random House, 1969.

May, R.   *Stability and complexity in model ecosystems.* Princeton, N.J.: Princeton University Press, 1973.

McNemar, Q.   Twin resemblances in motor skills and the effect of practice thereon. *Journal of Genetic Psychology,* 1933, *42,* 70–97.

Mead, G. H.   *Mind, self and society.* Chicago: University of Chicago Press, 1934.

Mehrabian, A.   Nonverbal communication. In J. Cole (Ed.), *The Nebraska Symposium on Motivation, 1971.* Lincoln: University of Nebraska Press, 1972.

Melton, A. W.   Individual differences and theoretical process variables. In R. Gagné (Ed.), *Learning and individual differences.* Columbus, Ohio: Chas. E. Merrill, 1967.

Melzack, R., & Wall, P. D.   On the nature of cutaneous sensory mechanisms. *Brain,* 1962, *85,* 331–56.

Mesarovic, M. D. (Ed.).   *Systems theory and biology: Proceedings.* New York: Springer-Verlag, 1968.

MESAROVIC, M. D., MACKO, D., & TAKAHARA, Y.   *Theory of hierarchical, multilevel, systems.* New York: Academic Press, 1970.

MESAROVIC, M. D., & PESTEL, E.   *Mankind at the turning point.* New York: Dutton, 1973.

MESSER, S. B.   Reflection-impulsivity: A review. *Psychological Bulletin,* 1976, *83,* 1026–52.

MESSICK, S.   Multivariate models of cognition and personality: The need for both process and structure in psychological theory and measurement. In J. R. Royce (Ed.), *Multivariate analysis and psychological theory.* London: Academic Press, 1973.

MESSICK, S., & KOGAN, N.   Differentiation and compartmentalization in object-sorting measures of categorizing style. *Perceptual and Motor Skills,* 1963, *16,* 47–51.

MICHENER, J. A., & DAY, A. G.   *Rascals in paradise.* New York: Random House, 1957.

MILES, W. R.   Measures of certain human abilities throughout the life span. *Proceedings of the National Academy of Science,* 1931, *17,* 627–33.

MILES, W. R.   Age and human ability. *Psychological Review,* 1933, *40,* 99–123.

MILLER, A.   *The death of a salesman.* New York: Bantam Books, 1951.

MILLER, D. L.   *Individualism: Personal achievement and the open society.* Austin: University of Texas Press, 1967.

MILLER, G. A., GALANTER, E., & PRIBRAM, K. H.   *Plans and the structure of behavior.* New York: Holt, Rinehart, & Winston, 1960.

MILLER, J. G.   *Living systems.* New York: McGraw-Hill, 1978.

MISCHEL, T.   Psychological explanations and their vicissitudes. In W. J. Arnold (Ed.), *Nebraska Symposium on Motivation 1975: Conceptual foundations of psychology.* Lincoln: University of Nebraska Press, 1976.

MISCHEL, W.   *Personality and assessment.* New York: John Wiley, 1968.

MISCHEL, W.   Continuity and change in personality. *American Psychologist,* 1969, *24,* 1012–18.

MISCHEL, W., EBBESEN, E. B., & ZEISS, A. M.   Determinants of selective memory about the self. *Journal of Consulting and Clinical Psychology,* 1976, *44,* 92–103.

MITTLER, P.   *The study of twins.* Middlesex, England: Penguin, 1971.

MOOS, R. H. (ED.).   *Human adaptation.* Lexington, Mass.: Heath, 1976.

MORRIS, C.   *Varieties of human value.* Chicago: University of Chicago Press, 1956.

MOS, L. P., LUKAWESKI, R., & ROYCE, J. R.   The effect of septal lesions on factors of mouse emotionality. *Journal of Comparative and Physiological Psychology,* 1977, *91,* 523–32.

MOS, L. P., ROYCE, J. R., & POLEY, W.   Effect of postweaning stimulation on factors of mouse emotionality. *Developmental Psychology,* 1973, *8,* 229–39.

MOS, L., VRIEND, J., & POLEY, W.   Effects of light environment on emotionality and the endocrine system of inbred mice. *Physiology and Behavior,* 1974, *12,* 981–89.

MUELLER, W. H.   Parent-child correlation for stature and weight among school aged children: A review of 24 studies. *Human Biology,* 1976, *48,* 379–97.

MULAIK, S. A.   *The foundations of factor analysis.* New York: McGraw-Hill, 1972.

MURRAY, H. A. (AND COLLABORATORS).   *Explorations in personality.* New York: Oxford, 1938.

NAESS, A.   *The pluralist and possibilist aspect of the scientific enterprise.* Oslo: Universitetsforlaget, 1972.

NAGEL, E.   *The structure of science: Problems in the logic of scientific explanation.* London: Routledge & Kegan Paul, 1961.

NASH, H.   The role of metaphor in psychological theory. *Behavioral Science,* 1963, *8*(4), 336–45.

NEISSER, U.   *Cognitive psychology.* Englewood Cliffs, N.J.: Prentice-Hall, 1967.

NEISSER, U.   *Cognition and reality.* San Francisco: Pergamon Press, 1976.

NESSELROADE, J. R., & BALTES, P. B.   Higher order factor convergence and divergence of two distinct personality systems: Cattell's HSPQ and Jackson's PRF. *Multivariate Behavioral Research,* 1975, *10,* 387–408.

NEUGARTEN, D. L., KERKOWITZ, H., CROTTY, W. J., GRUEN, W., GUTMANN, D. L.,

Lubin, M. I., Miller, R., Peck, F., Rosen, J. L., Shukin, A., Tobin, S. S., & Falk, M. (Eds.). *Personality in middle and late life.* New York: Atherton, 1964.

Oliver, J. N. The effect of physical conditioning exercises and activities on the mental characteristics of educationally sub-normal boys. *British Journal of Educational Psychology,* 1958, *28,* 155–65.

Oppenheimer, R. Analogy in science. *The American Psychologist,* 1956, *11,* 127–35.

Orwell, G. *1984.* New York: Harcourt Brace Jovanovich, 1949.

Pattee, H. H. *Hierarchy theory.* New York: George Braziller, 1973.

Pawlik, K. Concepts and calculations in human cognitive abilities. In R. B. Cattell (Ed.), *Handbook of multivariate experimental psychology.* Chicago: Rand McNally, 1966.

Pettigrew, T. F. The measurement and correlates of category width as a cognitive variable. *Journal of Personality,* 1958, *26,* 532–44.

Pettit, I. B., Pettit, T. F., & Welhowitz, J. Relationships between values, social class, and duration of psychotherapy. *Journal of Consulting and Clinical Psychology,* 1974, *42,* 482–90.

Pew, R. W. Human perceptual-motor performance. In B. H. Kantowitz (Ed.), *Human information processing: Tutorials in performance and cognition.* Hillside, N.J.: Lawrence Erlbaum Associates, 1974.

Pfaffmann, C. The afferent code for sensory quality. *American Psychologist,* 1959, *14,* 226–32.

Phares, E. J. *Locus of control in personality.* Morristown, N.J.: General Learning Press, 1976.

Phillips, J. *The second happiest day.* New York: Bantam Books, 1953.

Piaget, J. *The child and reality: Problems of genetic psychology.* Middlesex, England: Penguin, 1976.

Piaget, J. *Psychology and epistemology: Towards a theory of knowledge.* Middlesex, England: Penguin, 1977.

Pickford, R. W. A factorial analysis of colour vision. *Nature,* 1946, *157,* 700.

Pickford, R. W. *Individual differences in color vision.* London: Routledge & Kegan Paul, 1951.

Plutchik, R. *The emotions: Facts, theories, and a new model.* New York: Random House, 1962.

Plutchik, R. Emotions, evolution, and adaptive processes. In M. Arnold (Ed.), *Feelings and emotions.* New York: Academic Press, 1970.

Plutchik, R. *Emotion: A cycle evolutionary synthesis.* New York: Harper & Row, 1980.

Polanyi, M. *Personal knowledge.* Chicago: University of Chicago Press, 1958.

Poley, W., & Royce, J. R. Genotype, maternal stimulation, and factors of mouse emotionality. *Journal of Comparative and Physiological Psychology,* 1970, *71*(2), 246–50.

Poley, W., & Royce, J. R. Alcohol consumption, water consumption, and emotionality in mice. *Journal of Abnormal Psychology,* 1972, *79,* 195–204.

Poley, W., & Royce, J. R. Behavior genetic analysis of mouse emotionality: II. Stability of factors across genotypes. *Animal Learning and Behavior,* 1973, *1,* 116–20.

Poley, W., & Royce, J. R. Acrophobia factor scores as a function of pole height. *Multivariate Behavioral Research,* 1976, *11,* 189–94. (a)

Poley, W., & Royce, J. R. Factors of mouse emotionality at the second order, third order, and fourth order. *Multivariate Behavioral Research,* 1976, *11,* 63–76. (b)

Poley, W., Yeudall, L. T., & Royce, J. R. Factor analyses of alcohol and water consumption in laboratory mice. *Canadian Journal of Psychology,* 1970, *24,* 34–41.

Popper, K. R. *The logic of scientific discovery.* New York: Basic Books, 1959.

Popper, K. R. *Conjectures and refutations.* London: Routledge & Kegan Paul, 1963.

Powell, A., Holt, P., & Royce, J. R. The life-span development of individuality. Edmonton, Alberta: Center for Advanced Study in Theoretical Psychology, *Center Paper in Progess*, 1982.

POWELL, A., KATZKO, M., & ROYCE, J. R.   A multi-factor systems theory of the structure and dynamics of motor functions. *Journal of Motor Behavior*, 1978, *10*, 191–210.

POWELL, A., & ROYCE, J. R.   Paths to being, life style, and individuality. *Psychological Reports*, 1978, *42*, 987–1005.

POWELL, A., & ROYCE, J. R.   An overview of a multifactor-system theory of personality and individual differences: I. The factor and system models and the hierarchical factor structure of individuality. *Journal of Personality and Social Psychology*, 1981, *41*, 818–29.

POWELL, A., & ROYCE, J. R.   An overview of a multifactor-system theory of personality and individual differences: III. Life span development and the heredity-environment issue. *Journal of Personality and Social Psychology*, 1981, *41*, 1161–73.

POWELL, A., & ROYCE, J. R.   Cognitive information processing: The role of individual differences in the search for invariants. *Academic Psychology Bulletin*, 1982, *4*, 255–89.

POWELL, A., ROYCE, J. R., & VOORHEES, B.   Personality as a complex information processing system. *Behavioral Science*, in press.

PRIBRAM, K.   *Languages of the brain*. Englewood Cliffs, N.J.: Prentice-Hall, 1971.

PRIGOGINE, I., ALLEN, P. M., & HERMAN, R.   Long term trends and the evolution of complexity. In E. Laszlo & J. Bierman (Eds.), *Goals in a global community: The original background papers for "Goals for mankind."* New York: Pergamon Press, 1977, pp. 1–64.

RADNITZKY, G.   *Contemporary schools of metascience* (2nd ed.). Goteborg: Akademiforlaget, 1970.

RAPAPORT, A.   *Science and the goals of man: A study in semantic orientation*. New York: Harper & Row, 1950.

RIESMAN, D.   *The lonely crowd: A study in changing American character*. New Haven, Conn.: Yale University Press, 1950.

RIESMAN, D.   *Selected essays from individualism reconsidered*. New York: Free Press, 1954.

RIMOLDI, H. J. A.   Personal tempo. *Journal of Abnormal and Social Psychology*, 1951, *46*, 283–303.

ROGERS, C. R.   *Client-centered therapy: Its current practice, implications, and theory*. Boston: Houghton Mifflin, 1951.

ROGERS, C. R.   *On becoming a person*. Boston: Houghton Mifflin, 1961.

ROGERS, C. R.   Actualizing tendency in relation to "motives" and to consciousness. *Nebraska Symposium on Motivation 1963*. Lincoln: University of Nebraska Press, 1963.

ROGERS, C. R., & DYMOND, R. F. (EDS.)   *Psychotherapy and personality change: Co-ordinated studies in the client-centered approach*. Chicago: University of Chicago Press, 1954.

ROSSMAN, B. B., & HORN, J. L.   Cognitive, motivational and temperamental indicance of creativity and intelligence. *Journal of Educational Measurement*, 1972, *9*, 265–86.

ROUTTENBERG, A.   The two-arousal hypothesis: Reticular formation and limbic system. *Psychological Review*, 1968, *75*, 51–80.

ROYCE, J. R.   A synthesis of experimental designs in program research. *Journal of General Psychology*, 1950, *43*, 295–303.

ROYCE, J. R.   Factor theory and genetics. *Educational and Psychological Measurement*, 1957, *17*, 361–76. (a)

ROYCE, J. R.   Psychology in the mid-twentieth century. *American Scientist*, 1957, *45*, 57–73. (b)

ROYCE, J. R.   Toward the advancement of theoretical psychology. *Psychological Reports*, 1957, *3*, 401–10. (c)

ROYCE, J. R.   The development of factor analysis. *Journal of General Psychology*, 1958, *58*, 139–64.

ROYCE, J. R.   Heretical thoughts on the definition of psychology. *Psychological Reports*, 1960, *8*, 11–14.

Royce, J. R.   Factors as theoretical constructs. *American Psychologist,* 1963, *32,* 522–28.
Royce, J. R.   Psychological and philosophical reflections on the death of John F. Kennedy. *Review of Existential Psychology and Psychiatry,* 1964, *4,* 121–25. (a)
Royce, J. R.   *The encapsulated man: An interdisciplinary essay on the search for meaning.* Princeton, N.J.: D. Van Nostrand & Co., 1964. (b)
Royce, J. R.   Concepts generated from comparative and physiological psychological observations. In R. B. Cattell (Ed.), *Handbook of multivariate experimental psychology.* Chicago: Rand McNally, 1966. (a)
Royce, J. R.   Optimal stimulus parameters in avoidance conditioning of inbred strains of mice. *Multivariate Behavioral Research,* 1966, *1,* 209–17. (b)
Royce, J. R.   The present situation in theoretical psychology. In J. R. Royce (Ed.), *Toward unification in psychology.* Toronto: University of Toronto Press, 1970. (a)
Royce, J. R. (Ed.).   *Toward unification in psychology.* Toronto: University of Toronto Press, 1970. (b)
Royce, J. R. (Ed.).   *Multivariate analysis and psychological theory.* London: Academic Press, 1973. (a)
Royce, J. R.   The conceptual framework for a multi-factor theory of individuality. In J. R. Royce (Ed.), *Multivariate analysis and psychological theory.* London: Academic Press, 1973. (b)
Royce, J. R.   Cognition and knowledge: Psychological epistemology. In E. C. Carterette & M. P. Friedman (Eds.), *Handbook of perception. Historical and philosophical roots to perception.* New York: Academic Press, 1974.
Royce, J. R.   Epistemic styles, individuality and world-view. In A. Debons & W. Cameron (Eds.), *Perspectives in information science.* Leyden, The Netherlands: International Publishing Co., 1975.
Royce, J. R.   Psychology is multi: Methodological, variate, epistemic, world-view, systemic, paradigmatic, theoretic, and disciplinary. In W. J. Arnold (Ed.), *Nebraska Symposium on Motivation 1975: Conceptual foundations of psychology.* Lincoln: University of Nebraska Press, 1976.
Royce, J. R.   Guest Editorial: Have we lost sight of the original vision for SMEP and MBR? *Multivariate Behavioral Research,* 1977, *12,* 135–41. (a)
Royce, J. R.   On the construct validity of open-field measures. *Psychological Bulletin,* 1977, *84,* 1098–1106. (b)
Royce, J. R.   Toward an indigenous philosophy for psychology. *The Ontario Psychologist,* 1977, *9,* 16–32. (c)
Royce, J. R.   Genetics, environment and intelligence: A theoretical synthesis. In A. Oliverio (Ed.), *Genetics, environment and intelligence.* Amsterdam: Elsevier/North-Holland, 1977. (d)
Royce, J. R.   How we can best advance the construction of theory in psychology. *Canadian Psychological Review,* 1978, *19,* 259–76. (a)
Royce, J. R.   The lifestyle of a theory oriented generalist in a time of empirical specialists. In T. S. Krawiec (Ed.), *The psychologists* (Vol. 3). Brandon, Vt.: Clinical Psychology Publishing Co., 1978. (b)
Royce, J. R.   The factor-gene basis of individuality. In J. R. Royce & L. Mos (Eds.), *Theoretical advances in behavior genetics.* Alphen aan den Rijn, The Netherlands: Sijthoff & Noordhoff International Publishers, 1979. (a).
Royce, J. R.   Toward a viable theory of individual differences. *Journal of Personality and Social Psychology,* 1979, *37,* 1927–31. (b)
Royce, J. R., & Buss, A. R.   The role of general systems and information theory in multi-factor individuality theory. *Canadian Psychological Review,* 1976, *17,* 1–21.
Royce, J. R., Coward, H., Egan, E., Kessel, F., & Mos, L. P. Psychological epistemology: A critical review of the empirical literature and the theoretical issues. *Genetic Psychology Monographs,* 1978, *97,* 265–353.

ROYCE, J. R., & DIAMOND, S. R.   A multifactor system dynamics theory of emotion: Cognitive-affective interaction. *Motivation and Emotion*, 1980, *4*, 263–98.

ROYCE, J. R., HOLMES, T. M., & POLEY, W.   Behavior genetic analysis of mouse emotionality: III. The diallel analysis. *Behavior Genetics*, 1975, *5*, 351–72.

ROYCE, J. R., KEARSLEY, G. P., & KLARE, W. P.   The relationship between factors and psychological processes. In J. M. Scandura & C. J. Brainerd (Eds.), *NATO ASI on Structural/Process Models of Complex Human Behavior*. Alphen aan den Rijn, The Netherlands: Sijthoff and Noordhoff, 1978.

ROYCE, J. R., & McDERMOTT, J.   A multidimensional system dynamics model of affect. *Motivation and Emotion*, 1977, *1*, 193–224.

ROYCE, J. R., & MOS, L. P. (EDS.).   *Theoretical advances in behavior genetics*. Alphen aan den Rijn, The Netherlands: Sijthoff & Noordhoff International Publishers, 1979.

ROYCE, J. R., & MOS, L.   *Manual. Psycho-epistemological profile*. Edmonton: University of Alberta Printing Office, 1980.

ROYCE, J. R., & POLEY, W.   Acrophobia factor scores as a function of pole height and habituation. *Multivariate Behavioral Research*, 1976, *11*, 189–94.

ROYCE, J. R., POLEY, W., & YEUDALL, L. T.   Behavior genetic analysis of mouse emotionality: I. Factor analysis. *Journal of Comparative and Physiological Psychology*, 1973, *83*, 36–47.

ROYCE, J. R., & POWELL, A.   Toward a theory of man: A multi-disciplinary, multi-systems, and multi-dimensional approach. *Proceedings of the Sixth International Conference on the Unity of Sciences*. New York: International Cultural Foundation Press, 1978.

ROYCE, J. R., & POWELL, A.   Human nature, metaphoric invariance, and the search for self-knowledge. *Proceedings of the Seventh International Conference on the Unity of the Sciences*. New York: International Cultural Foundation Press, 1979.

ROYCE, J. R., & POWELL, A.   An overview of a multifactor-system theory of personality and individual differences: II. System dynamics and person-situation interactions. *Journal of Personality and Social Psychology*, 1981, *41*, 1019–30.

ROYCE, J. R., & SMITH, W. A. S.   A note on the development of the psycho-epistemological profile (P.E.P.). *Psychological Reports*, 1964, *14*, 297–98.

ROYCE, J. R., YEUDALL, L. T., & BOCK, C.   Factor analytic studies of human brain damage: I. First- and second-order factors and their brain correlates. *Multivariate Behavioral Research*, 1976, *4*, 381–418.

ROYCE, J. R., YEUDALL, L. T., & POLEY, W.   Diallel analysis of avoidance conditioning in inbred strains of mice. *Journal of Comparative and Physiological Psychology*, 1971, *76*, 353–58.

ROZEBOOM, W. W.   The art of metascience, or what should a psychological theory be? In J. R. Royce (Ed.), *Toward unification in psychology*. Toronto: University of Toronto Press, 1970.

SATINDER, K. P., ROYCE, J. R., & YEUDALL, L. T.   Effects of electric shock, D-amphetamine sulphate, and chlorpromazine on factors of emotionality in inbred mice. *Journal of Comparative and Physiological Psychology*, 1970, *71*(3), 443–74.

SCHAIE, K. W., & GOULET, L. R.   Trait theory and the verbal-learning processes. In R. Cattell & R. Dreger (Eds.), *Handbook of modern personality theory*. New York: John Wiley, 1977.

SCHEFF, T. J.   *Being mentally ill: A sociological theory*. Chicago: Aldine Publishing Co., 1966.

SCHEFFLIN, A. E.   Human communication: Behavioral programs and their integration in interaction. *Behavioral Science*, 1968, *13*, 44–55.

SCHMIDT, R. A.   A schema theory of discrete motor skill learning. *Psychological Review*, 1975, *82*, 225–60.

SCHMITT, R. C.   Density, health and social disorganization. *Journal of the American Institute of Planners*, 1966, *32*, 38–40.

SCHOPFLOCHER, D., & ROYCE, J. R.   An item factor analysis of the Psycho-Epistemological Profile. Center paper in progress. Edmonton, Alberta: Center for Advanced Study in Theoretical Psychology, 1982.

SCHRODER, H. M., DRIVER, M. J., & STREUFERT, S.   *Human information processing.* New York: Holt, Rinehart & Winston, 1967.

SEAVER, G.   *Albert Schweitzer: The man and his mind.* New York: Harper & Row, Pub., 1947.

SEIDMAN, C., GOLDING, S. L., HOGAN, T. P., & LeBow, M. D.   Interpretation and comparison of three A-B scales. *Journal of Consulting and Clinical Psychology,* 1974, *42,* 10–20.

SELIGMAN, M.   *Helplessness: On development, death, and depression.* San Francisco: W. H. Freeman & Company, Publishers, 1975.

SELYE, H.   *The stress of life.* New York: McGraw-Hill, 1956.

SHAFFER, L. H.   Intention and performance. *Psychological Review,* 1976, *83,* 375–93.

SHAVER, K. G.   Defensive attribution: Effects of severity and relevance on the responsibility assigned for an accident. *Journal of Personality and Social Psychology,* 1970, *14,* 101–13.

SHAW, R., & BRANSFORD, J. (EDS.),   *Perceiving, acting, and knowing: Toward an ecological psychology.* Hillsdale, N.J.: Lawrence Erlbaum Associates, 1977.

SHAW, R., & McINTYRE, M.   Algoristic foundations for cognitive psychology. In W. Weimer & D. Palermo (Eds.), *Cognition and the symbolic processes.* Hillsdale, N.J.: Lawrence Erlbaum Associates, 1974.

SHAW, R., McINTYRE, M., & MACE, W.   The role of symmetry in event perception. In R. B. MacLeod & H. Pick (Eds.), *Perception: Essays in honor of James J. Gibson.* Ithaca, N.Y.: Cornell University Press, 1974.

SHEPARD, R. N., & METZLER, J.   Mental rotation of three-dimensional objects. *Science,* 1971, *171,* 701–3.

SIESS, T. F., & JACKSON, D. N.   Vocational interests and personality: An empirical integration. *Journal of Counseling Psychology,* 1970, *17,* 27–35.

SINGER, R. N.   *Motor learning and human performance: An application to physical education skills* (2nd ed.). New York: Macmillan, 1975.

SKINNER, H. A., JACKSON, D. N., & RAMPTOM, G. M.   The Personality Research Form in a Canadian context: Does language make a difference? *Canadian Journal of Behavioral Science,* 1976, *8,* 156–68.

SKUDE, G.   Complexities of human taste variation. *Journal of Heredity,* 1960, *51,* 259–63.

SLOAN, H. N., GORLOW, L., & JACKSON, D. N.   Cognitive styles in equivalence range. *Perceptual and Motor Skills,* 1963, *16,* 1389–1404.

SMITH, K. V.   Cybernetic psychology. In R. N. Singer (Ed.), *The psychomotor domain: Movement behaviors.* Philadelphia: Lea & Febiger, 1972.

SMITH, W. A. S., ROYCE, J. R., AYERS, D., & JONES, B.   The development of an inventory to measure ways of knowing. *Psychological Reports,* 1967, *21,* 529–35.

SNOW, R. E.   *Research on aptitudes: A progress report.* Technical Report No. 1, Aptitude Research Project, Stanford University, 1976. (a)

SNOW, R. E.   *Theory and method for research on aptitude processes: A prospectus.* Technical Report No. 2, Aptitude Research Project, Stanford University, 1976. (b)

SNOW, R. E., MARSHALEK, B., & LOHMAN, D. F.   *Correlation of selected cognitive abilities and cognitive processing parameters: An exploratory study.* Technical Report No. 3. Aptitude Research Project, Stanford University, 1976. (c)

SNYDER, L. H.   Inherited taste deficiency. *Science,* 1931, *74,* 151–52.

SNYGG, D., & COMBS, A. W.   *Individual behavior: A new frame of reference for psychology.* New York: Harper & Row, 1949.

SOMMERHOFF, G.   The abstract characteristic of living systems. In F. E. Emery (Ed.), *Systems thinking: Selected readings.* Middlesex, England: Penguin, 1969.

SPENCE, K. W.   *Behavior theory and conditioning.* New Haven, Conn.: Yale University Press, 1956.

SPENCE, K. W.   Anxiety (drive) level and performance in eyelid conditioning. *Psychological Bulletin,* 1964, *61,* 129–39.

SPIELBERGER, C. D. (ED.).   *Anxiety and behavior.* New York: Academic Press, 1966.

SPUHLER, K. P.   *Family resemblance for cognitive performance: An assessment of genetic and environmental contributions to variation.* Unpublished dissertation, University of Colorado, 1976.

STAATS, A. W., GROSS, M. C., GUAY, P. C., & CARLSON, C. C.   Personality and social systems and attitude-reinforcer-discriminative theory: Interest (attitude) formation, function, and measurement. *Journal of Personality and Social Psychology,* 1973, *26,* 251–61.

STAGNER, R.   *Psychology of personality* (4th ed.). New York: McGraw-Hill, 1974.

STAGNER, R.   Homeostasis, discrepancy, dissonance: A theory of motives and motivation. *Motivation and Emotion,* 1977, *1,* 103–38.

STELMACH, G. E. (ED.).   *Motor control: Issues and trends.* New York: Academic Press, 1976.

STELMACH, R. M., BOURGEOIS, R. P., CHIAN, J. Y. C., & PICKARD, C. W.   Extraversion and the orienting reaction habituation rate to visual stimuli. *Journal of Research in Personality,* 1979, *13,* 49–58.

STERNBERG, R. J.   *Intelligence, information processing, and analogical reasoning: The componential analysis of human abilities.* Hillsdale, N.J.: Lawrence Erlbaum Associates, 1977.

STOULENMIRE, J.   Effects of muscle relaxation training on state and trait anxiety in introverts and extroverts. *Journal of Personality and Social Psychology,* 1972, *24,* 273–75.

STRICKER, L. J.   The Personality Research Form: Factor structure and response style involvement. *Journal of Consulting and Clinical Psychology,* 1974, *42,* 529–37.

STRONG, E. K.   *Vocational interests of men and women.* Stanford, Calif.: Stanford University Press, 1943.

STRONGMAN, K. T.   *The psychology of emotion* (2nd ed.). New York: John Wiley, 1978.

SULLIVAN, H. S.   *The interpersonal theory of psychiatry.* New York: W. W. Norton & Co. 1953.

SURWILLO, W. W.   Internal histograms of period of electroencephalogram and reaction time in twins. *Behavior Genetics,* 1977, *7,* 161–69.

TEGHTSOONIAN, M., & TEGHTSOONIAN, R.   How repeatable are Steven's power law exponents for individual subjects? *Perception and Psychophysics,* 1971, *10,* 147–49.

TERKEL, S.   *Working: People talk about what they do all day and how they feel about what they do.* New York: Pantheon Books, 1974.

THIESSEN, D. D.   *Gene organization and behavior.* New York: Random House, 1972.

THOMAS, J. B.   *Self-concept in psychology and education: A review of research.* New York: Humanities Press, 1973.

THORNDIKE, E. L.   Animal intelligence: An experimental study of the associative processes in animals. *Psychological Review Monograph,* 1898, *2*(Whole No. 8).

THORPE, W. H.   *Learning and instinct in animals.* London: Methuen, 1956.

THURSTONE, L. L.   Psychophysical analysis. *American Journal of Psychology,* 1927, *38,* 368–89.

THURSTONE, L. L.   *Multiple factor analysis.* Chicago: University of Chicago Press, 1947.

THURSTONE, T. G.   *An evaluation of educating mentally handicapped children in special classes and in regular classes.* Cooperative Research Project Contract Number OE-SAE-6452 of the U.S. Office of Education, School of Education, University of North Carolina, 1959.

TILLICH, P.   *Dynamics of faith.* New York: Harper and Row, 1957.

TINBERGEN, N.   *The study of instinct.* London: Oxford University Press, 1951.

TOBACH, E., BELLIN, J. S., & DAS, D. K.   Difference in bitter taste perception in three strains of rats. *Behavior Genetics,* 1974, *4,* 405–410.

TOYNBEE, A. J.   *A study of history.* New York: Oxford University Press, 1962.

TROLL, L. E.   *Early and middle adulthood.* Monterey, Calif.: Brooks/Cole, 1975.

UNDERWOOD, B. J.,   Individual differences as crucibles in theory construction. *American Psychologist,* 1975, *30,* 128–134.

VANDENBERG, S. G.   The hereditary abilities study: Hereditary components in a psychological test battery. *American Journal of Human Genetics,* 1962, *14,* 220–237.

VAN HOOF, J.A.R.A.M.   A structural analysis of the social behavior of a semi-captive group of chimpanzees. In M. von Cranach & I. Vine (Eds.), *Social communication and movement: Studies of interaction and expression in man and chimpanzee.* New York: Academic Press, 1973.

VERNON, P. E.   *The structure of human abilities.* London: Methuen, 1950.

VOORHEES, B.   Generation of some theoretical life-span development curves. *Center Paper in Progress.* Edmonton, Alberta: Center for Advanced Study in Theoretical Psychology, 1980.

VOORHEES, B.   Toward a theory of control in factor hierarchies: I. Hierarchical structure and macrodeterminism. *Center Paper in Progress.* Edmonton, Alberta: Center for Advanced Study in Theoretical Psychology, 1981. (a)

VOORHEES, B.   Toward a theory of control in factor hierarchies: II. Cycliccorrelations as template. *Center Paper in Progress.* Edmonton, Alberta: Center for Advanced Study in Theoretical Psychology, 1981. (b)

WALLIS, C. P., & MALIPHANT, R.   Delinquent areas in the county of London: Ecological factors. *British Journal of Criminology,* 1967, *7,* 3.

WANSCHURA, R. G., & DAWSON, W. E.   Regression effect and individual power functions over sessions. *Journal of Experimental Psychology,* 1974, *102,* 806–12.

WARDELL, D.   A note on style structure. *Perceptual and Motor Skills,* 1974, *38,* 774.

WARDELL, D., & ROYCE, J. R.   Relationships between cognitive temperament traits and the concept of "style." *Journal of Multivariate and Experimental Personality and Clinical Psychology,* 1975, *1,* 244–66.

WARDELL, D., & ROYCE, J. R.   Toward a multi-factor theory of styles and their relationships to cognition and affect. *Journal of Personality,* 1978, *46,* 474–505.

WECKOWICZ, T.   *Models of mental illness.* Unpublished manuscript. Edmonton, Alberta: The Center for Advanced Study in Theoretical Psychology, University of Alberta, 1982.

WEISS, P. A. (ED.)   *Hierarchically organized systems in theory and practice.* New York: Hafner, 1971.

WELFORD, A. T.   Motor performance. In J. E. Birren, & K. W. Schaie (Eds.), *Handbook of the psychology of aging.* New York: Van Nostrand Reinhold, 1977.

WENGER, M. A.   Studies of autonomic balance in Army Air Force Personnel. *Comparative Psychological Monographs,* 1948, *19*(4), 1–111.

WERNER, H.   *Comparative psychology of mental development* (Rev. ed.). New York: International Universities Press, 1948.

WERNER, H.   The concept of development from a comparative and organismic point of view. In D. B. Harris (Ed.), *The concept of development.* Minneapolis: University of Minnesota Press, 1957.

WERTHEIMER, M.   *Fundamental issues in psychology.* New York. Holt, Rinehart & Winston, 1972.

WHEELWRIGHT, P.   *The burning fountain.* Bloomington: Indiana University Press, 1968.

WHYTE, A. G., WILSON, A. G., & WILSON, D. (Eds.).   *Hierarchical structures.* New York: American Elsevier, 1969.

WIGNER, E. P.   *Symmetries and reflections.* Bloomington: Indiana University Press, 1967.

WILCOCK, J., & BROADHURST, P. L.   Strain differences in emotionality: Open-field and conditioned avoidance behavior in the rat. *Journal of Comparative and Physiological Psychology,* 1967, *63,* 335–38.

WILSON, S.   *The man in the grey flannel suit.* New York: Simon & Schuster, 1955.

WITKIN, H. A.   *Psychological differentiation: Studies of development.* Hillsdale, N.J.: Lawrence Erlbaum Associates, 1974.

WITKIN, H. A., DYK, R. B., FATERSON, H. F., GOODENOUGH, D. R., & KARP, S. A. *Psychological differentiation.* New York: John Wiley, 1962.

WITKIN, H. A., GOODENOUGH, P. K., & KARP, S. A.   Stability of cognitive style from childhood to young adulthood. *Journal of Personality and Social Psychology,* 1967, *7,* 291–300.

WOLD, H.   Soft modeling: Intermediate between traditional model building and data analysis. *Mathematical Statistics,* 1980, *6,* 333–46.

WOLITZKY, D. L., & WACHTEL, P. L.   Personality and perception. In B. B. Wolman (Ed.), *Handbook of general psychology.* Englewood Cliffs, N.J.: Prentice-Hall, 1973.

WOOD, N. E.   Auditory closure and auditory discrimination in young children. *Acta Symbolica,* 1974, *5,* 68–84.

WYLIE, R. C.   The present status of self theory. In E. F. Borgatta & W. W. Lambert (Eds.), *Handbook of personality theory and research.* Chicago: Rand McNally, 1968.

WYLIE, R. C.   *The self concept: A review of methodological considerations and measuring instruments* (Rev. ed.). Lincoln: University of Nebraska Press, 1974.

Index

AUTHOR INDEX

Numbers in italics refer to references

SUBJECT INDEX